O9-AIF-108

herbs& spices

herbs& spices

Jill Norman

Photography
Dave King

LONDON, NEW YORK, MUNICH,
MELBOURNE, and DELHI

For Paul, who made it possible

PROJECT EDITOR Frank Ritter
EDITOR Hugh Thompson
PROJECT ART EDITOR Toni Kay
ART EDITOR Sara Robin
MANAGING EDITOR Gillian Roberts
US EDITOR Norma MacMillan
ART DIRECTOR Carole Ash
CATEGORY PUBLISHER Mary-Clare Jerram
DTP DESIGNERS Sonia Charbonnier, Louise Waller
PRODUCTION CONTROLLER Joanna Bull

First American Edition, 2002
11 12 20 19 18 17
021-AS421-Oct/02

Published in the United States by
DK Publishing, Inc.
375 Hudson Street
New York, New York 10014

A Cataloging-in-Publication record for this book is available from the Library of Congress

ISBN 978-0-7894-8939-5

Color reproduction by Colourscan, Singapore
Printed and bound by Hung Hing, China

CONTENTS

Introduction 8

What defines an herb or spice, and why are they used in cooking? Regional cuisines derive much of their character from how specific herbs and spices are combined and used. With increasing availability of fresh herbs and spices from around the world, every cook can recreate authentic regional dishes at home, and try out new combinations to his or her personal taste.

Herbs

Introducing herbs 14

While robust herbs such as sage do not lose their flavors if dried, most herbs are meant to be eaten fresh. Herbs added at the beginning of cooking impart their flavor to foods; adding the herbs at the end ensures that their aroma is retained. In this directory, more than 60 herbs and their varieties are grouped by aroma and taste, with details of the parts used, buying and storing, growing your own, and culinary uses worldwide.

PURSLANE
Portulaca oleracea
MINER'S LETTUCE
Claytonia perfoliata

Fresh and mild herbs

Parsley 18 • Purslane 20 • Miner's lettuce 21 • Borage 22
Salad burnet 23 • Perilla 24 • Mitsuba 26 • Orache 27

Sweet herbs

Marigold 28 • Basil 30 • Asian basils 34 • Bay 36
Myrtle 38 • Angelica 39 • Scented geranium 40
Sweet cicely 43 • Lavender 44 • Woodruff 48 • Pandan 49

Other mints

Moroccan mint

Bowles' mint

Chocolate mint

Apple mint

Black peppermint

Mountain mint

Bitter or astringent herbs

Celery 84 • Lovage 86 • Hyssop 88 • Chicory 89

Pungent and spicy herbs

Oregano and marjoram 90 • Rosemary 94 • Sage 96
Thyme 100 • Savory 104 • Micromeria 107 • Cilantro 108
Culantro 110 • Rau ram 111 • Arugula 112 • Wasabi 114
Horseradish 116 • Watercress 118 • Epazote 120 • Mugwort 121

Citrus or tart herbs

Bee balm 50 • Lemon balm 52 • Vietnamese balm 53
Lemon verbena 54 • Sassafras 55 • Sorrel 56
Houttuynia 58 • Rice paddy herb 59

Licorice or anise herbs

Chervil 60 • Tarragon 62 • Dill 64 • Fennel 66 • Agastache 68

Minty herbs

Mint 70 • Calamint 74 • Catnip 75

Oniony herbs

Garlic 76 • Welsh onion 81
Chives 82
Garlic chives 83

Preparing herbs 122

Everything you need to know to explore the full potential of fresh and dried herbs.

Stripping, chopping, and pounding herbs 123 • Drying and rubbing herbs 126 • Making vinegars, oils, and butters 128

Spices

Introducing spices 132

Most spice plants are native to the Asian tropics and were used in cooking long before European powers fought for control of their trade. Traditionally many spices have been combined with others, and mixtures vary according to the dish and the cook. The directory of spices contains more than 60 spices and their variants, each placed in a family of taste and aroma. It is explained how the spices are used worldwide, which herbs and spices combine well, and which foods best complement each spice.

MACE
Myristica fragrans

Nutty spices

Sesame 138 • Nigella 140 • Poppy 141 • Mahlab 142
Wattle 143

Sweet spices

Cinnamon 144 • Cassia 146 • Coriander 148
Juniper 150 • Rose 152 • Vanilla 154 • Akudjura 158
Pink pepper 159 • Paprika 160

Acidic and fruity spices

Tamarind 162 • Sumac 164 • Barberry 166
Pomegranate 168 • Kokam 170 • Amchoor 172

Citrus spices

Lemon grass 174 • Kaffir lime 176 • Galangal 178
Lemon myrtle 181 • Citrus 182

Licorice or anise spices

Star anise 184 • Anise 186 • Licorice 188

Warm and earthy spices

Saffron 190 • Cardamom 194 • Black cardamom 196
Cumin 198 • Caraway 200 • Nutmeg 202 • Mace 206
Turmeric 208 • Zedoary 210 • Curry leaves 212 • Achiote 214

Bitter or astringent spices

Capers 216 • Ajowan 218 • Fenugreek 220
Mastic 222 • Safflower 223

Pungent spices

Pepper 224 • Cubeb 229 • Aromatic leaves 230
Mountain pepper 232 • Grains of paradise 234
Sichuan pepper and sansho 236 • Fresh ginger 238
Dried ginger 242 • Allspice 244 • Cloves 246
Asafetida 250 • Mustard 252 • Chili peppers 256

TURMERIC
Curcuma longa

Preparing spices 266

Simple, reliable descriptions of the techniques you need to get the best from every spice.

Bruising, grating, slicing, and shredding spices 267
Dry-roasting and frying spices 270
Grinding, crushing, and making spice pastes 272
Fresh chili peppers 274
Dried chili peppers 276

Recipes

Blending herbs and spices 280

How to create classic and modern herb and spice blends and use them, either applied directly to foods or mixed into sauces, condiments, and marinades.

Herb mixtures 280 • Spice mixtures 284
Sauces and condiments 296 • Marinades 304

blending herbs and spices

HERB MIXTURES 281

HERB MIXTURES

Dried or fresh herbs can be used in many combinations. The composition of even the classic mixtures is usually determined by the kind of dish they are to go with – a guiding principle, whether in European bouquets garnis, Iranian blends, or Latin American blends in which spices are often included with the herbs.

Bouquets garnis

Fines herbes

Persillade

Gremolata

Herbes de Provence

Winter herbs

Farcellets

Herbed pepper

Garlic and herb paste

Cooking with herbs and spices 306

Recipes for savory and sweet dishes that use herbs, spices, and mixtures in this book, enabling you to experience their aromas and flavors first-hand.

Soups and light dishes 306 • Fish 310 • Meats 312
Vegetables 317 • Pasta, noodles, and grains 319
Desserts and drinks 324

Bibliography 326

Sources of herbs and spices 328

Index 330

Acknowledgments 336

The definition of what constitutes an herb or spice is not as straightforward as it might seem. Broadly, we think of herbs as plants used by cooks for their flavor and aroma. The word herb derives from the Latin *herba*, meaning grass or, by extension, green crop: it was originally applied to a wide range of leaf vegetables in addition to the plants we now call herbs. Most of the culinary herbs we use grow in temperate climates. Spices, on the other hand, are products of tropical plants: aromatic roots, bark, seeds, buds, and fruits, usually used in dried form, whether whole or ground. Again our word derives from Latin, where *species* meant specific kind but, in later use, goods or merchandise – spices certainly being an important commodity even at the time of the Romans.

How the book is organized

I have followed standard European usage in defining herbs and spices, and have grouped both according to their dominant aroma and flavor. Some fitted easily into a specific category; others were difficult to define and could have been put into more than one group. Marigolds, for instance, are basically sweet, yet have a bitter note. Some Asian basils are more piquant than sweet. Ginger is pungent but it is also earthy and warm. Another difficulty is that the way we express our

awareness of flavors and aromas varies from individual to individual. Your perception of aromatics may not be the same as mine, and a different term may come to your mind from the one that came to mine.

In the US, the American Spice Trade Association defines "any dried plant used primarily for seasoning purposes" as a spice; this includes dried herbs, even dehydrated onions. In Southeast Asia, any aromatic plant used fresh is an herb, but once the same substance is dried it is classed as a spice. I have followed European usage and classed all herbs as herbs and all spices as spices, whether fresh or dried.

Health benefits of herbs and spices

The early use of herbs and spices was medicinal, and in many regions where they grow they are still valued for their medicinal properties. Often their use in cooking owed as much to their perceived ability to promote health, combat flatulence, or help digest fatty foods as to their appetizing fragrances. Fresh herbs and spices provided mineral salts and vitamins long before our need for these was understood. In tropical countries the vitamin C contained in chili peppers remains just as important to the diet as the lift that the chilies give to it.

Most cultures recognize the importance of providing a balance in food. Indian cooking follows Ayurvedic principles in using herbs and spices to provide flavor and to create physical and emotional wellbeing. In China, nutrition and medicine have long been integrated. Chinese cooking is based on a theory that wellbeing is brought about by the careful balancing of the five flavors – sweet, salty, bitter, sour, and pungent – with the texture and color of the food. Yin herbs such as mint and parsley slow down the metabolism, whereas yang spices such as chili and ginger activate it. Similar principles are followed in Iran, where the cook strives to maintain a balance between ingredients classed as hot or cold. In the West, herbs and spices have become important elements in adding flavor to low-salt and lowfat foods; and garlic has gained wider acceptance because it is said to lower cholesterol levels and help prevent heart disease.

Flavorings rooted in tradition

In the past herbs and spices were also important for their preservative properties: before the arrival of refrigeration their volatile oils and other compounds prolonged the useful life of many foodstuffs. Pickled or salted meat, fish, and vegetables would last through the winter months, and aromatics were used to improve their flavor. Although we no longer need these methods of preserving, we still use many of them simply because we have come to like the taste they impart to foods.

Herbs and spices are used to stimulate all the senses, not just the tastebuds, through their aroma, flavor, texture, and visual appeal. In all the regions of the world, traditional flavor combinations, using local ingredients, have come to characterize the foods of those regions. Saffron, pimentón, garlic, and nuts dominate in Spain; wine and herbs in France; basil, garlic, olive oil, and anchovy in Italy. In Britain, it is parsley, thyme, sage, and mustard; in eastern Europe, sour cream, dill, and caraway. The Middle East uses lemon, parsley, and cinnamon. In northern India, ginger, garlic, and cumin are the most important spices; in southern India, it is mustard seed, coconut, chili, and tamarind. Thailand has fish sauce, lemon grass, galangal, and chili; in China, it is soy sauce, ginger, and Sichuan pepper. Mexico remains faithful to its chilies, cilantro, and cinnamon.

New opportunities for experimental cooking

We are becoming increasingly aware of these traditional patterns as the demand for and availability of authentic ethnic food grows. The number of herbs offered in stores and markets, and of spices and spice mixtures sold in supermarkets and specialty stores, has dramatically increased, as has the number of forms in which herbs and spices are now marketed. Recent techniques, such as preserving chopped herbs in oil or freeze-drying, are showing promising results. Organic herbs and spices are frequently on offer; the spice merchants bring out ever more blends. We are becoming more knowledgeable, and more adventurous.

Herb and spice combinations

This leads me to end on a note of caution. Herbs and spices should not be overused, and only their skillful blending leads to a successful dish. Just as too much of a specific herb or spice can ruin a dish, flavors in herb and spice mixtures can cancel each other out. Experiment with combinations you think you will like, but do so with caution; you will find that herbs and spices can bring subtlety, harmony, and complexity to your cooking.

Jill Norman

herbs

Introducing herbs

While compiling the herb directory in this book I became conscious of the impact of world trade expansion on the sale of fresh herbs. It has long been accepted that spices, and to a lesser extent dried herbs, can travel great distances without damage, and in recent years air freight has also made it possible to import fresh spices, such as ginger, lemon grass, chili peppers, and zedoary (white turmeric). But herbs were always considered too fragile for long transportation; when I last wrote about herbs some five or six years ago it was almost impossible to find some Asian basils, or Japanese herbs such as perilla or mitsuba. Some of the herbs recorded here I had not seen or tasted then, some I was not even aware of. With fewer herbs readily available, I would bring back plants from my travels, willing them to grow in my London garden. Luckily most of them did, and several survived for more than one season.

New markets for fresh herbs

Today international trade brings herbs grown in Turkey, Cyprus, and Israel to my supermarket shelves as a matter of course. Deliveries from Japan, Thailand, and Singapore bring little-known tropical herbs at least once a week to specialty stores. At present, demand probably comes largely from immigrant communities and from restaurants, but my own visits to such markets revealed a great curiosity and a willingness to experiment on the part of other local enthusiasts. With these people in mind I have included a number of recent arrivals. In the US, and in other countries with sufficiently warm climates, many herbs are already being cultivated to meet demand not just from immigrants but also, increasingly, from a wider public. Perhaps in a few years my markets, too, will sell bunches of fresh culantro, rau ram, and epazote alongside familiar Western varieties.

The Western tradition

Many herbs remain essential in classic European cuisines: tarragon, thyme, bay, and garlic in France; basil, sage, and rosemary in Italy; oregano in Greece; dill in Scandinavia; parsley, sage, thyme, and bay in Britain. The traditional uses of these herbs are still reflected in the choices made by today's cooks, but the foods with which they are used and their flavor combinations are changing as other possibilities, afforded as much by our own curiosity as by increased availability, are explored. If you are a novice in cooking with herbs, start with classics such as chicken with tarragon, guacamole with cilantro and chili, grilled cod or tuna with salsa verde, roast potatoes with rosemary and garlic, or a beef stew with a bouquet garni and red wine. Once you begin to appreciate how the blending of flavors affects a dish, you will be drawn to experiment and adapt or devise combinations to your own taste.

ROSEMARY FLAT-LEAF PARSLEY BASIL GARLIC

We are rediscovering many herbs that once were in common use but have long been forgotten or neglected as weeds. In 17th-century Europe, salad herbs were grown and used widely. In 1699, John Evelyn's *Acetaria* recorded more than 30 salad herbs, including arugula, basil, balm, chicory, corn salad, clary sage, various cresses, dandelion, fennel, hyssop, mallow, mint, orach, purslane, and sorrel. In 1731, Philip Miller's *Gardener's Dictionary* instructed gentlemen gardeners in herb cultivation. Some have become easily available once more, in season and even all year round, but others – such as sweet cicely, clary sage, and hyssop – you will have to grow yourself. Specialist nurseries are constantly extending their stocks to meet the demand for a wider range of herbs. But there is also a trend to overuse certain herbs – arugula and chervil are currently the worst affected – which I hope will not lead to their disappearance once the fashion changes.

Choosing and using herbs

Generally, herbs are used to add fragrance and flavor rather than to provide the dominant taste. The light flavors of dill, parsley, and chervil are good with fish and seafood; the more pungent rosemary, oregano, and garlic will flavor braised or baked lamb or roast pork beautifully. Root vegetables respond well to thyme and rosemary, eggplant to Provençal herbs, green peas to chives, tomatoes to basil and parsley. It is important always to balance delicate and hearty flavors, and to use herbs judiciously.

The wealth of fresh herbs now available has had the beneficial effect of banishing from many kitchens a lot of small packets of stale dried herbs. Some herbs that are sold dried, such as basil and parsley, are never worth having; their aroma is musty at best, and their taste insipid. Such herbs are meant to be eaten fresh. The clean, herbaceous notes of fresh parsley, and the complex, sweet scent of anise and clove wafting from a bunch of basil, beguile first the sense of smell and later also the tastebuds. Unlike many herbs, these two are not overwhelming if used in large quantities – as they

CHOPPING HERBS
Chop herbs just before they are needed – freshly chopped herbs have the best aroma and flavor.

POUNDING LEAVES
Herbs intended for sauces or pastes can be pounded in a mortar. Other ingredients may be worked into the crushed herbs.

DRYING HERBS
Some herbs can be dried at home and their leaves stripped and kept in an airtight jar.

are in the basil sauce pesto and the parsley salad tabbouleh. Robust herbs, such as oregano, thyme, sage, savory, mint, and rosemary, respond well to drying, which preserves and often concentrates their flavor. Whether fresh or dried, these herbs should be used sparingly or they will overwhelm other flavors in the food instead of complementing them.

Herbs added early on in cooking will release their flavors into the dish. Dried herbs should always be put in at the beginning, and herbs with tough leaves, such as rosemary, lavender, winter savory, thyme, and bay, will withstand long cooking. If you add sprigs of herbs to a dish, remove them before serving. To restore the aroma of herbs used in a slow-cooked dish, stir a few finely chopped leaves into the pan toward the end of the cooking process. Strongly flavored herbs, such as mint, tarragon, fennel, marjoram, and lovage, can be added at any stage during cooking. The essential oils of delicate herbs, like basil, chervil, chives, dill, cilantro, perilla, and lemon balm, soon dissipate when heated. To keep them fresh in taste, texture, and color, add them just before a dish is served.

PARSLEY

Petroselinum crispum

Probably the only herb considered indispensable by most Western cooks, parsley is a truly versatile biennial, native to the eastern Mediterranean region. Today it is cultivated throughout most of the temperate world. Parsley root, which is valued for its root rather than its leaves, was first grown in Germany in the 16th century.

TASTING NOTES

Parsley has a lightly spicy aroma with hints of anise and lemon; its taste is tangy and herbaceous, and has a light, peppery note. Flat-leaf parsley has a more persistent and finer flavor than curly parsley and a finer texture. Both bring out the flavors of other seasonings.

PARTS USED

Fresh leaves are the most used, but stems are good for flavoring stocks; parsley root is grown for its roots.

BUYING AND STORING

Buy fresh parsley in large bunches; keep in a plastic bag in the refrigerator. Discard any sprigs that look slimy and it should keep for 4–5 days. Parsley can be chopped and frozen in small containers or in ice-cube trays with a little water. Don't buy dried parsley.

GROW YOUR OWN

Parsley seeds take some weeks to germinate, but soaking them overnight in hot water helps to speed up the process. Sow in the ground, and thin seedlings when they are big enough. Sow seeds every year, so that when one batch runs to seed in its second year a new batch is ready to use. Harvest from late spring.

Culinary uses

Parsley is liked for its clean, fresh taste and is rich in iron and vitamins A and C. It is used in sauces, salads, stuffings, and omelettes in many parts of the world. In Anglo-Saxon cultures its use as a flavoring ingredient (except in a parsley sauce) rather than simply as a garnish is quite recent. Add chopped parsley at the end of cooking time for a fresh flavor. Sprigs of dark green, deep-fried curly parsley make an excellent garnish for fried fish. Parsley root is used in soups and stews, but it can also be blanched and then roasted or cooked in other ways as a root vegetable. It mashes well with potato.

Essential to a number of traditional flavoring mixtures: French bouquets garnis, fines herbes, and persillade; Italian gremolata and salsa verde; and tabbouleh.

Good with eggs, fish, lemon, lentils, rice, tomatoes, most vegetables.

Combines well with basil, bay, capers, chervil, chili, chives, garlic, lemon balm, marjoram, mint, oregano, pepper, rosemary, sorrel, sumac, tarragon.

Curly parsley *P. crispum*

Good for garnishes, curly parsley also gives a light, herbaceous flavor and attractive green color to mayonnaise and other sauces.

Flat-leaf parsley

P. c. var. 'Neapolitanum'

Also called French or Italian parsley, flat-leaf parsley has the best flavor for cooking, and is most widely used throughout Europe and the Middle East.

STEMS
Parsley stems are coarser in flavor than the leaves. Tie them in a bundle and use in long-cooked stocks and stews; discard the stems when the cooking is finished.

Parsley root

P. c. var. *tuberosum*

Mostly cultivated in central and northern Europe, parsley root, also called Hamburg parsley, is no more difficult to grow than leaf parsley. It looks like a small parsnip or, if round, a turnip. Its flavor combines those of parsley and celery, with a light nuttiness. The leaves have a coarse flavor and texture.

PURSLANE

Portulaca oleracea

Purslane is a sprawling annual that grows wild throughout much of the world. It has been used as a food plant for centuries in southern Europe and the Middle East. An important source of iron and vitamin C, purslane is also one of the best plant sources of Omega-3, one of the fatty acids that help to maintain a healthy heart.

TASTING NOTES

Purslane has little aroma; the fleshy leaves and stems have a refreshing, lightly piquant, astringent, lemony taste, and a crunchy, juicy texture.

PARTS USED

Leaves and young shoots. The flowers can be added to salads. Purslane is always eaten fresh.

BUYING AND STORING

Fresh purslane will keep for 2–3 days in a plastic bag in the vegetable crisper of the refrigerator. In summer Greek and Turkish grocers usually have large bunches of purslane. In Mexico, you find it readily in markets.

GROW YOUR OWN

Purslane does best on moist, light soil in a sunny position. Seeds can be sown outdoors from early summer, and the leaves are ready to harvest about 60 days later. In hot, dry weather it will need more watering than other herbs. Cut purslane a little above the ground, leaving two leaves for regrowth. For salad, harvest young leaves regularly because older leaves become tough. Yellow flowers appear in summer, but only open for a short time around midday.

Culinary uses

Young leaves make an agreeable addition to a salad. In the Middle East, chopped purslane with a garlicky yogurt dressing is served as an accompaniment to grilled meats. The herb is also a standard ingredient of fattoush, the Lebanese salad.

Blanch older leaves to use as a vegetable. Cooking emphasizes their mucilaginous content, which provides a good thickening for soups and stews. In Turkey, large bunches of purslane are used in a traditional lamb and bean stew, and all around the Mediterranean it turns up in soups. The Mexicans cook it with pork, tomatillos, and chili peppers, especially smoky chipotles (*p.261*). Purslane combines well with spinach tossed in olive oil and lemon juice.

Good with beets, cucumber, eggs, fava beans, feta cheese, new potatoes, spinach, tomatoes, yogurt.

Combines well with arugula, borage, chervil, cresses, salad burnet, sorrel.

Fresh sprigs and flowers

Green purslane has oblong, thick, succulent leaves and a round stem tinged with red. Golden purslane (*P. sativa*) is a smaller plant and is less hardy.

MINER'S LETTUCE

Claytonia perfoliata

Miner's lettuce, also called claytonia and winter purslane, is a delicate-looking annual that makes an excellent winter salad herb. It is called miner's lettuce because miners in the California Gold Rush ate the wild plant to avoid scurvy – like the unrelated purslane *Portulaca oleracea* (*p.20*), miner's lettuce is high in vitamin C.

Culinary uses

Leaves, young stems, and flowers make a useful and pretty contribution to the salad bowl. I particularly like miner's lettuce for its winter usefulness, when other salad greens can be dreary. The leaves and stems can be cooked – try them alone or with other greens, stir-fried with a little oyster sauce. **Combines well with** arugula, chives, sorrel, watercress.

Fresh sprigs and flowers

Miner's lettuce leaves totally encircle the smooth stems. The tiny, white flowers are borne on thin stems from early summer.

TASTING NOTES

Miner's lettuce is not aromatic. It is mild, with a clean, fresh flavor.

PARTS USED

Leaves, young stems, and flowers.

BUYING AND STORING

Miner's lettuce can be gathered from the wild in shady grasslands in North America, its native habitat, but it is less commonly found in Europe. It is best picked and used at once, but can be kept in a plastic bag in the refrigerator for 1–2 days.

GROW YOUR OWN

A few herb nurseries now stock miner's lettuce, but it is also easy to grow from seed. Seeds sown in spring will produce plants for summer use; summer sowing will produce plants for winter picking. Miner's lettuce does survive near-freezing temperatures. It prefers a light soil, but is adaptable. Miner's lettuce makes a pretty garden edging plant.

BORAGE

Borago officinalis

This robust, annual herb, native to southern Europe and western Asia, is now naturalized throughout Europe and North America. It is worth growing just for its dazzling, blue, star-like flowers. The old herbalists held that borage made people cheerful and courageous; it is now known to stimulate the adrenal glands and have mild sedative and antidepressant effects.

TASTING NOTES

Borage has a gentle aroma and a somewhat stronger flavor of cucumber. It is cool and fresh-tasting, with a slight saltiness.

PARTS USED

Leaves and flowers. Avoid the bristly stems.

BUYING AND STORING

Borage is always used fresh. Leaves can be kept for a day or two in the vegetable crisper of the refrigerator, either wrapped in damp paper towel or placed inside a plastic bag. Flowers are best used soon after picking or they will wilt. Freeze them in ice cubes and serve in drinks.

GROW YOUR OWN

Grow borage in well-drained soil in a sunny spot. It is a large, ungainly plant and will self-seed easily. Plant borage only where you intend it to grow because it has a long taproot and does not like to be moved. Harvest young leaves in spring and summer, and pick the flowers as soon as they open.

Culinary uses

Borage is essentially a salad herb. Shred the young leaves, because their hairy texture is disagreeable if they are left whole. Combine the shredded leaves with cucumber tossed in yogurt or sour cream, and add them to dressings and salsas. Tough older leaves can be sautéed, or cooked in water and treated like spinach. The Italians use borage with spinach or with bread crumbs, egg, and Parmesan cheese to stuff ravioli and cannelloni. The Turks add the leaves to green pea soup. The flowers will impart a delicate cucumber note to salads, and they look wonderful floating on a creamy soup or flavoring a summer punch. They can also be candied to decorate cakes and desserts. Use borage sparingly.

Good with eel and other fatty fish, potato salad, white cheeses, yogurt; Pimm's and other summer punches.

Combines well with arugula, chervil, cresses, dill, garlic, mint, salad burnet.

Fresh leaves and flowers
Of borage species, only *B. officinalis* is edible. The white-flowered cultivated variety *B. o.* 'Alba' can be used in the same way as the blue- or purple-flowered varieties.

SALAD BURNET

Sanguisorba minor

Salad burnet is a graceful, bushy, perennial plant with sharply toothed, deep-green leaves. Although delicate in appearance, it is actually sturdy, its evergreen leaves often pushing up through a light covering of snow. Native to Europe and western Asia, salad burnet was taken to North America by early European colonists and is now naturalized there.

TASTING NOTES

Salad burnet is not aromatic, and has a mild, lightly astringent flavor reminiscent of cucumber with a hint of nuttiness. Old leaves become bitter and are best cooked.

PARTS USED

Leaves and young stems.

BUYING AND STORING

Salad burnet will keep for a day or two in a plastic bag in the vegetable crisper of the refrigerator. In some parts of Europe, you can buy bunches of burnet in the market, alongside other herbs and salad leaves.

GROW YOUR OWN

Easy to grow from seed, salad burnet flourishes in light, well-drained soil in sun or light shade. Remove the flowerheads and cut leaves regularly to encourage new growth. Divide after the second year to maintain tender growth.

Culinary uses

The subtle flavor of the young, feathery leaves is best appreciated by eating them raw. Add them to salads – they are particularly good in autumn and winter, when interesting salad leaves can be in short supply. Chop as a garnish for vegetables or egg dishes; combine with tarragon, chives, and chervil for fines herbes. The leaves are good scattered over soups and casseroles, and made into sauces and herb butters. Burnet is often recommended to flavor vinegar, but I have found this disappointing.

Good with cream cheese, cucumber, eggs, fava beans, fish, salad leaves, tomatoes.

Combines well with chervil, chives, miner's lettuce, mint, parsley, rosemary, tarragon.

Fresh sprigs
The tender, young leaves have the best flavor. The pretty red flowers have no taste.

PERILLA

Perilla frutescens

The aromatic leaves of perilla – or shiso, to give the plant its Japanese name – are widely used in Japan, Korea, and Vietnam. More recently they have been discovered by cooks in Australia, the US, and Europe. An annual herb, related to mint and basil, perilla is native to China. The flavor of dried perilla only palely reflects that of the fresh.

TASTING NOTES

Green perilla is sweetly yet strongly aromatic, with notes of cinnamon, cumin, citrus, and anise basil, and a pleasant warmth on the palate. Red perilla is less aromatic and has a more subdued flavor. It is faintly musty and woody with cilantro, cumin, and cinnamon overtones.

PARTS USED

Leaves, flowers, and sprouts. Seeds are harvested commercially for their oil.

BUYING AND STORING

Fresh perilla leaves are sold in Asian markets. The leaves keep for 3–4 days in a plastic bag in the vegetable crisper of the refrigerator. Red leaves are also sold pickled in vacuum packs. Dried perilla is available from Japanese markets; store in an airtight container for 6–8 months.

GROW YOUR OWN

Perilla is not demanding about soil or situation, but does not like to be waterlogged and does not tolerate frost. Well-drained, light soil is best and a sheltered spot in sun or partial shade. Pinch out the tops to produce bushy plants. Perilla self-seeds easily, especially the red variety.

Sprouted seeds
Sprouted perilla seeds are now available from some supermarkets and specialty stores. They are sold as growing shoots, similar to those of mustard.

Green perilla *P. frutescens*

Green perilla has soft, downy leaves with a crinkly edge. They look somewhat like stinging nettle leaves.

Red perilla *P. f.* var. *crispa*

Red perilla ranges from deep red to purple-bronze. The large leaves are crinkly or flat with a serrated edge and the flowerspikes are purple. It is a beautiful plant for the garden, providing vivid contrast to the more usual green herbs. It is sometimes called beefsteak plant because of the color of its leaves.

Culinary uses

In Japan, red perilla is mostly used for coloring and pickling umeboshi (salted and dried "plums"). Green perilla is served with sushi and sashimi – it is said to counteract parasites in raw fish. The leaves are also used in soups and salads and to wrap rice cakes. Coated with batter on one side only, they are deep-fried for tempura. The Vietnamese shred perilla and add it to noodles; they serve grilled meat, shrimp, and fish wrapped in green perilla leaves with a spicy dipping sauce; and they also use it in salads.

Chopped green perilla gives a wonderful flavor to cooked rice; substitute dried if necessary. In recent years I have become accustomed to growing perilla, and while I mostly use the red in salads and as a garnish, I increasingly extend my use of the green. I add it to slices of lemon or lime in the cavity of fish to be roasted or steamed, to sauces for fish and chicken, and to salsa verde instead of basil. Sometimes I use it instead of basil with tomatoes, or with pasta or noodles.

It has recently been discovered that oil extracted from perilla seeds is one of the richest sources of Omega-3 essential fatty acids.

Good with beef, chicken, fish, mooli, noodles and pasta, potatoes, rice, tomatoes, zucchini.

Combines well with basil, chives, fresh and pickled ginger, lemon grass, mitsuba, parsley, sansho, wasabi.

MITSUBA

Cryptotaenia japonica

Mitsuba is also known as Japanese parsley, Japanese chervil, and trefoil. This cool-climate, elegant perennial grows wild in Japan and is used extensively in Japanese cooking. It is now cultivated in Australia, North America, and Europe, initially to supply Japanese restaurants but increasingly to sell to herb enthusiasts.

TASTING NOTES

Mitsuba has little aroma but a distinctive, mild, restrained, and agreeable taste, showing elements of chervil, angelica, and celery, with something of the astringency of sorrel and a hint of clove.

PARTS USED

Leaves and stems.

BUYING AND STORING

You may find mitsuba is available in a Japanese or Asian market, otherwise buy a plant from a nursery. Leaves keep for 5–6 days if wrapped in damp paper towel or placed in a plastic bag in the vegetable crisper of the refrigerator.

GROW YOUR OWN

Mitsuba is a woodland plant and is easy to grow in light shade. It seeds itself readily. In summer mitsuba bears insignificant white flowers above the leaves. Leaves and slender stems are harvested from spring through to autumn or winter. Mitsuba is not long-lived; I have found it necessary to replace mine after 4–5 years.

Culinary uses

In Japan, mitsuba is used to season soups, simmered dishes (nabemono), and savory custards, in salads, and with fried or vinegared foods. It adds its highly individual, delicate flavor to matsutake no dobinmushi, a dish made only for a few weeks when the much-prized pine mushrooms are in season. The mushrooms are simmered in a broth and the mitsuba is added for a few seconds at the end. Small bundles of stems can be tied in a knot below the leaves and fried for tempura. Mitsuba is often blanched quickly to tenderize the leaves, or added to stir-fried foods at the last moment; overcooking destroys the flavor of the leaves. The sprouted seedlings are good in salads.

Good with eggs, fish and seafood, mushrooms, poultry, rice, and as a garnish for most vegetables, especially sweet roots such as carrots and parsnips.

Combines well with basil, chives, ginger, lemon balm, lemon grass, marjoram, sesame.

Fresh leaves
Mitsuba means "three leaves" in Japanese, from the three leaflets that make up the leaf. The meaning is echoed in the English name trefoil.

ORACH

Atriplex hortensis

Orach belongs to the goosefoot family, as does epazote (*p.120*). It grows wild in Europe and much of temperate Asia, and was formerly gathered and also cultivated for use as a vegetable. Its old popular name was mountain spinach. Out of fashion for a long time, orach has been rediscovered as an attractive salad herb.

TASTING NOTES

Orach is not aromatic; the leaves have a mild, agreeable, spinach-like flavor, which contrasts well with more pungent salad herbs.

PARTS USED

Young leaves.

BUYING AND STORING

Seeds and plants are available from specialist suppliers. It is best to use leaves straight after picking, but they will keep for a day or two in a plastic bag in the refrigerator vegetable crisper. Orach is sometimes included in gourmet mixtures of salad leaves.

GROW YOUR OWN

Orach produces bigger leaves if planted in rich, well-drained soil. Red orach benefits from partial shade, where the leaves will not scorch in hot sun. It grows fast, and it is best to sow seeds in late spring and again in summer for a continuous supply of young leaves. Orach has a tendency to grow tall and straggly, but the plants should remain bushy if you harvest leaves regularly and remove the flowerspikes as they begin to form. Orach is a self-seeding annual.

Culinary uses

Orach is best used as a salad herb, but it can also be cooked with spinach or sorrel (it alleviates the acidity of the latter). The triangular leaves, particularly of red orach, make an attractive addition to the salad bowl, and an ornamental asset in the garden (harvest leaves regularly).

Good with catalogna, corn salad, lettuce, mizuna, mustard greens, and other salad leaves.

Combines well with arugula, borage, chicory, cresses, dill, fennel, purslane, salad burnet, sorrel.

Fresh leaves
Green orach may have red-tinged stems; red orach has deep plum-colored leaves and stems.

MARIGOLD

Calendula officinalis and Tagetes species

Marigolds are used in many different ways. The dried, ground petals of pot marigold (*C. officinalis*) and French marigold (*T. patula*) are prized in the Georgian republic; in Mexico and the southern US, Mexican mint marigold (*T. lucida*) is used as a tarragon substitute; in Peru, huacatay (*T. minuta*) is an essential flavoring; in Europe, fresh petals are used as a garnish and in salads.

Pot marigold *C. officinalis*

This marigold is a long-lived annual with pale green, lance-shaped leaves and single or double flowers. The petals and young leaves should be used immediately after picking.

DRIED PETALS
Dried pot marigold petals from the Republic of Georgia have a sweet, musky aroma with hints of citrus peel.

TASTING NOTES

Pot marigolds have a sweet, resin-like aroma, French marigolds a distinctive muskiness with light citrus notes that reminds me of coriander seed. Fresh marigold petals have a delicate, aromatic bitterness and earthy taste. The leaves are slightly peppery.

PARTS USED

Fresh and dried petals, fresh young leaves.

BUYING AND STORING

Marigold petals can be dried in a low oven and then ground. Dried pot marigold petals can be bought from some herb and spice suppliers; dried marigold powder is less easily found. Store dried marigold petals and powder in airtight containers. The leaves of Mexican mint marigold will keep for a day or two in a plastic bag in the refrigerator.

GROW YOUR OWN

Marigolds thrive in any soil, but do best in a sunny position. Picking the flowers prolongs flowering, but if a plant goes to seed it will readily self-seed. Pot and French marigolds are annuals. Mexican mint marigold is a perennial, but should be taken indoors to overwinter where not hardy.

Culinary uses

Apart from adding a lively note to salads, marigold petals have long been used to color food and give it a slightly pungent flavor. Fresh petals can be added to cookies and small cakes, to custards, savory butters, and soups. Dried petals were often used to adulterate saffron; they can be used as an inexpensive substitute for coloring rice.

In the Republic of Georgia, dried marigold petals are an essential flavoring, used in spice mixtures and with other aromatic staples (chili peppers, garlic, walnuts). Georgians prefer the French marigold, and the flavor blends particularly well with cinnamon and cloves. They call it Imeretian saffron after the province of Imereti, where the dried petals are highly appreciated.

Mint marigold leaves are used with other indigenous American foods – avocado, corn, squash, tomatoes – as well as with fish, chicken, and other foods that marry well with tarragon. They also combine well with melon, summer berries, and stone fruits.

Huacatay, also called black mint, is strongly aromatic with citrus and eucalypt notes and a bitter aftertaste. It is hard to find fresh outside South America, but is sold as a paste in jars in the US. Use with chili peppers to season grilled meats, soups, and stews.

Mexican mint marigold *T. lucida*

The long, narrow leaves of Mexican mint marigold smell more of anise than mint, with light notes of hay and some spicy warmth.The plant's other common names, winter or Mexican tarragon, refer to its tarragon-like taste.

French marigold

T. patula

This marigold species is a bushy annual with divided, toothed leaves and flat single or frilly double flowers that vary in color from yellow to deep orange.

BASIL

Ocimum species

Lightly brushing basil leaves releases an aroma that promises warmth and sunlight – in every Greek village the intoxicating fragrance of basil fills the air. Basil belongs to the mint family, as is clear from the minty, anise notes that accompany its sweetness. Native to tropical Asia, where it has been cultivated for 3,000 years, it is now grown almost everywhere where the climate is warm enough.

TASTING NOTES

Sweet basil has a complex sweet, spicy aroma with notes of clove and anise. The flavor is warm, peppery, and clove-like with underlying mint and anise tones. Purple (opal) basil, bush basil, lettuce basil, and 'Ruffles' basils have rather similar flavors (*pp.31–33*).

PARTS USED

Fresh leaves; add buds from flowerspikes to salads or use as a garnish.

BUYING AND STORING

Most basil leaves bruise and wilt easily, so avoid bunches with drooping or blackened leaves. Store for 2–3 days in damp paper towel or a plastic bag in the refrigerator vegetable crisper. Thai basil (*p.34*) is more sturdy and will keep for 5–6 days. Basil leaves will freeze well for up to 3 months; one of the best ways is to purée them with a little water or olive oil and freeze in ice-cube trays.

GROW YOUR OWN

Most basils are tender annuals. Basil grows easily from seed, and needs a sheltered, sunny position in rich, well-drained soil. In cooler climates it prefers a greenhouse or a windowsill. Delay flowering and encourage bushiness by pinching out the tops. Harvest until the first frost.

Sweet basil *O. basilicum*

Also called Genoese basil, this plant has large, bright green, silky leaves and small, white flowers. Good for all Western cooking, it is the best basil for pesto, pistou, and tomato salads. It combines very well with garlic. One way to preserve the leaves is to put them in a jar with an airtight lid, layer lightly with salt, and cover with olive oil. Kept in the refrigerator, the leaves eventually blacken, but they flavor the oil beautifully.

Culinary uses

In Western cooking, basil is the natural companion of tomatoes, whether in salad, sauce, or soup. It is a good flavoring for poultry too – combine softened butter with chopped basil, garlic, grated lemon rind, and a few bread crumbs, then work the mixture under the skin of a chicken or chicken pieces before baking or pot-roasting. Use basil with fish and seafood, especially lobster and scallops, and with roast veal and lamb. It also has an affinity with raspberries. Purple basil makes a pretty, pale pink vinegar.

Sweet basil turns black when cooked in a tomato sauce or other acid medium, but retains its flavor. It quickly loses its aroma when cooked, so use it in a dish for depth of flavor, then stir in a little more to add fragrance when the cooking is finished. Basil leaves can be torn, or chopped or shredded with a knife, but cutting bruises them and they darken quickly.

Essential to pesto and pistou.

Good with corn, cream cheese, eggplant, eggs, lemon, mozzarella cheese, olives, pasta, peas, pizza, potatoes, rice, tomatoes, white beans, zucchini.

Combines well with capers, chives, cilantro, garlic, marjoram, oregano, mint, parsley, rosemary, thyme.

Purple basil *O.b.* var. *purpurascens*

This handsome plant, also called opal basil, has purple or almost black leaves and pink flowers. It is highly aromatic, with clear notes of mint and clove. Use with rice and grains and to add a splash of color to salads.

Other basils

There are many different basils, some of them with names that indicate their aroma or appearance. All have the underlying sweet, warm, clove-anise aroma of sweet basil, but different aspects are dominant: a pungent warmth in 'Ruffles', a peppery note in bush basil, anise in lettuce basil. In Mediterranean cooking, basil's natural partners are garlic, olive oil, lemon, and tomato. The herb is best known as the key ingredient of Genoese pesto and the related pistou of France.

O. b. 'Purple Ruffles'

'Purple Ruffles' is an ornamental plant with large, shiny, purple-maroon leaves with a ruffled edge, and pink flowers. Its flavor is warm and licorice-like. 'Green Ruffles' has big, lime-green leaves with a frilly edge and white flowers. Use both as sweet basil (*p.30*).

Bush basil *O. b.* var. *minimum*

Also called Greek basil, this makes a compact bush with small leaves, white flowers, and a peppery aroma. It is easy to grow in a pot. Use as sweet basil; add whole leaves to salads.

O. b. 'Cinnamon'

This variety is native to Mexico. The leaves are flushed purple and the flowers pink. It has a pronounced, sweet scent with clear cinnamon notes rising above hints of camphor. Serve it with bean and legume dishes and with spicy, stir-fried vegetables.

O. 'African Blue'

This variety has become one of my favorite basils for its striking appearance and excellent flavor. The leaves are mottled green-purple, the flowers purple. It is strongly scented with peppery, clove, and mint notes and a hint of camphor in the background. Use it with rice, vegetables, and meats; it is very good in potato salad and makes an outstanding pesto. Unlike most basils, it is a perennial as long as it is kept frost-free.

Lettuce basil *O. b.* var. *crispum*

This basil has large, floppy, wrinkled leaves with a soft texture. It is excellent in salads, or chopped and mixed with diced tomato and extra virgin olive oil to make a pasta dressing. Lettuce basil is much prized in southern Italy.

Asian basils

Asian basils (many are *Ocimum basilicum* varieties) are as numerous as Western basils, and herb nurseries now supply some of the common ones. Their flavors differ from those of Western basils because of the different chemical constituents of the essential oils. The dominant aroma constituent of sweet basil (*p.30*) is linalool (floral) with some methyl chavicol (anise) and a little eugenol (clove), but in Asian basils methyl chavicol is dominant with some eugenol and a little camphor.

Thai basil *O. b. horapa*

Thai bai horapa has a heady, sweet, peppery aroma backed by pronounced anise notes, and a warm, lingering, anise-licorice flavor.

Licorice basil *O. b. Anise*

This decorative plant, also called anise basil, has purple-veined leaves, reddish stems, pink flowerspikes, and an agreeable, anise-licorice aroma. Use as Thai basil.

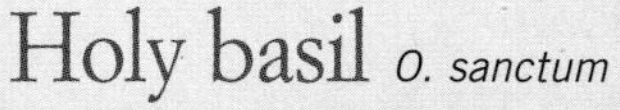

Holy basil *O. sanctum*

Holy basil, or bai gaprow, is intensely aromatic with a spicy, sweet pungency, hints of mint and camphor, and a touch of muskiness. If you can't find it, use sweet basil and a few mint leaves. The flavor is enhanced by cooking; when raw, the taste is slightly bitter. It is the essential ingredient in a Thai dish of stir-fried chicken with chili peppers and basil, and is much used in meat curries.

Culinary uses

Basil flavors Southeast-Asian salads, stir-fried dishes, soups, and curries. It is added at the end of cooking so that the aromatic leaves balance the spices in the dish. It is also used in Thai green curry paste.
Good with beef, chicken, coconut milk, fish and seafood, noodles, pork, rice.
Combines well with chili, cilantro leaf and root, galangal, garlic, ginger, kaffir lime, krachai, lemon grass, tamarind, turmeric.

Lemon basil *O. b. citriodorum*

This bushy, compact basil has a clean, lemon fragrance. In Indonesia, where it is called kemangie, it is fried with fish and seafood. Add it to salads, and scatter over poached scallops, grilled fish, or pork kebabs.

Thai lemon basil *O. canum*

Also called hairy basil, or bai manglak, this plant has an attractive lemon-camphor aroma and a peppery, lemony flavor. Thai cooks stir it into noodles or fish curry just before serving. The seeds are soaked and used in a coconut-milk dessert and in cooling drinks. It is sometimes sold as green holy basil.

Lime basil *O. americanum*

This basil is similar to *O. b. citriodorum*, but the leaves are slightly darker and the aroma is decidedly of lime, not lemon. Use in salads and with fish and seafood.

BAY

Laurus nobilis

The bay tree is native to the eastern Mediterranean, but has long been cultivated in northern Europe and the Americas. It came to symbolize wisdom and glory to the Greeks and Romans, who crowned kings, poets, Olympic champions, and victorious generals with wreaths of its glossy, leathery leaves. Although there are several varieties of bay, only *L. nobilis* is used in the kitchen.

TASTING NOTES

Bay has a sweet, balsamic aroma with notes of nutmeg and camphor, and a cooling astringency. Fresh leaves are slightly bitter, but the bitterness fades if you keep them for a day or two. Fully dried leaves have a potent flavor and are best when dried only recently.

PARTS USED

Fresh and dried leaves.

BUYING AND STORING

Fresh leaves can be used from a tree, but are less bitter if kept until wilted. To dry completely, lay leaves flat in a dark, well-aired place and leave until brittle. If stored in an airtight container, dried leaves will keep their aroma and flavor for at least a year; stale leaves have no flavor.

GROW YOUR OWN

Although bay does best in warm regions, it will survive in a sheltered, sunny position in cooler climates. It is a good container plant, and growing it like this has the advantage that it can be moved indoors for the winter where not hardy. In warm climates it produces small, yellow flowers in spring, followed by purple berries (which are not edible). Leaves can be picked throughout the year.

Fresh leaves
Fresh leaves need to be crushed or rubbed to release their aromatic compounds. Bay is indispensable in French and Mediterranean cooking.

Bouquet garni
A bouquet garni is a bundle of herbs used to flavor slow-cooked dishes. The classic includes a few sprigs of thyme and parsley with a bay leaf (*recipes, p.280*).

DRIED LEAVES
Dried bay leaves should remain a mat, sage green, and not turn yellow or brown. Crumble or grind the leaves only when you need them.

Culinary uses

Bay leaves yield their flavor slowly, so they are useful in stocks, soups, stews, sauces, marinades, and pickles. Put a leaf or two on top of a homemade pâté or terrine before baking it; add bay to any fish stew, or combine with lemon and fennel when filling the cavity of a fish to be baked; thread leaves onto kebabs (soak dried leaves in water first), or add them to a pilaf. Bay is always included in a bouquet garni, and to flavor the milk for béchamel sauce. It goes well with beans, lentils, and tomatoes, especially to flavor a tomato sauce.

The Turks use bay in steamed and slow-cooked lamb dishes, the Moroccans in chicken and lamb tagines; the French partner it with beef in Provençal daubes. Bay also gives a pleasant, unusual, spicy fragrance to baked custards and rice pudding and to poached fruit dishes. In Turkish spice bazaars, boxes of dried figs are often lined with bay leaves.

Two or three bay leaves flavor a dish for four to six people; if you put in too many, the flavor will be too strong. Remove the leaves before serving. Note also that in India, parts of the Caribbean, and South America, leaves of other species may be called bay leaves.

Essential to bouquets garnis, béchamel sauce.

Good with beef, chestnuts, chicken, citrus fruits, fish, game, lamb, lentils, rice, tomatoes, white beans.

Combines well with allspice, garlic, juniper, marjoram, oregano, parsley, sage, savory, thyme.

MYRTLE

Myrtus communis

Myrtle is native to the hilly regions of the Mediterranean basin and the Middle East, where for centuries it was used as a flavoring. Although mainland Europe came to prefer imported Oriental spices, myrtle continued to be an important flavoring on the Mediterranean islands of Crete, Corsica, and Sardinia.

TASTING NOTES

All parts of the plant are aromatic. The leaves are slightly resinous with a sweet, orange-blossom note; they taste juniper-like and astringent. The berries are sweet with notes of juniper, allspice, and rosemary. The flowers are more delicately scented.

PARTS USED

Leaves, flowers, berries. Leaves, flowerbuds, and berries can be dried.

BUYING AND STORING

Myrtle plants can be bought from specialist nurseries. Use leaves fresh from the plant or dry them in a dark, well-ventilated place until brittle, then keep in an airtight container. Dry buds and berries in the same way, and then store.

GROW YOUR OWN

Myrtle is an evergreen shrub with small, shiny, oval leaves. It bears scented, white flowers with pretty yellow stamens in summer and purple-black fruits in autumn. In cooler climates a young myrtle plant is best grown in a container and taken indoors in winter. Once established it can be planted out in a sunny, sheltered site. Myrtle leaves can be harvested throughout the year.

Culinary uses

Use myrtle flowers picked straight from the plant, in salads or as a garnish. The leaves make a good flavoring for pork and wild boar, for venison, hare, and squab. Use very sparingly and add toward the end of cooking if you are making a stew. Combine with thyme or savory to flavor meat and game, or with fennel to flavor fish. When grilling meat, add a few sprigs to the charcoal, to impart a juniper-like flavor. Place myrtle berries and a clove of garlic in the cavity of squab or quail to be roasted or fried, or use them as you would juniper berries. Crush dried buds and berries, and use as a spice.

Myrtle leaves are still used in southern Italy as a wrapping for small, newly made cheeses; as the cheeses cure, the leaves absorb their moisture, at the same time giving them a subtle flavor.

Fresh sprigs Common myrtle is most frequently used, but the compact *M. c.* subsp. *tarentina*, native to Corsica and Sardinia, where it is used with chicken and pork, has the same aromatic qualities.

ANGELICA

Angelica archangelica

A statuesque biennial – flower stalks may be over 6½ft (2m) high – angelica does best in cooler climates and is hardy enough to grow in northern parts of Scandinavia and Russia. Although it needs a lot of space, it is worth growing for its showy clump of bright green, serrated leaves and large domes of tiny, yellow-green flowers.

TASTING NOTES

The whole plant is aromatic. When rubbed, young stalks and leaves have a sweet, musky scent; the taste is musky and bittersweet, slightly earthy, and warm, with notes of celery, anise, and juniper. The flowers have a honeyed fragrance.

PARTS USED

Young leaves and stalks. Essential oil, distilled from the seeds and roots, is used to flavor drinks such as vermouths and liqueurs.

BUYING AND STORING

Fresh angelica is not available commercially, so it is necessary to grow your own. Young plants are available from some herb nurseries; it can also be grown from seed. Young stalks will keep in a plastic bag in the refrigerator for up to a week; leaves will wilt after 2–3 days.

GROW YOUR OWN

Angelica grows best in rich soil and partial shade. It produces long, tubular stalks in the first year, dies down in the winter, and then comes back vigorously the following spring. By late spring or early summer, purple-tinged flower stems rise up and open spectacular flowerheads. These eventually set to seed, after which the plant dies. If permitted, the plant will self-seed easily.

Fresh leaves and stalks
Young stalks and leaves are best cut during the first summer or early the following spring.

Culinary uses

Young stalks are candied. Young leaves and stalks can be used in marinades and poaching liquids for fish and seafood, or cooked as a vegetable – boiled or steamed angelica is very popular in Iceland and northerly parts of Scandinavia. Leaves can be added to salads, stuffings, sauces, and salsas.

Angelica's musky sweetness has a natural affinity with rhubarb for compotes, pies, and preserves – use a handful of sliced young stalks or chopped leaves to 2¼lb (1kg) of rhubarb. Angelica can also be infused in milk or cream for ice cream or a baked custard.

Good with almonds, apricots, hazelnuts, oranges, plums, rhubarb, strawberries; fish and seafood.

Combines well with anise, juniper, lavender, lemon balm, nutmeg, pepper, perilla.

SCENTED GERANIUM

Pelargonium species

TASTING NOTES

There are hundreds of varieties of scented geraniums, smelling of apple or citrus fruits, cinnamon, clove, nutmeg or mint, roses or pine. The best for cooking are rose- and lemon-scented plants.

PARTS USED

Fresh leaves. Flowers have little fragrance, but make a pretty garnish for desserts. Although leaves retain their aroma when they die on the plant or are dried, they are not good for cooking.

BUYING AND STORING

Nurseries have a good supply of scented geraniums each spring. Freshly cut leaves are quite sturdy and will keep in a plastic bag in the refrigerator crisper for 4–5 days. Flowers are best picked just before they are to be used.

GROW YOUR OWN

Scented geraniums are tender perennials that will wither at the first frost, but they grow well in pots and can be taken indoors or put in a sheltered spot for the winter. You can also grow them indoors. Leaves can be cut throughout the summer, and cuttings taken for propagation in early autumn.

Scented geraniums offer a profusion of perfumes that echo the scents of other plants. The plants were carried to Europe from South Africa in the 17th century and had reached America by the 18th. Their commercial potential was realized in the mid-19th century when the French perfume industry found a way to use oil from rose-scented geraniums in place of imported and costly attar of roses.

Lemon geranium *P. crispum*

This variety is a stiff plant with small, rough, crinkly leaves, lavender flowers, and a fresh, lemon scent.

FRESH LEAVES
Geranium leaves release their fragrance when they are brushed against or rubbed.

Culinary uses

Sugar scented with rose geranium leaves can be used in desserts and cakes. To make it, bury a handful of leaves in a jar of sugar and leave two weeks (remove the leaves before use). Also try scented sugar when cooking blackberries or mixed berries, or add a couple of leaves to the pan.

Geranium-leaf syrup can be used to make sorbets and poach fruits, or diluted for a refreshing drink. Bring to a boil ¾ cup (150g) sugar and 1 cup (250ml)) water; stir in 10–12 lightly crushed geranium leaves, remove from the heat, and let cool. Strain and add 2 tbsp lemon juice for lemon-scented leaves, or rose water for rose-scented ones. Store in an airtight jar in the refrigerator for a week or so.

Macerate summer berries in wine or syrup with a few geranium leaves. When making preserves, add leaves for the last few minutes of cooking; rose geranium goes well with apples, blackberries, and raspberries; lemon geranium with peaches, apricots, and plums. For ice creams and baked custard, infuse 10–12 lightly crushed leaves in 2 cups (500ml) heated cream or milk until cool, then strain and use.

Rose geranium leaves can be used to line the bottom of a cake pan before pouring in the batter; this will give a subtle flavor to a plain cake. Remove the leaves when the cake has cooled.

Rose geranium

P. graveolens

This variety is an upright plant with triangular, deep-cut leaves and small, pink flowers. The scent is a blend of rose and spice, reminiscent of Turkish delight.

P. 'Lady Plymouth'

This variegated variety has triangular, deep-cut leaves edged with cream, pink flowers, and a lemon-mint-rose scent.

Other geranium varieties

There are more than 250 species of geranium and they show great diversity of form and color. Leaves may be sculpted, lacy, fern-like, or frilled. Colors vary from deep to pale green, velvety gray-green, green and silver, or green and cream.

P. 'Prince of Orange'

A low, compact plant with slightly wrinkled leaves, this variety has pale pink flowers with deeper pink veins, and a sweet, orange scent.

Nutmeg geranium

P. 'Fragrans'

This variety has frilly, notched leaves and white flowers marked with red lines. The leaves have a distinct nutmeg fragrance.

SWEET CICELY

Myrrhis odorata

Sweet cicely is an underrated herb, a natural sweetener with a fine flavor, and its leaves remain green and edible from early spring to late autumn. A perennial indigenous to upland pastures from the far west of Europe to the Caucasus, it is long naturalized in northern Europe and is now cultivated in other temperate zones.

TASTING NOTES

Sweet cicely has an attractive, musky aroma with notes of lovage and anise; the flavor tends more to anise with a hint of celery and a pleasing sweetness. The whole plant is aromatic. The unripe seeds have the strongest flavor and a nutty texture. The glossy, black, ripe seeds have less flavor and are fibrous and chewy.

PARTS USED

Fresh leaves, flowers, and green seeds. In the past raw roots were added to salads or boiled and eaten as a vegetable.

BUYING AND STORING

Plants are available from herb nurseries, and can also be grown from seed. Sweet cicely is not available from supermarkets. The leaves are best used soon after picking, but they will keep for 2–3 days in damp paper towel or a plastic bag in the vegetable crisper of the refrigerator.

GROW YOUR OWN

Sweet cicely is easy to grow and prefers rich, moist soil and semi-shade. It self-seeds readily. Cut back the whole plant after flowering to encourage new growth. Cut leaves between spring and autumn. Harvest the flowers in spring, and the green, unripe seeds in summer.

Culinary uses

The leaves and green seeds reduce the tartness of fruits such as gooseberries and rhubarb when cooked together, although the flavor of the herb itself is dissipated. Leaves and seeds add an anise note to fruit salads and cream-cheese desserts, and sweetness and a hint of spice to cakes, breads, and fruit pies. Sweet cicely is a useful herb for savory dishes too, but to retain the flavor it is best to add it at the end of the cooking time. Young leaf tips give a subtle flavor to green salads and cucumber, and to cream and yogurt sauces made to accompany fish or seafood. Chop leaves into omelettes and clear soups, and stir them into a purée of carrot, parsnip, or pumpkin to enhance the sweetness. Use leaves as a garnish for cheese, and flowers to decorate salads.
Good with apricots, gooseberries, nectarines, peaches, rhubarb, strawberries, root vegetables; chicken, scallops, shrimp.
Combines well with chervil, chives, lemon balm, lemon verbena, mint, vanilla.

Fresh sprigs

By late spring the large, feathery plant bears sweetly scented, lacy, white flowers, followed by large, attractive seedheads.

LAVENDER

Lavandula species

The sight of the deep purple-blue lavender fields shimmering in the heat as you travel down the Rhône valley in France is, for me, the first real indication of reaching the warm south. Native to the Mediterranean region, lavender became a popular garden plant in Tudor England. Today, lavender is grown in many parts of the world for display, for the kitchen, and for its aromatic oils.

TASTING NOTES

Lavender has a penetrating, sweetly floral, and spicy aroma with lemon and mint notes; the taste echoes the aroma with undertones of camphor and a touch of bitterness in the aftertaste. The flowers have the strongest fragrance, but leaves can also be used.

PARTS USED

Fresh and dried flowers; leaves.

BUYING AND STORING

Well-stocked garden centers and herb nurseries have plentiful supplies of a variety of lavenders from spring to autumn. Fresh lavender flowers and leaves will keep in a plastic bag in the refrigerator for up to a week. Dried lavender will keep for a year or more. To dry flowers, hang stems in small bunches or spread on trays; when fully dry, rub the flowers from the stems and store in an airtight container.

GROW YOUR OWN

Lavender needs an open, sunny position and well-drained soil, whether in the garden or a container. The flowers are best harvested just before they are fully open, when their essential oils are most potent. Harvest leaves at any time during the growing season.

English lavender *L. angustifolia*

The gray-green foliage and lilac, purple, or white flowers of this evergreen shrub make it one of the most attractive garden plants. Also called common lavender, it is the best lavender for the cook because of its lower camphor content.

FRESH LEAVES
Like rosemary, lavender has tough leaves that must be chopped finely; flowers also have a firm base, but petals can be plucked out.

DRIED FLOWERS
Soft, floral-scented, English lavender is no less prized for its oils than the intensely aromatic original lavender from the Mediterranean.

French lavender *L. stoechas*

Also called Spanish lavender, this bushy shrub has narrow, green leaves and purple flowers topped by purple bracts. Some varieties are hardy, others are half-hardy and may survive the winter in a sheltered spot. *L. stoechas* has a more pungent camphor note than *L. angustifolia*.

Culinary uses

Lavender is very potent and must be used sparingly. A few dried lavender flowers immersed in a jar of sugar for a week or so will give it a fine, sweet aroma. Alternatively, grind fresh lavender flowers and sugar to a powder – this gives a stronger flavor since grinding breaks down the buds and the sugar absorbs the aromatic oils. Use the sugar for baking and in desserts.

Fresh flowers can be chopped and added to a cake batter or sweet pastry or shortbread dough before baking. Scatter petals over a cake or dessert to decorate it. Add flowers to preserves toward the end of the cooking time, or to fruit compotes for a sweetly spiced note. Infuse flowers in cream, milk, syrup, or wine to flavor sorbets and other desserts. Lavender ice cream is very good, or try adding lavender to chocolate ice cream or mousse.

Lavender is successful in savory dishes, too. Chop leaves for a salad or scatter flowers over the top. Fold chopped flowers into cooked rice. Use chopped flowers and leaves to flavor a leg of lamb, or roast or casseroled rabbit, chicken, or pheasant. Add lavender to marinades and rubs. Lavender also makes an excellent vinegar.

Around the Mediterranean, lavender is used in herb mixtures. In Provence, France, it is blended with thyme, savory, and rosemary; in Morocco, it is sometimes used in ras el hanout.

Good with blackberries, blueberries, cherries, mulberries, plums, rhubarb, strawberries; and chicken, lamb, pheasant, rabbit.

Combines well with marjoram, oregano, parsley, perilla, rosemary, savory, thyme.

LAVENDER *is grown commercially on a large scale, mainly to be distilled for its aromatic oils. Long neglected in the*

kitchen, the herb is slowly making a comeback as a versatile, unexpected flavoring in both savory and sweet dishes.

WOODRUFF

Galium odoratum

As its name suggests, woodlands are the natural habitat of this low, creeping, perennial herb. Native to Europe and western Asia, woodruff is now also found in temperate North America. Its pretty, star-like, white flowers and neat ruffs of narrow, shiny leaves make it a most attractive garden plant in spring.

TASTING NOTES

The fresh plant has a faint scent, but cutting releases the smell of new-mown hay and vanillin. Flowers are more lightly scented than leaves; the flavor echoes the scent.

PARTS USED

Leaves and flowers, whole stems.

BUYING AND STORING

Plants are available from garden centers and herb nurseries. Woodruff sprigs are best picked and kept for a day or two before using. The aroma strengthens when the leaves are wilted or dried, and the leaves keep their aroma when frozen. To freeze, spread the woodruff on a tray, and once frozen, store in a plastic bag in the freezer.

GROW YOUR OWN

Woodruff can be grown from seed, although it is slow to germinate. Once established it spreads readily in shady areas. Leaves and flowers can be picked in spring and early summer; later in the year the fragrance is less pronounced.

Culinary uses

The pleasant aroma of woodruff is at its best when the herb has wilted. The principal traditional use of the herb is in the Waldmeisterbowle (Waldmeister is the German name for woodruff) or Maibowle. These are both names for a punch made to celebrate May Day (and other occasions too) using white wine, herbs, sugar, and Sekt. Woodruff can also be infused in marinades for chicken and rabbit, in dressings for salads, in wine to make a sabayon or sorbet. Use only one or two stems and remove before serving or using the liquid. Woodruff flowers are decorative on salads.
Good with apples, melon, pears, strawberries.

Fresh leaves and flowers
Since woodruff contains coumarin, a substance that may cause liver damage if used in excess and is now thought to be carcinogenic, it should be used in very small amounts. Luckily just one or two stems will impart the herb's heady aroma.

PANDAN

Pandanus amaryllifolius, P. tectorius

Pandan or screwpine species grow in the tropics from India to Southeast Asia, northern Australia, and the Pacific islands. The leaves of *P. amaryllifolius* are used as a flavoring and a wrapping for food. Kewra essence, a favorite flavoring of the Moghul emperors of India, is extracted from *P. tectorius* flowers.

TASTING NOTES

Pandan leaf smells sweetly fresh and floral, lightly musky, with notes of new-mown grass. The taste is pleasantly grassy and floral. Leaves have to be bruised or cooked to release their flavor. Kewra essence has a sweet, delicate musk and rose aroma.

PARTS USED

Leaves, flowers.

BUYING AND STORING

Fresh pandan leaves may be found in Asian markets. They keep well in a plastic bag in the refrigerator for 2–3 weeks. Neither frozen nor dried pandan can match fresh leaves for fragrance. Bottled leaf extract has an unnaturally bright color and quickly loses what aroma it has. Pandan powder has a light grassiness that fades after a few months. Kewra essence or kewra water (essence mixed with water) will keep for 2–3 years if tightly closed and stored away from strong light.

HARVESTING

Pandan trees, with their shiny, sword-like leaves growing spirally around the trunk, can be seen in gardens throughout southern Asia. They grow easily, especially in damp areas. Leaves are harvested at any time; flowers are at their best soon after they open.

Culinary uses

To use pandan leaves, pound or scrape them with the prongs of a fork to release their flavor, then tie in a loose knot so that the fibers do not come loose.

Add a leaf or two to rice before cooking to give it a light fragrance, as they do in Malaysia and Singapore. Cooks there also use pandan leaf as a flavoring for pancakes, cakes, and creamy desserts made with sticky rice or tapioca. A knotted leaf is sometimes added to a soup or curry, and in Sri Lanka it adds its flavor to curry powder. Leaves are also used to wrap food. Thai cooks steam or fry parcels of pandan-wrapped chicken or weave leaves as containers for desserts.

Kewra essence is used in India to flavor pilafs and meat dishes as well as sweets and kulfi. It can be diluted with a little water and sprinkled into a dish just before serving. It also gives a special flavor to homemade lemonade.

Good with chicken, coconut, curried dishes, palm sugar, rice.

Combines well with chili, cilantro, galangal, ginger, kaffir lime, lemon grass.

Fresh leaves

Juice from the leaves is used for coloring food; to extract the juice, put 4–5 coarsely chopped leaves into a blender with a little water.

BEE BALM

Monarda didyma

Native to North America, the genus *Monarda* is named for the 16th-century Spanish physician, Nicolas Monardes, whose *Joyfull Newes Out of the Newe Founde Worlde* was the first American herbal. It is commonly called bee balm because the flowers attract bees. Another name, bergamot, probably derives from the similarity of the plant's aroma to that of the bergamot orange.

TASTING NOTES

The whole plant has a distinctive citrus aroma. The flavor is citrus with an added warm, spicy note. Flowers are more delicately flavored than the leaves.

PARTS USED

Fresh and dried leaves; flowers. Dried leaves are used for teas.

BUYING AND STORING

Plants are available from herb nurseries and garden centers. Flowers and leaves wilt quickly and are best used soon after picking. They can be chopped and frozen. Spread leaves and flowers on trays to dry, or hang bunches of stems in a dark, well-ventilated place. Store when dry in an airtight container. Dried bee balm can be bought as an herbal tea.

GROW YOUR OWN

A perennial of the mint family, bee balm thrives in most situations, but does best in a fertile, moisture-retaining soil, in sun or partial shade. Every 3 years, dig up the plant, discard the center, and replant the young outer parts. Pick flowers when fully open, and leaves throughout the summer.

Fresh leaves
All the cultivated varieties of bee balm, with their showy whorls of different colored flowers and slightly different scents, can be used in the same way.

Culinary uses

Use only fresh, young leaves and flowers for cooking. Add shredded leaves and petals to green and fruit salads. Bee balm goes well with duck, chicken, and pork; it can be chopped into yogurt or cream for a sauce, or added to a salsa. Flowers are good in sandwiches with cream cheese and cucumber.

Bee balm is also known as Oswego tea – named for the Oswego river and valley in the northeastern US, where Native American tribes made a tea from it, a practice that was adopted by early European settlers. Try adding a few fresh or dried flowers or leaves to a pot of tea, to homemade lemonade, or to summer punches for a lightly scented taste.

Good with apples, chicken, citrus fruits, duck, kiwi fruit, melon, papaya, pork, strawberries, tomatoes.
Combines well with chives, cresses, dill, fennel, garlic, lemon balm, mint, parsley, rosemary, thyme.

Other monardas
Wild bee balm, *M. fistulosa*, also known as horsemint, is less handsome and has a stronger and coarser fragrance than cultivated varieties. Use sparingly.

Another variety, *M. f.* var. *menthifolia*, resembles oregano in aroma and flavor and is sometimes used as a substitute for oregano in the southwestern US.

Bee-balm salsa
A salsa of chopped bee balm leaves, parsley, and orange is delicious with pork kebabs or barbecued fish.

LEMON BALM

Melissa officinalis

TASTING NOTES

When crushed, the young leaves have a fresh, lingering, lemon scent and a mild lemon-mint flavor. The aroma is subtle and pleasant, and not as penetrating as that of lemon verbena or lemon grass. Large, older leaves have a musty flavor.

PARTS USED

Leaves, fresh and dried.

BUYING AND STORING

Seeds and plants may be bought from specialist nurseries. Fresh leaves will keep for 3–4 days in a plastic bag in the vegetable crisper in the refrigerator. To dry leaves, hang small bunches of stems in a dark, airy place. Crumble the leaves when completely dry and store in an airtight container. They should keep their flavor for 5–6 months.

GROW YOUR OWN

Lemon balm is easy to grow from seed or by dividing the root stock in spring or autumn. Plants should be cut back after flowering to encourage new growth. Balm grows vigorously and will spread readily unless kept in check: in a small garden it is best grown in a pot. Leaves should be harvested early in the season since they can become rank later on.

Lemon balm is a perennial of the mint family, native to southern Europe and western Asia, and now cultivated widely in all temperate regions. With its crinkled, serrated leaves and tiny white or yellowish flowers, it is not a showy plant, but earns its place in the garden by attracting bees and by its agreeable lemon scent.

Culinary uses

Lemon balm's principal use is in a soothing, calming tea, made from fresh or dried leaves. Fresh leaves can be infused in summer punches or blended in smoothies. For cooking, the lemon-mint flavor of fresh leaves complements fish and poultry in sauces, stuffings, and marinades. Tear young leaves for green or tomato salads, or chop them to scatter over steamed or sautéed vegetables or to stir into rice or cracked wheat. Lemon balm makes a delicate herb butter and fragrant vinegar. The fresh flavor is good in fruit desserts and in creams and cakes. A strong tea, well sweetened, makes the basis for a good sorbet.

Good with apples, apricots, carrots, soft white cheeses, chicken, eggs, figs, fish, melon, mushrooms, nectarines, peaches, peas, summer berries, tomatoes, zucchini.

Combines well with bee balm, chervil, chives, dill, fennel, ginger, mint, nasturtium, parsley, sweet cicely.

Fresh leaves
Always cook with fresh leaves, and use generous amounts because the aroma is delicate. The variegated form, *M. o.* 'Aurea', can also be used.

VIETNAMESE BALM

Elsholtzia ciliata

Native to temperate eastern and central Asia, Vietnamese balm, or rau kinh gio'i, is a bushy plant with light green, serrated leaves and lavender flowerspikes. It somewhat resembles lemon balm in aroma, but the plants are unrelated. It is cultivated in Germany more than in other regions of Europe, and also in those parts of the US where there are large Vietnamese population centers. Stray plants also grow wild in parts of Europe and North America.

TASTING NOTES

Vietnamese balm has a clear, lemon aroma with floral undertones; the flavor is reminiscent of lemon balm, but is more concentrated, somewhat like lemon grass. If none is available, lemon balm and lemon grass can be combined as a substitute.

PARTS USED

Fresh leaves and young sprigs.

BUYING AND STORING

Vietnamese balm is grown mostly by nurseries that supply herbs to Southeast-Asian restaurants, and is sold by Asian markets, but it is not yet widely available in Europe or North America. Leaves keep for 3–4 days in a plastic bag in the refrigerator vegetable crisper.

GROW YOUR OWN

Vietnamese balm is a perennial, often grown as an annual. It can be grown from seed outdoors when the frosts are over, and is likely to become invasive in warm, moist conditions. Sprigs from an Asian market can be encouraged to root by standing them in water. Cuttings taken in autumn will root and survive if kept in a warm place. Harvest leaves from spring to early autumn.

Culinary uses

Vietnamese balm is used to flavor egg, vegetable, and fish dishes, in soups, and with noodles and rice. It is sometimes added to the platter of fresh herbs that accompanies many Vietnamese meals. In Thailand, it is most frequently cooked and served as a vegetable.

Good with carambola, cucumber, eggplant, lettuce, mushrooms, scallions, fish and seafood.

Combines well with Asian basils, chili, cilantro, galangal, garlic, mint, perilla, tamarind.

Fresh leaves

Vietnamese balm has been used as a culinary and medicinal plant for many years in Southeast Asia, but as yet is little known to Western cooks.

LEMON VERBENA

Aloysia citriodora

Lemon verbena is native to Chile and Argentina, and was taken to Europe by the Spaniards and to North America by a New England sea captain in the 18th century. In France, it was used by toilet-water manufacturers for its aromatic oils. Until 100 years ago it was widely grown as an ornamental garden plant; it certainly merits a place in any scented garden for its intoxicating, pure lemon fragrance.

TASTING NOTES

Lemon verbena has an intense, fresh lemon aroma. The taste echoes the aroma but is less strong; it is more lemony than a lemon, but lacks the tartness. Leaves keep their fragrance quite well when cooked. The aroma of dried leaves is retained for up to a year.

PARTS USED

Leaves, fresh and dried.

BUYING AND STORING

Specialist herb nurseries stock plants. Cut leaves can be kept for a day or two in the refrigerator. Sprigs can also be put in a glass of water for 24 hours. Leaves can be chopped and frozen in small pots or in ice cubes. To dry, hang stems in a dark, well-ventilated place. Dried lemon verbena is sold as a tisane, and that is the best use for dried leaves.

GROW YOUR OWN

Lemon verbena needs sun and well-drained soil. Leaves can be harvested throughout the growing season. Regular trimming will make the plant bushier, and it should be cut back in autumn to remove weak branches. It does not tolerate frost, so is best grown in a container and taken indoors in winter, when it will shed its leaves. Take outside only when frosts are over.

Culinary uses

Lemon verbena is a natural companion to fish and poultry: put some sprigs into the cavity, or chop and use in a stuffing or marinade. The vibrant, clean taste is also good with fatty meats such as pork and duck, in vegetable soup, and in a rice pilaf. Lemon verbena is used as a flavoring for desserts and drinks. Add sprigs to a syrup for poaching fruit, chop finely for a fruit salad or tart, or infuse in cream to make a fresh-scented ice cream. Lining a cake pan with leaves will give a lemon scent to a plain cake.

Good with apricots, carrots, chicken, fish, mushrooms, rice, zucchini.

Combines well with basil, chili, chives, cilantro, lemon thyme, mint, garlic.

Fresh sprigs
Add sprigs to iced tea or summer coolers, or make an infusion of fresh leaves. Lemon verbena makes one of the best and most refreshing of all teas.

SASSAFRAS

Sassafras albidum

Sassafras is an aromatic, ornamental tree native to the eastern US, from Maine to Florida. Native Americans showed early settlers how to make tea from the bark, roots, and leaves. The French-speaking Canadians (Cajuns) who went to Louisiana adopted a Choctaw method of using dried, ground sassafras leaves to flavor and thicken stews. The roots used to be an essential ingredient of root beer.

TASTING NOTES

Young leaves have an astringent, citrus-fennel aroma; the roots smell camphorous. Filé powder tastes sourish, rather like lemony sorrel with woody notes. Its flavor can be brought out by brief heating.

PARTS USED

Leaves and roots.

BUYING AND STORING

It is best not to use fresh sassafras, because in its natural form it contains safrole, a carcinogen. Root bark and leaves are now treated to remove safrole before they are sold or used commercially. Buy prepared filé powder, sassafras tea, or tea concentrate only if marked "safrole free." Filé powder will keep for 6 months, and sassafras tea for a year or more.

GROW YOUR OWN

Sassafras trees are mostly found in the wild. Only young specimens can be transplanted, because established trees have long taproots, and so they are seldom offered for sale. Leaves for making commercial filé powder are harvested in spring, then dried and ground.

Culinary uses

Filé powder, or gumbo filé, made from dried, ground sassafras leaves, is only used in the cooking of Louisiana, but it is the key to the texture and flavor of many Cajun and Creole soups and stews. In particular, it is used in gumbo, a substantial, spicy soup made with a variety of vegetables, seafood, or meat and served with rice. The mucilaginous quality of filé helps thicken the dish, provided it is stirred in when the pan is removed from the heat; prolonged cooking makes filé tough and stringy. Some brands of filé powder contain other ground herbs, such as bay, oregano, sage, or thyme, in addition to ground sassafras leaf.

Dried leaves
The large leaves, which provide dramatic autumn colors, may have one, two, or three lobes, even on the same branch.

FILE POWDER
Filé powder is essential to create the rich texture of Louisiana dishes. It also serves as a condiment to accompany them.

SORREL

Rumex acetosa, R. scutatus

A member of the dock family, sorrel grows wild in meadowlands throughout much of Europe and western Asia, and it is well worth growing in the garden. Garden sorrel, *R. acetosa*, is the common variety; French or buckler leaf sorrel, *R. scutatus*, has a more delicate, lemony flavor. Sorrel has been appreciated for the tartness it imparts to rich foods since the time of the ancient Egyptians.

TASTING NOTES

Sorrel has no aroma; the taste of garden sorrel ranges from refreshingly tangy and sharp to astringent, and large leaves may be slightly bitter. The texture is spinach-like. French sorrel has a milder, more lemony, and more succulent flavor.

PARTS USED

Fresh leaves.

BUYING AND STORING

Sorrel is seldom seen in supermarkets because it wilts quickly and is best used within a day or two of picking. Keep it in a plastic bag in the vegetable crisper of the refrigerator. It does not dry well, but leaves can be frozen. Steam the leaves until wilted, or cook in a little butter, then freeze in small pots.

GROW YOUR OWN

Garden sorrel grows best in rich, moist soil with partial, light shade. Too much hot sun will make the leaves bitter. French sorrel prefers a drier, warmer spot. Both are perennials that grow well from seed, or you can buy plants from an herb nursery. Plants grow to sizeable clumps and can be divided in autumn. Sorrel goes to seed quickly, so remove the flower stems to encourage leaf growth.

Garden sorrel *R. acetosa*

Sorrel leaves can be harvested from spring until the plant dies down in winter. The more you pick, the more prolifically they grow. I have recently started growing *R.a.* 'Abundance,' a cultivar from Canada that makes a compact, bushy plant. The leaves are dark green and round rather than oval, it doesn't go to seed, and the acidic flavor is restrained.

Culinary uses

Sorrel is high in vitamins A and C, and also in oxalic acid, which gives the herb its sour taste. It is best served in combination with other foods, and that is how it has been traditionally used.

Raw whole French sorrel and shredded garden sorrel make an agreeable addition to salads, but whisk a little honey or sugar into the dressing to counter the herb's acidity. A few shredded raw leaves add a welcome tartness to omelettes, baked and scrambled eggs, and creamy dishes and sauces, and also make a good garnish for fish.

Sorrel cooks very quickly and reduces greatly in volume. It turns a drab khaki color, which you can mask by using it in a soup or sauce, or by cooking it with spinach, as in the classic green Ukrainian borscht.

In Lithuania, slices of smoked sausage are used in a creamy sorrel soup; in Poland, a roux-based soup uses sorrel, half of it cooked and half raw; in France, potato usually forms the base of sorrel soup. Sorrel is one of the herbs used in Frankfurt green sauce. One Italian version of salsa verde is made from raw sorrel, watercress, and onion, chopped and blended to a creamy emulsion with oil and vinegar; serve with poultry or fish. For the classic French sorrel sauce, cook the sorrel in a little butter, add fish or chicken stock and cream, and stir until smooth.

Good with chicken, cucumber, eggs, fish (especially salmon), leeks, lentils, lettuce, mussels, pork, spinach, tomatoes, veal, watercress.

Combines well with borage, chervil, chives, dill, lovage, parsley, tarragon.

French sorrel

R. scutatus

This species is an attractive, carpeting plant with small, mid-green, shield-shaped leaves. There is also a silver variegated variety. Another name for French sorrel is buckler leaf sorrel.

HOUTTUYNIA

Houttuynia cordata

This perennial, water-loving plant is not appreciated as an herb by Western cooks, but it is widely used in Southeast Asia. Native to Japan, houttuynia now grows wild across much of eastern Asia. The dark green-leaved variety is most commonly used for cooking, but you can use the striking cultivated variety *H. c.* 'Chameleon,' which has green, red, pink, and yellow foliage. In Vietnam, houttuynia is called rau diep ca; the name is anglicized to vap ca in the West.

TASTING NOTES

Crushed leaves have a coriander aroma with citrus and sometimes fishy notes. The flavor is sourish and astringent with similarities to rau ram and cilantro but with fishy undertones; it is aptly known as fish plant and Vietnamese fish mint. Some plants smell rank, while others are pungent but pleasing. People either love or hate this herb.

PARTS USED

Fresh leaves.

BUYING AND STORING

Plants are available from nurseries and garden centers. Crush leaves to smell them before buying. Leaves will keep for 2–3 days in a plastic bag in the vegetable crisper of the refrigerator.

GROW YOUR OWN

Houttuynia can be grown in damp soil or in shallow water at the edge of a pond or stream, but it is invasive. If you grow the variegated variety, plant it in a sunny spot to get the most vivid foliage. Harvest leaves from spring to autumn. With its heart-shaped leaves and small, white flowers it makes a pretty ground-cover plant.

Culinary uses

In Japan, houttuynia is used as a vegetable rather than an herb, and simmered with fish and pork dishes. In Vietnam, where it is very popular, it is chopped and steamed with fish and chicken. Leaves can also be shredded into a clear soup. More often it is eaten raw, to accompany beef and duck, with raw vegetables to dip in fiery nam prik, or as a salad. Combine it with lettuce, mint, and young nasturtium leaves and flowers. I have shredded it into stir-fried vegetable and seafood dishes and into fish soups. Cilantro or rau ram could be used instead.

Combines well with chili, galangal, garlic, ginger, lemon grass, mint.

Fresh leaves
Japanese houttuynia shows clear orange and coriander aromas, whereas Chinese houttuynia smells more rank. *H. c.* 'Chameleon' has multi-colored leaves (*right*).

RICE PADDY HERB

Limnophilia aromatica

Rice paddy herb is native to tropical Asia. It is now available from nurseries in the US, but has yet to catch on in Europe. Brought to the US by Southeast Asian immigrants in the 1970s and 1980s, it is also known by its Vietnamese names, rau om and rau ngo. It is readily available in Vietnamese neighborhoods of US cities and deserves to be more widely known; its agreeable aroma should encourage experimentation.

TASTING NOTES

Rice paddy herb has an attractive floral-citrus, musky aroma and flavor with a hint of the pungent earthiness of cumin. It is a fragrant, delicate herb.

PARTS USED

Fresh young shoots and leaves.

BUYING AND STORING

Buy plants from nurseries. Keep stems for a few days in a plastic bag in the refrigerator vegetable crisper.

GROW YOUR OWN

A rather straggly plant, with long, mid-green leaves and lilac flowers, rau om grows wild in ponds throughout Southeast Asia, and is cultivated in flooded rice fields. It will grow in or at the edge of ponds, covered by an inch or so of water, and does well in sun or partial shade. It is a perennial but needs protection from frost. Leaves can be harvested throughout the growing season.

Culinary uses

The Vietnamese are enthusiastic users of rice paddy herb. They chop it into vegetable and sour soups just before serving them, include it in fish dishes, and frequently add it to the platter of herbs provided with most Vietnamese meals. Rice paddy herb is often eaten with freshwater fish. In northern Thailand, it is served with fermented fish and chili sauce, and in curries made with coconut milk. Malay cooks use rice paddy herb as a vegetable, rather like spinach. Its lemony fragrance also makes it suitable for sweet dishes.

Good with coconut milk, fish and seafood, lime juice, noodles, rice, shallots, green and root vegetables.

Combines well with chili, cilantro, lemon grass, galangal, tamarind.

Fresh sprigs
This small, trailing herb is easily recognized by the whorls of three long leaves along the thick stem.

CHERVIL

Anthriscus cerefolium

Native to southern Russia, the Caucasus, and southeastern Europe, chervil was probably introduced to northern Europe by the Romans. A traditional symbol of new life, the arrival of chervil in markets signals springtime, when chervil sauces and soups appear on menus in France, Germany, and Holland. Often seen in restaurants as a garnish, chervil deserves to be more widely used in domestic cooking.

TASTING NOTES

Chervil is sweetly aromatic. The taste is subtle and soothing, with light anise notes and hints of parsley, caraway, and pepper.

PARTS USED

Fresh leaves; flowers for garnish.

BUYING AND STORING

Chervil is not an herb for long keeping: in a plastic bag or in damp paper towel, it will keep for 2–3 days in the vegetable crisper of the refrigerator. Chopped and frozen in small containers it will keep for 3–4 months. Chervil butter can also be frozen. Dried chervil has almost no flavor and is not worth buying.

GROW YOUR OWN

Chervil is easy to grow from seed, and prefers rich, moist soil in semi-shade. Sow seed where you want the plants to grow, because chervil doesn't like to be transplanted. It does best in cool temperatures, so in summer, plant it between taller plants that will provide shade. Old leaves turn pink or yellow and no longer have a fresh flavor. Sow the first batch of seeds toward the end of winter, and then sow every 3–4 weeks to ensure a continuing supply.

Fresh leaves
Chervil grows quickly and can be harvested 6–8 weeks after sowing, but its lifespan is short – once it flowers it is of no use in the kitchen. Be rigorous about cutting out flower stems and harvest frequently, cutting outer leaves first to encourage new growth at the center of the plant.

Culinary uses

Chervil is one of the indispensable herbs of French cooking: in classic fines herbes it is combined with chives, parsley, and tarragon. Fines herbes – or chervil alone – stirred into eggs will make an excellent omelette or scrambled egg dish. In Holland and Belgium, there is a long tradition of making chervil soup, either based on potato and shallot or a richer version that uses cream and egg yolks.

Chervil is delicious in consommés, and gives a delicate flavor to vinaigrettes and to butter or cream sauces to serve with fish, poultry, and vegetables. It is a great addition to salads: try it in a warm potato salad or a beet salad with shallots or chives. Chervil is sometimes used with tarragon in béarnaise sauce, and its flavor can usually be detected in Frankfurt green sauce. A small amount of chervil brings out the flavor of other herbs, but you can use it lavishly on its own – for example, scatter it generously over freshly cooked vegetables. If you are using it in a hot dish, stir it in when the cooking is at an end, because the aroma and flavor quickly dissipate with heat.

Curly chervil, *A. c. crispum*, has the same properties as the flat-leafed variety.

Essential to fines herbes.

Good with asparagus, beets, carrots, cream cheese, eggs, fava beans, fennel, fish and seafood, green beans, lettuce, mushrooms, peas, potatoes, poultry, tomatoes, veal.

Combines well with basil, chives, cresses, dill, hyssop, lemon thyme, mint, mustard, parsley, salad burnet, tarragon.

Fines herbes

This classic French flavoring for egg, fish, and poultry dishes is a combination of chervil, chives, parsley, and tarragon (*recipe, p.281*).

TARRAGON

Artemisia dracunculus

Native to Siberia and western Asia, tarragon was unknown in Europe until the Arabs introduced it when they ruled Spain. During the 16th and 17th centuries, the development of classic French cooking extended its use in the kitchen. Indeed, the best cultivated variety is usually called French tarragon (or, in Germany, German tarragon) to distinguish it from the inferior Russian variety.

TASTING NOTES

The leaves are sweetly aromatic, with hints of pine, anise, or licorice; the flavor is strong yet subtle, with spicy anise and basil notes and a sweetish aftertaste. Long cooking diminishes the aroma but the flavor is not lost.

PARTS USED

Fresh leaves and sprigs.

BUYING AND STORING

Supermarkets sell tarragon in small quantities, so it is better to grow your own. Avoid the Russian variety when buying plants. Young sprigs keep for 4–5 days in a plastic bag in the vegetable crisper of the refrigerator. To dry, hang stems in bundles in an airy, dark place. Dried they lose much of their aroma; freezing the leaves, whole or chopped, retains more of the flavor.

GROW YOUR OWN

French tarragon can be propagated by cuttings or in spring by division of the brittle, white rhizomes – do this every 3 years to preserve the flavor of the plant. The more vigorous Russian tarragon will grow from seed. Tarragon needs a rich, dry soil and much sun. Until well established the roots of French tarragon may need winter protection.

French tarragon *A. d.* var. *sativa*

This tarragon has mid-green leaves and is the preferred culinary variety. The leaves can be harvested when required, and whole stems removed for drying in midsummer.

Culinary uses

Tarragon is an essential ingredient in French cooking, with fish, poultry, and egg dishes. Used discreetly, it lends a pleasant, deep note to green salads. It is very good in marinades for meat and game, and for flavoring goat cheeses and feta preserved in olive oil. Whole stems can be used under fish or with roast chicken and rabbit – "tarragon chicken" appears in nearly every cook's repertoire.

Tarragon makes one of the most versatile of herb vinegars and is often used in mustards and butters. It adds a fresh, herbal fragrance to mushrooms, artichokes, and ragouts of summer vegetables; with tomatoes it is almost as good as basil. Use tarragon in moderation and it will enhance the flavor of other herbs.

Essential to fines herbes and similar herb mixtures, to béarnaise,ravigote, and tartar sauces.

Good with artichokes, asparagus, eggs, fish and seafood, potatoes, poultry, salsify, tomatoes, zucchini.

Combines well with basil, bay, capers, chervil, chives, dill, parsley, salad herbs.

Other tarragons

Russian tarragon, *A. d.* var. *inodora*, or sometimes *A. dracunculoides,* is lighter in color and more coarse in appearance, and has a bitter taste. It is best avoided. When buying a tarragon plant, check that the label says French tarragon; if the type of tarragon is not specified, it may be the Russian variety.

Mexican tarragon, *Tagetes lucida*, is a species of marigold (*p.29*) that is often used in the southern states instead of French tarragon. It has a more pronounced licorice flavor.

Bouquet garni for fish

Intended to be added to the liquid of slow-cooked fish dishes, this bouquet garni comprises tarragon, thyme, parsley, and a strip of lemon peel (*recipes, p.280*).

DILL

Anethum graveolens

An annual plant native to southern Russia, western Asia, and the eastern Mediterranean, dill is widely grown for its feathery leaves (often called dill weed) and its seed. Indian dill, *A. g.* subsp. *sowa*, is grown primarily for its seed, which is lighter in color, longer, and narrower than European dill seed and has a more pungent taste. It is preferred for curry mixtures.

TASTING NOTES

Dill leaves have a clean, fragrant aroma of anise and lemon. The taste is of anise and parsley, mild but sustained. The seeds smell like a sweet caraway due to carvone in the essential oil; the taste is of anise with a touch of sharpness and a lingering warmth.

PARTS USED

Fresh and dried leaves; seeds.

BUYING AND STORING

Choose a bunch that looks crisp and fresh. If you have a large quantity, use it quickly; after 2–3 days kept in a plastic bag in the refrigerator it will droop. Dried dill stored in an airtight container will keep its flavor for up to a year. Similarly stored seed has a shelf life of 2 years. Ground dill seed does not keep.

GROW YOUR OWN

Dill is easy to grow from seed. Sow in a sheltered, sunny spot with well-drained soil in spring, and water well. Successive sowings will provide plants throughout the season. Dill seedlings are frail, so make sure the ground is weed-free. Flowerheads left to ripen will readily self-seed. Do not transplant; the long tap root is easily damaged. Avoid planting dill and fennel close to each other or they will cross-pollinate and create hybrids.

Fresh leaves
Freezing preserves the flavor of dill better than drying. Freeze the stems whole in a plastic bag and cut off sprigs when needed. Add dill leaves at the end of cooking because they lose their flavor if overheated.

FRONDS
The feathery fronds of *A. graveolens* resemble fennel, although the dill plant is much smaller.

DRYING LEAVES
Dill leaves can be dried, either by spreading them on a cloth and leaving in a dark, warm, well-ventilated place for a few days, or in the microwave. Dried leaves retain some of the aroma and flavor of the fresh plant.

SEEDS
The seeds are oval and flattish with five ribs, two of which form a broader rim. They are extremely light: 10,000 weigh less than 1oz (25g). Harvest seeds when they are light brown and fully formed; put the seedheads in a large paper bag and leave in a warm place until dry. When they have dried, rub the seedheads between your hands to separate seeds from husks. Use the seeds for slow-cooked foods.

Culinary uses

Fresh dill is an excellent partner for fish and seafood. Scandinavian dishes include herrings marinated with dill, gravad lax (salmon cured with salt and dill and served with a mustard and dill sauce), and crab, scallops, or shrimp with a creamy dill sauce.

In northern and central Europe, dill is used with root vegetables, cabbage, cauliflower, and cucumber. Some Russian cooks use it in borshcht, their classic beet soup, and dill combined with sour cream or yogurt and a little mustard also makes a good sauce for beets. German cooks make a similar sauce, but replace the mustard with horseradish and serve it with braised beef. In Greece, dill is added to stuffed grape leaves. In Turkey and Iran, dill flavors ricc, fava beans, zucchini, and celery root. Spinach with dill and shallots is a standard Iranian dish, echoed in a lentil and spinach dish of northern India that uses both dill leaves and seeds. Don't forget dill for salads and salad dressings, especially for potato salad.

Both leaves and seeds are used in pickling, as in the crunchy dill-pickled cucumbers of a New York deli and the garlicky version popular in Poland, Russia, and Iran. Seeds are added to breads and cakes in Scandinavia, where they are also used to flavor vinegar. In India, seeds and leaves are used in curry powders and masalas.

Leaves good with beets, carrots, celery root, cucumber, eggs, fava beans, fish and seafood, potatoes, rice, spinach, zucchini.

Leaves combine well with basil, capers, garlic, horseradish, mustard, paprika, parsley.

Seeds good with cabbage, onion, potatoes, pumpkin, vinegar.

Seeds combine well with chili, coriander seed, cumin, garlic, ginger, mustard seed, turmeric.

FENNEL

Foeniculum vulgare

This tall, hardy, graceful perennial, indigenous to the Mediterranean and now naturalized in many parts of the world, is one of the oldest cultivated plants. The Romans enjoyed fennel shoots as a vegetable; the Chinese and Indians valued fennel as a condiment and digestive aid. Today in India, fennel water is used to treat colic in babies. The herb should not be confused with the bulbous sweet or Florence fennel, *F. v.* var. *dulce*, which is eaten as a vegetable.

TASTING NOTES

The whole plant has a warm, anise-licorice aroma. The taste is similar: pleasantly fresh, slightly sweet, with a hint of camphor. Fennel seed is less pungent than dill, and more astringent than anise.

PARTS USED

Young leaves, flowers, pollen, stems, seeds.

BUYING AND STORING

Leaves will keep in a plastic bag in the refrigerator for 2–3 days. Stems can be used fresh or tied in bundles and hung up to dry; store in an airtight container and use within 6 months. Seed will keep for up to 2 years when stored in an airtight container. Wild fennel pollen, an intensely flavored, golden-green dust, can be bought via the internet.

GROW YOUR OWN

Fennel will grow in most conditions, but prefers a well-drained, sunny site. It grows to 5ft (1.5m) or more. Plants will self-seed very prolifically. Don't grow fennel near dill or they will cross-pollinate and produce hybrids. When the seed is yellowy green, cut off the seedheads, place them in a large paper bag, and keep in an airy, warm place until quite dry; then shake the seeds loose. Fennel plants should be replaced every 3–4 years.

Green fennel *F. vulgare*

Green fennel is a tall, stately plant with tangled, feathery foliage. All parts of the fennel plant are edible; the roots are no longer eaten, but the leaves, stems, and fruits (seed) are esteemed as flavorings. Fennel's anise character derives from anethole, the main constituent of its essential oil, which is most concentrated in the seed.

STEMS
Stems have a mild flavor that is retained when they are dried.

Culinary uses

In spring, fennel gives a fresh, lively note to salads and sauces. Later in the season a garnish of flowers or a sprinkling of pollen gives an anise fragrance to cold soups, chowders, and grilled fish.

Fennel is an excellent foil for oily fish. The Sicilians use it liberally in their pasta with sardines. In Provence, France, whole fish such as red mullet are baked or grilled on a bed of fresh or dried fennel stems, which imparts a delicate flavor.

Pollen gives a more heady flavor to fish, seafood, grilled vegetables, pork chops, and Italian breads.

Fennel seed can be added to pickles, soups, and breads – try combining ground fennel and nigella to flavor bread, as is done in Iraq. In Greece, leaves or seeds are combined with feta cheese and olives to make a well-flavored bread. Fennel seeds flavor sauerkraut in Alsace and Germany, and Italians use them with roast pork and in finocchiona, the renowned salami of Florence.

Fennel seed is one of the constituents of five spice powder, the principal Chinese spice blend used mostly with meat and poultry. Bengal, in northeast India, also has a five spice mixture, panch phoron, with fennel as an ingredient; the mixture is used with vegetables, beans, and lentils. Elsewhere in the Indian subcontinent, fennel appears in garam masala, in spiced gravies for vegetables or lamb, and in some sweet dishes. Indians also chew fennel seed after a meal as a breath-freshener and digestive aid.

Good with beans, beets, cabbage, cucumber, duck, fish and seafood, leeks, lentils, pork, potatoes, rice, tomatoes.

Combines well with chervil, cinnamon, cumin, fenugreek, lemon balm, mint, nigella, parsley, Sichuan pepper, thyme.

Bronze fennel *F. v.* 'Purpureum'

This is a less vigorous plant than green fennel and has a milder aroma and flavor.

LEAVES
Only young fennel leaves are suitable for use in the kitchen. They have a mild taste and are best used soon after picking.

SEEDS
Fennel seed has a stronger flavor than the leaves and a bittersweet aftertaste. Dry-roasting the seed brings out the sweetness. Seed color varies from light brown to greenish-yellow – the latter is the best quality. It is best to keep seed and grind it as needed.

AGASTACHE

Agastache species

The agastaches are handsome, perennials of the mint family that are just becoming known in Europe. Two are particularly worth the cook's attention – anise hyssop, *A. foeniculum*, native to North America, and Korean mint, *A. rugosa*, native to eastern Asia. Mexican giant hyssop, *A. mexicana*, is half-hardy and grows wild in Mexico, where the leaves and flowers are used to make a tea.

TASTING NOTES

Anise hyssop has a sweet, anise aroma and flavor; it has a natural sweetness, unlike many herbs that are bitter when tasted alone. Korean mint smells of eucalypt and mint, but the taste resembles that of anise hyssop, with a lingering anise aftertaste.

PARTS USED

Fresh leaves; flowers for garnishes.

BUYING AND STORING

Some specialist nurseries stock plants. Leaves are quite sturdy and will keep in a plastic bag in the vegetable crisper of the refrigerator for 4–5 days. Leaves can be frozen, but they are best used fresh. Dry leaves only to make teas – otherwise don't bother.

GROW YOUR OWN

Anise hyssop and Korean mint prefer a sheltered, well-drained spot in full sun. Both can be grown from seed. After 2–3 years plants can be divided and replanted. If you leave some flowers to seed, agastaches will self-seed, but the new plants come up quite late in the year. Harvest young leaves throughout the growing season. They are most aromatic just before the plant flowers.

FLOWERS
Anise hyssop smells of anise and its flowers resemble those of hyssop, but it is not related to either plant.

Anise hyssop

A. foeniculum

Anise hyssop, also called licorice mint, is an upright, branched plant with gray-green, oval leaves tinged with purple. The showy, lilac flowerspikes appear in late summer and attract bees.

Culinary uses

Anise hyssop and Korean mint can be used interchangeably in the kitchen. Commonly used in teas or summer drinks, they can also be used in similar ways to anise. Add the leaves to marinades and sauces for fish and seafood, chop them into rice, or add to chicken or pork dishes. Their natural sweetness complements the sweetness in vegetables such as beets, carrots, winter squash, and sweet potatoes, and they also work well with green beans, zucchini, and tomatoes. Use as a garnish, or stir in chopped leaves just before serving. A few leaves in a salad will add an elusive anise note; mix with other summery herbs to flavor pancake batter or an omelette, or to make a sauce for pasta with olive oil, crisp-fried bread crumbs, and garlic. Agastaches are also good with summer fruits such as apricots, blueberries, peaches, pears, plums, and raspberries. To make agastache honey, fill a small jar with leaves and flowers, pour in warmed clear honey, cover, and leave for a month.

Good with green beans, root vegetables, tomatoes, winter squash, zucchini; berries and stone fruits.

Combines well with basil, bee balm, chervil, marjoram, mint marigold, parsley, salad burnet, tarragon.

Korean mint *A. rugosa*

Korean mint is a very hardy, low, bushy shrub with spikes of purple-blue flowers. Its heart-shaped, serrated leaves are rougher than those of anise hyssop.

MINT

Mentha species

One of the most popular flavors in the world, mint is at once cooling and warming, with a sweet fragrance. Native to southern Europe and the Mediterranean, mints have long naturalized throughout the temperate world. They hybridize easily, leading to some confusion in their naming, but for the cook they broadly divide into two groups: spearmint and peppermint (*pp.72–73*).

TASTING NOTES

Spearmint is mellow and refreshing, with a sweet-sharp, pleasantly pungent flavor backed by hints of lemon. Peppermint has pronounced menthol notes and a fiery bite, yet is also slightly sweet, tangy, and spicy with a fresh, cool aftertaste.

PARTS USED

Leaves, fresh and dried; flowers for salads and garnishes.

BUYING AND STORING

Bunches of fresh spearmint will keep for 2 days in a glass of water in the kitchen, or in the refrigerator. Leaves can be chopped and frozen in small containers or mixed with a little water or oil and frozen in ice-cube trays. Mint dries well; pick before flowering and hang bunches in a dry, airy place, or dry sprigs in a low oven or microwave. Store dried mint in an airtight container.

GROW YOUR OWN

Mints are perennial plants and are easy to grow. They prefer partial shade or full sun, and need lots of water. They have a spreading habit, so unless you have space for mint to run wild it is best to grow it in a pot. Otherwise, plant in a large, bottomless pot or bucket.

Fresh leaves
The most widely grown mint, spearmint or garden mint (*M. spicata*), has pointed leaves and bears lilac flowers in late summer. This mint and its cultivated varieties suit all recipes calling for mint. Leaves can be picked thoughout the growing season, but are best harvested shortly before flowering, when the essential oils are at their strongest. The aroma of mints is due to menthol, which also leaves cooling and mild numbing sensations in the mouth.

Culinary uses

Mint has many uses worldwide. Fresh and dried mints are not usually used interchangeably in recipes.

Fresh mint

Western cooks use mint to flavor carrots, eggplant, peas, potatoes, tomatoes, and zucchini. Mint goes well with chicken, pork, veal, and the traditional spring lamb, whether as a marinade, mint jelly, mint sauce, or a salsa. Sauce paloise (a béarnaise sauce made with mint instead of tarragon) is a good accompaniment to grilled fish and chicken.

In the Middle East, mint is essential to tabbouleh and is part of the bowl of fresh herbs and salad vegetables that accompanies mezze. In Vietnam, it is added to salads and to platters of herbs that accompany spring rolls. Mint also finds its way into Southeast-Asian dipping sauces, sambals, and curries. The cooling notes of mint make it the perfect herb for chilled Iranian yogurt and cucumber soup, and the Indians emphasize its refreshing qualities in chutneys and raitas. Indian cooks also use the freshness of mint to counter the warmth of spices in vegetable and meat dishes. In much of South America, mint is combined with chili peppers, parsley, and oregano as a flavoring for slow-cooked dishes; Mexicans use a little with meatballs and chicken.

Mint's refreshing effect enhances fruit salads, fruit punches, and, of course, a mint julep. It makes a surprisingly good iced parfait, and minty notes are a welcome addition to several kinds of chocolate desserts and cakes.
Combines well with basil, cardamom, cloves, cumin, dill, fenugreek, ginger, marjoram, oregano, paprika, parsley, pepper, sumac, thyme.

Dried mint

Around the eastern Mediterranean and in the Arab countries, dried mint is often preferred to fresh. In Greece, dried mint, sometimes with oregano and cinnamon, seasons keftedes (meatballs) and the filling for grape leaves; the Cypriots use it for their Easter cheesecakes, called flaounes. Cacik, the Turkish cucumber and yogurt salad, is best with dried mint. A teaspoon of dried mint, quickly fried in a little olive oil or clarified butter and added just before serving, imparts a fine, lively aroma to some Turkish and Iranian dishes. Try it with lentil and bean soups, and lamb or vegetable stews.

DRIED LEAVES
Spearmint is the dried mint most commonly found commercially. The aroma is pungent and concentrated but lacks the sweetness of fresh.

Other mints

Spearmint and its relatives are the most important mints for the cook. Peppermint and its related varieties are too pungent for most culinary uses and are used primarily to flavor confectionery and toothpaste. Fresh or dried, mint has long been prized for its digestive properties, which helps explain its popularity in the yogurt drinks of Turkey, Iran, and India; sweet Moroccan mint tea served in small glasses; or French tisanes of mint or lime flowers and mint (tilleul-menthe).

Moroccan mint *M. s.* 'Moroccan'

This mint has bright green leaves and white flowers. It is prized for its fine, spicy aroma and is less sweet than spearmint. It is used in tea and for all minted dishes.

Bowles' mint

M. x *villosa* f. *alopecuroides*

This mint has soft, furry, round leaves and spikes of lilac flowers. It wilts rapidly after cutting. It has a fine flavor but the leaves should be chopped finely to eliminate the furry texture. Use for all dishes requiring mint.

Apple mint *M. suaveolens*

Apple mint has wrinkled leaves, and the whole plant is downy. Dense flowerspikes are pale pink. The plant smells subtly of mint combined with ripe apple and has a good flavor. The leaves have an unattractive texture and are best shredded.

Other mints

Peppermint *M.* x *piperita* This mint is a hybrid of spearmint and water mint. A vigorous plant with tall stems and long, green, slightly hairy leaves. Rather strident and pungent. Use sparingly for desserts, cooling drinks, and fresh or dried for teas. Grown commercially for its oil.

Tashkent mint *M. s.* 'Tashkent' This cultivated variety has large leaves and deep pink flowers. It has an intense aroma and flavor. Use as spearmint.

Pineapple mint *M. s.* 'Variegata' Smaller than apple mint, this mint has light green leaves edged with cream. Young leaves have a tropical fruit aroma; older leaves are more minty. Use young leaves to flavor salads, cool drinks, and fruit desserts.

Basil mint *M.* x *piperita citrata* 'Basil' The leaves of this mint are dark green with a purple tinge; they have a spicy scent with light notes of basil. Good with eggplant, tomatoes, and zucchini.

Field mint, corn mint *M. arvensis* This mint has downy, gray-green leaves and whorls of pink flowers on the stem. Pungently aromatic but fairly mild in flavor, it is often used in Southeast-Asian cooking. It has a high menthol content.

English pennyroyal *M. pulegium* There are upright and creeping varieties of this plant. It smells very strongly of peppermint and has an intense, bitter flavor. I recommend using it with caution.

Chocolate mint *M.* x *piperita citrata* 'Chocolate'

This mint has dark green to purple leaves and a scent of after-dinner chocolate mints. Good for chocolate desserts and as a garnish for ice creams and sorbets.

Black peppermint

M. x *piperita piperita*

This hybrid mint has deep purple stems, dark green leaves tinged with purple, and a fine if pungent aroma. Use as peppermint.

Mountain mint *Pycnanthemum pilosa*

This graceful plant is not a true mint, but young leaves and buds can be used as a mint substitute. Native to the eastern US, it smells and tastes of mint but is more bitter.

CALAMINT

Calamintha species

These aromatic, perennial plants deserve to be better known. For the cook, lesser calamint, *C. nepeta*, also called nepitella or mountain balm, is the most rewarding. Common calamint, *C. sylvatica*, is less fragrant but can be used in the same way. Large-flowered calamint, *C. grandiflora*, is a striking plant sometimes called showy savory; the leaves are used for teas. The calamints are related to savory.

TASTING NOTES

The whole plant smells warm and minty with notes of thyme and camphor; the taste is pleasantly pungent, warm, minty, and peppery with a light bitterness in the aftertaste. Lesser calamint has a stronger odor and flavor than large-flowered calamint.

PARTS USED

Leaves and sprigs; flowers for garnishes and salads.

BUYING AND STORING

Calamint is not available as a cut herb, but specialist nurseries stock plants. In North America, calamint is often available under the name nepitella. Sprigs will be good for 1–2 days if kept in a plastic bag in the refrigerator. Stems can be tied in bundles and hung to dry in a well-ventilated place; leaves are then stripped and crumbled. Store in an airtight container.

GROW YOUR OWN

Calamint prefers an alkaline, well-drained soil and full sun, although it will tolerate partial shade. It can be propagated by division or grown from seed. Large-flowered calamint makes a handsome garden plant; all are attractive to bees. Leaves may be harvested from spring to late summer.

Culinary uses

Lesser calamint is a favorite flavoring in Sicily and Sardinia, as well as in Tuscany where it is popular with vegetables and especially in mushroom dishes. The Turks use it as a mild form of mint. It is good with roasts, stews, game, and grilled fish; in stuffings for vegetables and meat; and in marinades and sauces. Fresh leaves are best for cooking; dried leaves are used for teas. Large-flowered calamint has large, slightly floppy leaves.

Good with beans, eggplant, fish, green vegetables, lentils, mushrooms, pork, potatoes, rabbit.

Combines well with bay, chili, garlic, mint, myrtle, oregano, parsley, pepper, sage, thyme.

Fresh sprigs
Lesser calamint is a bushy plant with downy, grayish foliage. It bears small, lilac or white flowers throughout the summer.

CATNIP

Nepeta cataria

The names catnip and catmint are used interchangeably, and catmint is also used for some of the ornamental species of *Nepeta*. Native to the Caucasus and southern Europe, this attractive plant is now widely cultivated in many temperate regions, as well as being found in the wild. The mint-like odor induces a state of bliss in cats, but only if the leaves have been bruised and the aroma released.

TASTING NOTES

When bruised, catnip leaves release a sweet, minty, camphorous aroma; the taste is also pungently mint-like with an acrid, bitter note. Use sparingly.

PARTS USED

Leaves and sprigs.

BUYING AND STORING

Plants are available from garden centers and specialist nurseries. Sprigs will keep for a day or two in a plastic bag in the vegetable crisper of the refrigerator.

GROW YOUR OWN

Catnip is a perennial that is easy to grow from seed, and left to seed it self-seeds readily. It grows best in partial shade and needs very little attention. It is as attractive to bees as it is to cats. Leaves can be harvested throughout the spring and summer.

Culinary uses

Catnip was a more important culinary herb in the past than it is today, although it is still used in Italy, in salads, soups, egg dishes, and stuffings for vegetables. A few of the sharply flavored leaves certainly give zest to a green or mixed herb salad. The robust flavor also goes well with fatty meats like duck and pork. It is widely used as an herbal tea.

Fresh sprigs
Catnip's gray-green, heart-shaped leaves are covered by a white down; the flowers are white to lavender, dotted with red spots.

GARLIC

Allium sativum

Garlic is native to the steppes of central Asia and spread first to the Middle East. It was one of the earliest cultivated herbs, but its early use was mainly medical and magical – except in ancient Egypt where it was eaten in quantity. When the first English settlers took it to America, it was still regarded as a medicinal herb. Today it is recognized for lowering blood pressure and cholesterol, but its culinary use has become vastly more important.

TASTING NOTES

Raw, dried garlic is pungent and hot; green garlic is milder. The disulphate allicin is formed when raw garlic is cut, and this accounts for the smell that raw garlic leaves on the breath. Cooking garlic degrades the allicin, but forms other disulphates that have less odor.

PARTS USED

Bulbs.

BUYING AND STORING

Garlic is available all year round. Choose unbruised, firm heads without signs of mold or sprouting. If your garlic is sprouting, remove the indigestible green shoots. Store garlic in a cool, dry place. Dehydrated garlic flakes, granules, and powder are available, as are garlic paste, extract and juice. Smoked garlic is chic but not especially useful.

GROW YOUR OWN

Garlic is propagated by the cloves. It grows best in rich, moist soil in a sunny position. Perennial or biennial, it is extremely hardy and survives long periods of cold. Harvest when the tops dry out and begin to collapse. Pull up the whole plant and hang in the shade to dry. As harvested garlic dries, the skin becomes papery and the flavor intensifies.

Fresh heads
At the beginning of the growing season, heads of new green garlic are succulent and mild, and have a soft, thick, white skin.

Culinary uses

If crushed with the flat blade of a heavy knife, dried garlic cloves are easy to peel. Once peeled, garlic can be pounded in a mortar. Avoid garlic presses because they can make the taste unpleasantly acrid.

Garlic can be used to enhance the flavor of many foods. Whole cloves cooked slowly have a mellow, nutty taste; cut garlic is more pungent, even when cooked. Similarly, a whole clove gently sautéed in oil and then removed will leave a delicate flavor: a minced clove leaves a much stronger one. Never let garlic burn or it will develop a bitter, acrid taste. Garlic roasted whole can accompany new potatoes or root vegetables. In European cooking, garlic is roasted with chicken or lamb; braised in wine; puréed, blanched, or sautéed. Young, green garlic can be used in summer vegetable stews without peeling. In Spain, young garlic shoots are fried for tapas. Raw garlic flavors salads, is rubbed over bread with tomato and oil, and is pounded with egg yolks and oil to make aïoli or, with nuts and basil, pesto. In Asia, where the consumption of garlic far exceeds that of the Mediterranean countries, its companions are lemon grass, fresh ginger, cilantro, chili peppers, and soy sauce. Garlic is used in stir-fried dishes, curry pastes, sambals, and nam prik. In Cuba, it is combined with cumin and citrus juice to make the ubiquitous table sauces called mojos. Garlic can also be steeped in oil for a few days, and in vinegar for at least two weeks. In Korea and Russia, garlic makes a much-loved pickle.

Essential to many sauces (aïoli, allioli, skordalia, rouille, tarator, pesto).
Good with almost anything savory.
Combines well with most herbs and spices.

DRIED CLOVES
Dried cloves of garlic may have a white, pink, or violet skin, depending on variety.

GARLIC *was one of the earliest herbs to be cultivated. Although its strong taste and smell were disliked by many,*

its medical and magical properties were never in doubt. Its culinary use is greatest in Southeast Asia and Europe.

Garlic varieties

Several plants have aromatic qualities similar to those of garlic. Slender rocambole is actually related to the leek. European wild garlic, or ramsons, comes closest to garlic in taste and has the advantage that it can be gathered early in spring. The huge cloves of elephant garlic, *A. ampeloprasum*, may be too mild for real garlic aficionados, but they are good roasted with other vegetables. North American wild garlic, *A. canadense*, has a flavor between garlic and leek.

Rocambole

A. s. var. ophioscorodon

Also called serpent garlic or sandleek, rocambole grows wild in southern Europe. The stalks turn into spirals and twirls as they mature, and the mauve flowers give way to purple bulbils. All parts can be used: early in the year the new, slender, pointed leaves as chives, and in summer the pea-sized bulbils and bulbs as a milder substitute for garlic.

Ramsons *A. ursinum*

Ramsons grow wild in much of Europe. The leaves resemble those of lily-of-the-valley, but with the smell of wild garlic; the flavor is milder than the smell. They are easy to cultivate, but invasive. Leaves are picked in late winter and early spring, and are best used fresh to garnish potato and egg dishes, in soups and creamy sauces, cooked briefly with spinach, or wrapped around fish fillets before steaming. American wild leek, *A. tricoccum*, grows from Canada to Carolina. Its other name ramps, derives from ramsons, and it can be used in the same ways as ramsons.

WELSH ONION

Allium fistulosum

Despite their name, Welsh onions are native to Siberia. Also called Japanese bunching onions or Japanese leeks, they are Asia's largest onion crop. Western cookbooks usually refer to them as bunching onions, but in books on Asian cooking they are most often called scallions, a name we often give to "spring" onions (*A. cepa*), which do resemble them but have a different taste.

TASTING NOTES

Welsh onions have only a faint onion aroma when cut. The onion flavor is pronounced if rather mild.

PARTS USED

White "stems" (the slightly bulbous leaf bases), and green leaves.

BUYING AND STORING

Welsh onions occasionally appear in markets; avoid any that look wilted and yellowed. To grow your own, buy seeds or plants from a nursery. Once cut, Welsh onions can be kept in the vegetable crisper of the refrigerator for about a week; wrap them well to prevent their smell from permeating other foods.

GROW YOUR OWN

Welsh onions are perennials and are grown from seed in well-drained, fertile soil, sometimes in stages for a continuing crop. They are non-bulbing, producing only a slight swelling at the base, but like most alliums multiply in clumps, which should be split occasionally. Harvest plants after 5–6 weeks, when they are about 10in (25cm) high. The Welsh onion has round, hollow leaves, whereas scallions have flatter leaves.

Culinary uses

Welsh onions are used as a flavoring and as a vegetable. They are essential to Asian cooking, often in combination with garlic and ginger. They are used with meats, fish, seafood, and poultry, finding a place in many soups, stews, and braises. They are usually added at the end of the cooking process, even in stir-frying, to preserve their color and crunchy texture. Chopped fine, they can be added to Western stews or potato and legume dishes, again shortly before the end of cooking. Raw, they can be used as a substitute for scallions.

Good with eggs, fish and seafood, meat, poultry, most vegetables.

Combines well with chervil, chili, cilantro, galangal, garlic, ginger, lemon grass, parsley, perilla.

Fresh stems

Asian varieties of the Welsh onion are stronger in flavor than those grown elsewhere. While most of them are green, some varieties have red stems.

CHIVES

Allium schoenoprasum

This smallest and most delicately flavored member of the onion family originated in northern temperate zones. Chives have long grown wild all over Europe and North America, but widespread cultivation in Europe does not seem to have begun until the later Middle Ages. The herb became popular only in the 19th century.

TASTING NOTES

All parts of chives have a light, onion aroma and a spicy, onion flavor.

PARTS USED

Stems and flowers.

BUYING AND STORING

Buy a clump from a nursery and divide the small bulbs as needed to guarantee a sufficient supply. Drying chives is pointless, but chopped and frozen they retain their flavor tolerably well and can be used straight from the freezer.

GROW YOUR OWN

Chives grow as grass-like clumps of hollow, bright green stems, with small, spherical, pink to purple flowerheads. They are perennials, easy to grow in any garden soil, but they must be watered well because the small bulbous roots remain very near the surface. Propagate by division. The plants die back in winter, but reappear very early in spring. They should be cut, not pulled, preferably the outer ones first to keep the clump neat. Always leave some top growth on the clumps to preserve the strength of the bulbs.

Culinary uses

Chives should never be cooked, since cooking quickly dissipates their taste. Chopped with a knife or with scissors, they can be added in generous measure to many dishes and salads. Their delicate onion flavor, crunchy texture, and fresh green appearance livens up potato salad and many a soup, and lends an equally upbeat note to any herb sauce. It has become traditional to serve chives with butter or sour cream as a dressing for baked potatoes. Stirred into thick yogurt, chives make a fresh relish for grilled fish. The attractive, bright flowers have a pleasant, light, onion taste and look good scattered over herb salads or added to omelettes.

Essential to fines herbes.

Good with avocados, cream cheese, egg dishes, fish and seafood, potatoes, smoked salmon, root vegetables, zucchini.

Combines well with basil, chervil, cilantro, fennel, paprika, parsley, sweet cicely, tarragon.

Fresh stems
Chives should be crisp, not floppy. Use quickly after cutting.

GARLIC CHIVES

Allium tuberosum

Garlic or Chinese chives are native to central and northern Asia, but grow also in subtropical China, India, and Indonesia. Records of the use of chives in China go back thousands of years. The plants have flat leaves rather than the hollow stems of ordinary chives, and the star-like flowers are white.

TASTING NOTES

Leaves and flowers have a stronger, more distinct garlic taste than those of ordinary chives; blanched leaves are milder. The taste is stronger in the flowers than in the leaves.

PARTS USED

Leaves and flowerbuds.

BUYING AND STORING

Specialty markets sell the chives in bundles, and blanched chives and the stiff flowerbud stems in smaller bundles. Once cut, chives wilt quickly – blanched garlic chives fastest of all. Green chives will keep for a few days in a plastic bag in the refrigerator, but the smell is strong.

GROW YOUR OWN

Garlic chives are robust; in warm climates they stay green all winter. The plants are taller than ordinary chives but tend to form neater and smaller clumps. They do not produce real bulbs and propagation is by the rhizome. Leaves can be cut for use at any time. Sometimes the plants are cut back and kept in the dark: the pale yellow shoots produced by this blanching are a prized delicacy. Flowers are harvested as buds, on the stems.

Culinary uses

Cut into short lengths, garlic chives can be quickly blanched to accompany pork or poultry. They are used in spring rolls and added at the last minute for pungency in stir-fried dishes of beef, shrimp, tofu, and many vegetables. Little bundles can be dipped in batter and deep-fried. The flowerbuds, sold separately on their stems, are a much-prized vegetable. In China and Japan, the flowers are ground and salted to make a spice. Blanched chives are a popular but expensive delicacy; they are stirred into soups, noodle dishes, and steamed vegetables at the last minute. Flower stems and leaves of garlic chives placed inside a bottle of white wine vinegar soon give it a light garlic flavor.

Leaves and flower stems
Bright green leaves, pale, blanched leaves, and bud stems are sold in specialty markets.

CELERY

Apium graveolens

Wild celery is an ancient European plant from which garden celery and celery root were bred in the 17th century. Cutting or leaf celery, also called smallage, resembles the original wild celery. Chinese celery is mid-green with leaves similar to those of garden celery. The unrelated water or Vietnamese celery, *Oenanthe javanica*, has upright stalks with small, serrated leaves; do not confuse it with the poisonous European water dropwort, *O. crocata*.

TASTING NOTES

Cutting celery leaves have an herbaceous, parsley-like aroma and taste combined with warmth and a bitter note. Chinese celery is similar in flavor. Water celery has a fresh taste; parsley notes are more dominant than celery's warm bitterness.

PARTS USED

Leaves, stalks, and fruits (seeds)

BUYING AND STORING

Cutting celery and leaves of garden celery can be kept for 4–5 days. Chinese celery is often sold with its roots and will last for a week if kept whole. Water celery keeps for 1–2 days. Store them all in plastic bags in the vegetable crisper of the refrigerator. Seed in an airtight container will remain aromatic for up to 2 years.

GROW YOUR OWN

Celery's natural habitat is marshland, but it is easily grown from seed in the garden in moisture-retentive soil; seed of cutting celery can be obtained from specialist suppliers. Harvest leaves throughout the growing season. Water celery grows wild in Southeast Asia; if you can find a plant, keep it in a pot because it spreads quickly. Water frequently.

Cutting celery *A. graveolens*
Cutting celery looks like a dark green, glossy version of flat-leaf parsley. It produces an abundance of leaves on erect stems to form a bushy plant.

SEEDS
Celery seed has an aroma and taste that is much more pronounced than that of the parent plant. It is penetrating, spicy, with hints of nutmeg, citrus, and parsley and it leaves a somewhat bitter, burning aftertaste.

Culinary uses

Cutting celery is used in Holland and Belgium rather as we use parsley, as a garnish or stirred into dishes just before serving. It is one of the herbs used for the traditional dish of eel in green sauce. In France, it is sold as a soup herb; in Greece, it is popular in fish and meat casseroles. Cutting celery is useful because you can pick leaves to add to bouquets garnis, soups, and stews, instead of having to use a celery stalk.

Chinese celery is used as a flavoring and as a vegetable. It is rarely eaten raw. Stalks are sliced and used in stir-fried dishes; leaves and stalks flavor soups, braised dishes, rice, and noodles throughout Southeast Asia. I have also enjoyed a very good Thai dish of fish steamed with Chinese celery.

Garden celery and celery root are eaten raw or cooked as vegetables, but you can also use their leaves as a flavoring. Cooking tempers the bitterness of all types of celery, but they retain their other aromatic properties. Water celery, with its mild taste, is very popular in Vietnam as a salad herb, or lightly cooked, when it is added to soups, fish, and chicken dishes. Thais use it in a similar way and serve it raw with larp or blanched with nam prik. The Japanese use it for sukiyaki. It also flavors tomato salad.

The Russians and Scandinavians add the seeds to soups, and a few lightly crushed seeds give a pleasant warmth to dressings for winter vegetable salads. Indian cooks also pair celery seed with tomato in curries. Try seeds in potato salad, in cabbage dishes, in stews, and in breads. Because they are so small, celery seeds are usually used whole. The flavor is strong, so use sparingly.

Good with cabbage, chicken, cucumber, fish, potatoes, rice, soy sauce, tomatoes, tofu.

Combines well with cilantro, cloves, cumin, ginger, mustard, parsley, pepper, turmeric.

Chinese celery *A. graveolens*

Chinese celery (kun choi) looks like a small head of green garden celery. The stalks are thin and hollow.

LOVAGE

Levisticum officinale

Lovage is native to western Asia and southern Europe, where it has been used since Roman times; outside Europe its use has never become popular. Wild and cultivated forms are indistinguishable, and the herb has long been naturalized elsewhere – even in Australia. In Italy, it is chiefly associated with Liguria – the name *levisticum* may be a corruption of *ligusticum*, or Ligurian. The Pilgrim Fathers are believed to have taken lovage to North America.

TASTING NOTES

Lovage is strongly aromatic, somewhat similar to celery (in French it is called *céleri bâtard*, or false celery) but more pungent, with musky overtones and notes of anise, lemon, and yeast. The aroma and taste are distinct and tenacious.

PARTS USED

Leaves, stems, roots, seeds.

BUYING AND STORING

Seeds and ground, dried roots can be bought from some spice merchants. Cut lovage is seldom sold, but it is easy to grow your own; buy seeds or plants from an herb nursery. Pick leaves at any time; in a plastic bag they will keep for 3–4 days in the refrigerator. Cut off stems at the base, the outer ones first. As the seeds turn brown, pick fruiting stems and hang upside-down to dry, with a paper bag over the seedheads. These will keep for a year or two.

GROW YOUR OWN

This perennial herb can be grown from seed or by division. It does equally well in shade or sun, but its deep roots need moist, fertile, well-drained soil. The plant dies down in winter but is extremely hardy.

Fresh stems
Lovage is a tall, stately umbellifer with rather large, dark-green, toothed leaves and ridged, hollow stems. The small but attractive yellow flowers bloom in late summer, then give way to huge heads of seeds.

Culinary uses

Lovage can be used as celery or parsley in almost any dish, but is much stronger than either of these and should be used with caution. Its pungency diminishes in cooking.

Leaves, chopped stems, and roots work well in casseroles, soups, and stews. In some diets it may be an advantage that lovage can be used as a salt substitute. Young leaves make a good simple soup, on their own or with potato, carrot, or Jerusalem artichoke, and are often used in seafood chowders. They are good in green salads; older leaves liven up bean or potato dishes and are good in stuffings for poultry.

A lovage-flavored potato and rutabaga gratin is worth trying, as are potato cakes with lovage and Cheddar or Gruyère, and creamy baked vegetable dishes with lovage. Whole or ground seeds can be used in pickles, sauces, marinades, breads, and crackers. The hollow stems can be blanched to use as a vegetable.

Good with apples, carrots, corn, cream cheese, egg dishes, ham, lamb, legumes, mushrooms, onions, pork, potatoes and other root vegetables, rice, smoked fish, tomatoes, tuna, zucchini.

Combines well with bay, caraway, chili, chives, dill, garlic, juniper, oregano, parsley, thyme.

Other lovages

Scots lovage, *Ligusticum scoticum*, is native to the northern temperate region. It does not grow as tall as *L. officinale* and is less pungent; it has white rather than yellow flowers. Use in the same ways as lovage.

Black lovage, *Smyrnium olusatrum*, or alexanders, is another tall umbellifer grown in southern and western Europe from antiquity and throughout the Middle Ages. Much loved in Elizabethan fish and seafood dishes, it was taken to North America in the 16th century. It is almost as easy to grow as lovage, looks much like it, and all parts can be used in the same way.

SEEDS
The tiny, ridged seeds (fruits) are aromatic and have a taste similar to that of the leaves, but with added warmth and a hint of clove.

DRIED LEAVES
Whether dried or frozen, the leaves retain most of their strength; dried leaves are more yeasty and celery-like than fresh ones.

HYSSOP

Hyssopus officinalis

Hyssop is a low, perennial shrub, semi-woody and semi-evergreen, that is native to northern Africa, southern Europe, and western Asia. It is a handsome, compact plant that has long been naturalized in central and western Europe. The Romans used it as a base for an herbal wine, and it was cultivated as a condiment and a strewing herb in monastic gardens during the early Middle Ages.

TASTING NOTES

Hyssop has a strong and pleasant aroma of camphor and mint. The taste of the dark green leaves is refreshing but potent, hot, minty, and bitterish – reminiscent of rosemary, savory, and thyme.

PARTS USED

Leaves and young shoots; flowers.

BUYING AND STORING

In a plastic bag in the vegetable crisper of the refrigerator hyssop will keep for about a week.

GROW YOUR OWN

Hyssop grows well from seed but can also be divided or propagated by cuttings. It likes dry, rocky, well-drained soils, needs sun but tolerates shade. Every 3 years or so, hyssop plants should be divided or they will become too woody. As hyssop is virtually evergreen, its leaves can be picked nearly year-round. The long, dense flowerspikes that appear in late summer are attractive to bees. Their color depends on the variety grown: *H. o. albus* has white flowers; *H .o.* subsp. *aristatus*, dark blue ones; *H. o. roseus*, pink.

Culinary uses

Hyssop leaves and young shoots can be used in salads (to which the flowers can make a robust garnish) or added to soups. The herb is particularly good in rabbit, kid, and game stews; rubbing it onto fatty meats such as lamb can make them easier to digest. It has long been used to flavor non-alcoholic summer drinks, digestives, and liqueurs. It is very good in fruit pies and compotes, and with sherbets and desserts made using assertively flavored fruits such as apricots, morello cherries, peaches, and raspberries. A sugar syrup made for a fruit dish will benefit from boiling with a sprig of hyssop.

Good with apricots, beets, cabbage, carrots, egg dishes, game, legumes, mushrooms, peaches, winter squashes.

Combines well with bay, chervil, mint, parsley, thyme.

Fresh sprigs
Hyssop should be used sparingly or it will overwhelm other flavors.

LEAVES
Both leaves and flowers retain much of their strength when dried. The tiny flowers have a more delicate flavor than the leaves.

CHICORY

Cichorium intybus

Chicory is a tall herbaceous perennial, native to the Mediterranean basin and Asia Minor. The modern cultivated forms originated in 16th-century Europe. In time they gave rise to two very different forced forms: in the late 18th century the Dutch grew the roots for use as a cheaper substitute for coffee – as an additive without caffeine it remains popular in Belgium, France, Germany, and the US; in 1845, the Belgians developed the blanched form grown under soil or sawdust that we still know as Belgian endive or witloof.

Culinary uses

Young leaves are used in salads; the edible flowers can also be added to salads as cheerful decoration. Older leaves benefit from quick blanching and are then used in cooked dishes – they are not appetizing in salads.

Good with fresh cheeses, lettuce and other salad greens, nuts.

Combines well with chervil, cilantro, cresses, parsley, purslane, salad burnet, sweet cicely.

TASTING NOTES

Chicory has no smell. It has a milky white juice containing inulin, which accounts for the bitter taste – quite pleasant in the crisp, young leaves but harsh in old ones. The flowers are not at all bitter.

PARTS USED

Young green leaves; flowers.

BUYING AND STORING

Seeds and plants can usually be bought from an herb nursery. Leaves will keep in a plastic bag in the vegetable crisper of the refrigerator for 2–3 days. Flowers need to be used immediately.

GROW YOUR OWN

Chicory is easily grown from seed in almost any water-retentive but reasonably well-drained soil that allows penetration by the very long taproots. The light green leaves are large at the base, smaller on the upper, branching stems. The large, light blue, daisy-like flowers, which last only a day or so and close in the midday sun, appear all through the summer and early autumn. Suppressing the flower stems early encourages leaf growth.

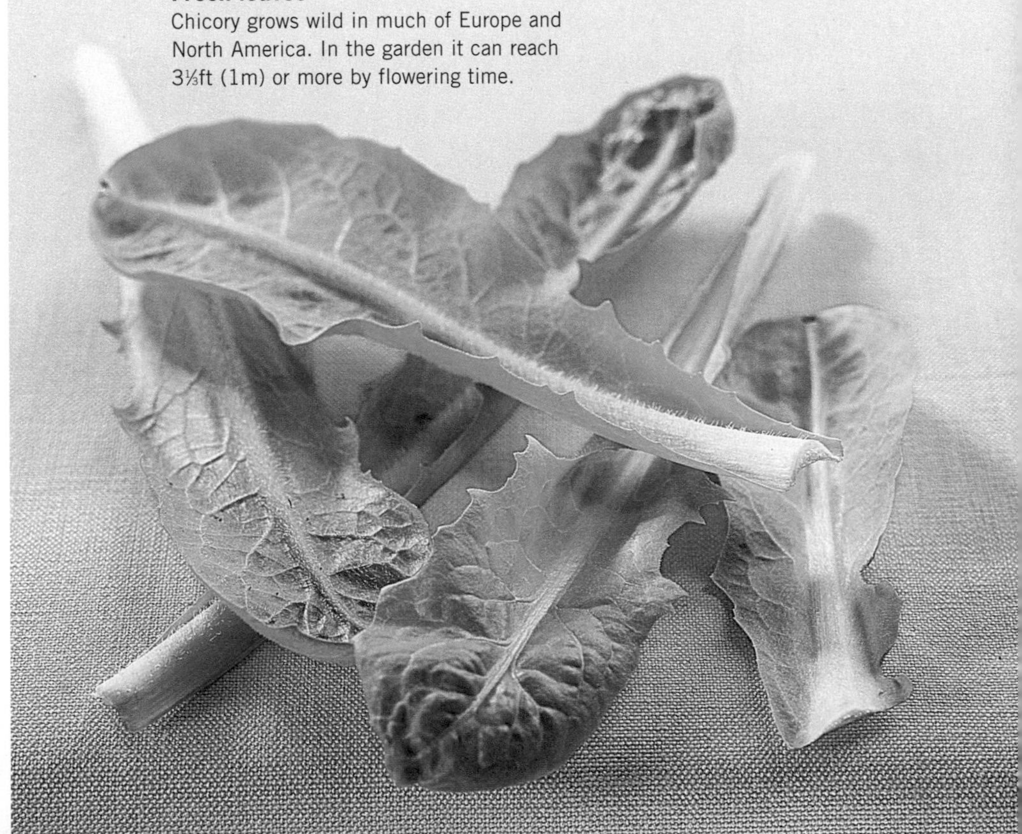

Fresh leaves
Chicory grows wild in much of Europe and North America. In the garden it can reach 3⅓ft (1m) or more by flowering time.

OREGANO AND MARJORAM

Origanum species

Low, bushy perennials of the mint family, the marjorams and oreganos are native to the Mediterranean and western Asia. The plants are often confused, partly because marjoram used to have its own genus, *Majorana*, but also because the word "oregano" is often used simply as a term for a certain type of flavor and aroma. Thus, unrelated plants with a similar aromatic profile may also be called oregano.

Common oregano

O. vulgare

This plant has reddish stems that are slightly woody; the leaves are mid-green and hairy underneath; the flowers deep pink, white, or mauve.

DRIED LEAVES
Dried marjoram and oregano are more intensely aromatic than fresh and have a stronger flavor. Several varieties of oregano are sold dried under the Greek name rigani.

TASTING NOTES

The basic taste is warm, slightly sharp, and bitterish with a note of camphor. To this, marjoram adds a sweet, subtle spiciness, even in temperate climates. Oregano is more robust and peppery, with a bite and often a lemony note. These qualities diminish in colder climates.

PARTS USED

Leaves, flowerknots.

BUYING AND STORING

Marjoram and oregano plants can be bought from herb nurseries. To dry the herbs, pick stems after the flowerbuds form and hang bunches in a well-ventilated, dry place. Rub the leaves off and store them in an airtight container. In supermarkets oregano is more easily available dried than fresh. Dried oregano keeps for a year.

GROW YOUR OWN

Most varieties are upright bushes with woody stems. They can be grown from seed or propagated by division. They need well-drained soil and much sun. Cutting back plants before winter prevents them from growing straggly. Leaves can be picked freely at any time; harvest for drying just after the flowerbuds form. Although perennial, marjoram is often grown as an annual in cooler climates.

Culinary uses

Oregano has become an essential ingredient in much Italian cooking, especially for pasta sauces, pizza, and roasted vegetables. For the Greeks it is the favorite herb for souvlaki, baked fish, and Greek salad. In Mexico, it is a key flavoring for bean dishes, burrito and taco fillings, and salsas. Throughout Spain and Latin America, it is used for meat stews and roasts, soups, and baked vegetables. Combined with paprika, cumin, and chili powder it flavors Tex-Mex chile con carne and other meat stews. Its strong flavor works well with grills and in stuffings, hearty soups, marinades, vegetable stews, even hamburgers. It will also flavor oils and vinegars.

The more delicate flavor of marjoram is easily lost in cooking, so it should be added only at the last moment. It is good in salads, egg dishes, and mushroom sauces, with fish and poultry. It makes more delicate stuffings than oregano. Fresh, it makes a great sorbet. Use leaves and flowerknots in salads, and with mozzarella and other young cheeses.

Sprigs of either marjoram or oregano placed on the coals of a grill give a fine flavor to whatever is cooked on top.

Good with anchovies, artichokes, beans, cabbage, carrots, cauliflower, cheese dishes, chicken, corn, duck, eggplant, eggs, fish and shellfish, lamb, mushrooms, onions, pork, potatoes, poultry, spinach, squash, sweet peppers, tomatoes, veal, venison.

Combines well with basil, bay, chili, cumin, garlic, paprika, parsley, rosemary, sage, sumac, (lemon) thyme.

Sweet marjoram *O. majorana*

This pretty plant, also called knotted marjoram, has gray-green, slightly hairy leaves and clusters of white flowers. Its taste is more delicate and somewhat sweeter than that of common oregano and it does not lend itself to long cooking.

Oreganos and marjorams

In addition to common oregano and sweet marjoram, there are many other varieties and plants of other species with similar characteristics. The flavor of oregano depends on the relative concentration of the phenols carvacrol and thymol in the volatile oil of the plants. Carvacrol is primarily responsible for the typical oregano flavor; its level is generally highest in Greek and some Mexican oreganos.

Cretan dittany *O. dictamnus*

Also called hop marjoram and native only to Crete and southern Greece, this plant grows less tall than most other varieties and has thick, silvery foliage and deep pink flowers. Its flavor is very similar to that of sweet marjoram. It goes well with grilled fish.

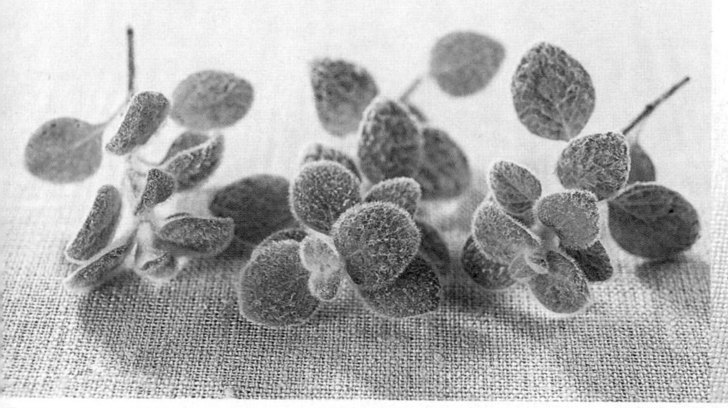

Pot marjoram *O. onites*

Sometimes called Sicilian marjoram but native to Greece and Asia Minor, this is a dwarf shrub with light green, downy leaves and white or pink flowers. A close relative of sweet marjoram, it is less sweet and more piquant.

Greek or Turkish oregano

O. heracleoticum (O. v. hirtum)

Also called winter marjoram, this plant is native to southeastern Europe and western Asia. In Turkey, it is sometimes labeled black oregano because of its dark green, almost black color. It has small, white flowers and a more peppery note than most oreganos. It is the species most widely cultivated in Greece and Turkey and the most important economically, being the source for much of the dried oregano sold in Europe and North America.

Other oreganos

There are a number of unrelated plants used and sold as oregano. **Cuban oregano,** *Plectranthus amboinicus*, is a tender perennial with an intense flavor, native to Malaysia, now widely cultivated in the tropics. Its pungent, long, thick leaves are good to eat raw; they are much used in the Philippines and in Cuba, especially for black beans. Plants grow easily from cuttings and like partial shade.

Also marketed as oregano are *Poliomintha longiflora* and *Monarda fistulosa* var. *menthifolia*. These grow in the southwestern US and Mexico, where they are prized for their pungent flavors. Cumin and cilantro are their natural partners in the kitchen.

Golpar, an Iranian spice often erroneously described as marjoram or angelica seed, is in fact the seed of *Heracleum persicum*, found in eastern Turkey and Iran. Whole seeds, yellow-green with brown markings in the center (*p.187*), can be bought from Iranian markets, as can the powdered spice. Golpar has a herbaceous, balsam aroma with yeasty overtones. The taste is mellow at first but has a persistent bitter note. When cooked, its mellow qualities dominate. It is used in soups (one of the best flavored with pomegranate molasses) and stews, in pickles, and over fava beans and potatoes.

Golden oregano

O. v. 'Aureum'

This oregano is a handsome ground-cover plant with dense foliage. It can be used in the same way as ordinary oregano but has a much milder flavor.

Mexican oregano

Lippia graveolens

This is an attractive plant with gray-green, oval leaves and creamy-white flowers. Related to lemon verbena, it has a high volatile oil content.

Syrian oregano *O. syriacum*

This oregano is cultivated for culinary use in the Middle East. Its flavor is pungent, reminiscent of thyme, marjoram, and oregano but sharper. It is sometimes sold as za'atar (*p.102*).

ROSEMARY

Rosmarinus officinalis

Rosemary is a dense, woody, evergreen perennial, native to the Mediterranean but long cultivated in temperate zones throughout Europe and America. It has been grown in England since Roman times. In the early 9th century, Charlemagne, in his *Capitulaire de Villes*, included it in the list of essential plants to be grown on the imperial estates; in the later Middle Ages it was still used as a strewing or incense herb.

TASTING NOTES

Strongly aromatic, warm and peppery, resinous and slightly bitter, with notes of pine and camphor. Nutmeg and camphor are present in the taste; the aftertaste is woody, balsamic, and astringent. The flavor dissipates after leaves are cut. Flowers have a milder flavor than leaves.

PARTS USED

The small needle-like leaves, sprigs, stems, flowers.

BUYING AND STORING

Buy plants from a nursery, or grow from cuttings. Fresh sprigs are available from supermarkets and can be kept for several days in the refrigerator or in a vase. They are available all year round, so there is little use for dried rosemary, although this retains most of its flavor and the leaves can easily be crumbled for use.

GROW YOUR OWN

Rosemary is hard to grow from seed but easy to propagate by cutting or layering. It needs light, well-drained soil and ample sun. There are creeping varieties as well as upright ones. Fairly hard spring pruning will keep plants bushy. The attractive, small flowers are usually blue, sometimes pink or white. Leaves and sprigs can be cut at any time of the year.

Fresh leaves
Rosemary leaves can be tough, so they are best chopped before being added to any dish in which they will be eaten.

Culinary uses

The flavor of rosemary is strong and unsubtle; it is not diminished by long cooking, so use rosemary judiciously, even in slow-cooked stews. In Mediterranean cuisines it is much used with vegetables fried in olive oil; in Italy, it is popular with veal. Whole sprigs are good in marinades, especially for lamb, and will give a subtle, smoky flavor when placed under meat or poultry being grilled or roasted. Older, stronger stems can be used as skewers for kebabs, or as basting brushes. Rosemary is very good in cookies and crackers, and in foccaccia and other breads. Young sprigs can be used to flavor olive oil, infused in milk, cream, or syrup for desserts, or steeped for summer drinks such as lemonade. Flowers frozen in ice cubes make a pretty garnish for such drinks. Crystallized rosemary flowers are pretty, but quite fiddly to make.

Essential to herbes de Provence.

Good with apricots, cabbage, cream cheese, eggplant, eggs, fish, lamb, lentils, mushrooms, onions, oranges, parsnips, pork, potatoes, poultry, rabbit, tomatoes, veal, winter squashes.

Combines well with bay, chives, garlic, lavender, lovage, mint, oregano, parsley, sage, savory, thyme.

Herbes de Provence
Used with meat, game, vegetable, and tomato dishes, this herb blend can be fresh or dried. This version includes rosemary, thyme, marjoram, savory, and bay (*recipe, p.281*).

SAGE

Salvia species

The sages are native to the north Mediterranean and are mostly perennial, shrubby plants that thrive on warm, dry soils. The great variety of their textured, velvety foliage – from pale gray-green to green splashed with silver or gold, as well as the dark leaves of purple sage – makes them attractive garden plants as well as an invaluable addition to the cook's repertoire of seasonings.

TASTING NOTES

Sage can be mild, musky, and balsamic, or strongly camphorous with astringent notes and a warm spiciness. Generally, variegated species are milder than common sage. Dried sage is more potent than fresh and can be acrid and musty; it is best avoided, except for tea.

PARTS USED

Leaves, fresh or dried. All sages have attractive, hooded flowers that make pretty garnishes.

BUYING AND STORING

Fresh sage leaves are best picked and used as soon as possible. If you buy them, wrap them in paper towel and keep in the salad crisper of the refrigerator for no more than a few days. Dried sage will keep for up to 6 months if stored away from light in an airtight container.

GROW YOUR OWN

Sage does best on warm, dry soils. Its aromatic strength varies according to soil and climate. Leaves can be harvested from spring to autumn. Plants are best cut back after flowering. Purple, variegated, and tricolor sages (*pp.97–99*) are less hardy than common sage, and pineapple sage (*p.98*) needs protection from freezing temperatures.

Common sage *S. officinalis*

There are broad and narrow-leaved varieties of common sage. Young, green leaves are less pungent than the older, gray ones. Narrow-leaved sage has pretty lilac, blue, or white flowers. Broad-leaved sage seldom flowers.

Culinary uses

Sage aids the digestion of fatty and oily foods and is traditionally used as a partner for them. In Britain, sage is associated with pork, goose, and duck, and works well in stuffings for these meats. In the US, sage and onion stuffing is often used for the Thanksgiving turkey. Sage also makes an excellent flavoring for pork sausages, and in Germany it accompanies eel. The Greeks use it in meat stews and with poultry, and also in a tea. Italians use sage with liver and veal (saltimbocca alla romana is the classic dish), and to flavor focaccia and polenta; they make a well-flavored pasta sauce by gently heating a few leaves in butter. Sage is not a subtle herb, so use sparingly.

Good with apples, dried beans, cheese, onions, tomatoes.

Combines well with bay, caraway, cutting celery, dried ginger, lovage, marjoram, paprika, parsley, savory, thyme.

Purple sage

S. o. Purpurascens Group

This sage has musky, spicy tones and is slightly less pungent than common sage. It rarely flowers, but when it does the blue flowers look stunning against the foliage.

Bouquet garni for meats

Little bundles of herbs such as this can be varied to suit the dish to be cooked. Sprigs of thyme, sage, cutting celery, and parsley make a fine flavoring for stews (*recipes, p.280*).

Other sages

Pungent common sage, *Salvia officinalis*, has many cultivated varieties grown mainly for the color of their foliage or flowers; all can be used for cooking, and each has its own flavor. Others have milder tastes and distinctly fruity fragrances: pineapple and black-currant sages smell like their eponymous fruits; clary sage, a statuesque biennial with large, wrinkled leaves, has a delicate scent of muscat grapes.

S. o. 'Tricolor'

Perhaps the most striking of all the sages, this has mottled green, cream, and pink leaves, and blue flowers. The flavor is quite gentle.

Black-currant sage *S. microphylla*

Rub the leaves in your hands for a rich scent of black currant; the flavor is less pronounced, however. Deep purple-pink flowers appear in late summer.

Greek sage *S. fruticosa*

The large, gray-green, downy leaves of this species are intensely aromatic, with dominant resinous notes. Use very sparingly in cooking, or as a tea.

Clary sage *S. sclarea*

This aromatic biennial has a scent reminiscent of muscat grapes; the taste is slightly bitter and balsam-like. The leaves can be used for fritters, while the flowers make a beautiful, edible garnish.

Variegated golden sage

S. o. 'Icterina'

This cultivated variety has pretty gold-and-green variegated foliage, but rarely flowers. The flavor is considerably milder than that of common sage.

Pineapple sage *S. elegans*

Overwintered indoors, this sage grows into a large shrub. The long leaves have a clear, pineapple scent but the flavor is less marked. Striking red flowers appear in autumn. Leaves can be placed in a cake pan to scent a plain cake.

THYME

Thymus species

Thyme is a small, hardy, evergreen shrub with small, aromatic leaves, indigenous to the Mediterranean basin. It grows wild on the hot, arid hillsides of its native region, where it has infinitely more flavor than it ever achieves in cooler regions. Wild thyme tends to be woody and straggly. Cultivated varieties have more tender stems and a bushy form; there are hundreds of them, each with a slightly different aroma, and they have a tendency to cross-breed as well.

Common thyme *T. vulgaris*

The basic thyme for cooking, also called garden thyme, is a cultivated variety of wild Mediterranean thyme. It forms a sturdy, upright shrub with gray-green leaves and white or pale lilac flowers. There are a number of garden thymes, including English "broad-leaf" and French "narrow-leaf" varieties.

TASTING NOTES

The whole plant has a warm, earthy, and peppery fragrance when lightly brushed. The taste is spicy, with notes of cloves and mint, a hint of camphor, and a mouth-cleansing aftertaste.

PARTS USED

Leaves and sprigs; flowers for garnishes.

BUYING AND STORING

Many varieties of thyme are sold by nurseries, but make sure they smell when brushed lightly by hand. Common and lemon thyme are available fresh from supermarkets. Fresh leaves will keep for up to a week stored in a plastic bag in the refrigerator. Dried thyme will retain its flavor through the winter.

GROW YOUR OWN

All thymes need very well-drained, sandy soil and as much sun as they can get. They benefit from the heat reflected off patio stone paving and the rocks in rock gardens. Propagation is easiest by division. Pick leaves when needed – the more often the better, or the plant may become straggly and woody. Harvest thyme for drying just before it flowers.

Culinary uses

Thyme is an essential flavoring in much Western and Middle-Eastern cooking. Unlike most herbs, it withstands long, slow cooking; used with discretion it enhances other herbs without overpowering them, and in stews and casseroles combines well with onions, beer, or red wine. Thyme has become indispensable in every French stew, from pot-au-feu to cassoulet, but equally in Spanish ones and, by extension, those of Mexico and Latin America, where it is often used in combination with chili peppers. It is widely used to flavor pâtés, thick vegetable soups, tomato and wine-based sauces, and in marinades for pork and game. In Britain, it is used in stuffings, pies, and jugged hare. The dried herb is essential in the Creole and Cajun cooking of Louisiana, where it appears in gumbos and jambalayas; elsewhere in the US, fresh thyme is used as a traditional flavoring in New England clam chowder.

Essential to most bouquets garnis.

Good with cabbage, carrots, corn, eggplant, lamb, leeks, legumes, onions, potatoes, rabbit, tomatoes, wild mushrooms.

Combines well with allspice, basil, bay, chili, clove, garlic, lavender, marjoram, nutmeg, oregano, paprika, parsley, rosemary, savory.

Lemon thyme *T. citriodorus*

This is a compact, upright shrub with mauve-pink flowers that gives a fresh lemony note to fish and seafood, roast chicken, or veal; it can be used in cookies, breads, and fruit salads. For the cook lemon thyme is the most important variety after garden thyme.

Other thymes

Cultivated varieties of common thyme (*T. vulgaris*) and lemon thyme (*T. citriodorus*) as well as other species offer different flavors to the cook. In the Middle East, the Arab name za'atar is given to thyme, to *Thymbra spicata*, and to other herbs with a thyme-savory-oregano aroma: Syrian oregano (*p.93*), conehead thyme (*p.103*), and thryba (*p.106*). Any of these can be combined with sesame (*p.138*) and sumac (*p.164*) to make the spice mixture also called za'atar.

Caraway thyme *T. herba-barona*

This is a trailing plant native to Corsica and Sardinia, with red stems, narrow glossy leaves, and pink flowers. Its taste has a light caraway note that goes well in root vegetable and cheese dishes, and cream sauces.

Creeping thyme *T. serpyllum*

This thyme grows throughout the Mediterranean region and also in central and northern Europe. It is milder than common thyme and should only be used fresh. Scatter the tiny leaves over salads or grilled vegetables. It combines well with hyssop.

Za'atar *Thymbra spicata*

This is a dark-leaved, woody shrub, rather like savory, is native to the Middle East. Its showy clusters of purple flowers make it a great rock-garden plant.

Conehead thyme *T. capitatus*

The Arabic for this variety is za'atar farsi, or Persian thyme; in the Middle East, it is the most widely used thyme.

Variegated thyme *T.c.* 'Golden Queen'

This variegated thyme has a mild flavor. The aromatic properties of thyme varieties vary according to the composition of their essential oils, and in particular the amount of thymol contained in the oils.

Orange-scented thyme

T. c. 'Fragrantissimus'

Leaves of this cultivated variety of thyme can be used as a flavoring in place of a piece of orange peel.

Lemon-scented thyme

T. sp. 'Lemon Mist'

This lemon-scented thyme has narrow leaves and a mounding growth habit. It is used in salads and as a flavoring for tea. A few chopped leaves added in the last few minutes of cooking will add zest to soups.

SAVORY

Satureja species

Highly aromatic, as the name suggests, savory was one of the strongest flavorings available before spices reached Europe. Summer savory *(S. hortensis)* is native to the eastern Mediterranean and the Caucasus; winter savory *(S. montana)* to southern Europe, Turkey, and North Africa. Both were taken to northern Europe by the Romans and to North America by early settlers.

Summer savory *S. hortensis*

This savory is a slender plant with soft, grayish leaves and white or pinkish flowers. Summer savory leaves are tender, whereas those of winter savory are tough.

FRESH SPRIGS
The leaves have the most intense aroma if harvested just before flowering.

TASTING NOTES

Savories have a peppery bite. Summer savory has a subtle, herbaceous scent and flavor – agreeably piquant, slightly resinous, and reminiscent of thyme, mint, and marjoram. Winter savory has a more assertive, penetrating aroma and flavor, with notes of sage and pine.

PARTS USED

Leaves and sprigs; flowers for garnishes and salads.

BUYING AND STORING

Savory is not available as a cut herb, but plants are available from nurseries. Summer savory will keep for 5–6 days, winter savory for up to 10 days, in a plastic bag in the refrigerator. Savory retains its flavor well if frozen, chopped or as sprigs. To dry summer savory, hang the stems in an airy, dark place.

GROW YOUR OWN

Summer savory is an annual, winter savory an evergreen perennial. Both can be grown from seed, and winter savory can be propagated by division in spring. Both prefer light, well-drained soils and full sun. Summer savory does best in a rich soil; cut back on flowering to encourage new growth. Winter savory will grow in poorer soils.

Culinary uses

Because they are pungent, both savories are good flavorings for long-cooked meat and vegetable dishes and stuffings. Savory is frequently associated with beans, as its German name Bohnenkraut (bean herb) indicates. Summer savory is best with green and fava beans, whereas either can be used with white beans and other legumes. Savory is also good with cabbage, root vegetables, and onions, and reduces their strong cooking smells.

Summer savory is often added to bouquets garnis for lamb, pork, and game dishes. It is also good with oil-rich fish such as eel and mackerel. Chopped finely, it can be added to salads; it is especially good with potato, bean, and lentil salads.

Winter savory (called poivre d'âne or pebre d'aï – donkey pepper – in Provence, France) is more widely used around the Mediterranean. Chopped leaves and flowers are added to soups, fish stews, frittate, pizza, rabbit, and lamb dishes. It is also used to coat Banon, a Provençal goat or sheep milk cheese.

Good with beans, beets, cabbage, cheese, eggs, fish, legumes, potatoes, rabbit, sweet peppers, tomatoes.

Combines well with basil, bay, cumin, garlic, lavender, marjoram, mint, oregano, parsley, rosemary, thyme.

Winter savory *S. montana*

This is a woody, compact shrub with stiff, glossy, dark green leaves and lavender or white flowers. Although the savories can be used interchangeably to some extent, both should be used judiciously, and winter savory in much smaller amounts than summer savory.

FRESH SPRIGS
Winter savory leaves can be harvested year-round.

Other savories

The genus *Satureja* encompasses many plants with pungent, spicy aromas in the mint-thyme-oregano spectrum; they have a variety of common names. Many are used as flavorings in their native habitat. There is also some confusion with the *Micromeria* species in the naming of certain plants.

Yerba buena, *S. douglasii*, is a pretty, trailing plant with small, heart-shaped, toothed leaves and tiny, white flowers. It has a rather synthetic, sweet smell with notes of mint (a little like chewing gum) and a minty, bitterish taste. Yerba buena means the good herb; in the past it was used to make a restorative tea (use it sparingly). Also called Indian mint, it is native to Western and Central America, and probably was given this name because it was used by Native Americans. In Mexico, yerba or hierba buena is the common name used for any minty plant, whether it be spearmint or one of the *Satureja* varieties.

Costa Rican or Jamaican mint bush, *S. viminea*, has small, oval, glossy, light leaves and an agreeable, minty smell and flavor. Native to Central America and the Caribbean, it grows in the southern and western regions of the US. In Trinidad and Tobago, it is used as a meat flavoring, but is mostly used for tea elsewhere.

Thryba *S. thymbra*

Also called thyme-leaved savory, this is a small, woody perennial found in Sardinia, Crete, and the Aegean islands, and on the western coast of Turkey. Its scent is of thyme, mint, and savory, and the taste has an agreeable bite. Leaves and flowertips are used to flavor meat, game, and vegetable stews, and grilled meats, and in cures for olives.

MICROMERIA

Micromeria species

Micromerias are perennial herbs or dwarf shrubs native to southern Europe, the Caucasus, southwestern China, and western America. In these regions they are regularly used as a culinary herb and to make teas. In Europe, they thrive particularly in the Balkan peninsula; in Croatia, one species appears on postage stamps. Micromerias are closely related to savories (*Satureja* species, *p.104*), and there is some confusion and duplication in the naming of certain plants.

TASTING NOTES

The flavors of some micromerias tend toward mint, others toward thyme and savory. *M. juliana* (also called *Satureja juliana*) resembles savory. *M. fruticosa* resembles English pennyroyal (*p.73*).

PARTS USED

Fresh leaves.

BUYING AND STORING

Micromerias are not available as cut herbs, but plants are stocked by some specialist nurseries. They can also be picked from the wild. Sprigs will keep for a few days in a plastic bag in the vegetable crisper of the refrigerator.

GROW YOUR OWN

In the wild, micromerias thrive on thin soils on dry, exposed cliffs and rocky meadows. They can be grown from seed, or by plant division, in loamy, well-drained soil in pots or in the garden. They make attractive ornamental plants for rock gardens, with their bushy habit and thin stems bearing white, red, or purple flowers above the foliage. Harvest leaves from spring to late summer.

Culinary uses

Among the micromerias the species *M. thymifolia* has the finest flavor: warmly aromatic with delicate notes of thyme and savory. It is also rich in unsaturated fatty acids. Italian cooks use young leaves with thyme-savory aromas to flavor soups, marinades, and frittate, in stuffings for meat and vegetables, and with roast chicken or squab. Finely chopped leaves are added to pasta sauces or sprinkled over meat or poultry before grilling. In Balkan cooking the leaves are used like thyme. Micromeria brings out the flavor of ripe tomatoes and soft, fresh cheeses. A few chopped leaves give a depth of flavor to summer berry desserts.

A minty tea is made from *M. fruticosa*. Pulegone, the main constituent of that herb's essential oil, is known to be toxic, but, taken in normal quantities, the tea is not likely to cause health problems. Emperor's mint is the micromeria most commonly available; it can be used sparingly in place of garden mint.

Emperor's mint *M. species*

Emperor's mint has an assertive, minty aroma, reminiscent of spearmint, and a bitterish minty flavor.

CILANTRO

Coriandrum sativum

Native to the Mediterranean and western Asia, coriander is now grown worldwide. It is both herb and spice, and a fragrant staple in many cuisines. The fresh leaves, commonly called cilantro, are essential to Asian, Latin American, and Portuguese cooking. Thai cooks also use the thin, spindly root. In Western cooking the fruit or seed is used as a spice; in the Middle East and India, both are common in the kitchen. Another name for the herb is Chinese parsley.

TASTING NOTES

Leaves, roots, and unripe seeds all have the same aroma. Some people are addicted to its refreshing, lemony-ginger aroma with notes of sage; others hate it and find it soapy and disagreeable. The flavor is delicate yet complex, with a suggestion of pepper, mint, and lemon.

PARTS USED

Leaves and sprigs, roots.

BUYING AND STORING

Cilantro is available from specialty markets and supermarkets; bunches are sold with roots intact in Asian markets, or you can grow your own. In a plastic bag, cilantro will keep for 3–4 days in the refrigerator vegetable crisper. Frozen cilantro retains its flavor fairly well; chop and freeze in small pots or in ice-cube trays covered with a little water. Dried cilantro is not worthwhile and is never used in Asian cuisines.

GROW YOUR OWN

Coriander is an annual that grows easily from seed in a warm, sunny spot. Leaves can be gathered throughout the growing season. Clusters of small, white or pinkish flowers produce the seeds. Seeds should be harvested when fully ripe; to dry them, hang bunches of stems in a warm place and put a paper bag over the seedheads.

Fresh sprigs
Cilantro was called a "very stinking herbe" by Gerard, the 16th-century herbalist, and is known as the "fragrant plant" by the Chinese. The herb's aroma continues to provoke both dislike and enthusiasm today.

ROOTS
The roots are more pungent and musky than the leaves, with a light, citrus smell.

Culinary uses

Except when they are used in a curry or similar paste, cilantro leaves are always added at the end of cooking; high or prolonged heat reduces their flavor. Cilantro leaves are used lavishly throughout most of Asia, in delicately flavored soups, in stir-fried dishes with ginger and scallions, in curries and braised dishes. Thai cooks use the roots for curry pastes and combine leaves with basil, mint, and chili peppers.

In India, cilantro garnishes many savory dishes and is combined with other herbs and spices in green masala pastes. India and Mexico share a liking for cilantro with green chili peppers in chutneys, relishes, and salsas. Mexicans also combine cilantro and chilies with garlic and lime juice to make a dressing for vegetables, or for a sauce in which to cook fish.

In Bolivia and Peru, cilantro, chilies, and huacatay flavor a very assertive table sauce. In the Middle East, cilantro is essential to Yemeni zhug and hilbeh, both pungent spice pastes, and is combined with nuts and spices, lemon juice, and olive oil to make flavoring mixtures. The Portuguese are the only Europeans who have continued to use cilantro to the same extent as it was used in the 16th century. They partner it with potatoes and fava beans, and with their excellent clams.

Essential to hilbeh, zhug, chermoula, ceviche, guacamole.

Good with avocados, coconut milk, corn, cucumber, fish and seafood, legumes, lemons and limes, rice, root vegetables.

Combines well with basil, chili, chives, dill, galangal, garlic, ginger, lemon grass, mint, parsley.

Yemeni zhug paste

This mixture of cilantro, hot chili peppers, garlic, cumin, and cardamom is used as a condiment (*recipe, p.290*).

CULANTRO

Eryngium foetidum

This tender biennial grows wild on many Caribbean islands and is variously called shado beni (Trinidad), chadron benee (Domenica), and recao (Puerto Rico). Also grown in Southeast Asia, it reaches Europe with names like Mexican cilantro, long or spiny coriander, sawleaf herb, and Chinese or Thai parsley.

TASTING NOTES

Culantro has an intense aroma with a fetid element, as its Latin name indicates. The taste is earthy, pungent, and quite sharp – a concentrated version of cilantro with a bitter note at the finish.

PARTS USED

Fresh leaves.

BUYING AND STORING

Plants are available at some herb nurseries. Leaves, tied in bundles, sometimes with rootlets attached, are sold in Asian markets. They keep for 3–4 days in the refrigerator. I have not come across culantro as a dried herb, but it freezes well. Remove the thick central rib and purée the leaves with a little water or sunflower oil, then freeze in ice-cube trays.

GROW YOUR OWN

Culantro grows best in well-drained soil in partial shade. Shade produces plants with bigger, greener, and more pungent leaves, whereas hot sun encourages the plant to go rapidly to seed. Remove flower stems to encourage more leaf growth. Culantro has long, tough leaves with serrated edges that may be prickly. Leaves can be picked throughout the growing season by cutting off at soil level.

Culinary uses

In its indigenous regions, culantro is consumed enthusiastically. It flavors soups, stews and curries, rice and noodle dishes, meat and fish dishes. It is a key ingredient in Trinidadian fish and meat marinades, and in Puerto Rican sofrito, a mixture of garlic, onion, green sweet and chili peppers, cilantro, and culantro that forms the basis of many of the island's dishes. Mexican cooks use it in salsas. In Asia, it is often used to temper the smell of beef, which many people find too pungent. For northern Thai cooks it is common in larp, a fiery dish of lightly cooked or raw beef served with sticky rice. In Vietnam, young culantro leaves are always in the bowl of herbs that accompanies every meal.

Combines well with chili, cilantro, galangal, garlic, kaffir lime, lemon grass, mint, parsley.

Fresh leaves

If leaves are spiny, remove the spines or make sure they are cooked. Culantro can be used in dishes calling for cilantro but less culantro should be used.

RAU RAM

Polygonum odoratum

Rau ram seems increasingly to be the accepted name for this popular tropical Asian herb, but it is also sold as Vietnamese coriander or cilantro, Vietnamese mint, daun kesom (its Malay name), and laksa leaf. Vietnamese emigrants took it to France in the 1950s and the US in the 1970s, where it now has an enthusiastic and growing following.

TASTING NOTES

Rau ram smells rather like a more penetrating version of cilantro with a clear citrus note; the taste is similar, refreshing with a hot, biting, peppery aftertaste. Some people find the aroma soapy.

PARTS USED

Fresh, young leaves.

BUYING AND STORING

Plants are available from specialist nurseries and bunches of stems are sold in Asian markets. In a plastic bag, these will keep in the refrigerator vegetable crisper for 4–5 days if bought in good condition.

GROW YOUR OWN

A bushy herb, rau ram grows wild on the banks of ponds and streams in its native habitat. A tender perennial, it is often grown as an annual. It overwinters in a sheltered spot outside unless there are very hard frosts. Rau ram grows best in partial shade and rapidly becomes invasive in rich, moist soil. Lower stems tend to become woody. In the tropics it bears red or pink flowers. Keep trimming the plant to encourage new growth. It roots easily if stems are left in a glass of water for 2–3 days, after which it can be planted out.

Culinary uses

Rau ram is used as a flavoring for fish, seafood, poultry, and pork. The Vietnamese make an excellent chicken and cabbage salad flavored with rau ram, chili peppers, and lime juice. Thai cooks also serve the leaves raw with nam prik, or shred them and add to larp and curries. One of its most popular uses in Singapore and Malaysia is as an aromatic garnish for laksa, a spicy soup made with fish, seafood, and coconut milk. Use rau ram as you would cilantro: add shredded or torn leaves to stir-fries, soups, and noodles.

Good with coconut milk, egg dishes, fish and seafood, meat, poultry, noodles, bean sprouts, red and green sweet peppers, water chestnuts.

Combines well with chili, galangal, garlic, ginger, lemon grass.

Fresh leaves

Rau ram withstands cooking better than cilantro and will impart a subtle flavor to cooked dishes if added part way through the cooking. The leaves can also be used as a component of a salad platter.

ARUGULA

Eruca vesicaria subsp. sativa

Arugula is native to Asia and southern Europe and naturalized in North America. It was a popular herb in Europe until the 18th century, when it virtually disappeared everywhere but in Italy. After nearly two centuries of neglect it is having a well-deserved revival, and is currently the most fashionable salad herb in both the US and Europe (where it is variously known as rucola, roquette, and rocket).

TASTING NOTES

Arugula's toothed leaves have a warm, peppery smell that rises from the bed as soon as the first leaf is picked. The taste is pleasantly pungent. The small, white or yellow, edible flowers have a faint orange aroma; they make an attractive garnish.

PARTS USED

Leaves and flowers.

BUYING AND STORING

Arugula is now readily available in supermarkets, either on its own or in bags of mixed salad leaves. All the same it is well worth growing from seed, as it needs no looking after and is at its best freshly picked. It can be stored in a plastic bag in the refrigerator vegetable crisper for a few days. Drying arugula is a waste of time, nor does it freeze well, but as fresh leaves can be obtained easily this matters little.

GROW YOUR OWN

Arugula and wild arugula are both very easy to grow from seed, and staggered sowing will give a useful crop virtually throughout the year. They thrive in partial shade. Arugula is an annual, wild arugula a perennial; both self-seed only too readily. Leaves are ready for picking in 6–8 weeks.

Culinary uses

Whole leaves can be added to any salad of mixed leaves or potato salad, or will make a strongly flavored salad on their own, especially with a nut oil dressing. Arugula leaves can also be used as a fragrant bed on which to present other salads, poached eggs, or roasted sweet red peppers. Arugula and prosciutto makes a good sandwich filling, and with mushrooms or cheese a filling for ravioli. Shredded leaves are good in herb butter for seafood or herb dressings, especially for pasta. Arugula can also be used to make pesto, with or without basil.

Good with goat cheese, lettuce, potatoes, salad herbs, tomato.

Combines well with basil, borage, cilantro, cresses, dill, lovage, mint, parsley, salad burnet.

Arugula *E. v.* subsp. *sativa*

The leaves become progressively more peppery the longer they stay on the plant, but once the flowers fully develop their taste diminishes.

Wild arugula

Diplotaxis muralis

Wild arugula has narrower, more sharply toothed leaves and a more peppery taste than its cultivated counterpart. It can be bought as growing plants from herb nurseries or specialist suppliers.

Turkish arugula *Bunias orientalis*

Turkish arugula grows wild in parts of Asia. It has a sharp and coarse flavor, rather like horseradish, and a tinge of sulfur. Called rokka, it can often be bought in large bunches from Turkish markets. It is better cooked, for instance in a vegetable frittata, than used raw.

WASABI

Eutrema wasabi

This herbaceous perennial grows primarily in cold mountain streams in Japan; recently some cultivation has started in California and New Zealand. The name translates as mountain hollyhock. In the West the plant is sometimes called Japanese horseradish, a reference to its pungency and the fact that the gnarled and knobby root, on average about 4–5in (10–12cm) long, is the edible part.

TASTING NOTES

Wasabi has a fierce, burning smell that makes the nose prickle, and a bitingly sharp but fresh and cleansing taste. Dried wasabi only develops its penetrating aroma and flavor when mixed with water and left to steep for about 10 minutes.

PARTS USED

Roots.

BUYING AND STORING

Some specialty produce markets sell fresh wasabi, but more usually it is sold either in tubes as a paste or in cans as powder. Fresh wasabi will keep for a week, wrapped in plastic wrap, in the vegetable crisper of the refrigerator. Powdered wasabi has a shelf life of several months but can develop a rather stale aftertaste. Tubes of paste must be refrigerated after opening. The paste loses its potency more quickly than the powder.

HARVESTING

Wasabi can only be cultivated in cold, pure, running water; commercial growing is normally done in flooded terraces, usually in partial shade. It is very expensive to produce.

Fresh root
Fresh wasabi root is sold in tubs of water. The tough, brownish-green skin is removed to reveal pale green flesh.

Culinary uses

Wasabi does not retain its flavor when cooked, so it is generally served with or added to cold food. In Japan, it accompanies most raw fish dishes. Sashimi and sushi plates always have a tiny mound of grated wasabi or wasabi paste, which is then mixed to individual taste with a soy dipping sauce. In sushi it often appears as an ingredient as well as a garnish, between raw fish and the vinegared rice. With soy sauce and dashi (soup stock), wasabi makes the popular wasabi-joyu sauce. On its own, wasabi can be used to give a sharp piquancy to dressings and marinades. It also makes a good butter that keeps in the refrigerator for weeks; this makes an interesting change served on filet mignon or other steaks.

Essential to sashimi, sushi.

Good with avocado, beef, raw fish, rice, seafood.

Combines well with ginger, soy sauce.

GRATED ROOT
In Japan, peeled wasabi root is grated finely on an oroshigane, a flat grater tightly set with thin spikes. Made of stainless steel, tinned copper, or plastic, these can be bought from Japanese stores.

WASABI PASTE
Because wasabi is so expensive, harsher-tasting horseradish mixed with mustard and green coloring is frequently passed off as wasabi paste or powder. Real paste costs twice as much as fake and has a shorter shelf life.

HORSERADISH

Armoracia rusticana

Horseradish is a perennial native to eastern Europe and western Asia, where it still grows wild in the steppes of Russia and the Ukraine. Its culinary use probably originated in Russia and eastern Europe, spreading to central Europe in the early Middle Ages, later to Scandinavia and western Europe. English settlers took it to North America, and cultivation was established by German and eastern European immigrants around 1850. By about 1860, bottled horseradish was available as one of the first convenience condiments.

TASTING NOTES

Horseradish root is very pungent and mustard-like when just grated, enough to make your eyes water and your nose run. The taste is acrid, sharp, and hot. The leaves are also pungent when crushed; the taste is sharp, but much milder than that of the root.

PARTS USED

Fresh young leaves; fresh or dried roots.

BUYING AND STORING

Fresh roots are sold in supermarkets, particularly near Passover (horseradish is one of the five bitter herbs of the Seder). Fresh roots taken from the garden will keep for months in dry sand, bought ones for 2–3 weeks in a plastic bag in the refrigerator, even after being cut and part-used. Grated horseradish can be frozen. Dried roots can be bought powdered or flaked.

GROW YOUR OWN

Horseradish is propagated from root cuttings. It grows very easily in sandy loam soil with good drainage, but is invasive – the tiniest bit left in the soil will be enough to overrun a patch, so plant in a container, as one does mint. The roots can be lifted throughout the winter, if the ground is not frozen.

Fresh root
Slicing a long, thick, hairy, yellowish-brown horseradish root reveals white flesh. Grating releases its highly pungent volatile oil, but this dissipates very quickly and does not survive cooking.

Culinary uses

Freshly grated horseradish can be stabilized with a little lemon juice. It is good on salads of potatoes or root vegetables, and aids the digestion of oily fish. A traditional accompaniment to roast beef – and to tongue in Germany – it also goes well with boiled beef. Why it is served with oysters – often alongside tomato ketchup and Tabasco sauce – is a mystery to me, since it masks the oysters' flavor completely.

Horseradish is easily made into a sauce by blending it with cream and vinegar, or with sour cream alone, with or without sugar. A popular Austrian condiment is Apfelkren, made by mixing horseradish with grated apples and a little lemon juice. With apricot preserve and a little mustard, horseradish makes a good glaze for ham. Mixed with mustard into butter it is good with corn-on-the-cob or carrots. A few tender, young leaves will give a pleasant, sharp taste to a green salad. Processed horseradish browns as it ages and loses its strength. Many condiments have too much added sugar, which masks the fresh and pungent flavor.

Good with apple, avocado, baked ham, beef, beets, oily or smoked fish, potatoes, pork sausages, seafood.

Combines well with capers, celery, chives, cream, dill, mustard, tomato paste, vinegar, yogurt.

GRATED ROOT
Sprinkle lemon juice on grated horseradish to preserve its white color and pungency. Vinegar is used to prevent browning and loss of flavor in commercial horseradish condiments.

WATERCRESS

Nasturtium officinale

TASTING NOTES

Watercress has little aroma; sprigs and leaves are crisp and have a peppery, slighty bitterish taste.

PARTS USED

Sprigs and leaves.

BUYING AND STORING

Seeds for watercress, upland and garden cress, and nasturtiums can be obtained from nurseries. Fresh watercress is available all year round in supermarkets, usually in small bunches or in bags of mixed salad greens. In a plastic bag in the vegetable crisper of the refrigerator, all of the cresses will keep for 4–5 days. Nasturtium flowers should be used immediately. Seeds can be harvested in autumn to sow the next year.

GROW YOUR OWN

Watercress grows speedily near springs and open running watercourses – conditions that are imitated in its commercial hydroponic cultivation. It can be grown fairly easily from seed in a tub, where its shining, bright green leaves will soon cover the entire surface.

Watercress is a hardy perennial native to Europe and Asia, widely naturalized in North America, and has been introduced also into the West Indies and South America. Its use as a salad herb can be traced back to the Persians, Greeks, and Romans. Its cultivation in northern Europe started relatively late – Germany began growing it in the 16th century, and Britain had not started before 1800.

Culinary uses

Watercress is used in an amazing variety of soups, made either with stock, cream, or yogurt. Best known is French potage au cresson (potato and watercress soup), served hot or cold; Italians use cress in minestrone and other vegetable soups; the Chinese in egg-drop and wonton soups and in Cantonese seafood broths. In the American southwest, watercress soup may be served with a red-pepper rouille. The herb is also served with fish, often with ginger; made into a sauce, much like sorrel, it works well with salmon. In China, watercress is popular blanched, chopped, and tossed in light sesame oil, or stir-fried with salt, sugar, and a little rice wine.

Good with chicken, cucumber, fish, onion, oranges, potatoes, salmon.

Combines well with fennel, ginger, parsley, other salad herbs, sorrel.

Fresh sprigs
In the West, watercress is mostly eaten raw, as a garnish or in sandwiches and salads, either on its own or combined with, for instance, cucumber, fennel, orange sections, papaya, or red onion.

Other cresses

There are many plants resembling or used like watercress but not necessarily related to *N. officinale*. Nasturtium is the common name of a South American genus cultivated widely for its vivid flowers. The transfer of the name came about because the leaves taste similar to watercress, although few people take advantage of nasturtiums in the kitchen.

Upland cress *Barbarea verna praecox*

As one of its other names, winter cress, indicates, this biennial plant is very hardy; it is also called land cress. Like watercress, its small, tender leaves have a spicy flavor and make a welcome addition to winter's limited array of fresh greens. It can be grown from seed.

Garden cress *Lepidium sativum*

This cress has dark green leaves, which may be curled, and a strong, peppery flavor. Quite hardy, it prefers cold and dry conditions, and tolerates almost any soil. In combination with mustard seed, it is sprouted as a cut-and-come-again seedling crop in Britain.

Nasturtium or Indian cress *Tropaeolum majus*

Neither the leaves nor the flowers of this plant have much aroma, but both have an agreeably peppery, cress-like taste – the flowers are slightly sweeter and more delicate. Young leaves can be used in salads; the flowers look and taste great scattered over a green salad or one of potato or white beans, or floated on a bowl of fruit punch. Flowerbuds and seeds can be pickled and used instead of capers.

EPAZOTE

Chenopodium ambrosioides

Native to central and southern Mexico, epazote was an essential ingredient of Mayan cuisine in the Yucatán and Guatemala. It is now widely cultivated and used in southern Mexico, the northern countries of South America, and the Caribbean islands. Its use is spreading in North America, where it is often found as a weed along roadsides and in towns; it is grown commercially in the south. It still has to make its mark in Europe, although it grows wild there also.

TASTING NOTES

Not everyone likes epazote. The aroma is described as that of turpentine or putty by those who hate it, while it reminds others of savory, mint, and citrus. I think of it as camphorous, earthy, and minty. The taste is pungent and refreshing, bitterish with lingering citrus notes and a curious, oddly addictive rankness.

PARTS USED

Leaves, fresh or dried.

BUYING AND STORING

It is difficult to obtain fresh epazote, except in Latin markets, unless you grow it yourself; dried epazote has much less taste but is still good in cooking. Make sure you get the leaves, not the stems, which are also sold dried – these are fine for tea but less good in cooking.

GROW YOUR OWN

Epazote can easily be grown from seed in dry soil. Its flavor will depend on the amount of sun it gets – in colder climates it is less aromatic. It is an annual but will reseed itself only too readily. Once established, it should be possible to overwinter plants indoors.

Culinary uses

The fresh herb is commonly used in Mexican bean dishes, partly for its flavor and partly because it reduces flatulence. Chopped finely, it is used in soups and stews. Although used raw in salsas, its flavor works best in cooking; add for only the last 15 minutes or so to avoid bitterness. It is essential to mole verde, a green cooking sauce of tomatillos and green chili peppers, thickened with nuts or seeds. Use epazote lightly: it easily overwhelms other flavors, and in larger doses it is somewhat toxic and can cause dizziness.

Essential to black bean dishes, mole verde, quesadillas, salsas.

Good with chorizo, corn, fish and shellfish, green vegetables, legumes, lime, mushrooms, onion, pork, rice, squash, sweet peppers, tomatillos, white cheese.

Combines well with chili, cilantro, cloves, cumin, garlic, oregano.

Fresh leaves
The taste of epazote is too pungent for many people. Its name, deriving from Nahuatl, an Aztec language still spoken around Mexico City, refers to a disagreeable odor – *epatl* means skunk and *tzotl* sweat.

DRIED LEAVES
Use dried leaves only when fresh are unavailable.

MUGWORT

Artemisia vulgaris

Mugwort is an herbaceous perennial that grows wild in many habitats throughout most of North and South America, Europe, and Asia. In the Middle Ages, it was used instead of hops as a bittering agent in brewing beer. In the 18th century, it was one of the most used kitchen herbs in Europe, but it has since gone out of fashion except in Germany, where it is popular as Gänsekraut, goose herb.

TASTING NOTES

The aroma of mugwort is of juniper and pepper, lightly pungent with a hint of mint and sweetness. The flavor is similar, with a mild, bitter aftertaste.

PARTS USED

Fresh young shoots; leaves and flowerbuds, both fresh and dried.

BUYING AND STORING

Buy plants from a nursery. Pick young leaves as needed. Flower stems are dried by hanging in a dark, warm place. This can take 3 weeks, or 4–6 hours if left in a warm oven. Once dry, buds and leaves can be stored in an airtight container for up to a year. Dried mugwort is available from Japanese markets.

GROW YOUR OWN

Mugwort is quite adaptable, but does prefer full sun and a rich, moist soil. It can be propagated from seed or by division of the rhizomes. It should be kept in check or it will run rampant. Numerous small, reddish-brown florets bloom in late summer and early autumn on panicled spikes. Harvest just before the flowerbuds open: the flowers can get unpleasantly bitter.

Culinary uses

Mugwort works well with oily fish, fatty meat, and poultry such as duck or goose, helping in their digestion. It is good in stuffings and marinades, and also flavors stock quite well. Its aroma develops with cooking, so it should be added early. It has no natural partners among herbs, but garlic and pepper go well with it. Called yomogi in Japan, it is used as a vegetable, as a popular ingredient in mochi (rice cakes), and as a seasoning for soba noodles. Young leaves are boiled or stir-fried thoughout Asia. Young leaves can also be shredded over a green salad or stirred into the dressing. Cider vinegar in which mugwort has been steeped for some weeks is good for salad dressings and marinades.

Good with beans, duck, eel, game, goose, onions, pork, rice.

Combines well with garlic, pepper.

Fresh leaves
Leaves are smooth and green on top, downy white underneath.

DRIED LEAVES
In Germany, mugwort is available fresh and dried; elsewhere it is necessary to grow your own, or buy dried via the internet.

preparing herbs

STRIPPING, CHOPPING, AND POUNDING HERBS

Some herbs – chives, chervil, and cilantro – have soft stems, but in most cases leaves must be stripped from the stems before being used. Small leaves and sprigs are used whole in salads or as a garnish, but most leaves are chopped, sliced, or pounded, depending on the dish being prepared. Chop, slice, or pound herbs just before you need them or their flavors will dissipate.

Stripping leaves

When stripping herbs you may find that you are not able to go right to the top of the stem because it is too tender and will break. Such upper stems are likely to be soft enough to chop with the leaves. Some herbs are easier to strip from the top down, particularly those with large leaves.

Stripping tough stems ▲
Hold the bottom of the stem firmly in one hand, place the thumb and first finger of the other hand on either side of the stem, and, using the thumb to guide, pull upward, stripping the leaves onto a board.

Stripping tender stems ▶
Strip fennel and dill from the bottom of the stem, pulling the leaf sprays upward with one hand. Take out any thick stems that remain and strip off the leaves.

Chopping leaves

Herbs are chopped according to the dish for which they are needed. Finely chopped herbs integrate well with other ingredients. They provide immediate flavor because so much of their surface is exposed, allowing the essential oils to blend into the food quickly, but they may lose their flavor in cooking. Coarsely chopped herbs keep their identity, flavor, and texture longer and survive cooking better than finely chopped herbs, but are less attractive in a smooth-textured dish.

Using a mezzaluna ▶
Some cooks prefer to use the curved mezzaluna for large amounts of herbs. This implement is rocked backward and forward to great effect. Herbs can also be chopped in the small bowl of a food processor: use the pulse button and chop briefly. Make sure the herbs are completely dry or they will turn out unattractively pastelike. It is more difficult to obtain uniformly chopped leaves in a processor.

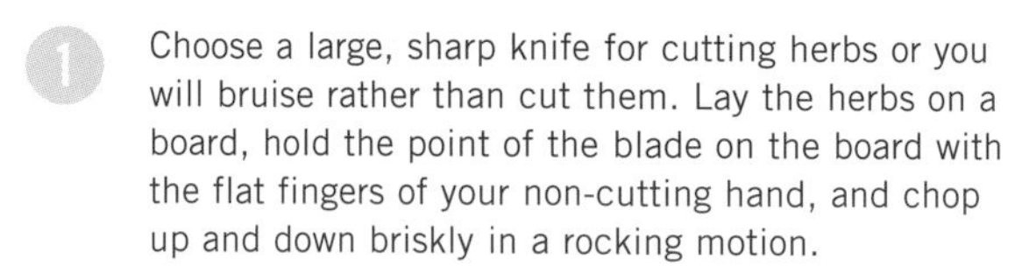

1 Choose a large, sharp knife for cutting herbs or you will bruise rather than cut them. Lay the herbs on a board, hold the point of the blade on the board with the flat fingers of your non-cutting hand, and chop up and down briskly in a rocking motion.

2 Scoop the herbs back into a pile from time to time with the flat of the blade. Continue the chopping action until the herbs are cut as finely as you need.

Making a chiffonade

Any finely shredded vegetable used as a garnish is termed a "chiffonade." Shredded herb leaves make an attractive garnish and also keep their texture well in a sauce.

1. If using leaves such as sorrel, remove the thick vein from each one beforehand.
2. Stack a few similar-sized leaves one on top of the other and roll them up tightly.
3. ▶ Using a sharp knife, cut the roll of leaves into very fine slices.

Pounding herbs

Herbs can be pounded to a paste using a mortar and pestle, and garlic is easily puréed in a mortar with a little salt. A smoother result is achieved more quickly in a food processor.

1. ▲ Pesto (*recipe, p.296*) is the classic pounded herb sauce. Start by pounding some basil and garlic in a large mortar.
2. ▶ Gradually work in some pine nuts, grated Parmesan, and olive oil, and mix to a paste.

DRYING AND RUBBING HERBS

Drying does not suit all herbs. Those with woody stems and tough leaves, such as thyme, rosemary, oregano, and lemon verbena, dry best and keep their flavor well, while those with soft leaves and stems, such as basil, parsley, chervil, and marjoram, lose their flavor almost completely. Mint is an exception: although it has soft leaves, it dries well. The traditional way to dry herbs is to hang them in bunches, but they also dry well in a microwave oven. For the best flavor, harvest herbs just before their flowerbuds open, when the essential oils are at their most concentrated, and pick early in the day.

Freezing herbs

Soft herbs that do not dry well can be frozen. Frozen herbs keep their fragrance for 3–4 months. Use for soups, stews, braised dishes, and sauces.

◀ **Freezing chopped herbs**
Wash and dry the herbs well, chop, and freeze in small pots or in ice-cube trays with a little water or oil. Store the cubes in plastic bags.

▲ **Freezing puréed herbs**
Alternatively, purée each herb with a little oil in a food processor and freeze in bags or plastic pots.

Drying herbs

Herbs hanging in a well-ventilated place will dry within a few days to a week. Those kept in a steamy kitchen will not dry well. Avoid direct sunlight or too much heat because they will cause the essential oils to evaporate.

Microwaving herbs ▶
Scatter two handfuls of cleaned leaves and sprigs evenly on a double layer of paper towel and microwave on high for 2½ minutes. Bay leaves may need a little longer. Microwaving preserves color well. Store as below.

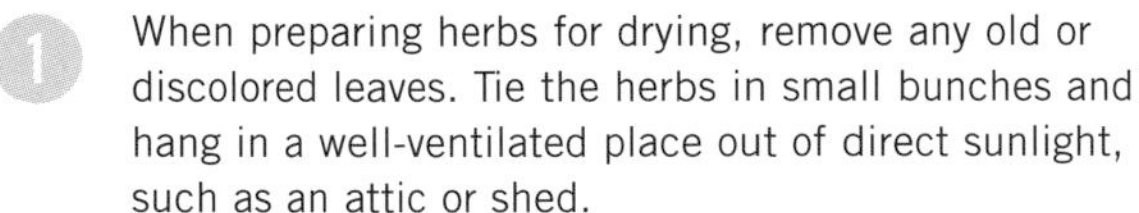

1 When preparing herbs for drying, remove any old or discolored leaves. Tie the herbs in small bunches and hang in a well-ventilated place out of direct sunlight, such as an attic or shed.

2 Drying is complete when the leaves feel brittle. Large leaves or small flowerbuds can be rubbed between the palms of your hands to crumble them. Otherwise, strip the leaves from the stems. Store in airtight containers.

MAKING VINEGARS, OILS, AND BUTTERS

Flavored vinegars and oils are useful for sauces, dressings, and marinades, and for stirring into soups and stews just before serving. Basil, dill, garlic, lavender, lemon verbena, rosemary, tarragon, and thyme make excellent vinegars; among spices try chili peppers, peppercorns, and dill, fennel, mustard, or coriander seeds. For oils, try basil, bay, dill, garlic, mint, oregano, rosemary, savory, or thyme, or chili peppers and cumin, dill, or fennel seeds. Herb and spice butters provide a quick dressing for broiled or fried fish, poultry, and meat, and steamed or boiled vegetables, as well as a good sandwich spread.

Making herb vinegar or oil

Flavored vinegars will keep in a cool, dark place for several years, mellowing as they age. Oils will keep for up to 2 weeks and should be refrigerated.

1. To make an herb or spice vinegar, take about 2oz (60g) of herb sprigs or whole spices – about 1½ cups herb sprigs and 2–4 tbsp whole spices – and crush to bring out their flavor.

2. ◀ Put them into a large jar and cover with 2 cups (500ml) white wine vinegar, cider vinegar, or rice vinegar. Close the jar and let infuse for 2–3 weeks. Flavors will develop more quickly if the jar is placed in the sun.

3. Strain into bottles, add a fresh herb sprig or a few fresh spices to each one for decoration, close with a cork or plastic-lined cap, and label the bottle.

Making herb oil

Follow the above method, but instead of vinegar fill up the jar with virgin olive oil, sunflower oil, or grapeseed oil. Let infuse in a cool, dark place or the refrigerator. When the flavors have developed, strain and bottle.

Making herb or spice butter

Most fresh herbs make fine flavored butters; among spices, choose ground cumin, black pepper, cardamom, allspice, paprika, or cayenne – 1½–2 tbsp per ⅔ cup (150g) butter. If you combine spices with herbs, use less. Butters keep for a week if refrigerated, or can be frozen.

1. Beat ⅔ cup (150g) softened butter in a bowl with 1–2 tbsp lemon juice and 4–5 tbsp chopped herbs, or blend the butter and lemon juice with the same quantity of herbs in a food processor.

2. Lay a sheet of plastic wrap on a flat surface and spoon the flavored butter into the center. Press the butter into an elongated shape. Wrap in another sheet of plastic wrap to prevent tearing.

3. Taking care to avoid folding the wrap into the butter, roll the butter into a sausage shape. Twist the ends of the plastic wrap to compress the butter, wrap in foil, and refrigerate.

spices

Introducing spices

I have long had a passion for spices and a fascination with their origins and production, as well as their culinary possibilities. What people eat in any particular region is, or was, largely determined by what grew and was reared there. The style of cooking originally depended on local conditions, such as the availability of fuels, but what really differentiates the great cuisines of the world is the spices they use and how they blend them.

Produce of tropical Asia

Most of the important spice plants – cinnamon, cloves, galangal, ginger, nutmeg, pepper – are native to the Asian tropics. They have been used and traded for millennia, and much has been written about the history of their trade – the fortunes and empires founded on it, the brutal conquests, piracy, and greed; but our view of these developments has always been a Western one. We know about the overland routes from China to Byzantium, we are aware of the role Arab seafarers played in the introduction of spices to the Tigris-Euphrates basin and later to the Mediterranean ports, and we have read about the Portuguese, Dutch, and English monopolies. But we know little about the equally important early Asian trade, dominated at different times by the large merchant fleets first of the Korean kingdom of Silla (early 7th to mid-9th centuries), then of southern China under the Sung dynasty (960–1276), and of Sri Lanka. We know even less of the much earlier Indian traders who, from 600 BC, established new Hindu or Buddhist states in Sri Lanka, Malaysia, and some of the Indonesian islands, and supplied them with spices from their homeland.

When Columbus "discovered" America, the cultures of the continent were already old and highly developed, and the spices of the American tropics and subtropics – allspice, chili peppers, vanilla – had played their part in those cultures for a very long time. Here Europeans can indeed be said to have been of importance, for the rapid spread of chilies throughout their colonies transformed the diet of half the world.

The spread of spices

Europe itself had already contributed much to the world of spices. Many of the aromatic seeds – coriander, fennel, fenugreek, mustard, poppy – are native to the Mediterranean region, and Europe's colder regions have contributed caraway, dill, and juniper. European trade remained mainly within the continent and with western Asia, but settlers sailing to the New World took many of their familiar spices with them.

Not all the spread of spices has been due to trade. Some resulted from the breaking of jealously guarded monopolies; French botanists and explorers were particularly effective in smuggling plants to new destinations, where plantations were established.

CARDAMOM POPPY LEMON GRASS GINGER

VANILLA
Cured vanilla beans, containing tiny, sticky seeds, flavor ice cream, cakes, and sweet syrups. Vanilla also goes well with seafood and chicken.

TURMERIC
Grated turmeric rhizome imparts a warm, earthy flavor to many Indian and Caribbean dishes, as well as giving them their rich yellow color.

TAMARIND
Tamarind is used to give a fruity acidity to many Asian dishes and preserves. Tamarind pulp is soaked in water before use.

Migration has had a more lasting effect than trade on the spread of spices. For example, ships from southern China carried ginger, planted in troughs, as a necessity of life, and so it came to be cultivated throughout the Pacific region. Immigrant communities, whether established by colonial force or economic plight, brought their own traditional ingredients and married them to local produce – hence Cape Malay and Cajun cooking, the "rijsttafel" of Holland, and the use of Colombo powder in the French West Indies.

The desire for authenticity

Today there is a growing awareness of and demand for authentic regional foods. We have learned that there is no such thing as Italian food, because every Italian region has something different to offer. We also know that what used to be the standard food in Chinese restaurants is Cantonese, and that the cooking in Beijing, Sichuan, and Hunan is quite different. The contrast between northern and southern Indian cooking is attracting attention, as is the difference between northern and southern Thai food.

Vietnamese, Japanese, Mexican, Turkish, Moroccan, and even Ethiopian restaurants now exist in most big cities. What determines their individuality has much to do with how they use herbs and spices.

It has been said that chemistry is like cooking, but now it would be more accurate to say that cooking is becoming like chemistry. Food companies are constantly formulating new flavors and trying to synthesize others. They use electronic noses and tongues and other sophisticated apparatus to produce "aroma-fingerprints." They "collect headspace" – that is, gather

QALAT DAQQA
(*recipe, p.291*)

aroma molecules from spices, herbs, and fruits or from finished dishes for reproduction in a laboratory, eventually to be unleashed in ready-prepared foods. The results are certainly impressive, but many of the cultural, tactile, and nutritive values of the original foods are lost.

Successfully making your own blend of spices gives a sense of achievement that nothing squeezed out of a tube or poured from a bottle can equal. In countries where such blends are used regularly there is no such thing as an immutably fixed recipe. Regional tradition, family tastes, and individual preference determine the ingredients, and even fairly standard mixtures will be adapted to the dish they are made for – masalas, bumbus, rempahs, and the like are infinitely variable.

GROUND WATTLE

GRATING GINGER
Fresh ginger rhizome yields a highly aromatic juice. After fine grating, the ginger shavings are wrapped in cloth and the juice squeezed out.

GRINDING SPICES
Spices are best stored whole and ground only when needed. Many spices start to lose their aroma within hours of grinding.

FRYING SPICES
For some dishes the spices are fried in oil beforehand to impart their flavor. The oil is then used to flavor the dish.

Choosing and using spices

Complex flavors are built up in mixtures by using spices (or herbs) that complement each other. Some are used for their taste, others for their aroma. Some have souring properties; in others, the color is important. The moment at which spices are added to a dish makes a crucial difference. Whether or not they are dry-roasted beforehand, they will impart their flavor to the dish if added at the beginning of cooking; if sprinkled on toward the end of cooking, it is their aroma that will be emphasized in the finished dish.

Toward the end of the book I have given recipes for mixtures from many different parts of the world. These should be regarded as basic formulas, the fundamentals of specific styles of cooking, and fully open to improvisation and experiment. By all means try them first as they are written, then adapt them to your taste and the dish you want to make.

SESAME

Sesamum orientale

Sesame is one of the earliest recorded plants grown for its seeds. The Egyptians and Babylonians used ground seeds in their breads, a practice that continues in the Middle East today. Excavations in eastern Turkey have found evidence of oil being extracted from the seeds as early as 900BC. High in polyunsaturated fatty acids, the oil pressed from raw seeds is excellent for cooking and is highly stable, with the advantage that it does not turn rancid in hot climates.

TASTING NOTES

Sesame seeds are not very aromatic but they have a mildly nutty, earthy odor. This is more marked in the taste, which develops even greater richness after dry-roasting or grinding to a paste. Black seeds have an earthier taste than white and are not usually ground.

PARTS USED

Seeds, whole and as a paste, and oil.

BUYING AND STORING

Sesame seeds are available from supermarkets and Middle Eastern and wholefood stores, as are the pale brown sesame paste (tahini), darker Chinese sesame paste and sesame oils (light and nutty sesame oil and darker, stronger Asian sesame oil). Golden seeds, with their richer aroma, are preferred by Japanese cooks, but these are harder to find. Store seeds in airtight containers and toast them as needed.

HARVESTING

Plants are harvested before the seed pods are fully ripe, when they burst open. The pods are dried and hulled, usually mechanically.

Whole seeds
Produced by an annual tropical plant, sesame seeds may be pale gold or white, red, brown, or black, depending on the variety. The seeds are small, flat, and oval, shiny and waxy because of their oil content, and fairly soft. The creamy white seeds are the most common.

Culinary uses

Sesame is scattered over breads or ground and added to the dough before baking. It is essential to the Middle Eastern spice blend za'atar, and to Japanese seven-spice powder. It is the main ingredient of the Middle Eastern sweetmeat, halva. In India, sesame is used in sweets such as til laddoos, which are balls of sesame and jaggery flavored with cardamom. Indian cooks use pale golden sesame oil, called gingili or til oil, for cooking. Tahini and the oil are made from raw seeds.

Deep brown Chinese sesame paste and amber-colored Asian oil are made from dry-roasted seeds; this enhances the nutty flavor and gives the darker color. These products are used in Chinese, Korean, and Japanese cooking. Asian oil is a seasoning oil, not a cooking oil, because it burns at low temperatures. Chinese sesame paste has a dense texture and is used in dressings for noodles, rice, and vegetables.

The Chinese like the crunchy texture of sesame seeds to coat shrimp balls and shrimp toasts. In Japan, white or golden sesame is blended with soy sauce and sugar to dress cold chicken, noodles, and vegetable salads.

Black sesame is used in Chinese and Japanese cooking as a garnish for rice and vegetables, and to coat fish and seafood before cooking. It is often said to be bitter if dry-roasted, but I have not found it so if done lightly, and Japanese cooks frequently use it dry-roasted. Blended with coarse salt it makes the Japanese condiment, goma shio, which is sprinkled over vegetables, salads, and rice. In China, black seeds coat deep-fried toffee apples and bananas.

Essential to za'atar, goma shio, seven-spice powder.

Good with eggplant, fish, green vegetables, honey, legumes, lemon, noodles, rice, salad greens, sugar, zucchini.

Combines well with cardamom, cassia, chili, cinnamon, cloves, coriander, ginger, nutmeg, oregano, pepper, sumac, thyme.

ASIAN SESAME OIL
Asian oil is usually added to dishes before serving. Combined with chili, garlic, and ginger, it is popular in Sichuan cooking.

TAHINI
In the Middle East, pale brown tahini is blended with garlic and lemon juice to make a paste, used as a basis for dressings for vegetable and fish dishes, and as the flavoring for the chickpea dip, hummus.

NIGELLA

Nigella sativa

TASTING NOTES

Nigella does not have a strong aroma; when rubbed it is herbaceous, somewhat like a mild oregano. The taste is nutty, earthy, peppery, rather bitter, dry, and quite penetrating; the texture is crunchy.

PARTS USED

Seeds.

BUYING AND STORING

Buy whole seeds because they keep better; ground seeds may be adulterated. In an airtight container they will keep their flavor for 2 years. Nigella is stocked by spice merchants and by Indian and Middle Eastern markets.

HARVESTING

Nigella seeds are mat black, small, and teardrop-shaped. Their surface is rough. The seed capsules are gathered as they ripen but before they burst, then dried and lightly crushed so that the seeds can be removed easily.

Nigella is the botanical name of love-in-a-mist, the pretty garden plant with pale blue flowers and feathery foliage. The species grown for its seed is a close but less decorative relative, native to western Asia and southern Europe, where it grows wild and in cultivation. India is the largest producer of nigella and a large consumer. The small, black seeds are often misnamed and sold as black onion seed.

Culinary uses

Nigella is sprinkled on flatbreads, rolls, and savory pastries, alone or with sesame or cumin. Cooks in Bengal combine it with mustard seeds, cumin, fennel, and fenugreek in the local spice mixture, panch phoron, which gives a distinctive taste to legume and vegetable dishes. Elsewhere in India, nigella is used in pilafs, kormas, and curries, and in pickles. In Iran, it is a popular pickling spice used for fruit and vegetables. It is good with roast potatoes and other root vegetables. Ground with coriander and cumin, it adds depth to a Middle-Eastern potato or mixed vegetable omelette.

Essential to panch phoron.

Good with breads, legumes, rice, green and root vegetables.

Combines well with allspice, cardamom, cinnamon, coriander, cumin, fennel, ginger, pepper, savory, thyme, turmeric.

Whole seeds
Indian cooks usually dry-roast or fry the seeds to develop their flavor before sprinkling them over vegetarian dishes and salads.

POPPY

Papaver somniferum

The opium poppy – *Papaver somniferum* means "sleep-inducing poppy" – is a plant of great antiquity, native from the eastern Mediterranean to central Asia. It has been cultivated since earliest times for opium, a narcotic latex that oozes from unripe seedpods if they are cut, and for its ripe seeds. Neither the seeds nor the dried pods from which they are harvested have narcotic properties.

TASTING NOTES

The aroma of dark seeds is lightly nutty and sweet; the flavor is stronger and somewhat almond-like. White seeds are lighter and more mellow in flavor. Both the aroma and flavor are enhanced by dry-roasting or baking. Poppy seeds are rich in protein and oil.

PARTS USED

Seeds.

BUYING AND STORING

Poppy seeds may be slate-blue, creamy-white, or mid-brown. The latter are common in Turkey and the Middle East; the blue-gray seeds are most used in Europe, and the creamy-white seeds in India. Blue poppy seeds are available from supermarkets; the white and brown can be bought from spice merchants or in Asian and Middle Eastern markets. The seeds tend to go rancid quickly because of their high oil content, so buy in small amounts and use quickly. Store in an airtight container, or in the freezer if you intend to keep them longer than a few months.

HARVESTING

Plants are harvested mechanically when the seedheads turn yellow-brown; the capsules are cut off and dried.

Culinary uses

In the West, poppy seeds are sprinkled over or incorporated into breads, bagels, pretzels, and cakes. Ground to a paste with honey or sugar, they are used to fill strudels and other pastries. In Turkey, roasted, ground seeds are made into halva or desserts with syrup and nuts. In India, the roasted seeds are ground and combined with spices to flavor and thicken kormas, curries, and gravies. They are used extensively in Bengali cooking in shuktas (bitter vegetable stews) and to coat crusty, dry-textured vegetables. Use poppy seeds, with or without other spices, in dressings for noodles or to garnish vegetables.

Good with eggplant, green beans, breads and pastries, cauliflower, potatoes, zucchini.

Whole seeds

Poppy seeds do not grind easily, but dry-roasting followed by a blitz in a spice mill or coffee grinder can help. If they are to be used to thicken a dish, cover them with a little water and soak for several hours, then process them briefly together with the liquid.

MAHLAB

Prunus mahaleb

TASTING NOTES

Mahlab is sweetly perfumed and floral with hints of almond and cherry. It has a mouthwatering flavor that is nutty with a soft, almond sweetness, but then finishes with a bitter aftertaste.

PARTS USED

Kernels.

BUYING AND STORING

Mahlab is best bought whole and ground as needed: once ground, it loses its flavor quite quickly. Store mahlab in an airtight container. Spice merchants and Middle Eastern or Greek markets are the best sources.

HARVESTING

The soft kernels are extracted from the cherry pits and dried. They are small, oval, and beige or light tan in color.

This agreeable spice, little known outside the Middle East, comes from a sour cherry tree that grows wild throughout the region as well as in southern Europe. The trees bear small, thin-fleshed, black cherries, the kernels of which are used to flavor breads and pastries. Mahlab is used in Greece, Cyprus, Turkey, and the neighboring Arab countries, from Syria to Saudi Arabia.

Culinary uses

Ground mahlab is primarily used in baking, especially in breads and pastries for festive occasions. A piquant note of mahlab spices the braided Greek Easter bread, tsoureki; Armenian sweet rolls called chorek; Arab ma'amool (little pastries stuffed with nuts or dates baked by Lebanese Christians for their Easter celebrations); and Turkish kandil rings, made for the five religious feast nights each year when the mosques are illuminated. It is also used to flavor sweetmeats. Try adding a little to spiced or fruit breads or to pastry to be used with fruit. Mahlab is best ground in a spice mill or coffee grinder. If difficult, add a little salt or sugar, according to the recipe, to help break down the mahlab. **Good with** almonds, apricots, dates, pistachio nuts, rose water, walnuts. **Combines well with** anise, cinnamon, cloves, mastic, nigella, nutmeg, poppy seed, sesame.

Whole kernels
Beige mahlab kernels are creamy white inside; their texture is soft and chewy.

GROUND KERNELS
Ground mahlab should be pale cream in color; if it is dark or turning yellow it is too old.

WATTLE

Acacia species

Several hundred acacia species are native to Australia, but only a few have edible seeds. *A. victoriae* and *A. aneura*, the latter locally called the mulga tree, are two of those most regularly harvested for wattle seed. When dried, roasted, and ground, the green, unripe seeds are transformed into a rich, deep brown powder that resembles ground coffee. Wattle is gaining popularity with food enthusiasts.

TASTING NOTES

Wattle seed has a rich, toasty aroma that is faintly like coffee. The flavor has notes of coffee and roasted hazelnuts, with a hint of chocolate.

PARTS USED

Roasted, ground seeds.

BUYING AND STORING

In Australia, wattle seed is sold by spice merchants and gourmet markets. In the northern hemisphere a few spice merchants and even supermarkets are beginning to stock it. In an airtight container it should keep for up to 2 years.

HARVESTING

Wattle seed is quite expensive because it is gathered from the wild and its preparation is extremely labor-intensive. Green seed pods are steamed open, the whole green seeds are roasted with embers and, once cooled and cleaned of ash, they are ground. The preparation is still mostly done in the bush by Aboriginal women.

Culinary uses

Wattle seed yields its flavor when infused in a hot liquid. Do not let the seed boil or the flavor will become bitter. The liquid can be strained and used alone, or the ground seed can be left in for its texture. Wattle seed is used to flavor desserts, especially cream- or yogurt-based desserts such as mousses, ice creams, and cheesecakes, and in cream fillings for cakes. I have added it to a sweet bread dough quite successfully, and a sprinkling gives a good flavor to a traditional bread and butter pudding. Wattle liquid is sometimes drunk as an alternative to coffee.

Ground seeds
Highly nutritious wattle seed has long provided food for indigenous Australians. New interest in bush foods has created a demand that at present exceeds supply.

CINNAMON

Cinnamomum zelanicum

True cinnamon is indigenous to Sri Lanka. Like cassia, it is the bark of an evergreen tree of the laurel family. For 200 years a highly profitable monopoly of the island's cinnamon was controlled first by the Portuguese, then the Dutch, and finally by the English. By the late 18th century, cinnamon had been planted in Java, India, and the Seychelles, and the monopoly could no longer be sustained.

TASTING NOTES

Cinnamon has a warm, agreeably sweet, woody aroma that is delicate yet intense; the taste is fragrant and warm with hints of clove and citrus. The presence of eugenol in the essential oil distinguishes cinnamon from cassia, giving it the note of clove.

PARTS USED

Quills of dried bark, ground cinnamon.

BUYING AND STORING

Ground cinnamon – the paler its color, the finer its quality – is widely available, but it loses its flavor quite quickly, so buy in small amounts. Whole quills are available from specialty spice merchants and some supermarkets. They keep their aroma for 2–3 years if stored in an airtight container.

HARVESTING

The Sri Lankan cinnamon gardens lie on the coastal plains south of Colombo. Seedlings grow in thick clumps, with shoots about the thickness of a thumb. In the rainy season the shoots are cut off at the base and peeled. The harvesters work with extraordinary dexterity to cut the paper-thin pieces of bark and then roll quills over 3ft (up to 1m) long by hand. The quills are then gently dried in the shade.

Quills
Pale brown or tan strips of dried bark are rolled one into another to form long, slender, smooth quills.

GRADES OF CINNAMON
There are many grades of cinnamon; quills are classified as Continental, Mexican, or Hamburg, according to their thickness; the thin Continental quills have the finest flavor. Quillings are quills broken in handling; featherings are the small inner pieces of bark not large enough to use in quills; and chips are shavings, the lowest grade of cinnamon. Featherings and chips are mostly used to produce ground cinnamon.

Culinary uses

Cinnamon's subtle flavor is well suited to all manner of desserts and spiced breads and cakes; it combines particularly well with chocolate and with apples, bananas, and pears. Use it in apple pie or with baked apples, with bananas fried in butter and flavored with rum, and in red wine used for poaching pears. It also makes an excellent flavoring for many meat and vegetable dishes in Middle Eastern and Indian cuisine. Moroccan cooks use it widely in lamb or chicken tagines, in the stew to accompany couscous, and above all to flavor bstilla, a pie of crisp, layered pastry filled with squab and almonds. The glorious Arab stew of lamb with apricots – mishmisheya – uses cinnamon and other spices, and it plays a role in many an Iranian khoresh (stews that accompany rice). In India, cinnamon is used in many masalas (spice mixtures), in chutneys and condiments, and in spiced pilafs.

Mexico is the main importer of cinnamon, which is used to flavor coffee and chocolate drinks; cinnamon tea is popular throughout Central and South America. Once popular for spicing ale, cinnamon, together with cloves, sugar, and sliced oranges, makes an excellent flavoring for mulled wine.

Good with almonds, apples, apricots, bananas, chocolate, coffee, eggplant, lamb, pears, poultry, rice.

Combines well with cardamom, cloves, coriander, cumin, ginger, mace, mastic, nutmeg, tamarind, turmeric.

GROUND BARK
Ground cinnamon is immediately aromatic; quills tend to hide their aromatic properties until broken or cooked in a liquid.

CASSIA

Cinnamomum cassia

Cassia is the dried bark of a species of laurel tree native to Assam and northern Burma. It is recorded in a Chinese herbal in 2700BC, and today most cassia is exported from southern China and Vietnam. The finest quality comes from northern Vietnam. Cassia and cinnamon are used interchangeably in many countries. In the US, cassia is sold as cinnamon or cassia-cinnamon, and is preferred to true cinnamon because of its more pronounced aroma and flavor.

TASTING NOTES

Cassia has a more intense aroma than cinnamon, because it has a higher content of volatile oil. It is sweetish with a distinct pungency and an astringent edge. Vietnamese cassia has the highest volatile oil content and the strongest flavor.

PARTS USED

Dried bark and quills, ground bark; dried unripe fruits, called cassia buds; tejpat leaves.

BUYING AND STORING

Cassia is difficult to grind, so it may be better to buy a small amount of ground cassia as well as pieces or quills. The latter will keep their flavor much longer, up to 2 years if stored in an airtight container. Buy bark, buds, and leaves from specialist spice dealers and keep in an airtight container.

HARVESTING

Harvesting starts in the rainy season when the bark can be stripped easily. As it dries it curls to make quills, which are graded according to their essential oil content, length, and color. Quills are reddish-brown and the layers are thicker than in cinnamon quills. Cassia bark is thicker and coarser than cinnamon, and the corky outer layer is often left on when it is sold in pieces.

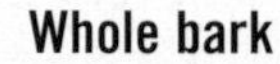

Whole bark
The color of the smooth inner bark is reddish-brown, the rough outside is gray-brown.

QUILLS
Cassia bark is thick and tough and its quills are simple, crude curls, whereas the thinner, softer bark of cinnamon is rolled more tightly.

Buds

Cassia buds are a bit like small cloves. The hard, red-brown seed is just visible in the wrinkled gray-brown calyx. The buds have a warm, mellow aroma and the flavor is musky, sweet, and pungent, but less concentrated than that of the bark.

Dried tejpat leaves

Leaves of the related *C. tamala* are oval in shape with three long veins. They are used in the cooking of north India. Dried tejpat leaves have an immediate smell of spiced tea. A prolonged sniff reveals a warm, musky aroma of clove and cinnamon with citrus undertones.

Culinary uses

Cassia is an essential spice in China, where it is frequently used whole to flavor braised dishes and sauces for cooking meat and poultry; and ground cassia is a constituent of five-spice powder. In India, it is found in curries and pilafs, and in Germany and Russia, it is often used as a flavoring for chocolate. I prefer cinnamon to cassia for delicate desserts, but it is good with apples, plums, dried figs, and prunes.

Cassia is used in spice blends for baking and sweet dishes. The pungency of cassia is better suited than cinnamon to rich meats such as duck or pork, and it goes well with pumpkin and other winter squashes, with sweet potatoes, and with lentils and beans. Cassia buds are used in sweet pickles in the Asia, and they can be used, whole, in place of cassia. They are particularly good in fruit compotes.

Tejpat leaves are often called Indian bay leaves, because both come from species of laurel and because they are both used in long-cooked dishes and removed before serving. However, tejpat leaves are quite different from bay aromatically and a clove or a small piece of cassia make a better substitute than bay if you can't find tejpat leaves. The leaves are used extensively in the biryanis and kormas of northern India and in some garam masalas.

Indonesian or Korintje cassia, *C. burmannii,* from Sumatra has a deep color and a pleasantly spicy flavor, but lacks the depth of Vietnamese or Chinese cassia.

Essential to five-spice powder.
Good with apples, plums, prunes, legumes, meat and poultry, root vegetables.
Combines well with cardamom, cloves, coriander, cumin, fennel, ginger, mace, nutmeg, Sichuan pepper, star anise, turmeric.

CORIANDER

Coriandrum sativum

A few plants serve cooks as both herb and spice, and of these coriander is undoubtedly the most widely used in both its forms. As a spice crop it is grown in eastern Europe, India, the US, and Central America, as well as in its native habitat of western Asia and the Mediterranean. In all of these regions it is used extensively, sometimes in combination with its leaf, commonly called cilantro.

TASTING NOTES

Ripe seeds have a sweet, woody, spicy fragrance with peppery and floral notes; the taste is sweet, mellow, and warm with a clear hint of orange peel.

PARTS USED

Dried fruits (seeds).

BUYING AND STORING

Coriander is widely available. Buy whole seeds. They are easy to grind as needed, but their aromatic properties diminish quickly after grinding. In some Indian markets you may find a blend of whole or ground coriander and cumin seeds called dhana-jeera, which is popular throughout the subcontinent.

HARVESTING

Seeds are harvested when they change color from green to beige or light brown. Traditionally, plants are cut, left to wither for 2–3 days, then threshed and dried in partial shade. If not fully dry they may be put in full sun before being sifted and packed. In some regions the seeds are dried artificially.

Whole Moroccan seeds
Spherical Moroccan seeds are more commonly available than the oval Indian variety.

GROUND SEEDS
Seeds are brittle and easy to grind; dry-roasting before grinding enhances the flavor.

Culinary uses

Cooks use coriander seeds in larger amounts than they do many other spices because the flavor is mild. After dry-roasting, coriander forms the basis of many curry powders and masalas. North African cooks use it in harissa, tabil, ras el hanout, and other spice mixtures. Georgian khmeli-suneli and Iranian advieh mixtures usually include it, as do Middle Eastern baharat blends; throughout the region coriander is a popular flavoring for vegetable dishes, stews, and sausages. Crushed green olives that are flavored with coriander are a specialty of Cyprus. In Europe and the US, coriander serves as a pickling spice and gives a pleasant, mild flavor to sweet-sour pickles and chutneys. West Indian cooks use it in masalas, and in Mexico it is often paired with cumin. French vegetable dishes à la grecque are flavored with coriander. It is a useful spice to add to marinades, to court-bouillon for fish, or to stock for soup. It is also a constituent of English mixed sweet spice, much used in cakes and cookies. Its flavor combines well with those of autumn fruits – apples, plums, pears, quinces – baked in pies or stewed in compotes.

Essential to harissa, tabil, dukka, most masalas.

Good with apples, chicken, citrus fruit, fish, ham, mushrooms, onions, plums, pork, potatoes.

Combines well with allspice, chili, cinnamon, cloves, cumin, fennel, garlic, ginger, mace, nutmeg.

Whole Indian seeds

Although coriander seeds and leaves smell and taste quite different, they complement each other in Indian and Mexican dishes.

GROUND SEEDS

Indian coriander has a sweeter flavor than Moroccan.

JUNIPER

Juniperus communis

Juniper is a prickly, evergreen shrub or small tree that grows throughout much of the northern hemisphere, especially on chalky, hilly sites. It is a member of the large cypress family, the only one with edible fruit. The berries were used by enterprising Romans to adulterate pepper, and were burned in the Middle Ages (and well beyond) to clean the air of pestilence. Juniper's use as a flavoring for gin and other spirits dates back at least to the 17th century.

TASTING NOTES

The aroma of juniper is pleasantly woody, bittersweet, and unmistakably like gin. The taste is clean and refreshing, sweetish with a slight burning effect, and has a hint of pine and resin.

PARTS USED

Berries, fresh or dried.

BUYING AND STORING

Juniper berries are always sold whole and are usually dried. They are quite soft and bruise easily, so make sure those you buy are whole and dry. They will keep for several months in an airtight jar.

HARVESTING

A juniper bush makes a handsome garden plant all year round. The purple-black, smooth berries are about the size of a small pea. They take 2–3 years to ripen, so green and ripe berries occur on the same plant. There is some cultivation of juniper and also berries are gathered in the wild – a hazardous undertaking because of the very sharp, spiky leaves. Berries are picked when ripe, in autumn. Freshly picked berries have a green-blue bloom that disappears during drying.

Whole berries
Berries growing in southerly latitudes have more flavor. If you come across them in the wild, ripe and blue-black, it is well worth picking them.

Culinary uses

Juniper is perhaps best known as the flavoring for gin as well as for other spirits and cordials, but the berries also have many culinary uses. Juniper is a natural foil for game and for fatty foods. The Scandinavians add it to marinades for pickled beef and elk and to red-wine marinades for roast pork. In northern France, juniper appears in venison dishes and pâtés; in Belgium, it is used with veal kidneys flamed in gin; and in Alsace and Germany, it is a flavoring for sauerkraut.

Easily crushed in a mortar, the berries impart a mild but pungent flavor that can benefit many dishes, both savory and sweet. Mixed with salt and garlic they can be rubbed onto lamb, pork, game birds, and venison. Another dry-salting mixture that relies on juniper is that for Elizabeth David's spiced beef. Crushed berries also go into brines and marinades; chopped finely, just a few liven up stuffings and pâtés and make good sauces for hearty meats. Crush or grind juniper just before using it: in contact with the air the essential oils are quickly lost.

Good with apples, beef, cabbage, duck, game, goose, pork.

Combines well with bay, caraway, celery, garlic, marjoram, pepper, rosemary, savory, thyme.

A rub for meats

Juniper berries crushed in a mortar with garlic and coarse salt make a well-flavored rub for lamb, pork, and venison.

ROSE

Rosa species

Western cooks seldom think of roses as a flavoring ingredient, but throughout the Arab world, Turkey, and Iran, and as far east as northern India, dried rosebuds or petals and rose water are consumed in a variety of ways. Turkey and Bulgaria are the biggest producers of attar of roses (the essential oil) and rose water, but roses are also grown commercially in Iran and Morocco – their fragrance greets you as you approach the valleys where they grow. Most of the flowers are processed to make rose water, but you can also buy the wonderfully scented, dried pink buds.

TASTING NOTES

Only intensely fragrant roses are used; the highly perfumed damask rose, *R. damascena*, is the one preferred in the Balkans, Turkey, and most of the Middle East. In Morocco, a musk-scented rose is grown. Dried buds keep their perfume well.

PARTS USED

Buds, petals.

BUYING AND STORING

Rose water and rose oil are available from Middle Eastern, Indian, Iranian, and Turkish markets, as is very sweet but well-flavored rose-petal preserves, which may come from Bulgaria, Turkey, or Pakistan. Some markets also carry dried rosebuds, which can be kept in an airtight container for up to a year. Grind in an electric mill as needed.

HARVESTING

Rosebuds and petals are harvested in early summer and either dried or distilled to make rose essence (attar of roses), which may be diluted to make rose water.

Dried rosebuds
Buds and flowers are picked very early in the morning to capture their fragrance before it is lost to the sun.

Culinary uses

In India, powdered, dried rose petals are used in marinades and in delicately flavored kormas. In Bengal and Punjab, rose water features prominently in desserts such as gulab jamun (*gulab* means rose) and rasgulla, in sweet lassi (a cooling yogurt drink), and in kheer (a rich rice pudding). Its flavor can also be detected in much Turkish delight, in Middle Eastern pastries, and in some savory dishes. Fresh or dried petals are infused in syrups to make desserts and drinks. A delicately flavored rose sherbet is served at Turkish ceremonial functions. Rose petals can also be put into a jar of sugar to infuse it with a delicate rose scent that will flavor creams and cakes.

Iranian cooks use rosebuds quite extensively: a blend of ground, dried petals and cinnamon, sometimes with cumin or cardamom, makes a heady flavoring for rice. A more complex blend with powdered dried lime is used to flavor stews. Crushed rose petals may garnish a yogurt and cucumber salad or cold soup. In Morocco, rose water is used more than rosebuds, although buds are a constituent of ras el hanout.

Tunisian cooks seem to appreciate rosebuds most of all, using them in several spice blends for a wide range of dishes. A simple bharat of finely ground cinnamon and rosebuds is used together with black pepper to flavor roast meats, stews using fruits such as quinces or apricots, and couscous with fish or lamb. In Tunisian Jewish cooking the same flavorings are used in meatballs to accompany couscous.

Essential to Iranian advieh, ras el hanout, Tunisian bharat.

Good with apples, apricots, chestnuts, lamb, poultry, quinces, rice, desserts and pastries.

Combines well with cardamom, chili, cinnamon, cloves, coriander, cumin, pepper, saffron, turmeric, yogurt.

Advieh for rice
Rose petals, cinnamon, and cumin seeds are used in this Iranian flavoring for rice (*recipe, p.289*).

VANILLA

Vanilla planifolia

Vanilla is the fruit of a perennial, climbing orchid, native to Central America. It is not known when vanilla was first cured and used as a flavoring, but tribes ruled by the Aztecs had fairly sophisticated methods of fermenting the bean-like fruits to extract vanillin crystals. The Spanish conquistadors drank chocolate flavored with vanilla at the court of Moctezuma. They took to it and shipped both chocolate and vanilla back to Spain. They also gave the fruit its name: vanilla is the diminutive of *vaina*, meaning pod. Today, vanilla is exported from Mexico, Réunion, Madagascar, Tahiti, and Indonesia.

Whole dried beans
Good vanilla beans are deep brown or black, long and narrow, somewhat wrinkled, moist, waxy, supple, and immediately fragrant.

SEEDS
The tiny, sticky, black seeds can be scraped from the bean with the point of a knife.

TASTING NOTES

Fresh vanilla beans have no aroma or taste. After fermentation they develop a rich, mellow, intensely perfumed aroma with hints of licorice or tobacco matched by a delicate, sweetly fruity or creamy flavor. There may also be hints of raisin or prune, or smoky, spicy notes.

PARTS USED

Cured pods (beans).

BUYING AND STORING

You are more likely to get better grade beans from a specialty food store or mail order than a supermarket. Stored away from the light in an airtight container, vanilla beans will keep for 2 years or more. When buying extract, look for bottles labeled "pure vanilla extract," which by law must contain 35 percent alcohol by volume.

HARVESTING

Vanilla pods are picked when they begin to turn yellow. Further maturation is prevented by plunging them into boiling water, then they are sun-dried by day and sweated by night, wrapped in blankets. The pods shrivel and darken, and enzymes cause a chemical change that produces aromatic compounds, notably vanillin. About 11lb (5kg) of fresh pods yields 2¼lb (1kg) cured vanilla beans.

Culinary uses

Bourbon vanilla from Madagascar and Réunion has a rich, creamy flavor; Mexican was traditionally considered to be the most delicate and complex; Tahitian smells heady, floral, and fruity; Indonesian vanilla has a smoky, strong flavor. The best beans have a light, white frosting, called givre, of vanillin crystals.

Whole or split beans are most used to flavor creams, custards, and ice cream. The presence of tiny black specks, the sticky seeds, in the dishes indicates authenticity. A whole vanilla bean that has been infused in a syrup or cream can be rinsed, dried, and reused. Vanilla flavors cakes, tarts, and syrups used for poaching fruit. Cut beans can be laid over fruit to be baked in the oven. Vanilla's original use with chocolate is still widely practiced, and it also enriches tea and coffee. Vanilla is less commonly thought of as a spice for savory foods, but it goes well with seafood, particularly lobster, scallops, and mussels, and with chicken. It enhances the sweetness of root vegetables, and in Mexico, it is used with black beans.

Good with apples, melon, peaches, pears, rhubarb, strawberries, fish and seafood, cream, milk, eggs.

Combines well with cardamom, chili, cinnamon, cloves, saffron.

FLAVORED SUGAR
Rather than buy expensive boxes of vanilla-flavored sugar, granulated sugar can be perfumed beautifully simply by putting a vanilla bean in the jar or canister.

EXTRACT
Made by macerating pods in alcohol, vanilla extract has a sweet aroma and a delicate taste. Avoid synthetic vanilla, derived from pulp waste, which has a cloying smell and a disagreeable, bitter aftertaste.

VANILLA *is the second most expensive spice after saffron, because, like saffron, its production is very labor-intensive.*

Pollination of the plants has to be done by hand, harvesting the pods is difficult, and there is a lengthy curing process.

AKUDJURA

Solanum species

TASTING NOTES

The aroma of akudjura suggests baked caramel and chocolate. The taste is of caramel, tamarillo, and tomato, with a bitterish, lingering aftertaste that is quite refreshing.

Akudjura, *S. centrale*, is the name of an edible member of a group of wild tomatoes, native to the deserts of western and central Australia – the "bush" that gave the fruit its popular name of bush tomato. Several plants in the group are poisonous. The edible ones have always been gathered by the Aborigines for staple food stores, but recently they have attracted wider attention as a spice. Also collected is *S. aviculare,* which has larger fruit, known as kangaroo apple.

PARTS USED

Dried fruit.

BUYING AND STORING

Bush tomatoes are sold whole – these must be soaked for 20–30 minutes before use – and, more frequently, ground to an orange-brown powder, which is always called akudjura.

HARVESTING

There is, as yet, no cultivation of the bush tomato – what is available has been gathered in the wild. The yellow fruits are left to dry on the plant; they shrink to grape size, turn chocolate brown, and acquire a chewy texture reminiscent of raisins – hence their other name, desert raisins. Drying also reduces the level of alkaloids, especially potentially harmful solanine.

Culinary uses

Akudjura can be used in place of sun-dried tomato or sweet paprika. Those who have become accustomed, even addicted, to its special taste sprinkle it on salads, soups, egg dishes, and steamed vegetables. In Australia, it is used whole in casseroles and in an interesting version of damper, the traditional bread-like "bush tucker." The powder goes into cookies, chutneys, dressings, relishes, and salsas. A mixture of wattle, mountain pepper, and akudjura is used the same way as Cajun blackening spice, especially for fish; in other mixtures akudjura is used for grilling and for marinating meat, especially the very lean kangaroo meat.

Good with apple, cheese dishes, fish, lean meats, onions, sweet peppers, potatoes.

Combines well with coriander, lemon myrtle, wattle.

Whole fruit
Akudjura suits both sweet and savory dishes. It gives a distinct flavor to tomato-based sauces and to meat stews, particularly goulash.

CRUSHED FRUIT
Akudjura may be orange-red or brownish, depending on rainfall in the growing season.

TASTING NOTES

The aroma of crushed berries is pleasantly fruity, with a clear note of pine. The taste is fruity, resinous, and sweetly aromatic, similar to juniper but not as strong. It shares with true black pepper one important constituent, piperine oil, but it has none of pepper's heat.

PARTS USED

Dried fruit.

BUYING AND STORING

Dried pink pepper is sold by spice merchants and supermarkets – freeze-dried berries have the best color and flavor. It is also available in brine, vinegar, or water, bottled or canned. Dried berries are added, for color effect, to black, white, and green peppercorns, to which they are not related. Keep pink peppercorns whole in an airtight container, and crush or grind them as needed.

HARVESTING

In autumn, clusters of tiny, white flowers form green and juicy berries that ripen to a bright red. They are harvested when ripe.

PINK PEPPER

Schinus terebinthifolius

Pink pepper is the fruit of the Brazilian pepper tree, native not just to Brazil but to Argentina and Paraguay as well. The tree has been introduced in many places as an ornamental or shade tree. It is aggressively invasive and now grows in almost every temperate zone in the world. Mono-terpenes in the volatile oil can cause intestinal irritation, but not in the quantities used in a normal recipe. Réunion is the only place where pink pepper is commercially grown.

Culinary uses

Pink peppercorns flavor a variety of dishes. Use in small amounts, and not, for example, in the quantity needed to prepare a pepper steak. Pickling softens the berries and they can be crushed easily. Dried berries have a brittle, papery outer shell enclosing a hard seed. Pink pepper is mostly recommended for fish or poultry, but goes well with game and other rich foods in the same way as juniper. Pink pepper flavors quite delicate sauces to accompany such varied ingredients as lobster, veal scallops, and pork.

Good with fish, game, rich and fatty meats, poultry.

Combines well with chervil, fennel, galangal, kaffir lime leaves, lemon grass, mint, parsley, black and green pepper.

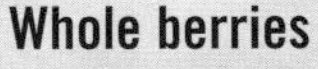

Whole berries
The berries are easily crushed with a mortar and pestle or under the blade of a big knife.

PAPRIKA

Capsicum annuum species

Capsicums are native to the Americas and were first planted in Spain after the voyage of Columbus in 1492. It was the Spanish who first dried and ground the peppers to make pimentón, or paprika. Later, seeds reached Turkey and were planted there and throughout the Ottoman Empire. Ornamental Turkish pepper was recorded in Hungary in 1604. A century later paprika was mentioned there as a spice used by peasants; it was not until the 19th century that it was considered suitable for "sophisticated stomachs."

TASTING NOTES

The aroma of paprika tends to be restrained and delicate; caramel notes, fruitiness, or smokiness characterize some paprikas, while others have a nose-prickling, light heat. Flavors vary from sweetly smoky to rounded and full-bodied, or gently pungent with bitter notes.

PARTS USED

Dried fruits. There is no single paprika pepper: it is made from a number of different red capsicums.

BUYING AND STORING

Hungarian paprika is somewhat hotter than Spanish. Portuguese and Moroccan paprika tend to resemble Spanish; that from the Balkan states is closer to Hungarian. Paprika from the US is mild. All paprika should be kept in an airtight container and away from light, otherwise it will lose its vibrancy. Paprika paste and paprika sauce are also produced in Hungary.

HARVESTING

Once dried, stems are removed, seeds and veins are separated, then the wall of the fruit and the seeds are ground separately and blended according to the type of paprika being made. For Spanish pimentón, the peppers are dried over oak fires for a smoky flavor.

Ground paprika
Paprika can be sweet, bittersweet, or hot, depending on whether it is produced from mild or lightly pungent peppers, and also on the amount of ground seeds and veins included in the powder.

HUNGARIAN PAPRIKA
Hungarian cooks usually have different grades of paprika in the kitchen and select the one best suited to the dish being prepared.

Culinary uses

Paprika is the predominant spice and coloring in Hungarian cooking. Fried gently with onion in lard (the main cooking fat), it forms the basis of goulash, veal or chicken paprikás, and duck or goose pörkölt; it gives color and flavor to potato, rice, and noodle dishes and many vegetables. Serbian cooks use paprika in similar ways. In Hungary, the Balkan countries, and Turkey, it is more usual to find paprika or chili flakes on the table than black pepper.

In Spain, paprika is used in sofrito, the mixture of onions and other ingredients fried in olive oil that forms the basis of many slow-cooked dishes. It appears in rice and potato dishes, is appreciated with fish and in omelettes, and is essential to romesco sauce. In Morocco, it is widely used in spice blends, in chermoula (a marinade and sauce for fish), and in tagines; in Turkey, it flavors soups, vegetables, and meat dishes, especially variety meats. In India, its principal use is to add a red color to dishes. Everywhere it is used as an essential flavoring for sausages and other meat products.

Paprika should never be overheated since it becomes bitter.

Essential to romesco sauce.

Good with beef and veal, white cheeses, chicken, duck, most legumes and vegetables, pork, rice.

Combines well with allspice, caraway, cardamom, garlic, ginger, oregano, parsley, pepper, rosemary, saffron, thyme, turmeric, sour cream and yogurt.

SPANISH PAPRIKA
The denomination of origin of pimentón de la Vera quarantees the consumer a hand-made, high-quality paprika with its characteristic smoky aroma and taste.

Paprika classifications

Paprika is usually sold in sealed cans or bags bearing labels of authenticity.

Hungarian paprika comes from two regions, Szeged and Kalocsa, whose names appear on the packaging.

Különleges (special, delicate) is bright red, finely milled to a silky powder; with only a tiny percentage of seeds, it is sweet with a barely perceptible heat. It has a long shelf life.

Édesnemes (noble sweet) is darker red, sweet, rounded, with restrained heat and no bitterness. Quite finely ground.

Delicatess (delicatessen) is fruity, slightly hot, and bright, light red.

Félédes (semi-sweet) contains more veins, and is therefore less sweet and more pungent.

Rozsa (rose) is pinkish red and has more heat; it is made from the whole fruit.

Eros (strong) is made from lesser-grade whole fruits and has more pungency and a bitter aftertaste. Brownish-red and coarse, it is more like a ground hot chili.

Most Spanish paprika comes from La Vera and carries a denomination of origin; a small amount of sweet paprika from the ñora pepper is produced in Murcia.

Dulce (sweet, mild) is a brick-red powder with a smoky aroma and a tangy flavor.

Agridulce (bittersweet) is deep red and piquant with an acrid, bitter note.

Picante (hot) is rust-red and has a sharp, pleasant heat. Spanish paprika is marketed in different quality grades: extra, select, and ordinary.

TAMARIND

Tamarindus indica

Tamarind is obtained from the bean-like pods of the tamarind tree, native to eastern Africa, probably Madagascar, which makes it the only important spice of African origin. The tall, evergreen trees with their handsome crowns were already growing in India in prehistoric times; the name comes from the Arabic *thamar-i-hindi*, fruit of India. Tamarind trees remain productive for up to 200 years. The spice has long been imported – principally from India – for the manufacture of such condiments as Worcestershire sauce.

TASTING NOTES

Tamarind has little smell, and a sourish but also sweet and fruity taste. The sour element is due to tartaric acid. Different locations give different levels of sourness in the pulp. Thai tamarind has a more rounded, less tart taste than Vietnamese or Indonesian tamarind.

PARTS USED

Pulp of ripe pods; leaves.

BUYING AND STORING

In East Indian and Asian markets, tamarind (also called Indian date) is available as a dried block, with or without seeds, as a thick, fairly dry paste, or as a more liquid, brown-black concentrate or syrup. In all processed forms tamarind keeps almost indefinitely. Occasionally fresh leaves, slices of dried pulp, and powdered dried tamarind can be found.

HARVESTING

Tamarind trees produce clusters of pale yellow flowers that turn into long, rust-colored pods. The pods contain a dark brown, sticky, and very fibrous pulp. The pulp is extracted from the brittle outer shell of the pod and pressed into flat cakes; these often include the shiny, black seeds. Further processing results in tamarind paste and concentrate.

Whole pods
In Vietnam and Thailand, unripe pods are used in tart soups and stews. In the regions where tamarind grows, especially Thailand and the Philippines, young, feathery leaves and flowers are sometimes used in curries and chutneys.

Culinary uses

In India and Southeast Asia, tamarind is used as an acidulant (much as the West uses lemon and lime) in curries, sambhars, chutneys, marinades, preserves, pickles, and sherbets. Tamarind gives many hot south Indian dishes, such as Goan vindaloo and Gujarati vegetable stews, their characteristic sourness. With raw sugar and chili peppers, it is simmered to a syrupy dipping sauce for fish. It goes into Thai tom yom soup and Chinese hot-and-sour ones. In Indonesia, where the word *asem* means both tamarind and sour, it is used in sauces, both savory and sweet, and for marinades. On Java, it is preferred to lemon for the island's sweet-sour dishes. In India, ground seeds are used in cakes. In Iran, stuffed vegetables are baked in a rich tamarind stock. In the Middle East, a lemonade-like drink made from tamarind syrup is popular; Central America and the West Indies also have tamarind drinks, which are consumed on their own or in tropical fruit punch, or made into milk shakes with ice cream. Jamaica uses tamarind in stews and with rice; in Costa Rica it makes a sour sauce. In Thailand, Vietnam, the Philippines, Jamaica, and Cuba, tamarind pulp is eaten as a sweetmeat, dusted with sugar or candied. Try using tamarind with salt as a rub for fish or meat before cooking, or with soy sauce and ginger in a marinade for pork or lamb.

Essential to Worcestershire sauce.

Good with cabbage, chicken, fish and shellfish, lamb, lentils, mushrooms, peanuts, pork, poultry, most vegetables.

Combines well with asafetida, chili, cilantro, cumin, galangal, garlic, ginger, mustard, shrimp paste (blachan, trassi), soy sauce, (brown or palm) sugar, turmeric.

BLOCK
To use tamarind from a block, soak a small piece, about the equivalent of 1 tbsp, for 10–15 minutes in a little hot water. Stir to loosen the pulp, squeeze out, and strain to remove fiber and, if they are present, seeds.

CONCENTRATE OR SYRUP
Tamarind concentrate has a "cooked" smell reminiscent of molasses, and a distinct sharp, acid taste. To use a concentrate, stir 1–2 tsp into a little water.

PASTE
Adding prepared tamarind to dishes moderates the heating effect of fiery chili peppers and hot spices.

SUMAC

Rhus coriaria

Sumac is the fruit of a decorative, bushy shrub that grows to a height of about 10ft (3m) and has light gray or reddish stems. The shrub grows wild on sparsely wooded uplands and high plateaux around the Mediterranean, especially in Sicily, where it is widely cultivated. Sumac also grows in parts of the Middle East, notably in Turkey (Anatolia) and in its native Iran.

TASTING NOTES

Sumac is only slightly aromatic; the taste is pleasantly tart, fruity, and astringent.

PARTS USED

Dried berries.

BUYING AND STORING

Outside the growing regions sumac is normally only available as a coarse or fine powder. In an airtight container this will keep for several months. Whole berries can be kept for a year or more.

HARVESTING

In the autumn sumac leaves turn a beautiful red, and the white flowers eventually develop into dense, conical clusters of fruit – small, round, russet-colored berries. The berries are picked just before they are fully ripe, dried in the sun, and crushed to a brick-red or red-brown powder.

Whole berries
Sumac thrives on rocky terrains; the higher it grows, the better the berries.

Culinary uses

Sumac is an essential ingredient in Arab and, especially, in Lebanese cooking, where it is used as an acidulant (just as the Western world employs lemon juice and Asia uses tamarind). It has little taste of its own, but brings out the flavors of the food to which it is added, much as salt does. If the berries are used whole they are cracked and soaked in water for 20–30 minutes, then squeezed out well to extract all the juice, which is used for marinades and salad dressings, in meat and vegetable dishes, and also to make a refreshing drink. Sumac powder is rubbed onto food before cooking: the Lebanese and Syrians use it on fish, the Iranians and Georgians on kebabs, the Iraqis and Turks on vegetables. In Turkish and Iranian kebab houses a small bowl of sumac is usually on the table alongside a bowl of chili flakes. Sumac is often sprinkled on flatbreads; it provides the tart element in the Lebanese bread salad, fattoush, and is an essential part of the spice and herb blend za'atar. Sumac is also used in chicken or vegetable casseroles, in stews, and in stuffings for chicken. With sliced raw onion it is used as an appetizer. Mixed into yogurt with fresh herbs, it makes a dipping sauce or side dish.

Essential to fattoush, za'atar.

Good with chicken, chickpeas, eggplant, fish and seafood, lamb, lentils, raw onion, pine nuts, walnuts, yogurt.

Combines well with allspice, chili, coriander, cumin, garlic, mint, paprika, parsley, pomegranate, sesame, thyme.

GROUND BERRIES
Berries vary in color from brick red to red-brown or maroon, depending on where they come from.

ZA'ATAR
Ground sumac berries are combined with sesame seeds and crushed, dried thyme in this Middle Eastern spice mixture (*recipe, p.290*).

BARBERRY

Berberis vulgaris

Many species of the *Berberis* genus and of the closely related genus *Mahonia* grow wild in temperate zones of Europe, Asia, northern Africa, and North America. They are dense, spiny, perennial bushes with toothed leaves, and they all have edible berries – the *Berberis* berries some shade of red, the *Mahonia* ones blue. Barberries are used as a spice in central Asia and the Caucasus region. In New England, ripe barberries are used in pies, preserves and syrups; green (unripe) barberries are sometimes pickled.

TASTING NOTES

The ripe berries are pleasantly acidulous. Dried berries have a light aroma, reminiscent of currants, but with a tart note. The taste is agreeably sweet-tart, with an underlying sharpness that derives from malic acid.

PARTS USED

Berries, fresh and dried.

BUYING AND STORING

Dried barberries are difficult to buy outside their region of production, except from Iranian markets. Plants can be found in nurseries and make attractive ornamental shrubs. If you grow one, or have found a bush in the wild, you can easily gather your own berries (provided you wear gloves to do so) and dry them. Dried berries will keep for several months. They retain their color and flavor best if stored in the freezer.

HARVESTING

The small, oblong berries hang down in tight clusters and can be picked from July until late summer. In Iran, the Caucasian republics, and countries further east, barberries are still gathered from the wild, sun-dried, and stored for use in the kitchen.

Whole dried berries
The small, oblong berries have a soft texture and a pleasant, sourish flavor. Berries should be red; dark berries are likely to be old and will have little flavor.

Culinary uses

Barberries are usually preserved in syrup or vinegar to make a tart flavoring. Being rich in pectin they are easily made into preserves. In central Asia and in Iran, dried berries are used to add a sour flavor and a splash of color to pilafs; they also go into stuffings, stews, and meat dishes.

Dried berries soon release their flavor if fried gently in butter or oil. They are sprinkled over some rice dishes. In Georgia, I was given a mixture of crushed barberries and salt – this is rubbed on lamb kebabs before grilling, giving the meat a tart piquancy. In India, dried berries are added to desserts, rather like sour currants. Fresh berries strewn over lamb or mutton for the last minutes of roasting will burst and coat the meat with their tart juice. Barberries make a good decoration for any dish with which you might otherwise use lemon juice. In the past the berries were also made into sweetmeats and comfits; the famous confitures d'épine vinette, which are made in Rouen, France, are the last remnant of that tradition.

The bluish berries of the Oregon grape, *Mahonia aquifolium*, are gathered in the wild and used in similar ways to the barberry.

Good with almonds, lamb, pistachios, poultry, rice, yogurt.

Combines well with bay, cardamom, cinnamon, coriander, cumin, dill, parsley, saffron.

CRUSHED BERRIES
Barberries can be crushed in a mortar for use with herbs and spices to flavor meatballs, pâtés, and marinades, or with salt, as here, to be rubbed onto lamb kebabs before grilling.

POMEGRANATE

Punica granatum

The pomegranate is a small, deciduous tree with narrow, leathery leaves, brilliant orange-red flowers, and large, beige to red-skinned fruits. Native from Iran to the Himalayas, it has been cultivated since ancient times all around the Mediterranean basin. Pomegranates now grow throughout the drier parts of subtropical India and Southeast Asia, Indonesia, and China, as well as in tropical Africa. The trees are very long-lived, but their vigor declines after only 15–20 years.

TASTING NOTES

The seeds are fleshy and taste both sweet and acidic. Middle Eastern pomegranates tend to be sweeter than those grown in India, which can have a slightly bitter aftertaste. The juice varies in color from a light pink to a deep red; it is sweet but with a refreshing sharpness.

PARTS USED

The seeds are used fresh and dried.

BUYING AND STORING

Pomegranates will keep for weeks in a cool place, and storing improves both flavor and juice content. Once extracted, the seeds or the juice can be frozen. Pomegranate molasses is a dark, thick, sticky syrup, stocked in Iranian and Middle Eastern markets and in some supermarkets. Anardana (dried berries) can be found in Indian markets, either whole, when they should be a deep, dark red, or ground. Anardana and molasses keep well.

HARVESTING

The fruit ripens in October and must be picked before it splits open to release the seeds. In northern India, the seeds of the sour and bitterish wild pomegranate are sun-dried for 2 weeks to make anardana.

Whole fruit
Choose fruit with the deepest color you can find. The seeds are really transparent juice sacs holding pulp and one (usually very hard) seed.

ANARDANA (DRIED SEEDS)
Dried seeds are pleasantly tart to smell and have a sweet-sour taste.

MOLASSES
Pomegranate molasses may be sweet or sweet-sour, the fruity sweetness tempered by an attractive tartness. The flavor is more concentrated than that of grenadine syrup.

Culinary uses

In the Middle East and central Asia, fresh, whole seeds are sprinkled over salads and pastes like hummus or tahina, or as a garnish on desserts. They are very good with chicken, can be added to stews, and will liven up a fruit or cucumber salad.

The seeds can be pressed, and the juice of the sweeter varieties is a popular beverage in the Middle East; in Georgia, tart juice is widely used in sauces for meat and fish.

Pomegranate molasses, a thick, dark syrup, is also made from the juice. Molasses can be brushed onto chicken or meat to act as a marinade, or added to slow-cooked dishes. Its taste and degree of sourness vary greatly from region to region. Arab and Indian molasses tends to be quite tart, even sour. Iran produces a sweeter version, which is an essential ingredient of muhammarah, a Middle-Eastern dip made with hot chili peppers and walnuts, and of fesenjan, a richly flavored Iranian duck or chicken dish made with walnuts. There is also a good Iranian winter soup based on pomegranate molasses.

Anardana (dried berries), which look like red-black raisins, are sticky but have a hard crunch. Their fruity, tangy flavor is much liked in northern India. They go into curries and chutneys, into stuffings for bread and savory pastries, and into braised vegetable dishes. In Punjabi cooking they flavor legumes. They give the food a more subtle sweet-sour taste than amchoor would, and are either soaked in water like tamarind, or crushed and sprinkled directly onto food.

Good with avocado, beets, cucumber, fish, lamb, legumes, pine nuts, poultry, spinach, walnuts.

Combines well with allspice, cardamom, chili, cinnamon, cloves, coriander, cumin, fenugreek, ginger, golpar, rosebuds, turmeric.

KOKAM

Garcinia indica

TASTING NOTES

Kokam has a slightly fruity, balsamic smell; a sweet-sour, tannic, astringent taste, often with a salty edge; and a lingering, sweetish aftertaste of dried fruit. Its sourness comes from malic and tartaric acids. The texture is surprisingly soft.

PARTS USED

Whole fruit or rind.

BUYING AND STORING

Dried rind can be bought from Indian markets and spice merchants; they may also have kokam paste. In an airtight jar both will keep for up to a year. The deeper the skin color, the better the kokam. Kokam is often labeled black mangosteen.

HARVESTING

Kokam is a smallish, round, sticky fruit, the size of a plum but with an uneven surface. It is dark purple when ripe and ready for picking, in April or May. The fruit is dried whole or split – which leaves the pulp full of the half dozen or more fairly big seeds. Alternatively, the rind is removed, soaked in the liquid of the pulp, and then dried in the sun. Its local name is *amsul*, literally sour rind. The dried rind comes folded into small strips that have a leathery appearance.

Kokam is the fruit of a slender, graceful, evergreen tree that is related to the mangosteen. It is native to India and grows almost exclusively in the tropical rainforests along a thin ribbon of the Malabar (Malwani) coast of India, from Mumbai to Cochin. In its native region, which includes Maharashtra, Karnataka, and Kerala, it is used as an acidulant, much as tamarind is in other parts of India. Fairly recently it has become popular in the US, the Middle East, and Australia, but it still has to make its mark in Europe.

Whole or sliced dried fruits
Whole fruits or slices can be added to flavor a dish and removed before eating – beware of the very hard seeds that may be left behind.

Culinary uses

Kokam is used as a souring agent, milder than tamarind. Dried fruit or rind are usually soaked in water; the pulp softens and is pressed dry, and the liquid is used for cooking beans or vegetables. Kokam rinds are often rubbed with salt to speed the drying; when using them, check that the dish does not become too salty.

Kokam saar – made by boiling pieces of kokam in water, straining the liquid, and flavoring it with different combinations of fresh ginger, onion, chili peppers, cumin, or coriander – is served both as an appetizer and as a cooling accompaniment to fiery, coconut-based fish curries. In Kerala, kokam is known as "fish tamarind."

With coconut milk, and with or without jaggery, kokam makes sol kadhi, a fragrant, carmine-colored beverage, which may be served with rice, taken as an appetizer, or drunk as a digestive. With sugar syrup kokam is also used for making cooling summer sherbets, some of which are marketed commercially. Kokam butter, made from kokam seeds and in the West sold as a skin cream, is edible and can be used as a vegetarian alternative to ghee.

Good with beans, eggplant, fish and shellfish, lentils, okra, plantain, potatoes, squash.

Combines well with cardamom, chili, coconut milk, coriander, cumin, fenugreek, garlic, ginger, mustard seed, turmeric.

Other kokams

G. atroviridis is a closely related Asian spice that is marketed, confusingly, as tamarind slices. Its properties, like those of kokam, resemble those of tamarind.

G. cambogia is another closely related species. Malwani cooks use it in the same way as kokam. Its fruit contains hydroxycitrate, a fruit acid that prevents the body from converting carbohydrates to fat, and which is used in slimming products.

DRIED RINDS
Dried rinds feel like fine-quality leather on the outside and are slightly sticky inside.

AMCHOOR

Mangifera indica

Amchoor is made from mangoes. The evergreen mango, a big, spreading tree with a massive, gray trunk and dark green leaves, is native to India and Southeast Asia and is now widely cultivated for its fruit. The trees crop every other year and continue to do so for well over a century. Every part of the tree is utilized in some way – bark, resin, leaves, flowers, seeds. The fruits are eaten fresh; both green (unripe) and ripe mangoes are made into chutneys and pickles. The spice is made from unripe fruit and is produced in India only.

TASTING NOTES

Amchoor has a pleasant, sweet-sour aroma of dried fruit and a tart, astringent, but also sweetish, fruity flavor. Its acidity comes from citric acid.

PARTS USED

Dried fruit, sliced or ground.

BUYING AND STORING

Amchoor is available from Indian and Asian markets, usually as a powder. It may be labeled "mango powder" – the English translation of the Hindi name *am-choor*. Dried slices are normally light brown and look like rough-textured wood. Slices keep for 3–4 months. The finely ground powder has a slightly fibrous texture, and is sandy-beige. It keeps for up to a year in an airtight jar.

HARVESTING

Unripe (green) mangoes are taken as windfalls or picked from the many semi-wild trees. They are peeled, sliced thin, and sun-dried. Sometimes a little turmeric is dusted over the slices to prevent insect damage. Dried slices are marketed whole, but most of the crop is pulverized to make amchoor powder.

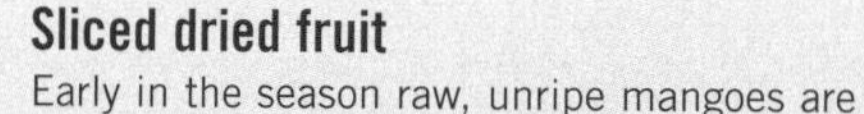

Sliced dried fruit
Early in the season raw, unripe mangoes are used as souring agents in pickles, curries, and dals. Slices are also sun-dried for use whole or powdered later in the year.

Culinary uses

Amchoor is used in north Indian vegetarian cooking to give a tang of tropical fruit to vegetable stews and soups, potato pakoras, and samosa fillings. It is good with stir-fried vegetables and in stuffings for breads and pastries. It is an essential ingredient in chat masala, a fresh-tasting and astringent spice blend from the Punjab, used for vegetable and legume dishes and for fruit salads. Amchoor is used as an acidulant in the way tamarind is in southern India. Dried slices are often used for pickles; if added to curries they should be removed before serving. Amchoor is particularly good in marinades used to tenderize poultry, meat, and fish. It is an important ingredient in the preparation of meats to be grilled in the tandoor. It is also much used as a sourish flavoring in dals and chutneys. The chutneys have been taken to the West Indies by Indian immigrants, where they have been adapted to take advantage of local ingredients. One teaspoon of amchoor has the equivalent acidity of three tablespoons of lemon juice.

Essential to chat masala.

Good with cauliflower, eggplant, legumes, okra, potatoes.

Combines well with chili, cloves, coriander, cumin, ginger, mint.

AMCHOOR POWDER
This lumpy powder is easily crushed and provides acidity without adding moisture.

LEMON GRASS

Cymbopogon citratus

TASTING NOTES

The flavor of lemon grass is refreshingly tart, clean, and citruslike with peppery notes. Freeze-dried lemon grass keeps its aroma quite well, but air-dried lemon grass loses its volatile oils; grated lemon rind gives more flavor than dried lemon grass.

PARTS USED

The lower part of the stalk, white and tinged with pale green.

BUYING AND STORING

Fresh lemon grass can be found in Asian markets and specialty produce markets. Buy firm stalks; they should not be wrinkled or dry. Fresh lemon grass will keep for 2–3 weeks in the refrigerator if wrapped in plastic. It also freezes well for up to 6 months. Freeze-dried lemon grass is quite fragrant and has a long shelf life in an airtight container. Dried lemon grass and lemon grass purée are available, but lack flavor.

HARVESTING

Most gardens in Singapore, Thailand, and Vietnam have a patch of lemon grass from which the cook can pluck a stalk or two. Commercial harvesting is done every 3–4 months. The leaves are removed before lemon grass is sold.

A showy, tropical grass with fibrous, sharp-edged leaves, lemon grass soon forms into large, dense clumps. It flourishes in temperate climates if it is overwintered indoors. The bulbous base imparts an elusive aromatic and lemon fragrance to the cooking of Southeast Asia. Previously hard to find outside that region, fresh lemon grass is now more widely available, thanks to the increased appreciation of Thai, Malay, Vietnamese, and Indonesian food. It is cultivated in Australia, Brazil, Mexico, West Africa, and in Florida and California.

Whole fresh stalks
Lemon grass contains citral, the flavor component of lemon rind. It gives the plant a subtle but sustained lemon fragrance.

Culinary uses

Remove the two outer layers and bruise the stalk if the lemon grass is to be used whole to flavor a stew or curry; take it out before serving. If the lemon grass is intended to be eaten as an ingredient of a soup or salad, discard the top part and slice the rest into very fine rings. Start at the bottom and stop slicing when the stalk becomes too hard – big pieces are unpleasantly fibrous to chew. Pounded with other spices and herbs, lemon grass goes into pastes to flavor curries, stews, and stir-fried dishes.

Lemon grass is a key ingredient in the Nonya cooking of Singapore and the southern part of the Malay peninsula. It is used in Thai larp, curries, and soups; in Vietnamese salads and spring rolls; in Indonesian bumbus (spice blends) for chicken and pork. Sri Lankan cooks use it in combination with coconut. Although it grows in India, it is not much used there except to make tea. If you grow the plant, the upper part of the leaves makes a pleasant, refreshing tea.

Lemon grass has a place in Western cooking, too. It suits all fish and seafood, especially crab and scallops. Add it to the stock for poaching fish or chicken. To flavor a vinaigrette, steep a few chopped stalks in it for 24 hours. Lemon grass is also good with fruit: use it, alone or with ginger or fennel seeds, to flavor syrups made for poaching peaches or pears.

Good with beef, chicken, fish and seafood, noodles, pork, variety meat, most vegetables.

Combines well with basil, chili, cilantro, cinnamon, cloves, coconut milk, galangal, garlic, ginger, turmeric.

FINELY SLICED STALK
Slices cut from fresh lemon grass often show purplish rings.

BRUISED STALKS
Bruising releases the volatile oils that impart flavor.

KAFFIR LIME

Citrus hystrix

Harvested from a shrubby, evergreen tree native to Southeast Asia, the rind and leaves of the kaffir lime have long imparted a clean, citrus flavor to the dishes of the region. Kaffir lime is now also grown in Florida, California, and Australia. The English name kaffir may originate in colonial usage or be a corruption of another word; some cooks may prefer to call this spice by its Thai name, makrut lime.

TASTING NOTES

Leaves have an explosive fragrance, cleanly floral and citrus – not quite lemon, not quite lime. Their aroma and flavor are assertive and lingering, yet delicate. The rind of the fruit is slightly bitter with a strong citrus note. Dried leaves and dried rind lack the intense aroma of fresh.

PARTS USED

Leaves and rind, preferably fresh.

BUYING AND STORING

Fresh leaves are available from Asian markets and some supermarkets. They keep for weeks in a plastic bag in the refrigerator. The leaves freeze well for up to a year, losing neither texture nor aromatics. Fruits should be firm and feel heavy for their size. Store in the refrigerator or in a cool room, as other citrus fruits. Dried leaves and rind are available; leaves should be green, not yellow or dingy-looking. Store both in airtight containers. Leaves will keep for 6–8 months. Some markets also stock rind preserved in brine.

HARVESTING

Leaves and fruit are picked and sold fresh or dried.

Whole fresh leaves
The leathery leaves grow in an unusual double form, as two on a single petiole. The upper side is dark green and glossy, the underside lighter and mat.

SHREDDED FRESH LEAVES
If the leaves are to be eaten, rather than removed before serving, break apart the pairs and remove the thick, central rib. Stack several leaves and shred finely.

Culinary uses

Lime leaves are responsible for the tangy, citrus perfume of many Thai soups, salads, stir-fries, and curries. Grated rind goes into curry pastes, larp, and fish cakes. Both are used in some fish and poultry dishes in Indonesia and Malaysia. Always use fresh leaves when available and never use dried in a salad. Whole leaves may be removed from a dish before serving, but if leaves are to be eaten, for example as a garnish for a clear soup, shred them very finely – as fine as a needle – with a small, sharp knife. The leaves keep their flavor well when cooked.

If you buy rind in brine, rinse it well and scrape off the pith before using; shredded, dried rind is best soaked briefly before being added to slow-cooked dishes. The pith makes dried rind bitter, so use sparingly. To give a citrus flavor to a Western dish, use leaves in chicken casseroles, with braised or roasted fish, or in sauces to serve with chicken or fish.

Essential to Thai curry pastes, Indonesian sambals.

Good with fish and seafood, mushrooms, noodles, pork, poultry, rice, green vegetables.

Combines well with Asian basils, chili, cilantro, coconut milk, galangal, ginger, lemon grass, rau ram, sesame, star anise.

Whole fresh fruit

The fruit is pear-shaped, bumpy, and wrinkled, lime green in color, and 2½–3in (7–8cm) long. What little juice it yields is sour and seldom used.

GRATED FRESH RIND

The very thin rind is best removed with a small-holed grater rather than a citrus grater, whose fine perforations will reduce the rind to a mushy mass. Proceed with caution to avoid including the bitter pith.

GALANGAL

Alpinia species

There are two main types of galangal: greater galangal, *A. galanga*, is native to Java; lesser galangal, *A. officinarum*, is native to the coastal regions of southern China. Greater galangal indeed grows taller than lesser and has larger rhizomes. Both are cultivated extensively throughout Southeast Asia, Indonesia, and India. The popularity of lesser galangal has long declined in favor of greater galangal, which continues to be used in the kitchen, principally in Southeast Asia. The English name stems from the Arabic *khalanjan*.

TASTING NOTES

The aroma of greater galangal is mildly gingery and camphorous; the taste has a lemony sourness with a flavor resembling ginger and cardamom mixed. Lesser galangal is more pungent, with a hint of eucalypt; its taste is piquant, suggesting a mix of pepper and ginger.

PARTS USED

Rhizome.

BUYING AND STORING

Fresh greater galangal can be bought from Asian markets, possibly under its local names – it is called kha in Thailand, lengkuas in Malaysia, and laos in Indonesia – or called Laos, Siamese or Thai ginger. It will keep for 2 weeks and can be frozen. Dried slices and powdered galangal (labeled laos) are more widely available. Powdered galangal can be kept for 2 months; slices keep their flavor for at least a year. Galangal in brine can be substituted for fresh; rinse it thoroughly before use. Lesser galangal rhizomes, which are reddish-brown outside and pale red inside, are seldom seen in the US.

HARVESTING

The rhizomes are lifted, cleaned, and processed much like those of turmeric or ginger.

Greater galangal *A. galanga*

Whole rhizomes of greater galangal are large and knobby, light orange-brown outside, and marked with darker rings. Young shoots have a pink hue.

SLICED RHIZOME The flesh is fibrous and buff-colored. Unless very young, the rhizomes are tougher and woodier than those of ginger.

Culinary uses

Throughout Southeast Asia, greater galangal is used fresh in curries and stews, in sambals, satays, soups, and sauces. In Thailand, it is an essential ingredient in some curry powders, as it is in the laksa spices of Malay Nonya cooking. In Thai cooking it is often preferred where other Asian cuisines would use ginger, especially to neutralize the smells of fish and seafood. It is good with chicken and in many hot and sour soups: it provides the key flavoring in tom kha kai, the popular chicken and coconut milk soup.

Like ginger, fresh galangal is easy to peel and grate or chop. It is always preferred to dried, but dried slices can be added to soups and stews; first soak them in hot water for about 30 minutes. They should be taken out before serving because they remain unpleasantly woody to chew. Powdered galangal is used in spice blends throughout the Middle East and across North Africa to Morocco (in ras el hanout). Grated galangal and lime juice are used to make a popular tonic in Southeast Asia. The use of lesser galangal appears to be largely restricted to tonic and healing soups.

Essential to Thai curry pastes.

Good with chicken, fish and seafood.

Combines well with chili, coconut milk, fennel, fish sauces, garlic, ginger, lemon grass, lemon juice, kaffir lime, shallots, tamarind.

SLICED DRIED RHIZOME
Dried slices are satisfactory for flavoring soups and stews and should be soaked in water before use.

GROUND RHIZOME
Tan-colored lesser galangal powder is gingerlike and sharp; greater galangal is sandy-beige, with a sour aroma and a milder ginger flavor.

Other galangal varieties

Several plants with similar properties to lesser galangal, *Alpinia officinarum*, are also referred to, confusingly, as lesser galangal. While it is often quite hard to make reliable distinctions, at least two of these appear to have individual characteristics and uses.

Aromatic ginger *Kaempferia galanga*

The young leaves of this small, wild plant, also known as the resurrection lily, kencur in Indonesia, cekur in Malaysia, and pro hom in Thailand, are served raw to accompany Thai fish curries and in Malay salads. The reddish-brown rhizome is usually no more than 2in (5cm) long, with yellowish-white flesh. In Indonesia, pounded kencur is added to a number of dishes; in China, the pounded rhizome is mixed with salt and oil, and served with baked chicken. In Sri Lanka, it is roasted and ground for biryanis and curries. Kencur is sold dried, in slices or ground. More like ginger than galangal, the pungent, camphorous rhizome is used in very small quantities. Confusingly, the word kencur is also used for zedoary (*p.210*).

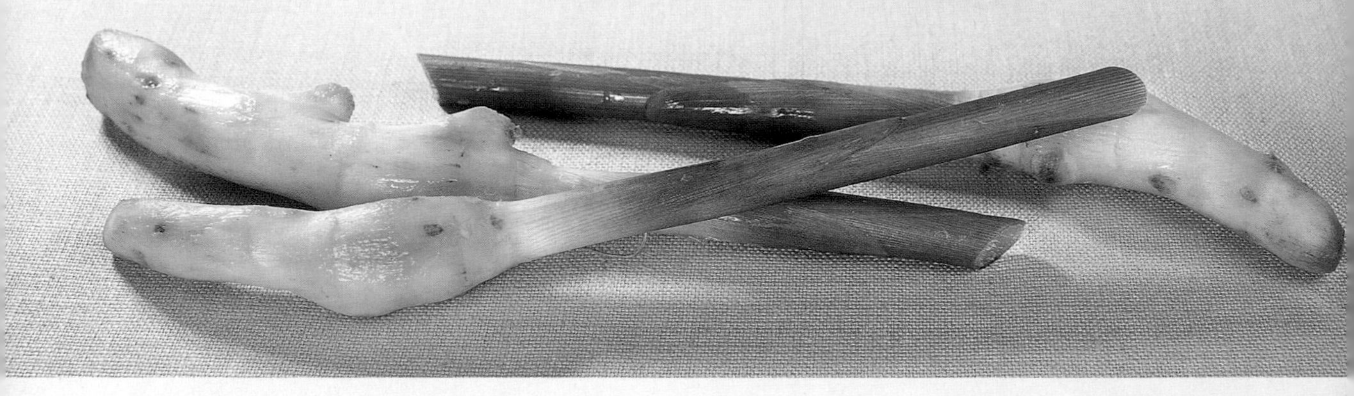

Fingerroot

Boesenbergia pandurata/Kaempferia pandurata

Also called Chinese keys, fingerroot grows throughout Southeast Asia. It is a small plant, up to 20in (50cm) high, with an underground rhizome and slender storage roots. In Thailand, it has a range of culinary uses; elsewhere it tends to be used as a medicinal herb. The clusters of thin fingers are yellowish-brown outside and yellow inside. The rhizome has a crisp texture, a sweet aroma, a refreshing, lemony taste, and lingering warmth, somewhere between galangal and ginger. As krachai it is essential to some Thai curry pastes; with vegetables, or just basil or a mixture of herbs, it is used to make soup. In the West, it is found fresh or in dried slices, which are soaked for 30 minutes. The Malay and Indonesian name for it is temu kunci.

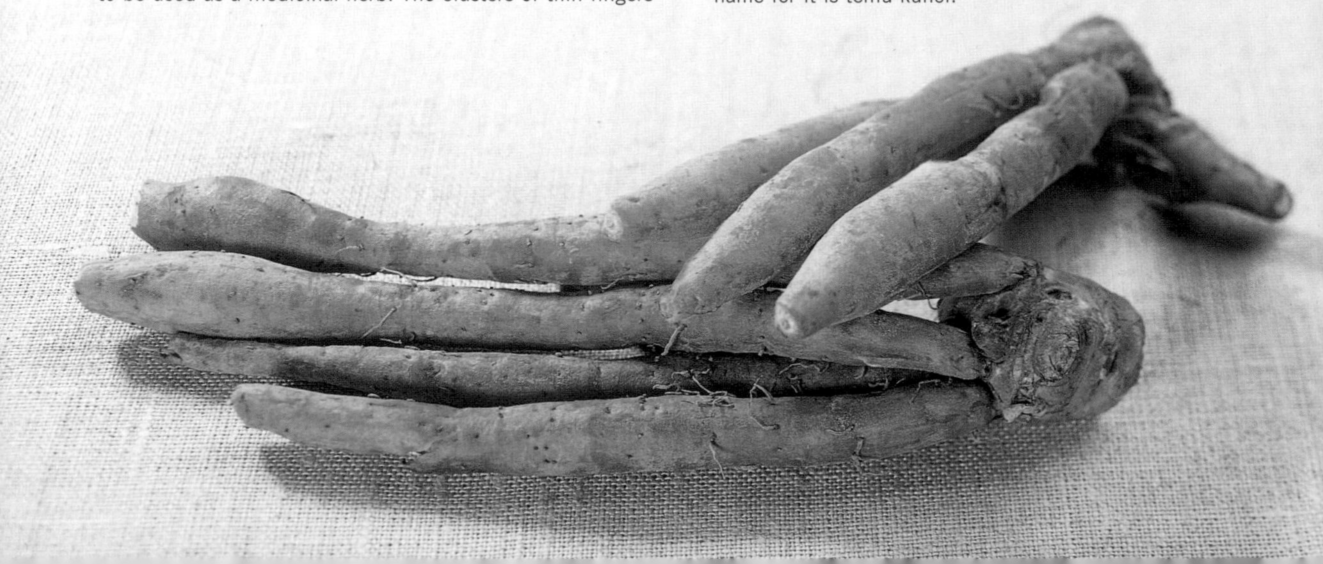

LEMON MYRTLE

Backhousia citriodora

The tall lemon myrtle tree is native to coastal Australian rainforests, mostly in Queensland. The trees have been introduced to southern Europe, the southern US, and South Africa, and are grown for their essential oil in China and Southeast Asia. So far, lemon myrtle has gained a place in the kitchen only in Australia, and even there quite recently, but it is slowly becoming more widely appreciated.

TASTING NOTES

The aroma is refreshing and intensely lemony, like that of lemon grass and lemon verbena, and is even more pronounced when the leaves are crushed. The taste is stronger still, more like lemon rind. The aftertaste is a lingering note of eucalypt or camphor.

PARTS USED

Fresh and dried leaves.

BUYING AND STORING

Lemon myrtle can be bought as whole, dried leaves or as a coarse, light green powder from herb or spice merchants and some supermarkets. It can also be found via the internet. Both forms should be stored in airtight containers in the dark. Buy powdered leaf only in small quantities.

HARVESTING

Mature, dark leaves are picked all year round. Drying intensifies their flavor, so dried leaves of good quality may taste even better than fresh ones.

Culinary uses

Lemon myrtle is versatile and can be used wherever lemon grass or lemon rind is called for. It is best used sparingly. If cooked for too long, the lemony flavor is lost and an unpleasant eucalypt note can take over. It is therefore better used in shortbread and other cookies, and in batters for things like pancakes than in longer-baked cakes, and also goes well in stir-fry dishes. It is excellent for fish cakes; with vinegar, sugar, basil, and olive oil it can be used as a dipping sauce for the cakes or as a salad dressing. It makes good vinegar as well as a lemonade and an herbal tea. It gives a lift to mayonnaise, sauces, and marinades for chicken or seafood. Combined with other spices it makes a good rub for chicken or fish to be grilled.

Good with chicken, fish and seafood, most fruit, pork, rice.

Combines well with akudjura, anise seed, basil, chili, fennel, galangal, ginger, mountain pepper, parsley, pepper, thyme, yogurt.

Whole dried leaves
The powerful lemon taste is due to a very high concentration of citral in the volatile oil (30 times that of lemon).

GROUND DRIED LEAVES
Outside Australia, lemon myrtle is usually only available ground.

CITRUS

Citrus species

Citrus fruits are universal providers of tartness in the kitchen. The Japanese use the peel of a small citron, called yuzu; the Chinese favor dried orange or tangerine peel; in the Gulf States and Iran, dried limes are preferred; in Tunisia, bitter orange peel and fruit are used for pickling liquids. In the West, cooks use juice and grated rind for their acidity, and candied peel in desserts and cakes. In the Caribbean islands and Mexico, it would be unthinkable to cook without limes.

TASTING NOTES

Japanese citron peel has an attractive, delicate aroma; crushed and ground dried limes have a sour smell backed by a dried-fruit sweetness; whole limes are less aromatic. Orange peels have a clear, orange scent; the flavors are tart or bitter, depending on the variety.

PARTS USED

Fresh and dried peel; juice.

BUYING AND STORING

Fresh yuzu is seldom available outside Japan, but dried peel is found in Asian markets, as well as dried tangerine peel. Middle Eastern and Iranian markets have dried bitter-orange peel, all forms of dried limes, and Moroccan preserved lemons. In North America, commercial mojos and sour orange marinades are sold in Latin markets, but it is easy to prepare your own. Stored in airtight containers, dried or candied peel and fruits will keep indefinitely.

HARVESTING

Yuzus are only in season for a brief period from November to January; bitter oranges come onto the market in January and February, and there is now an early autumn crop from Chile. Other citrus fruits and dried peels are available all year round.

Preserved lemons
The chopped peel of salted lemons preserved in their juice is used to flavor Moroccan tagines; it combines particularly well with green olives in a renowned chicken dish. The salty juice is good in salad dressings.

Sliced dried peel

Commercial dried tangerine or orange peel is dark brown and brittle. To dry your own after eating an orange or tangerine, remove all pith from the peel, put the peel on a rack, and leave to dry for 4–5 days. It will remain flexible. The flavor improves with age.

Whole dried limes

Dried limes are pierced and added whole to stews; they soften in cooking and are served as part of the dish, to be squeezed to extract all the juice.

Culinary uses

Slivers of fresh yuzu peel, or dried, crumbled peel, add fragrance to Japanese soups, simmered dishes (nabemono), and aromatic yuzu-miso condiments. Yubeshi, a traditional sweet, is made by steaming the shells of yuzus filled with glutinous rice, soy sauce, and sweet syrup. They are dried and sliced to serve.

Dried tangerine peel is used mostly in the cooking of Sichuan and Hunan. It is soaked in warm water for 15 minutes, then chopped finely for stir-fried dishes or used whole in rich dishes of braised pork or duck. It combines well with Sichuan peppercorns and star anise, with dark soy sauce and rice wine.

In the Gulf States, small, dried limes, often called Oman limes, or dried lime powder are used in fish, poultry, and lamb stews and pilafs. Gulf dishes call for a lot of spicing, and dried limes marry well with cardamom, cloves, allspice, pepper, ginger, cinnamon, and coriander. To the north, in Iran, they are used in the same way to flavor stews, especially lamb stews, but the Iranians prefer herbs – cilantro, dill, parsley, fenugreek – and green vegetables – leeks, scallions, spinach – in their lime-scented dishes. In some parts of Iran, bitter oranges are customary; often the juice and rind are added to stews. These flavorings are particularly good with duck, chicken, and rabbit.

The mojos of the Caribbean and South America are made with lime, lemon, grapefruit, or bitter orange juice to which garlic, spices, fruits, and fresh herbs are added. They are used as marinades, dips, and salad dressings, or as refreshing sauces to accompany vegetables, fish, and grilled or roasted meats.

STAR ANISE

Illicium verum

Certainly the prettiest spice, star anise is native to southern China and Vietnam, where it has a long history of medicinal and culinary use. It was known in Europe in the 17th century, and old recipes indicate that it was used to flavor syrups, cordials, and preserves. Today Western cooks use it as a flavoring for fish and seafood, in syrups for poaching figs and pears, and to spice tropical fruits.

TASTING NOTES

The aroma is fennel- and anise-like – star anise and anise seed both contain essential oil with anethole. Star anise has licorice notes and an assertive warmth. The flavor is pungent and sweet with a mildly numbing effect, and the aftertaste is fresh and agreeable.

PARTS USED

Whole star anise, or pieces; ground powder.

BUYING AND STORING

Star anise is best bought whole or in pieces. It will last for a year if kept out of bright light in an airtight container. Buy ground spice in small quantities; it should last for up to 2–3 months if kept as the whole spice.

HARVESTING

Star anise is the fruit of a Chinese evergreen magnolia tree, which now also grows in India, Japan, and the Philippines. The tree grows to about 26ft (8m) and has small yellow-green flowers. It fruits in its sixth year and continues to bear fruit for up to a century. The fruits are picked before ripening and sun-dried, which hardens and darkens the carpels and develops the aromatic compounds.

Whole pods and seeds
Used whole, star anise makes a decorative addition to a dish. The star anise seedpod is in the shape of an irregular, eight-pointed star. Up to 1¼in (3cm) across, complete pods are tough and red-brown or rust-colored.

CARPELS
Each carpel is canoe-shaped and slightly open, revealing a lustrous, brittle, brown seed. The carpels are more aromatic than the seeds.

Culinary uses

In Chinese cooking star anise is used in soups and stocks, in marinades for steamed chicken and pork, and in "red-cooked" chicken, duck, and pork – the meat is turned a red-brown color by braising in a dark broth flavored with spices and soy sauce. Star anise also colors and flavors marbled tea eggs. It is the main ingredient of Chinese five-spice powder. Vietnamese cooks also use it in simmered dishes, in stocks, and in pho (beef and noodle soup). The flavor of star anise can be detected in some of the cooking of Kerala in southern India; in some dishes of north India it may be used as a cheaper substitute for anise seed.

Star anise is little used in Western cooking except as a flavoring in drinks such as pastis and anisette, and in chewing gum and confectionery. In addition to flavoring fish and seafood and some fruit dishes, it enhances the sweetness of leeks, pumpkin, and root vegetables.

Essential to five-spice powder.

Good with chicken (in stock for poaching), fish and seafood (in court-bouillon), figs, tropical fruits, leeks, oxtail, pork, pumpkin, root vegetables.

Combines well with cassia, chili, cinnamon, coriander, fennel seed, garlic, ginger, lemon grass, lime peel, Sichuan pepper, soy sauce, dried tangerine peel.

BROKEN PODS
The dried pods are easily broken into pieces when only a little is needed. Star anise is potent, so use it sparingly.

GROUND PODS
For the best flavor, the pods and seeds should be ground in a mortar or electric spice mill and used immediately.

ANISE

Pimpinella anisum

This delicate plant, native to the eastern Mediterranean and Middle East, is related botanically to caraway, cumin, dill, and fennel. It is now widely established throughout Europe, Asia, and North America. Its earliest use was medicinal, but the Romans introduced it as a flavoring in food, especially in cakes served at the end of a meal to aid digestion. The plant is cultivated for its seeds (anise seed or aniseed), but young leaves are also used as an herb.

TASTING NOTES

The aroma and taste of the seeds are sweet, licorice-like, warm, and fruity, but Indian anise can have a hint of bitterness. The leaves have the same fragrant, sweet, licorice notes, with mild peppery undertones. The seeds are more subtly flavored than fennel or star anise.

PARTS USED

Seeds, leaves.

BUYING AND STORING

Anise can be grown from seed, and plants are available from some herb nurseries. As a spice, anise seed is best bought whole; check that there is only a minimum of stems and husks. In an airtight container it will retain its flavor for at least 2 years.

HARVESTING

Just before the fruit ripens, plants are pulled up and left to dry. They are threshed and the seeds spread on trays in partial shade to dry further. To dry anise you have grown yourself, put the seedheads in paper bags and hang them in a well-ventilated place.

Whole seeds
The small, oval seeds vary in color from pale brown to green-gray, with lighter colored ridges. Bits of thin stem are often attached to the seeds.

GROUND SEEDS
As the aroma of ground anise seed dissipates quickly, grind as needed.

Culinary uses

In Europe, anise seed is mostly used to flavor cakes, breads, cookies, and sweet fruit dishes. It flavors some rye breads, Scandinavian pork stews, and root vegetable dishes. The Portuguese add a handful of anise seed to the water when boiling chestnuts to impart a delicate fragrance. Figs and anise have a natural affinity; in Catalonia, cakes are made of chopped, dried figs and almonds flavored with anise, and in Italy, a fig and dried fruit "salami" is flavored with anise and anisette. Around the Mediterranean, anise often flavors fish stews, and its essential oil is in demand to flavor aperitifs and liqueurs such as ouzo, pastis, and anisette. These too can make an anise contribution in the kitchen: add a few drops of pastis to crab, mussels, fish soup, or mayonnaise to serve with fish.

In the Middle East and India, anise seed is mostly used in breads and savory foods. Indian cooks dry-roast the seeds to enhance the aroma before using them in vegetable or fish curries, or quickly fry them in hot oil as a garnish for lentils. Anise seed is also valued for its digestive properties; along with betel leaves, nuts, and other spices it is offered in the traditional paan at the end of a meal. In Morocco and Tunisia, anise flavors breads; in Lebanon, it goes into fritters and spiced custards. Anise leaves may be added to salads; they also make a garnish for carrots, beets, parsnips, and fish soups.

Good with apples, chestnuts, figs, fish and seafood, nuts, pumpkin, root vegetables.

Combines well with ajowan, allspice, cardamom, cinnamon, cloves, cumin, fennel, garlic, nigella, nutmeg, pepper, star anise.

Pickling spices blend

This blend of spices is used in Iran for pickling many vegetables and fruits. It includes anise seed, coriander, ginger, golpar (*p.93*), powdered lime, cinnamon, cumin, and nigella (*recipe, p.289*).

LICORICE

Glycyrrhiza species

Licorice plants are perennial shrubs with blue or lilac, pea-like flowers. The most important species are *G. glabra*, native to southeastern Europe and southwestern Asia; *G. glandulifera*, which grows further east and is known as Russian or Persian licorice; and *G. uralensis*, the main form used in Asia, native to the steppes of northern China. Licorice has been cultivated in Europe for about 1,000 years, in China at least twice as long. It is still used medicinally as a cough-repressant, an expectorant, and a gentle laxative.

TASTING NOTES

The aroma of licorice is sweet, warm, and medicinal; the taste is very sweet, earthy, and anise-like with a lingering, bitter, salty aftertaste.

PARTS USED

Rhizomes and roots.

BUYING AND STORING

Dried licorice roots can be bought from spice merchants. They keep almost indefinitely if they are quite dry; they can be sliced or ground as needed. Powdered licorice, gray-green and rather strong, needs an airtight container. Sticks and slabs, too, last well if kept dry.

HARVESTING

Licorice plants are easily grown from seed or root cuttings. They need rich, sandy soil and plentiful sun. The roots can be dug up in autumn; drying them takes several months. Roots are usually crushed to a pulp, which manufacturers boil to a thick consistency and reduce further by evaporation. The resulting soluble substance is called extract of licorice. Some manufacturers extract glycyrrhizic acid for use as a flavoring.

Dried roots
Licorice plants have deep taproots that send out a horizontal network of rhizomes. Both are harvested after about 4 years.

SLICED ROOTS
Sliced roots are bright yellow; their smell suggests their sweetness.

Culinary uses

The greatest amount of licorice flavoring is used for tobacco; cough syrups and toothpaste come a distant second. In the form of drinks such as sambuca and pastis the flavor enters a variety of dishes, both sweet and savory. A soft drink is made with it in Islamic countries during Ramadan. Licorice candies are made with powder, which is made into a malleable paste with sugar, water, gum arabic, and flour; they often derive their taste from anise oil and only their sweetness from licorice. In Morocco, the powder flavors snail and octopus dishes and is often an ingredient in ras el hanout. A little licorice improves Chinese five-spice powder; it also flavors Chinese soy sauce. Asian spiced stocks or marinades often contain licorice along with other spices.

The Dutch extrude the extract into black, salty licorice, called *drop*, in a bewildering variety of shapes and strengths; the English have multi-colored licorice allsorts and Pontefract cakes – lozenges named after the Yorkshire monastery where they originated in the 16th century. Licorice sticks are popular in Asia for chewing – they are bitter at first, and then become sweeter. In Turkey, fresh roots are eaten and powder is used in baking. In the West, licorice is becoming a fashionable flavoring for ice cream.

Licorice should be used sparingly or its bitterness may come through too strongly.

Combines well with cassia, cloves, coriander, fennel seed, ginger, Sichuan pepper, star anise.

SHAPED EXTRACT
Extract of licorice, produced by boiling licorice roots, is hard, black, and glossy. Manufacturers mold it into sticks, disks, and other shapes.

POWDER
Finely powdered licorice, with its woody, sweet aroma, is most readily available from Chinese markets.

SAFFRON

Crocus sativus

Saffron consists of the dried stigmas of the saffron crocus, or roses as they are called. Native to the Mediterranean and western Asia, it was used by the ancient civilizations of the region as a dye and to flavor food and wine. Spain is the main producer; at harvest time on the plain of La Mancha, a heady, sensual aroma explodes around you as the stigmas are toasted. It takes about 80,000 roses to yield 5lb (2.5kg) of stigmas, which produce 1lb (500g) of saffron after toasting. No wonder it is the most expensive spice in the world.

TASTING NOTES

The smell of saffron is unmistakable: rich, pungent, musky, floral, honeyed, and tenacious. The taste is delicate yet penetrating, warm, earthy, musky, bitter, and lingering. The aromatic properties vary slightly depending on the saffron's place of origin.

PARTS USED

Stigmas.

BUYING AND STORING

Buy dried stamens (known as filaments or threads); ground saffron is easily adulterated. Threads keep their flavor for 2–3 years if stored in an airtight container in a cool, dark place. Buy saffron only from a reliable source; in tourist markets around the world turmeric, marigold petals, and safflower are passed off as saffron. None has saffron's penetrating aroma, so smell before buying. If you use saffron regularly, buy it in larger quantities from a spice merchant.

HARVESTING

The violet-colored crocus flowers in autumn. The flowers are picked at dawn and the three red stigmas are plucked from each one. Small quantities are toasted on a drum sieve over a low fire. Dried stamens are deep red to orange-red, wiry, and brittle.

Whole threads

The best-quality saffron is deep red; this is called coupe for Spanish and Kashmiri saffron, sargol for Iranian. A proportion of thicker, yellow threads from the style of the flower is included in the next grade, Mancha if Spanish or Kashmiri, poshal or kayam if Iranian. Good-quality saffron is also produced in Greece and Italy. Lesser grades tend to have a brownish color and stubby, rather untidy threads.

IRANIAN POSHAL
This saffron has deep red, wiry threads with a few yellow styles.

KASHMIRI COUPE
This saffron has a rich, burgundy color. The threads are very long, firm, and smooth.

Culinary uses

Saffron has long been renowned as a dye, whether for the robes of Buddhist monks or for paella and risotto. For most dishes saffron is infused in liquid. If an infusion is added in the early stages of cooking it will impart more color; added at a later stage it contributes more aromatics. Avoid overuse: it can give a bitter, medicinal taste to foods. If a dish does not call for liquid, threads can be ground and stirred in. If they are not quite dry, dry-roast lightly before grinding.

Several cultures flavor specific dishes with saffron, often dishes associated with festivals or celebrations. Saffron provides the characteristic flavor for many Mediterranean fish soups and stews of which Provençal bouillabaisse and Catalan zarzuela are the best known. It adds class to a simple stew of mussels and potatoes or a fish baked in white wine. Saffron rice is excellent whether as a Valencian paella, risotto alla Milanese, an Iranian polo, a Moghul biryani, or a simple vegetable pilaf. In Sweden, saffron buns and cakes are made for the festival of light on December 13, St Lucia's Day. Traditional Cornish saffron cakes and breads have all but disappeared from Britain, but they are not difficult to make and have a fine, rich flavor. Saffron ice cream, whether in the European style, Middle Eastern with mastic, or Indian kulfi, is also worth a try.

Good with asparagus, carrots, chicken, eggs, fish and seafood, leeks, mushrooms, pheasant, rabbit, spinach, winter squashes.

Combines well with anise, cardamom, cinnamon, fennel, ginger, mastic, nutmeg, paprika, pepper, rosebuds, rose water.

SPANISH MANCHA
Spanish Mancha saffron is more orange-red in color with yellow styles.

GROUND THREADS
Ground saffron is easily adulterated with cheaper and inferior spices.

SAFFRON *is the costliest spice on earth, ten times as dear as vanilla, because its production still depends on intensive*

manual labor. The fragile stigmas of about 80,000 crocus flowers are needed to produce just 1lb (500g) of the spice.

CARDAMOM

Elettaria cardamomum

Cardamom is the fruit of a large, perennial bush that grows wild in the rainforests of the Western Ghats (also known as the Cardamon Hills) in southern India; a closely related variety grows in Sri Lanka. Both are now cultivated in their regions of origin and in Tanzania, Vietnam, and Papua New Guinea; Guatemala has become the main exporter. Cardamom has been used in India for some 2,000 years. It reached Europe along the caravan routes, and the Vikings took it from Constantinople to Scandinavia, where it is still very popular.

TASTING NOTES

The aroma of cardamom is strong but mellow, fruity, and penetrating. The taste is lemony and flowery, with a note of camphor or eucalypt due to cineole in the essential oil; it is pungent and smoky, with a warm, bittersweet note, yet is also clean and fresh.

PARTS USED

Dried seeds.

BUYING AND STORING

Pods will keep for a year or more in an airtight jar, but will slowly fade in both color and aroma. Exposed to air, the seeds quickly lose their volatile oils; grinding speeds up the loss. Ground cardamom is easy to adulterate and in any case usually includes the hulls, so it is better to grind your own when needed.

HARVESTING

Fruits ripen from September to December and are harvested at intervals while about three-quarters ripe, otherwise they split open. They are dried in the sun for 3–4 days, or more quickly in drying sheds. Dried pods are hard; the best are green to green-amber. Green pods from Kerala traditionally set the standards of quality and price, but Guatemalan cardamom is nearly as good.

Whole pods
Cardamom is best bought as whole pods, which should be plump and green. White pods are bleached green ones; less well flavored, their production is declining.

SEEDS
Inside each oval seed pod, triangular in section, are 15–20 tiny, dark brown or black, sticky seeds. Stickiness is the best indication of freshness.

Culinary uses

Cardamom enhances both sweet and savory flavors. In India, it is one of the essential components in many spice mixes. It goes into sweetmeats, pastries, puddings, and ice creams (kulfi), and is used in a digestive and breath-freshening paan with fennel and anise seeds and areca nuts. In India, it is also much used to flavor tea, while in Arab countries coffee is flavored with cardamom, often by pouring it over pods put in the spout of the pot – in Bedouin culture the cardamom used is first displayed to guests, bright green and pristine, as a mark of respect. Cardamom is an essential component of spice mixes in Lebanon, Syria, the Gulf States (baharat), and Ethiopia (berbere). Scandinavia is still the biggest importer in Europe; there and in Germany and Russia, cardamom is widely used for spiced cakes, pastries, and breads, and occasionally also in hamburgers and meat loaf.

Whole pods, lightly crushed, can be used to flavor rice, poached and braised dishes, and casseroles. They are an important ingredient in many Indian slow-braised meat dishes (kormas), which use a thick marinating liquid to develop a creamy sauce. Hulled seeds can be either lightly bruised and fried, or toasted and ground, before being added to a dish. Cardamom is good in baked apples, poached pears, and fruit salads. It combines well with orange and coffee in desserts, but is equally at home with roast duck or poached chicken, in marinades or spiced wine. It is useful in pickles.

Essential to berbere, curry powders, dals, masalas, pilafs, Indian rice pudding (kheer), zhug.

Good with apples, oranges, pears; legumes, sweet potatoes, and other root vegetables.

Combines well with caraway, chili, cinnamon, cloves, coffee, coriander, cumin, ginger, paprika, pepper, saffron, yogurt.

Spices for pilafs

Indian pilafs are flavored with whole spices, including green cardamom pods, pieces of cinnamon, cloves, cumin seed, and black peppercorns, which are simply added to the rice before it is cooked (*recipe, p.322*).

BLACK CARDAMOM

Amomum and Aframomum species

The larger seeds of several species of *Amomum* and *Aframomum* are widely used in the regions where they are grown, and sometimes they are sold, ground, as cheap substitutes for green cardamom. In color they are various shades of brown and their taste is usually more camphorous than that of green cardamom. The most important is Greater Indian or Nepal cardamom, *Amomum subulatum*, native to the eastern Himalayas. This particular variety, usually referred to as black cardamom, is never used as a substitute for green cardamom and has a distinct and separate role in Indian cooking.

TASTING NOTES

The seeds have a tarry smell and a taste of pine with an astringent, smoky, earthy note. They are used to give depth to masalas and tandoori-style spice mixtures.

PARTS USED

Dried seeds.

BUYING AND STORING

Buy pods that are whole, not broken, and store in an airtight container.

HARVESTING

Harvesting takes place from August to November, somewhat earlier than that of green cardamom (*p.194*), and drying is always done in sheds. The resulting color is a very dark brown.

Whole pods
Black cardamom has ribbed, often hairy, fruits that become deep red when ripe.

GROUND SEEDS
Seeds quickly lose their volatile oil when ground, so grind only when needed.

SEEDS
Seeds are sticky, but once removed from the pod they soon dry out.

Culinary uses

In contrast to green cardamom, which is considered a "cooling" spice, black cardamom is a "heating" spice. It is therefore an important ingredient in combination with cloves, cinnamon, and black pepper in any garam masala, the hot spice mixture that can be used either at the start of cooking or sprinkled over for a stronger effect toward the end. Black cardamom also occasionally finds its way into confectionery and pickles. When pods are used whole in vegetable or meat stews they should be removed before serving, but crushed seeds will dissolve into the sauce. The flavor is intense, so use sparingly.

Essential to garam masala.
Good with pilafs and other rice dishes, meat and vegetable curries.
Combines well with ajowan, green cardamom, cassia leaves, chili, cinnamon, cloves, coriander, cumin, nutmeg, pepper, yogurt.

Other cardamoms
Bengal cardamom, *A. aromaticum*, is very similar to the Greater Indian and used in the same way.
Chinese cardamom, *A. globosum*, is round, quite large, and dark brown. The flavor is astringent and cooling, leaving a numbing sensation in the mouth. Although mostly used medicinally in China, it combines well with star anise in stir-fry dishes. It is often on sale in Asian markets.
Javanese winged cardamom, *A. kepulaga*, is much used in Southeast Asia.
Cambodian cardamom, *A. krevanh*, from the Krevanh hills of Thailand and Cambodia, is also traded extensively within Southeast Asia.
Ethiopian cardamom, *Afr. korarima*, has a dull, slightly smoky aroma and a rather coarse flavor.
Grains of paradise, *A. melegueta*, is a different spice (*p.234*).

Standard garam masala
This is a basic blend of black cardamom, coriander seeds, black peppercorns, cloves, cinnamon, and tejpat leaves (*recipe, p.286*).

CUMIN

Cuminum cyminum

Cumin is the seed of a small, herbaceous umbellifer, native to just one locality, the Nile valley of Egypt, but long cultivated in most hot regions – the eastern Mediterranean, North Africa, India, China, and the Americas. It was used in medicines in Egypt and Minoan Crete at least 4,000 years ago. The Romans used it the way we use pepper. During the Middle Ages cumin was popular in Europe, but gradually caraway took its place. Spanish explorers took it to Latin America, where it is has become a very popular spice.

TASTING NOTES

The smell of cumin is strong and heavy, spicy-sweet, with acrid but warm depth. The flavor is rich, slightly bitter, sharp, earthy, and warm, with a persistent pungency. Use sparingly.

PARTS USED

Dried seeds (fruits).

BUYING AND STORING

Cumin seeds are widely available, either whole or ground. Black cumin can be bought from Asian markets, as can dhana-jeera, a blend of cumin and coriander seeds. Seeds will keep their pungency in an airtight jar for several months, but ground cumin has a very short shelf life.

HARVESTING

Cumin stems are cut when the plants begin to wither and the seeds turn brown; they are threshed and the seeds dried in the sun. In many countries the harvest is still done manually.

Whole seeds
Cumin seeds are oval, brownish-green in color, about ¼in (5mm) long. They look like caraway but are straighter and show a characteristic pattern of longitudinal ridges.

GROUND SEEDS
For the best flavor, only grind seed as needed.

Culinary uses

The aroma of cumin is enhanced if the seeds are dry-roasted before they are ground, or fried in oil if they are used whole. Early Spanish dishes combined cumin, saffron, and anise seed or cinnamon. Now cumin is found in Moroccan couscous, in the merguez sausages of North Africa, in Tex-Mex chile con carne, and more sparingly in the spice mixes of Mexico itself. It is added to pretzels in Alsace, pork sausages in Portugal, cheese in Holland, pickled cabbage in Germany, the tapas known as Moorish kebabs (pinchitos morunos) in Spain, fish dishes in Lebanon, köfte in Turkey, and a pomegranate and walnut sauce in Syria. In all countries that like spicy food it is used in breads, chutneys, relishes, savory spice mixes, and meat or vegetable stews. It is present in curry powders and masalas, and in commercial chili powders. The combination of ground cumin and coriander gives much Indian food its characteristic pungent smell – although authentic Indian recipes can confuse the user because the word for cumin, *jeera*, is sometimes wrongly translated as caraway.

Essential to Iranian advieh, baharat, berbere, Cajun spice blend, curry powders, dukka, masalas, panch phoron, sambhar powder, zhug.

Good with beans, bread, cabbage, hard or pungent cheeses, chicken, eggplant, lamb, lentils, onions, potatoes, rice, sauerkraut, squash.

Combines well with ajowan, allspice, anise seed, bay, cardamom, chili, cinnamon, cloves, coriander, curry leaves, fennel seed, fenugreek seed, garlic, ginger, mace and nutmeg, mustard seed, oregano, paprika, pepper, thyme, turmeric.

Other cumins

True black cumin (*kala jeera*) is an expensive variety grown in Kashmir, northern Pakistan, and Iran. It is used there and in the Gulf States in the same way as ordinary cumin is used elsewhere. Black cumin should not be confused with two other spices sometimes given that name, *Nigella sativa* and *Bunium persicum*; the latter grows wild in the Middle East and is used locally.

Whole black seeds

Darker than ordinary cumin seeds, black cumin seeds are also smaller. They have a sweeter smell and a complex, mellow flavor that is somewhere between cumin and caraway. Dry-roasted seeds go into pilafs and breads.

CARAWAY

Carum carvi

TASTING NOTES

Caraway has a pungent aroma that, like the flavor, is warm and bittersweet, sharply spicy, with a note of dried orange peel and a slight but lingering hint of anise.

Caraway is a hardy umbellifer native to Asia and northern and central Europe. It is cultivated as a biennial, not only in its regions of origin but also in Morocco, the US, and Canada. The Romans used it with vegetables and fish, medieval cooks as a flavoring for soups and bean or cabbage dishes. In 17th-century England, it was popular in bread, cakes, and baked fruit; coated with sugar the seeds made comfits. Nowadays Holland and Germany are the major producers. The essential oil flavors spirits such as aquavit and Kümmel.

PARTS USED

Dried seeds (fruits).

BUYING AND STORING

Caraway seed can be bought ground, but is often used whole and is best bought that way: the seed will keep for at least 6 months in an airtight jar. The seed is easy to grind or pound when needed, but once ground it will lose strength quite quickly.

HARVESTING

Stems are cut when the fruit is ripening, dried for 7–10 days to complete the ripening, then threshed. In the home garden, caraway plants can be grown from seed in well-drained soil in full sun. Their own seeds will not ripen until the second year. Cut ripe seed clusters early in the morning when dew is on them, or the seeds may scatter too freely and the plant will self-seed. To dry, hang up the stems with a paper bag tied around the seedheads.

Whole seeds
The fruit splits into two curved seeds with tapered ends; the hard, brown shell has five lighter-colored ridges.

Culinary uses

In central Europe, and especially in the Jewish cooking originating there, caraway is used to flavor brown or rye breads, crackers, seedcakes, sausages, cabbage, soups, and stews. It gives many south German and Austrian dishes their characteristic flavor, be it pumpernickel bread or roast pork; it is used in coleslaw and in combination with juniper for sauerkraut. It accompanies Munster cheese in Alsace; the seeds are also used in Geromé, another local cheese, and in pain d'épices.

Caraway is used in the cooking of North Africa, mostly in vegetable dishes and in spice blends, such as Tunisian tabil and harissa. Morocco has a traditional caraway soup – as does Hungary, where caraway also figures prominently in goulash. Mention of caraway in Indian recipes usually stems from a mistranslation of the word for cumin; caraway itself is used only in northern India – it grows wild in the Himalayas. Turkish recipes may cite "black caraway," which is not true caraway but nigella (*p.140*).

Young leaves, less pungent than the seeds and resembling dill in taste and appearance, are an interesting addition to salads, soups, or fresh white cheese. They make a good garnish for lightly cooked young vegetables and most other dishes for which parsley could be used.

Essential to tabil, harissa.

Good with apples, breads, cabbage, duck, goose, noodles, onions, pork, potatoes and other root vegetables, sauerkraut, tomatoes.

Combines well with coriander, garlic, juniper, parsley, thyme.

Tunisian tabil spices

Used for stews and vegetable and beef dishes, tabil is a blend of caraway seeds, coriander seeds, garlic, and chili (*recipe, p.291*).

NUTMEG

Myristica fragrans

This spreading, evergreen tree, native to the Banda islands of Indonesia, often called the Spice Islands, produces fruit that yields two distinct spices, nutmeg and mace (*p.206*). In the 6th century both spices formed part of the caravan trade to Alexandria; they were probably taken to Europe by the crusaders. Their early use, in China, India, Arabia, and Europe alike, was medicinal. When the Portuguese started trading direct from the islands, nutmeg gained importance as a spice, and by the 18th century a real craze for it developed in England.

TASTING NOTES

Nutmeg and mace have a similar rich, fresh, and warm aroma. Nutmeg smells sweet but is more camphorous and pine-like than mace. The taste of both is warm and highly aromatic, but nutmeg has hints of clove and a deeper, bittersweet, woody flavor.

PARTS USED

Kernel of the seed.

BUYING AND STORING

Nutmeg is best bought whole. In airtight containers it keeps almost indefinitely and is easily ground or grated as required. Once ground, nutmeg loses its flavor rather quickly. Banda and Penang nutmeg and mace are considered to be superior to the West Indian ones.

HARVESTING

The yellowish, apricot-like fruits are gathered when ripe and the outer skin, white flesh, and mace are stripped off. The seeds, covered by a hard brown-black shell, are dried on trays for 6–8 weeks, until the kernel – the nutmeg – rattles in its shell. The shells are then cracked open and the smooth, brown nutmegs are removed and graded by size. The yield of nutmeg is about ten times that of mace, which makes the latter comparatively costly.

Whole seeds
Nutmeg seeds can be bought intact, with the kernel still inside its hard shell, and the lacy aril still clinging to the shell.

NUTMEG
The hard, outer shells are stripped from the kernels and discarded.

Culinary uses

In India, nutmeg is used more than mace because of the latter's high cost; both are used sparingly, mainly in Moghul dishes. The Arabs have long used both spices in delicately flavored mutton and lamb dishes. In North Africa, they are found in such spice mixtures as Tunisian qâlat daqqa and Moroccan ras el hanout. The Europeans have used nutmeg and mace most extensively, in both sweet and savory dishes.

Nutmeg is widely used in honey cakes, rich fruit cakes, fruit desserts, and fruit punch. It goes well in stews and in most egg and cheese dishes, as does mace. The Dutch add nutmeg lavishly to white cabbage, cauliflower, vegetable purées, meat stews, and fruit puddings; the Italians add rather more subtle quantities to mixed vegetable dishes, spinach, veal, and fillings or sauces for pasta. In France, it is used with pepper and cloves in slow-cooked stews and ragoûts. Half-ripe nutmeg, pricked all over (as is done with unripe walnuts) and soaked before being boiled twice in syrup, was once a popular sweetmeat from Malaysia.

In very large quantities nutmeg's hallucinogenic properties become toxic; drinking alcohol greatly increases the harmful effect.

Essential to baking or dessert spices, quatre épices, ras el hanout, Tunisian five spices.

Good with cabbage, carrots, cheese and cheese dishes, chicken, eggs, fish and seafood chowders, lamb, milk dishes, onion, potato, pumpkin pie, spinach, sweet potato, veal.

Combines well with cardamom, cinnamon, cloves, coriander, cumin, rose geranium, ginger, mace, pepper, rosebuds, thyme.

GRATED NUTMEG
Nutmeg kernels are best kept whole and only grated when needed. Some graters (*below*) have a lidded compartment in which the kernels can be stored.

NUTMEG *and* MACE *grow together in the same fruit; mace is the bright red aril that shows first when the fruit splits open.*

Both spices are big business in several parts of the world, yet processing them from the pods is still done largely by hand.

MACE

Myristica fragrans

Inside the apricot-like fruit of *Myristica fragrans* lies a hard seed, the kernel of which is the spice nutmeg (*p.202*). Around this seed is a lacy covering or aril; this is the second spice, mace. Both nutmeg and mace became important commodities in a trade started by the Portuguese in the 16th century, developed by the Dutch, and taken over by the English when they captured the Spice Islands in 1796. Planting began in Penang, Sri Lanka, Sumatra, and the West Indies, where Grenada now produces almost a third of the world's crop.

TASTING NOTES

Mace has nutmeg's rich, fresh, and warm aroma, but the smell is stronger and shows a lively, floral character with notes of pepper and clove. The taste of mace is warm, aromatic, delicate, and subtle with some lemony sweetness, yet it finishes with a potent bitterness.

PARTS USED

Aril surrounding the seed.

BUYING AND STORING

Ground mace is more commonly available than whole pieces (the pieces are called blades), but the latter are worth seeking out. They keep almost indefinitely in an airtight container and can be ground in a spice mill.

HARVESTING

The ripe fruit of nutmeg trees is collected and the outer skin and white flesh removed to reveal the seed. The thin, leathery, lacy, bright scarlet aril, the mace, that covers the seed is removed, pressed flat, and dried for a few hours only. Mace from Grenada is then stored in the dark for about 4 months, during which time it turns a deep orange-yellow; Indonesian mace remains orange-red.

Mace and nutmeg
Produced by the same tree, these spices are similar in taste. Mace is preferred when the dish requires a lighter flavoring.

BLADES
Mace blades are brittle, yet they exude oil when pressed with the fingernails.

GROUND BLADES
Ground mace keeps its flavor reasonably well, longer than some other ground spices.

Culinary uses

In Southeast Asia and China, mace and nutmeg are used more for their medical than for culinary properties. Elsewhere mace and nutmeg tend to be used interchangeably by cooks, although nutmeg is more widely used because it is cheaper.

Mace gives a lift to béchamel and onion sauces, clear soups, shellfish stock, potted meat, cheese soufflés, chocolate drinks, and cream cheese desserts. Mace should be used in preference to nutmeg to preserve the delicate color of a dish. Whole blades of mace can be used to flavor soups and stews, but should be removed before serving.

In Indonesia, after the mace and kernel have been removed from the nutmeg fruit, the outer flesh is candied. In Sulawesi, in particular, it is cured in the sun and sprinkled with palm sugar, whereupon it becomes almost translucent.

Essential to pickling spices.

Good with cabbage, carrots, cheese and cheese dishes, chicken, egg dishes, fish and seafood chowders, lamb, milk dishes, onion, pâtés and terrines, potato, pumpkin pie, spinach, sweet potato, veal.

Combines well with cardamom, cinnamon, cloves, coriander, cumin, rose geranium, ginger, nutmeg, paprika, pepper, rosebuds, thyme.

Aromatic garam masala

Cardamom subtly dominates the flavor of this mild masala blend, made from green or black cardamom, cinnamon, mace, black peppercorns, and cloves (*recipe, p.286*).

TURMERIC

Curcuma longa

A member of the ginger family, turmeric is a robust perennial, native to southern Asia and appreciated there since antiquity as a flavoring, a dye, and a medicine. It is one of the cheapest spices, yet throughout the region it is valued on ritual and ceremonial occasions, whether to color rice for an Indonesian wedding or to dye the skin of cows (as I once saw during the Sankali festival in Mysore). India is the main producer of turmeric and more than 90 percent of the crop is used domestically. Other producers include China, Haiti, Indonesia, Jamaica, Malaysia, Pakistan, Peru, Sri Lanka, and Vietnam.

TASTING NOTES

Fresh turmeric is crunchy, has gingery, citrus aromas, and an agreeably earthy flavor with citrus overtones. Dried turmeric has a complex, rich, woody aroma with floral, citrus, and ginger notes. The taste is slightly bitter and sour, moderately pungent, warm, and musky.

PARTS USED

Fresh and dried rhizomes.

BUYING AND STORING

Fresh turmeric is available from Asian markets. Store it in a cool, dry place or in the refrigerator vegetable crisper for up to 2 weeks; it also freezes well. Dried turmeric keeps for 2 years or more in an airtight container. Alleppey and Madras are the best Indian grades of ground turmeric. Alleppey has the higher percentage of essential oil and curcumin (yellow coloring matter), giving it a darker color and more intense flavor. Stored in an airtight container, it retains its flavor for up to a year.

HARVESTING

Rhizomes are lifted and sold fresh, or boiled to stop further maturation and then sun-dried for 10–15 days. When dry and hard, turmeric is polished, graded, and usually ground. It loses three-quarters of its weight during processing.

Whole fresh rhizome
Fresh turmeric should be firm and plump. The rhizomes are used sliced, chopped, or grated.

SLICED FRESH RHIZOME
Add pared, sliced turmeric to pickles and relishes; it has a wonderful color and taste, and is also a preservative.

Culinary uses

Turmeric binds and harmonizes the other spices with which it appears in many combinations. Use it sparingly. Fresh turmeric is used throughout Southeast Asia in spice pastes made with lemon grass, galangal, garlic, shallots, tamarind, chili peppers, and sometimes dried shrimp paste and candlenuts. Chopped or grated, it goes into laksas, stews, and vegetable dishes. Juice extracted from crushed turmeric flavors and colors rice dishes for festive meals in Indonesia and Malaysia. The fragrant leaves are used to wrap foods in Malaysia, and the shoots are eaten as a vegetable in Thailand.

In India and the West Indies, dried, ground turmeric combined with other spices is the basis of masalas, curry powders, and pastes. It imparts a warm flavor and yellow-orange color to many regional vegetable, bean, and lentil dishes. It occurs in North African tagines and stews, most notably in the Moroccan spice blend ras el hanout, and in harira, the national soup. In Iran, turmeric and dried limes flavor gheimeh, a rich stew-sauce that is spooned over rice. In the West, turmeric is used as a colorant for cheese, margarine, and some mustards. It is widely used in pickles and relishes of both eastern and western manufacture.

Essential to masalas, curry powders and pastes, ras el hanout.

Good with beans, eggplant, eggs, fish, lentils, meat, poultry, rice, root vegetables, spinach.

Combines well with chili, cilantro, cloves, coconut milk, coriander, cumin, curry leaf, fennel, galangal, garlic, ginger, kaffir lime leaves, lemon grass, mustard seeds, paprika, pepper, rau ram.

GRATED DRIED RHIZOME
Turmeric stains fingers, utensils, and clothes, so be careful when using it.

WHOLE DRIED RHIZOME
Dried rhizomes look like tough, yellow wood; they are almost impossible to grind at home, but can be grated.

ZEDOARY

Curcuma species

TASTING NOTES

Fresh zedoary has a pleasant, musky taste somewhat similar to young ginger, clean and crisp with a hint of bitterness. The taste is sometimes described as resembling that of green mango, and one of the Indian names reflects this: *amb halad* means mango turmeric.

PARTS USED

Fresh or dried rhizome; young shoots, flowerbuds, and leaves.

BUYING AND STORING

Fresh zedoary is available from Asian markets, often as "white turmeric." It has a thin, brown skin and lemon-colored, crisp flesh. It keeps in the refrigerator for 2 weeks. Dried zedoary slices can also be bought in Asian markets. The spice is often available ground; the powder is usually colored reddish-brown artificially.

HARVESTING

The fleshy, yellow rhizomes take 2 years to reach full development. Then they are lifted and sold fresh, or boiled or steamed, cut into slices, and dried. Dried slices are grayish-brown, hard, and have a rough, somewhat hairy texture.

Native to subtropical wet forest zones of Southeast Asia and Indonesia, zedoary was brought to Europe in the 6th century, when it was used as a source for medicines and perfume. During the Middle Ages it became popular in the kitchen alongside its close relation, galangal; its culinary use is now largely restricted to Southeast Asia. Increased European interest in the food of that region has led to the availability of fresh zedoary, but the dried spice remains almost unknown. In Indonesia, it goes by the misleading name of kencur, which is also used for aromatic ginger, *Kaempferia galanga*.

CRUSHED DRIED RHIZOME
The aroma of dried zedoary is musky and agreeable, with a hint of camphor. The flavor is pungent, resembling that of dried ginger, less acrid but rather bitter and finishing on a citrus note.

Culinary uses

In Indonesia, young zedoary shoots are eaten and the flowerbuds are used in salads; the long, aromatic leaves wrap and flavor fish. In Thailand, peeled and shredded or finely sliced fresh zedoary is added to salads or raw vegetables to serve with nam prik. In Mumbai, a fresh zedoary and vegetable soup is popular. In Indonesia and India, fresh zedoary goes into pickles. Chopped fresh zedoary mixed with shallots, fresh lemon grass, and cilantro makes a good spice paste for cooking vegetables in coconut milk. In Southeast Asia, dried zedoary is used in the preparation of curries and condiments, and in dishes for which dried turmeric or dried ginger might be used. It goes well with chicken and lamb in southern Indian and Indonesian dishes.

Good with chickpeas, curries and stews, fish, lentils, poultry, Asian soups, green vegetables.

Combines well with chili, cilantro, coconut milk, garlic, ginger, kaffir lime leaves, lemon grass, turmeric.

Other zedoaries

Used interchangeably as a spice by cooks, *C. zedoaria* has round and stubby rhizomes and *C. zerumbet* has long ones. The latter has a milder taste and, because its pale yellow color contrasts sharply with the darker hue of similar-looking turmeric, it is often called white turmeric, khamin khao in Thai.

The roots of two other species, *C. leucorrhiza* and *C. angustifolia*, are used to make the starch called Indian arrowroot or tikor, used as a thickening agent and for baby food.

Fresh rhizome

C. zerumbet is increasingly available in fresh form. Combine with other fresh spices or use as a crisp garnish. The brown skin is removed before use.

CURRY LEAVES

Murraya koenigii

Curry leaves come from a small, deciduous tree that grows wild in the foothills of the Himalayas, in many parts of India, northern Thailand, and Sri Lanka. The tree has been cultivated in southern India for centuries, mostly on a small scale in private gardens for use in the kitchen, but more recently also on a commercial scale. Plantations have recently been established in northern Australia.

TASTING NOTES

When bruised, fresh leaves are intensely aromatic, giving off a musky, spicy odor with a citrus note. The taste is warm and pleasant, lemony and faintly bitter. Dried leaves have virtually no flavor – doubling the amount asked for in a recipe has very little effect on the taste.

PARTS USED

Leaves.

BUYING AND STORING

Fresh curry leaves can be bought in Asian markets, where they may be labeled meetha neem or kari (or kadhi) patta. They are best stored in an airtight plastic bag in the freezer, but even in the refrigerator will keep for a week or more. Dried leaves can be found in Asian markets too, but don't bother with them.

HARVESTING

Although the tree is deciduous, leaves are available for picking most of the year in the tropics. From the farms of Tamil Nadu and Andhra Pradesh, the stems are shipped fresh, to be sold in small bundles. Vacuum-drying is the best way to retain the fresh color and preserve at least some of the aroma.

Fresh leaves
The slender stems may have as many as 20 small, bright green leaves.

Culinary uses

Curry leaves are stripped from the stems just before they are added to the dish. They are used extensively in the cooking of south India, much as cilantro is used in the north. From many domestic gardens they go straight into the vegetarian dishes of Gujarat. They are also used in long-simmered meat stews and in the fish curries of Kerala and those of Chennai (Madras), the only region of India where curry leaves are a standard ingredient in curry spice mixes. Elsewhere they are usually added to curry dishes only for the last five minutes of cooking.

Sri Lankan curry mixtures also routinely include curry leaves. These mixtures are darker in appearance and taste than the Indian ones: the ingredients are more highly toasted and include spices native to the island, such as cinnamon and cardamom. Indian emigrants took curry leaves to Fiji, while others made them an important ingredient in South African Tamil cooking.

Quickly shallow-fried in ghee or oil with mustard seeds, asafetida, or onion, curry leaves can be used as a flavoring at the start of cooking, before other ingredients are added. More often the same combination of spices is used as a tempering, added at the end, for instance as the basic bagaar or tadka that goes over most lentil dishes. Chopped or crushed leaves are used in chutneys (notably coconut chatni), relishes, and marinades for seafood. Whole leaves are added to pickles.

Westerners are just beginning to appreciate the delicate, spicy flavor the leaves impart to curries without the heat often also associated with those dishes. Beginners may want to use whole sprigs and remove them before serving, but cooked leaves are quite soft and the taste soon becomes pleasantly addictive.

Good with fish, lamb, lentils, rice, seafood, most vegetables.

Combines well with cardamom, chili, cilantro, coconut, cumin, fenugreek seed, garlic, mustard seed, pepper, turmeric.

Sri Lankan curry powder

This curry powder is made from curry leaves, coriander, cumin, fenugreek, rice, chili, black peppercorns, cloves, green cardamom, and cinnamon (*recipe, p.288*).

ACHIOTE

Bixa orellana

Achiote is the orange-red seed of the small evergreen annatto tree, native to tropical South America. In pre-Columbian times the seeds were already widely used as a colorant for food, fabrics, and body paint; in the Western world they are still used as such in butter, cheese, smoked fish, and in cosmetics. Brazil and the Philippines are the main producers, but the tree grows throughout Central America, the Caribbean, and in parts of Asia. Also sometimes called annatto seed, achiote is its name in the Nahuatl language of Mexico.

TASTING NOTES

The seeds have a faint flowery or peppermint scent, and a delicate, earthy, slightly peppery taste with a hint of bitterness. They impart an agreeably earthy taste to food if used in quantities much larger than those required for coloring only.

PARTS USED

Dried seeds.

BUYING AND STORING

Achiote seeds are available, whole or ground, from Latin American, Spanish and East Indian markets. Seeds should be a healthy rust-red; avoid any that are dull and brownish. Powdered achiote is often mixed with cornstarch, sometimes with other spices such as cumin. Seeds and powder should be kept in an airtight jar out of the light. Seeds will keep for at least 3 years.

HARVESTING

The large, rose-like flowers develop into prickly, orange-red pods at the end of the branches; each contains about 50 brick-red, angular seeds. When ripe the pods are harvested, split open, and macerated in water. The pulp embedding the seeds is pressed into cakes for processing into dyes; the seeds are dried as a spice.

GROUND SEEDS
Dried achiote seeds are very hard and are most easily ground in an electric spice mill.

Whole dried seeds
Whole seeds are mostly used as a colorant. Soak ½ tsp in 1 tbsp boiling water for 1 hour, or until the water is a deep orange color.

Culinary uses

Achiote seeds can be soaked in hot water to obtain a colored liquid for stocks and stews, or to color rice. In the Caribbean, the seeds are fried in fat, over low heat, then discarded before the now deep-golden or orange fat is used for cooking. The fat, or oil treated the same way, can be stored in a sealed glass jar in the refrigerator for several months.

In Jamaica, achiote may be used with onion and chili peppers in the sauce for saltfish and ackee, often called the national dish. In the Philippines, achiote is ground and added to soups and stews, mostly for color effect; it is an essential ingredient in the famous pork-and-chicken dish, pipián. In Peru, it is used in marinades, especially for pork. In Venezuela, it is combined with garlic, paprika, and herbs to make a popular condiment called aliño criollo. In Mexico, it goes into achiote paste – the Yucatán recado rojo – basis of the region's best-known dish, pollo pibil (marinated chicken wrapped in banana leaves and cooked in a pit oven); the paste is equally good spread on fish or pork before grilling. In Mexico, achiote is also sometimes added to the dough for tamales, the stuffed cornmeal-paste rolls steamed in a corn-husk wrapping. In Vietnam, cooks use oil dyed with achiote as the base of braised dishes to give them color.

Essential to pipián, recado rojo.
Good with beef, egg dishes, fish (especially salt cod), legumes, okra, onions, pork, poultry, rice, squash, sweet peppers, sweet potatoes, tomatoes, most vegetables.
Combines well with allspice, chili, citrus juice, cloves, cumin, epazote, garlic, oregano, paprika, peanuts.

Recado rojo
Red achiote paste is indispensable to the cooking of Mexico's Yucatán peninsula. Achiote seeds are combined with black peppercorns, cloves, cumin and coriander seeds, dried oregano, garlic, and bitter orange juice or wine vinegar. Small hot red chili peppers may be added (*recipe, p.295*).

CAPERS

Capparis species

The caper bush is a small shrub that grows wild all around the Mediterranean, as far south as the Sahara and as far east as northern Iran, although it may have originated in dry regions of western and central Asia. Capers are successfully cultivated in many countries with a similar climate. In really hot countries the wild variety is likely to be *C. spinosa*, which has, as the name suggests, spines; the cultivated caper is usually *C. inermis*, without spines. In northern India, the variety used is *C. decidua*.

TASTING NOTES

The taste of pickled capers (once the vinegar or salt is rinsed off) is piquant, fresh, salty, and somewhat lemony. The pungency in its flavor derives mainly from a mustard oil, glycoside, not unlike those found in horseradish and wasabi.

PARTS USED

Unopened flowerbuds; unripe fruits.

BUYING AND STORING

Capers from southern France are graded from nonpareilles to capottes, according to size – the smaller ones being the best. Other important producers are Cyprus, Malta, Italy, Spain, and California. Pickled capers keep for a long time provided they are kept covered by the pickling liquid, which should not be renewed or added to, least of all with vinegar.

HARVESTING

Caper buds are picked by hand when they are the right size, wilted for a day or two, graded to size, then put in vinegar or dry-salted. The intensely flavored, large, Sicilian capers are always dry-salted, as are top-quality small ones. Salting preserves taste and texture better than pickling does.

Capers
Capers are commonly pickled in vinegar or dry-salted. Their quality depends on their place of origin, the preserving method, and on their size.

Culinary uses

Capers are an important ingredient in many sauces, such as ravigote, remoulade, tartar, and tomato-based salsa alla puttanesca. English caper sauce, still mentioned as traditional with mutton, is equally good with firm fish. Most fish can be cooked or garnished with capers in a variety of ways; so can chicken. Salt cod is often accompanied by capers and green olives, a standard combination for fish dishes in Sicily and the Aeolian islands; in Spain, with fried fish, capers are combined with almonds, garlic, and parsley. With black olives, capers are the basis of tapenade and are also good in casseroles of chicken or rabbit. On their own capers enhance many dishes of the fattier meats, and have become one of the standard garnishes on pizza. In Hungary and Austria, they flavor Liptauer cheese. Both capers and caper berries can be eaten on their own, like olives, or used as a relish with cold meats, smoked fish, and cheese. Used with discretion they can liven up a salad.

Pickled or salted capers should be rinsed before use. When capers are used in cooked dishes they should be added toward the end as lengthy cooking tends to bring out an undesirable, bitter flavor.

Essential to tapenade, various sauces.
Good with artichokes, eggplant, fish, green beans, gherkins, fatty meats (lamb), olives, potatoes, poultry, seafood, tomatoes.
Combines well with anchovies, arugula, basil, celery, garlic, lemon, mustard, olives, oregano, parsley, tarragon.

Caper berries

Caper berries are the small, semi-mature fruit of *Capparis* species. They are usually preserved in vinegar. Their taste is similar to but less intense than that of capers.

Leaves and shoots

Lightly pickled leaves and shoots are available in jars. The leaves and immature buds have a pleasant caper flavor, but the thicker stems can be spiny and are best discarded.

AJOWAN

Trachyspermum ammi

Ajowan, native to southern India, is a small, annual umbellifer closely related to caraway and cumin. The seeds are a popular spice throughout India, and the plant is also grown and used in Pakistan, Afghanistan, Iran, and Egypt. Ajowan's essential oil was the world's main source of thymol (an antiseptic phenol) until the introduction of synthetic thymol.

TASTING NOTES

When crushed, ajowan seeds have a strong, rather crude smell of thyme. The taste, largely determined by thymol in the essential oil, is hot and bitter. If chewed on their own, ajowan seeds numb the tongue.

PARTS USED

Dried seeds.

BUYING AND STORING

Ajowan can be bought from Indian markets, where it may also be called ajwain or carom. The seeds will keep indefinitely in an airtight jar. Bruise them before use to release their flavor; they are easily ground in a mortar.

HARVESTING

Ajowan stems are cut in May or June, when the seeds are ripe; they are dried, then threshed.

GROUND SEEDS
Seeds are often used whole or crushed. Do not grind until needed.

Whole seeds
The seeds are small, ridged ovals, grayish-green to reddish-brown, and resemble celery seeds.

Culinary uses

Ajowan should be used judiciously: too much will make a dish taste bitter. Cooking mellows the flavor to resemble that of thyme or oregano, but stronger and with a peppery note.

Ajowan has a natural affinity with starchy foods, and in southwestern Asia is used in breads (paratha), savory pastries (pakora), and fried snacks (especially those made with chickpea flour). It is also used to flavor pickles and root vegetables. It is often cooked with dried beans – it relieves flatulence and for that reason is also chewed as a digestive – and is an ingredient in some curry mixes. It is very popular in the vegetarian cuisine of Gujarat, where it is used in batters for bhajias and pakoras, and with chili peppers and cilantro to flavor the crêpes called pudlas. In northern India, ajowan is fried in ghee with other spices before being added to a dish. Probably its best-known use in the West is in the flavoring of a crunchy snack called Bombay mix. With lemon juice and garlic it makes an excellent rub for fish fillets; leave the fish to marinate for an hour or two before frying.

Ammi majus, a related umbellifer known as bishop's weed or false Queen Anne's lace, and also as Ethiopian cumin, is said to be the ajowan used in Ethiopian cooking.

Essential to berbere, chat masala.
Good with fish, green beans, legumes, root vegetables.
Combines well with cardamom, cinnamon, cloves, cumin, fennel seed, garlic, ginger, pepper, turmeric.

Chat masala

Used in small quantities with fruit and vegetable salads, this masala includes ajowan seed, amchoor powder, asafetida powder, black peppercorns, black salt, cumin seeds, ground hot chili, dried pomegranate seeds, and dried mint (*recipe, p.287*).

FENUGREEK

Trigonella foenum-graecum

Native to western Asia and southeastern Europe, fenugreek has a long history of use as a flavoring and medicine. The Latin name *Trigonella* refers to the triangular shape of the flowers, and *foenum-graecum* means Greek hay, a reference to its use as a fodder crop in classical times, a use for which it is still better known in Europe today. Although prized in Middle Eastern and Indian cooking, fenugreek has yet to capture the imagination of Western cooks.

TASTING NOTES

Fresh leaves are grassy and mildly pungent with astringent tones. In dried leaves there is a fragrant note of hay. The aroma of the raw seeds can be identified as the overriding smell of some curry powders. Their taste is celery- or lovage-like and bitter; the texture is floury.

PARTS USED

Fresh and dried leaves; seeds.

BUYING AND STORING

Iranian and Indian markets may have fresh leaves; keep in the refrigerator and use within 2–3 days. Dried leaves should be green with no yellowing; store in an airtight container. Seeds are available from the same sources and from spice merchants; store them in the same way and they will keep their flavor for a year or more. Ground fenugreek soon loses its flavor, so roast and grind it as needed. Wholefood markets may sell fenugreek sprouts.

HARVESTING

An annual, fenugreek can be grown from seed in rich soil in full sun. If you grow it you can gather both seeds and leaves. Plants bear white or yellow flowers that develop into narrow, beaked, light brown seedpods. These are harvested when ripe and the seeds dried.

Fresh leaves
Fenugreek is a small, slender plant with leaves that somewhat resemble loosely shaped clover leaves.

SPROUTED SEEDS
Dress fenugreek sprouts with vinaigrette and serve as a salad with tomatoes and black olives.

WHOLE SEEDS
Brief dry-roasting or frying mellows the flavor of the seeds and gives them a nutty, burnt-sugar or maple-syrup taste, but do not heat for too long or the bitterness is intensified. Use immediately after roasting. Seeds should be soaked for several hours if they are to be used in a paste.

Culinary uses

A good source of protein, minerals, and vitamins, fenugreek is widely used by vegetarians in India.

Indian cooks make extensive use of fresh fenugreek (methi) leaves as a vegetable, cooked with potatoes, spinach, or rice. The leaves are also chopped and added to the dough for naans and chapattis. Dried leaves are used to flavor sauces and gravies. Fenugreek often contributes bitterness to the Bengali vegetable stews called shuktas. Fresh or dried leaves are essential to the classic Iranian herb and lamb stew, ghormeh sabzi, and are often used to flavor herb omelettes.

Seeds are used in Indian pickles and chutney, in the southern spice blend sambhar powder, and in panch phoron from Bengal. They go well with lentils and with fish, are much used in dals and fish curries in the south, and ground with flour to make the local dosai breads. In Egypt and Ethiopia, fenugreek also flavors breads, and it is a constituent of Ethiopian berbere spice mixture. In Turkey and Armenia, ground fenugreek is combined with chili and garlic and rubbed onto pastirma, the excellent dried beef of the region. In Yemen, fenugreek seeds, first soaked in water to reduce their bitterness, are used in hilbeh, a potent dip that is spread on bread or, on grander occasions, served with a meat broth and dishes of vegetables.

The maple flavor of roasted fenugreek has led to its use in baked goods and artificial maple syrup.

Essential to sambhar powder, panch phoron, berbere, hilbeh.

Good with fish curries, green and root vegetables, lamb, legumes, potatoes, rice, tomatoes.

Combines well with cardamom, cinnamon, cloves, coriander, cumin, fennel seed, garlic, dried limes, nigella, pepper, turmeric.

MASTIC

Prunus mahaleb

Mastic is a resin produced by cutting the bark of one variety of lentisk tree native to the Greek island of Chios. The tree has many veins, rich in mastic, just beneath the bark of the trunk. The pieces of resin, some oval, some oblong, are called tears. They are semi-transparent, with a light, golden color. Mastic has a brittle texture, but when chewed it takes on the consistency of chewing gum.

TASTING NOTES

Mastic has a light, pine aroma; the taste is pleasantly mineral-like, lightly bitter, and very mouth-cleansing.

PARTS USED

Tears of dried resin. Mastic is powdered before use so that it blends evenly into a dish.

BUYING AND STORING

Mastic is expensive and is sold in small quantities, but you need only a small amount at a time. It is available from Greek and Middle Eastern markets and from spice merchants. Store in a cool place.

HARVESTING

The slow-growing evergreen trees start to produce mastic when 5–6 years old, and continue producing for another 50–60 years. Mastic is harvested from July to October. The gnarled trunks are cut diagonally and the sticky resin oozes out; some collects on the trunk, some falls to the ground. In contact with the air the resin hardens into "tears," which are collected, washed, then cleaned by hand and laid out to dry.

Culinary uses

Mastic's main use is in baking, desserts, and sweetmeats. Greeks use mastic to flavor festive breads, especially the Easter bread tsoureki, and Cypriots in their Easter cheese pastries, flaounes. Most of the crop is exported to Turkey and the Arab states. With sugar and rose or orange-flower water, mastic is used to flavor milk puddings, dried fruit and nut fillings for pastries, Turkish delight, and preserves. It gives a pleasant, chewy texture to ice creams. Mastic soup, mastic stew, and a mastic sweetmeat are made in Izmir, the Turkish port city in sight of Chios.

Good with almonds, apricots, fresh cheese, dates, milk desserts, pistachio nuts, rose water and orange-flower water, walnuts.

Combines well with allspice, cardamom, cinnamon, cloves, mahlab, nigella, poppy seed, sesame.

Mastic tears
Used as a breath-freshener and digestive aid, mastic was the original chewing gum.

SAFFLOWER

Carthamus tinctorius

The thistle-like safflower is an ancient crop, traditionally grown on small plots for local consumption, whether as medicine, dye, food colorant, or spice. Today it is grown in many parts of the world, mainly as an oilseed crop. Unscrupulous merchants sometimes pass it off to tourists as the much more expensive saffron, and indeed it is known as bastard or false saffron in some countries.

TASTING NOTES

Safflower has little aroma, but smells herbaceous and somewhat leathery; the flavor is bitter and lightly pungent. Although safflower contains the coloring agents carthamin and saflor yellow, it lacks essential oils to provide aroma.

PARTS USED

Dried flowers.

BUYING AND STORING

Safflower is available from some spice merchants, and in countries where it is used it can be bought in markets. It may be sold as loose, dried petals or as compressed flowerheads. In Turkey, where it is in common use, it may be sold as Turkish saffron. Store in an airtight container. The flavor fades after 6–8 months.

GROW YOUR OWN

Flowers are gathered in summer and sun-dried, then crushed.

Culinary uses

Safflower will color rice, stews, and soups a light gold, although it does not give the depth of color or complex flavors of saffron. It is often used in this way in India and in the Arab world. Petals may be added straight to the dish or infused in warm water to obtain a coloring liquid. Portuguese cooks use safflower in seasoning pastes for fish stews and in the vinegar sauces that accompany fried fish. In Turkey, it may be used in cooking, but more frequently it is a garnish for meat and vegetable dishes. Safflower oil is high in the monounsaturated fatty acids that are beneficial in the prevention of heart disease.
Good with fish, rice, root vegetables.
Combines well with chili, cilantro, cumin, garlic, paprika, parsley.

Dried petals
Safflowers are the globe-shaped flowers of a tall, upright plant with prickly edged, oval leaves. When growing, the flowers are deep red with yellow tips; when dried, they are yellow to bright orange to brick-red in color.

PEPPER

Piper nigrum

The history of the spice trade is essentially about the quest for pepper. Peppercorns and long pepper from India's Malabar coast reached Europe at least 3,000 years ago; trade routes were fiercely protected, empires were built and destroyed because of it. In 408AD the Goths demanded pepper as part of their tribute when they laid siege to Rome; later, pepper was traded ounce for ounce for gold, and used as currency to pay rents, dowries, and taxes. In volume and value pepper remains the most important spice. India, Indonesia, Brazil, Malaysia, and Vietnam are the main producers.

TASTING NOTES

Black pepper has a fine, fruity, pungent fragrance with warm, woody, and lemony notes. The taste is hot and biting with a clean, penetrating aftertaste. White pepper is less aromatic, and can smell musty, but it has a sharp pungency with a sweetish afternote.

PARTS USED

Immature and ripe fruits.

BUYING AND STORING

Sun-drying is preferable for peppercorns: if dried at high temperatures in artificial heat some of the volatile oils are lost. Black and white pepper rapidly lose their aroma and flavor when ground, so it is best to buy whole berries and grind in a pepper mill or crush in a mortar, as needed. In airtight containers pepper-corns will keep for a year.

HARVESTING

To produce black pepper, immature green berries are picked, briefly fermented, and then dried. During drying the pepper shrivels, becomes wrinkled, and turns black or dark brown. For white peppercorns, berries are picked when yellowish-red and almost ripe, then soaked to soften and loosen the outer skin. Once this is removed they are rinsed and sun-dried.

Whole peppercorns
Large, uniform, dark brown to black peppercorns command the highest price. Aroma and flavor are more important than pungency. The best white pepper is considered to be Muntok from Indonesia.

CRUSHED PEPPER
Crushed peppercorns can be pressed into steaks to be grilled, and release their flavors in marinades.

GROUND PEPPER
Ground white pepper is more attractive in creamy sauces than black.

Pepper has different characteristics in different places of origin and is therefore classified according to where it is grown. Broadly speaking, the flavor of pepper is determined by its essential oil content, while its content of the alkaloid piperine accounts for its bite. Black pepper has both aroma and pungency. White pepper contains less essential oil than black because the oil is present in the hull and is removed in cleaning; that also explains why white pepper, although pungent, has little aroma. Over time the strength of the flavor compounds in the essential oil diminishes.

The essential oil and piperine content varies according to the origins of the pepper. Pepper of the best quality is Indian Malabar; it has a fruity aroma and a clean bite. Tellicherry is the grade with the largest berries. Indonesian lampong pepper has more piperine and less essential oil, so it is more pungent than aromatic; the berries are smaller and gray-black in color. Sarawak pepper from Malaysia has a milder aroma than Indonesian berries, but is hot and biting. Brazilian pepper has a low piperine content and is rather bland. Vietnamese is light in color and mild.

RED PEPPERCORNS
Red or pink peppercorns are fully ripe fruits, usually available preserved in brine or vinegar. They have a soft outer shell with a delicate, almost sweet, fruity taste. The inner core provides a moderate, lingering heat.

GREEN PEPPERCORNS
Green pepper has a light aroma, and an agreeable, fresh pungency; it is not overpoweringly hot. Green peppercorns are preserved by freeze-drying or dehydration, or packed in brine or vinegar. Keep fresh green and red pepper berries in the refrigerator.

PEPPER *growing peacefully on its vine gives no hint of the fierce warfare and empire-building that have marked its past.*

As the condiment that invariably accompanies salt in the West, pepper remains the most important spice in volume and value.

Culinary uses

Pepper is neither sweet nor savory, merely pungent. Although mostly used in savory foods, it can be used with fruits and in some sweet breads and cakes. It brings out the flavor of other spices and retains its own flavor well during cooking.

The aroma of black pepper can be detected in foods all round the world. Even the chili lovers of Latin America and southern Asia reach for the peppercorns to flavor cooking liquids, stocks, salad dressings, and sauces, or crush them to add to spice mixtures and marinades. Ground pepper is rubbed on fish and meat to be grilled or baked; it flavors rich stews and curries; and it is used to season simple buttered vegetables and smoked fish.

White pepper is used in pale sauces and cream soups to preserve their attractive appearance. Use it judiciously because the bite is sharp.

In France, mignonette pepper, a mixture consisting of black and white peppercorns, black for aroma and white for strength, is often used.

Rinse brined peppercorns before using. Green pepper combines beautifully with sweeter spices, such as cinnamon, ginger, bay, fennel seed, and lemon grass, to flavor pork, chicken (rub butter mixed with crushed peppercorns and ginger under the skin before roasting), lobster, crab, and fish, especially salmon. It also makes an excellent steak au poivre and combines well with Dijon mustard. Red peppercorns can be used in similar ways.

Essential to baharat, berbere, garam masala, ras el hanout, quatre épices.
Good with most foods.
Combines well with basil, cardamom, cinnamon, cloves, coconut milk, coriander, cumin, garlic, ginger, lemon, lime, nutmeg, parsley, rosemary, thyme, turmeric.

Mignonette pepper
Black and white *P. nigrum* peppercorns are combined in this French seasoning.

Long pepper *P. longum* and *P. retrofactum*

The long pepper species *P. longum* and *P. retrofactum* originated in India and Indonesia respectively. Long pepper is mostly used in Asia, East Africa, and North Africa in slow-cooked dishes and pickles. The spikes of minute fruits are harvested green and sun-dried, when they resemble gray-black catkins. Long pepper is usually used whole. It smells sweetly fragrant, and initially resembles black pepper in taste, but it has a biting, numbing aftertaste. Indonesian long pepper is slightly longer and more pungent than the Indian.

CUBEB

Piper cubeba

Cubebs are the fruit of a tropical vine of the pepper family native to Java and other Indonesian islands. They were cultivated in Java from the 16th century and for 200 years cubebs were a popular substitute for black pepper in Europe. By the 19th century they had become almost unobtainable. Cubebs are now scarcely known in the West, but there is a revival of interest in them among spice aficionados.

TASTING NOTES

Cubebs have a warm, pleasant aroma, lightly peppery but also allspice-like, with a whiff of eucalypt and turpentine. When raw the flavor is strongly pine-like, pungent, and glowing with a lingering, bitter note, but cooking brings out the allspice flavor.

PARTS USED

Immature fruits.

BUYING AND STORING

Cubebs are not easy to find, except from some spice merchants. Buy sparingly: although they keep their aromatic properties well, they are only used in small amounts. Stored whole in an airtight container they will keep for 2 years or more. Grind as needed.

HARVESTING

Cubebs are harvested green and sun-dried to a deep brown-black.

Culinary uses

Cubebs, also known as Java pepper and tailed pepper, are used locally in Indonesian cuisine and to a lesser extent in Sri Lanka, where they are also grown. They were traded from the 7th century by Arab merchants and formerly had a role in Arab cooking, one that persists mainly in their presence in the Moroccan spice mixture ras el hanout. Cubebs are used to flavor North African lamb or mutton tagines, and as a substitute for allspice in long-cooked stews. Cubebs are best suited to meat and vegetable dishes.

Cubebs are sometimes confused with the Ashanti pepper, *P. guineense*, an African species, and the Benin pepper, *P. clusii* – these also have stems and are often called false cubebs.

Combines well with bay, cardamom, cinnamon, curry leaf, rosemary, sage, thyme, turmeric.

Whole fruits
Cubebs are furrowed and wrinkled, slightly larger than peppercorns, and have a short, straight tail. Some berries contain a single seed, others are hollow.

AROMATIC LEAVES

Various species

The aromatic leaves of a variety of trees are used as flavorings in many parts of the world. They are often described, somewhat misleadingly, as being rather like bay leaves. The way they are used may be similar, but their aromatic properties are very different. Included here are a few that are little known, but which are slowly becoming available outside their region of origin.

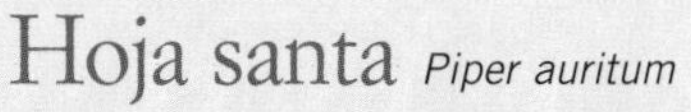

Hoja santa *Piper auritum*

This relative of *P. nigrum* grows in Central America and in Texas. Fresh leaves have a lightly pungent, musky aroma and flavor, with a hint of mint and anise; dried leaves have a warm, anise-fennel aroma with a citrus note.

Lá lót *Piper sarmentosum*

The lightly spicy leaves of this pepper are used in Thailand (where it is called chaa phluu) and Vietnam (where it is lá lót). These large, glossy, round to heart-shaped leaves are sometimes mistaken for betel pepper leaves (*P. betle*), which are chewed in India as a digestive aid.

TASTING NOTES

For aromas and flavors, see individual captions.

PARTS USED

Fresh and dried leaves.

BUYING AND STORING

Most dried aromatic leaves are available by mail order and via the internet. Dried leaves hold their flavor quite well, but if you can get fresh leaves it is worth freezing them between sheets of freezer wrap. Fresh and dried hoja santa leaves are available in Latin markets, fresh lá lót leaves in Southeast Asian markets, dried avocado leaves in Latin markets, and dried salam leaves in Indonesian markets.

HARVESTING

Avocado trees are sold in some nurseries. Aromatic leaves can be picked at any time from the tree and used fresh. Leaves are also laid out in the shade to dry before being packed for sale.

Culinary uses

Large, soft, heart-shaped hoja santa leaves feature in Mexican cooking, particularly in the states of Veracruz and Oaxaca. They are used to wrap fish or chicken to be steamed or baked; to line or layer casseroles of fish or chicken; and as a flavoring for tamales. They are also used with other herbs in green mole sauces. The leaves work well with chili peppers, garlic, Mexican mint marigold, and paprika. Avocado leaves make a differently flavored substitute as a wrapping; chopped fennel leaves in tamales will achieve a flavor similar to that of hoja santa.

The Thais wrap morsels of food – roasted coconut, peanuts, young ginger, shallots, chili peppers, and cubes of lime or other fruits – in lá lót leaves and serve them as a snack. In Vietnam, the leaves are used to wrap spring rolls and small pieces of beef to be grilled, and are added to soups.

Salam leaves are used fresh in soup-like mixed vegetable dishes, in stir-fried vegetables, or with beef, braised chicken, or duck, and in Bali with roast or grilled pork. Dried leaves are less fragrant than fresh. The aroma and flavor develop with cooking. Salam leaf combines well with other Southeast Asian aromatics: galangal, ginger, garlic, chili peppers, lemon grass, tamarind, and coconut milk, as well as pepper, cinnamon, cloves, and nutmeg.

Avocado leaves are used, fresh and dried, in some regions of Mexico to flavor tamales, stews, or grilled meats, or as wrappers. The leaves are usually toasted lightly and used whole or ground.

Salam *Eugenia polyantha*

The salam tree, a relative of the clove tree, is native to Malaysia and Indonesia. The leaf is used in Indonesian cooking. There is no real replacement for the lemony, aromatic leaves, but you could try curry leaves.

Avocado *Persea americana*

The glossy leaves of the avocado have a light hazelnut-anise or licorice flavor. If you live in a climate where the avocado will grow, it is worth cultivating for its wonderful fruit alone; the scented leaves come as a bonus.

MOUNTAIN PEPPER

Tasmannia lanceolata

Mountain pepper comes from a genus of small trees native to Australia (the uplands of Tasmania, Victoria, and New South Wales); it is unrelated to the pepper vine, *Piper nigrum*. Aboriginal peoples may never have used the leaves and berries of the tree as a flavoring, but early colonists soon discovered that ground berries could be used as a condiment; in 1811, the colonial historian Daniel Mann noted that this "spice tree possesses a more pungent quality than pepper."

TASTING NOTES

All parts of the tree are aromatic. The leaves have a warm, woody aroma with a citrus note; the taste is similar. Fresh berries initially taste of sweet fruit; a camphor-turpentine note soon follows, with an intensely pungent bite that leaves a numb sensation in the mouth.

PARTS USED

Fresh and dried leaves; fresh and dried berries.

BUYING AND STORING

In Australia, fresh and dried whole leaves and berries are available; fresh berries will keep for several weeks in a sealed plastic bag in the refrigerator. Berries are more potent than leaves, and both are stronger than true pepper, so use with caution. Elsewhere, dried, ground leaf is most commonly found. Buy both leaf and berries in small quantities since they are used sparingly and the flavor diminishes once they are ground, even when stored in an airtight container.

HARVESTING

Leaves may be used fresh, or dried flat in the same way as bay leaves. Ripe berries are dried or preserved in brine.

Fresh leaves
Mountain pepper leaves have a lingering heat and a kick that recalls Sichuan pepper (*p.236*) rather than black pepper. Dried leaves are stronger than fresh.

DRIED BERRIES
Dried mountain pepper berries can be ground in a peppermill and are often sold crushed, looking rather like oily, cracked black pepper.

Culinary uses

When substituting mountain pepper for true pepper, use half the amount of ground leaf as you would true pepper, and even less if you are using the berries. Mountain pepper is often used in combination with other Australian bush spices, such as wattle (*p.143*) and lemon myrtle (*p.181*). A mixture of mountain pepper leaf, lemon myrtle, and thyme is good in marinades or as a dry rub for lamb; in Australia, the same mixture is used with local meats such as kangaroo and emu.

The berries are very potent. The best way to use them is to add a few, crushed or whole, to long-cooked meat stews and hearty bean dishes or mixed vegetable soups; prolonged cooking dissipates their sharpness and pungency somewhat and allows the flavor of the pepper to permeate the dish. The berries could also go into a classic French sauce poivrade, which is good with beef and rich, well-flavored game, in particular hare or venison.

The leaves and berries of a related tree, *T. stipitata*, are sold as Dorrigo pepper, named for the Dorrigo mountains where it grows.

Good with game meats, beef, lamb, legumes, pumpkin and other winter squashes, root vegetables.

Combines well with bay, garlic, juniper, lemon myrtle, marjoram, mustard, oregano, parsley, red wine, rosemary, thyme, wattle.

Australian dry rub for lamb

Using ingredients from two indigenous Australian plants, this dry rub combines ground mountain pepper leaf and ground lemon myrtle leaf, with the additional flavor of crushed thyme.

GRAINS OF PARADISE

Amomum melegueta

Grains of paradise are the seeds of a perennial, reed-like plant with showy, trumpet-shaped flowers, indigenous to the humid tropical coast of West Africa, from Liberia along the Gulf of Guinea to Nigeria. Among their other names are Guinea pepper, Melegueta pepper, and, less often, alligator pepper. The spice, originally brought to Europe in the 13th century via Saharan caravan routes, was appreciated as a replacement for true pepper. Present-day production is still in the same region, with Ghana the main exporter.

TASTING NOTES

Grains of paradise are related to cardamom, but their taste does not have that spice's camphor element. Grains of paradise taste pungently hot and peppery, with a fruity note. The aroma is similar but fainter.

PARTS USED

Seeds.

BUYING AND STORING

Grains of paradise are not easy to obtain, but they are stocked by some spice merchants and can be bought from West Indian or African markets. Stored whole in an airtight container they will keep their flavor for several years. Grind them as needed.

HARVESTING

The fruit is a capsule, yellow streaked with red, fig-shaped and fig-sized. The capsule dries and becomes brown, hard, and nut-like; the seeds are chestnut brown and look like tiny, blunt pyramids.

GROUND SEEDS Grains of paradise grind down into a fine, aromatic powder.

CRUSHED SEEDS Crushing breaks down the red-brown coats of the seeds to reveal the white flesh inside.

Whole seeds The seedhead encloses a white pulp in which there are embedded 60–100 small, red-brown seeds, the grains of paradise.

Culinary uses

Grains of paradise are little used in Western cooking now, but did remain popular long after true pepper became more readily and cheaply available. They were used to spice wine and beer, and in hot sack (Spanish white wine) they were a popular 17th-century tonic. But by the mid-19th century, interest in the spice had all but disappeared. In Scandinavia, they are still used in akvavit. Only in West Africa, and to a lesser degree in the West Indies, are they still a much-used seasoning; in the Mahgreb they are one of the components of Moroccan ras el hanout and Tunisian qâlat daqqa. Grains of paradise are excellent in mulled wine, in braised lamb dishes, and with vegetables, including eggplant, potatoes, and pumpkin. Grind them before use and add at the last stage of cooking. Pepper mixed with a little cardamom and ginger may be used as a substitute.

Essential to qâlat daqqa, ras el hanout.

Good with eggplant, lamb, potatoes, poultry, rice, squash, tomatoes, root vegetables.

Combines well with allspice, cinnamon, cloves, cumin, nutmeg.

Qâlat daqqa

This Tunisian five-spice blend is mainly used with lamb and vegetable dishes. It comprises grains of paradise, black peppercorns, cloves, nutmeg, and cinnamon (*recipe, p.291*).

SICHUAN PEPPER AND SANSHO

Zanthoxylum simulans and Z. piperitum

These two spices, the one traditional to the cooking of Sichuan province in China, the other to Japan, are the dried fruits of prickly ash trees. Also called flower pepper, Japanese pepper, and formerly fagara (the prickly ashes are no longer classified in the genus *Fagara*), the spice should not be confused with black and white peppercorns harvested from the *Piper nigrum* vine.

TASTING NOTES

Sichuan pepper is very fragrant, woody, somewhat pungent, with notes of citrus peel. Sansho is tangy and quite sharp. Both have a numbing or tingling effect in the mouth. Sansho leaves, called kinome and used as a garnish in Japan, have a minty-basil aroma.

PARTS USED

Dried berries; fresh leaves.

BUYING AND STORING

Sichuan pepper is sold whole or ground in Asian markets and by spice merchants. Sansho is usually available as a coarse powder from the same sources. Split berries will keep their fragrance longer than the powder; store in an airtight container. The season for kinome is short and the leaves are not easily found outside Japan. If you do find them, keep for a few days in a plastic bag in the refrigerator.

HARVESTING

The reddish-brown berries are sun-dried, then split open and the rather bitter, black seeds are usually discarded. Kinome leaves are gathered and used fresh in spring.

Whole and split berries
Remove the bitter seeds from whole berries. Split berries are sold with the seeds removed, but check the package and discard any seeds you find.

GROUND BERRIES
Berries are dry-roasted alone or with salt, then ground and used as a condiment.

Culinary uses

Sichuan pepper is an important constituent of Chinese five-spice powder. For many dishes the berries are dry-roasted for 3–4 minutes. The dry-roasting releases their aromatic oils, but they smoke as they get hot, so control the heat carefully and discard any blackened berries. Let cool, then grind; an electric mill does the job well. Sift and discard the husks, then store in an airtight container to use as a condiment. It is best to make only a little at a time because the flavor soon dissipates. The roasted pepper is also used to make spiced salt. Sichuan pepper is used with poultry and meat to be roasted, grilled, or fried, and also with stir-fried vegetables. Try it with green beans, mushrooms, and eggplant.

Sansho is used as a table condiment in Japan, and is also an ingredient of seven-spice blend, shichimi togarashi. The spice is most commonly used with fatty fish, meat, and poultry to mask the smell.

Kinome has a refreshing, mild flavor and a tender texture, which make it a popular flavoring herb or garnish for soups, simmered dishes, grills, and cooked salads.

Essential to five-spice powder, Chinese spiced salt (Sichuan pepper); seven-spice blend (sansho).

Combines well with black beans, chili, citrus, garlic, ginger, sesame oil and seeds, soy sauce, star anise.

Seven-spice powder

This is the Japanese spice blend shichimi togarashi, or "seven-flavors chili," which is used to flavor udon (wheat noodles), soups, nabemono (one-pot dishes), and yakitori. In addition to chili flakes and sansho, it includes black and white sesame seeds, dried tangerine peel, flakes of nori (laver), and poppy seeds (*recipe, p.284*).

FRESH GINGER

Zingiber officinale

TASTING NOTES

Fresh ginger has a rich and warm aroma with a refreshing, woody note and sweet, citrus undertones. The flavor is hot and tangy, and has a bite. Rhizomes harvested young are milder and less fibrous than those harvested later in the season.

PARTS USED

Fresh rhizomes.

BUYING AND STORING

Fresh ginger rhizomes should be hard, unwrinkled, plump, and heavy. They keep well in the vegetable crisper of the refrigerator for a week to 10 days. Ginger is also available chopped and preserved in an acid medium, and frozen as a paste. Ginger in syrup and crystallized ginger will keep for up to 2 years in a cool, dry place. Pickled ginger keeps for 6 months.

HARVESTING

Ginger rhizomes are dug up 2–5 months after planting, while still tender. For use fresh, they are washed, dried for a few days, and then stored. Ginger to be preserved or crystallized is peeled, cut into pieces, and soaked in brine for some days, then in water. It is boiled in water, then in syrup, and either left in syrup or dried and dusted with sugar.

Ginger is a rhizome, an underground stem of a lush plant that is somewhat like a small bamboo. It has been an important spice for more than 3,000 years. Cultivated in the southern provinces of China and in India, it was a staple in the diet of Confucius, and Sanskrit literature records its pungent spiciness in Indian cooking. In Asia, ginger is most commonly used fresh, except in masalas and other dry spice mixtures. Most recently ginger has begun to be cultivated in Queensland in northern Australia.

Whole fresh rhizome
Fresh ginger has a pale tan skin stretched tautly around the yellow flesh, which should be crisp and not fibrous.

SLICED FRESH RHIZOME
Sliced rhizome can be left unpeeled for use in marinades or dishes from which it will be removed before serving.

Culinary uses

Fresh ginger is used in savory dishes throughout Asia. In China, it is grated, chopped, sliced, or shredded for cooking fish and seafood, meat, and poultry because it neutralizes fishy and meaty smells. Large, crushed pieces are left unpeeled for extra flavor and discarded when the dish is ready. Among vegetables it is particularly used with cabbage and greens. It goes into soups, sauces, and marinades. In Japan, fresh ginger has many uses, one of which, as in China, is to mask fish odors. Freshly grated ginger and its juice are used in tempura dipping sauce, in dressings, and with grilled and fried foods. Koreans add a little chopped ginger to many dishes, and the popular pickle, kimchi, relies on ginger and garlic for its flavor.

Galangal is generally preferred to ginger in Southeast Asia, although the two are used together in some dishes. Ginger and garlic are natural partners: many north Indian dishes are based on a ginger-garlic-onion paste, used to flavor cooking oil before meat or vegetables are added. In the south the combination is more likely to be ginger, garlic, chili peppers, and turmeric. It goes into chutneys and relishes, marinades for meat and fish, and into salads. Ginger and lime juice with chat masala makes a good salad dressing for legumes; or with chili peppers, sugar, fish sauce, and water a Vietnamese dipping sauce for fish.

To obtain ginger juice, grate fresh ginger (a fine Japanese grater does the job well) or grate pieces in a food processor, then squeeze the juice from the shredded or chopped ginger through cheesecloth. You could also add a little water to ginger in the processor and then strain. Ginger juice is used in sauces and marinades where a subtle flavor of ginger is needed, and is also sprinkled on meat.

Combines well with basil, chili, cilantro, coconut, fish sauce, galangal, garlic, kaffir lime, lemon grass, lime juice, mint, scallions, soy sauce, tamarind, turmeric.

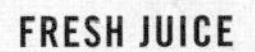

FRESH JUICE
Fresh ginger rhizomes are easily grated to produce an aromatic juice for use in sauces and dressings.

Young or spring ginger
Very pale, young ginger with a moist, translucent skin is sometimes found in Asian markets in springtime. The flesh is creamy-white, the tips of the shoots pink, and the flesh crisp. It has a pure, clean fragrance; the taste is definitely of ginger, but without bite. The tender rhizomes can be used without peeling. Slices can be stir-fried and eaten as a vegetable or lightly cooked with fish and seafood, especially crab. In China, it is often pickled. Add finely sliced young ginger and green garlic to salads of green beans, tomatoes, or baby beets. It is surprisingly good with cold roast beef.

Pickled ginger
In Japan, knobs of ginger are pickled in sweet vinegar and served in wafer-thin slices with sushi as a digestive condiment, called gari. The taste is quite mild and pickling turns the ginger pink. I have found that well-drained gari can be shredded and used to good effect in fish, seafood, and vegetable salads.

Beni-shoga is shredded ginger, dyed to a striking red by pickling and by being preserved with perilla leaves. More pungent than gari, it is good with crab and other seafood.

Hajikami shoga are pickled ginger shoots that are served with

PICKLED SHOOTS
Sometimes garishly colored, sometimes a delicate pink, hajikami shoga is made with the tender, young shoots of the ginger plant.

SHREDDED RHIZOME
Pungent beni-shoga is preserved first in salt, then vinegar. This vivid red pickle offers a sharp contrast in color and taste when served with seafood.

SLICED RHIZOME
Familiar to sushi lovers, gari is finely sliced ginger rhizome that is pickled in sweet vinegar.

grilled fish. Gari, beni-shoga, and hajikami shoga are all available from Asian markets.

Preserved ginger
Ginger in syrup and crystallized ginger can be eaten as sweetmeats on their own or used as flavorings for sweet sauces, ice cream, cakes, and tarts. China and Australia are the main producers and both kinds are widely available.

Mioga ginger
The Japanese and Koreans share an enthusiasm for the mildly flavored young shoots and buds of mioga ginger, *Z. mioga*. They are sliced and used to flavor soups, tofu, salads, vinegared dishes, and pickles to accompany grilled foods. This cold-tolerant ginger is now being grown in New Zealand for export. It is available pickled, and fresh when in season, from Asian markets.

Ginger flower
Also called torch ginger, the showy flowers of a wild ginger, *Nicolaia elatior*, are used in Thailand and Malaysia. Buds and young shoots are eaten raw with nam prik, sliced into salads, shredded over laksa soups, or used to add a mild pungency to fish curries. The buds are difficult to find outside Asia.

Aromatic ginger, *see p.180*.

CRYSTALLIZED GINGER
To make this lightly pungent sweetmeat, knobs of young ginger are cooked in a thick syrup, air-dried, and rolled in sugar.

GINGER IN SYRUP
Knobs of young ginger are poached several times in a dense syrup so that the syrup penetrates the flesh. It is sometimes called stem ginger because both stems and rhizomes are used.

FRESH MIOGA BUDS
Mioga buds are gathered in spring. They are fragrantly herbal rather than hot, and have a delicate, crunchy texture.

DRIED GINGER

Zingiber officinale

Middle Eastern and European dishes developed using dried ginger rather than fresh because it was in the dried form that ginger arrived via the caravan routes. The Assyrians and Babylonians used it in cooking, as did the Egyptians, Greeks, and Romans. Ginger was in use as a table condiment throughout Europe by the 9th century; such was the demand by the 16th century that the Spanish and Portuguese were planting it in their new tropical territories.

TASTING NOTES

Whole, dried ginger is less aromatic than fresh (*p.238*), but once bruised or powdered it is warm and peppery with light, lemony notes. The taste is fiery, pungent, and penetrating.

PARTS USED

Dried rhizomes.

BUYING AND STORING

Dried ginger can be bought as pieces of rhizome, slices, and powder. Quality is important in buying dried ginger; the best is pungent and lemony; poor-quality ginger is sharp and biting with a fibrous texture. Rhizomes are hard to grind; they can be rasped on a fine grater, but it is easier to buy a small amount ready-ground. Stored in an airtight container, good-quality rhizomes will keep their flavor for 2 years or more.

HARVESTING

Ginger to be dried is harvested 9–10 months after planting, when it is fully mature, more pungent, and more fibrous. The rhizomes are dried in the sun. For the best quality the skin is scraped off first; other grades may be left unpeeled, or boiled before peeling and drying. Ginger may also be bleached.

GROUND DRIED RHIZOME
Ground ginger is essential to many breads, cakes, and pastries. Dried ginger has a different taste to fresh, and the one should not be substituted for the other.

Dried rhizome pieces
Dried, pale beige rhizomes release a warm aroma when bruised. Whole pieces are most used in pickling spices.

Culinary uses

In Asia, dried ginger is used in many pungent spice mixtures. In the West, it was one of the cornerstones of early spice blends and today is used in quatre épices and pickling spices. It is an excellent flavoring for carrots, pumpkin and other winter squashes, and sweet potato. In the Arab countries, it is used with other spices in tagines, couscous, and slow-cooked meat dishes with fruit. It is a popular baking spice for cakes and cookies, and in commerce is much used for drinks such as ginger beer and ale. Fruits marry well with ginger, especially bananas, pears, pineapples, and oranges, and it is good for spicing preserves.

Essential to berbere, curry and masala blends, five-spice powder, pickling spices, quatre épices, ras el hanout.

Combines well with cardamom, cinnamon, cloves, dried fruits, honey, nutmeg, nuts, preserved lemons, paprika, pepper, rose water, saffron.

Types of dried ginger

The quality and flavor of ginger vary greatly according to its origin. In commerce, different grades indicate how the ginger has been prepared before drying. Peeled Jamaican ginger has long been considered the best for its delicate aroma, pale color, and fine-textured powder. It is expensive and in short supply. India is the main exporter of dried ginger; the best quality is Cochin, which is light brown, partly peeled, and has a pungent, lemony odor and taste. Chinese dried ginger is more lemony and less pungent than Cochin. The African varieties, principally from Sierra Leone and Nigeria, are often unpeeled and tend to be harsh and peppery with a note of camphor. Ginger from Australia has distinct lemon notes.

Quatre épices

This classic French blend is used in the preparation of pork and other meats. The four spices are black peppercorns, cloves, dried ginger, and nutmeg (*recipe, p.293*).

ALLSPICE

Pimenta dioica

TASTING NOTES

Allspice has a pleasantly warm, fragrant aroma. The name reflects the pungent taste, which resembles a peppery compound of cloves, cinnamon, and nutmeg or mace. Most of the flavor is in the shell rather than in the seeds it contains.

PARTS USED

Dried berries.

BUYING AND STORING

Allspice can be bought whole or ground. Whole berries, which look like large, brown peppercorns, are infinitely preferable; they crush easily if you need just a little allspice, and they keep in an airtight jar almost indefinitely.

HARVESTING

In Jamaica, berries are mostly harvested from trees cultivated in plantations. They are hand-picked when full size but still green. After a few days' sweating they are dried on black concrete platforms for up to a week. As they dry the berries turn red-brown. When dry – determined by the seeds rattling inside the shell – they are winnowed and graded by size. Larger, inferior, wild berries are still gathered in the rainforests of Mexico and Guatemala.

Allspice is native to the West Indies and tropical Central America. Columbus found it growing in the Caribbean islands and thought he had found the pepper he was looking for, hence allspice's Spanish name *pimienta* (pepper), which was anglicized as pimento. That name was later altered to Jamaica pepper because most of the crop, and certainly the best quality, came and still comes from that island. Allspice is the only important spice that still comes almost exclusively from its region of origin – which also makes it the only one grown almost exclusively in the New World.

Whole dried berries
Jamaican allspice has the highest level of the essential oil that determines the taste. One of the main components of the oil is eugenol, which is also the principal flavoring element of cloves.

GROUND BERRIES
Ground allspice can lose its strength rather quickly.

Culinary uses

Long before the discovery of the Americas, the people of the islands used allspice to preserve meat and fish. The Spaniards learned from them and used allspice in escabeches and other preserving liquids. In Jamaica, it is still an important ingredient in jerk seasoning pastes that are rubbed onto chicken, meat, or fish for grilling. It is also used extensively, crushed rather than ground, in breakfast breads, soups, stews, and curries. In the Middle East, allspice is used to season roasted meats. It is used in pilafs and goes into some Indian curries. In Europe, allspice is either used whole, as a pickling or mulling spice, or ground, to give a gentle, warm flavor to cakes, desserts, preserves, and fruit pies. Allspice enhances the flavor of pineapple, plums, black currants, and apples. Most of the world's crop goes to the food industry for use in commercial ketchups and other sauces, as well as sausages, meat pies, Scandinavian pickled herrings, and sauerkraut.

Essential to jerk spice mixtures.

Good with eggplant, most fruit, pumpkins and other squashes, sweet potatoes and other root vegetables.

Combines well with chili, cloves, coriander, garlic, ginger, mace, mustard, pepper, rosemary, thyme.

Sweet baking spice

Ground together, allspice berries, coriander seeds, cloves, mace, nutmeg, and cinnamon make up the sweet baking spice that is called mixed spice in Britain (*recipe, p.293*).

CLOVES

Syzyium aromaticum

The clove tree is a small, tropical evergreen with fragrant leaves. Its crimson flowers seldom develop, as unopened flowerbuds constitute the spice. Native to the Moluccas, volcanic islands now part of Indonesia, cloves reached Europe overland through Alexandria in Roman times. The Spice Islands were conquered by the Portuguese and then the Dutch, who harshly defended their monopoly until, in 1772, a French official smuggled seedlings to Ile-de-France (Mauritius). These days Zanzibar, Madagascar, and Pemba in Tanzania are the main exporters; Indonesia uses nearly all its vast production itself.

TASTING NOTES

The aroma of cloves is assertive and warm, with notes of pepper and camphor. The taste is fruity but also sharp, hot, and bitter; it leaves a numbing sensation in the mouth. As in allspice, eugenol in the essential oil is mainly responsible for the characteristic taste.

PARTS USED

Dried flowerbuds.

BUYING AND STORING

Whole cloves vary greatly in size and appearance, but should be clean and intact. Good cloves exude a small amount of oil if pressed with a fingernail. They will keep for a year in an airtight jar. They are hard and must be ground in an electric mill. Ground cloves should be dark brown; lighter, gritty powders are likely to be mostly made from flower stems, which contain less of the volatile oil. The powder loses its strength quite quickly.

HARVESTING

Clove buds appear in small clusters, twice a year, from July to September and November to January. They are picked before flowering, when they are mature but only just turning pink at the base. Drying in the sun on woven mats, they lose most of their weight and turn reddish to dark brown.

GROUND CLOVES
Ground cloves contribute their assertive warmth to most masalas and curry powders, to five-spice powder, berbere, and baharat.

Whole cloves
Good-quality cloves have reddish-brown stems and a lighter crown. They are rough to the touch and should snap cleanly.

Culinary uses

Cloves must be used sparingly, for they easily overpower other spices. They are equally good with sweet and savory foods. They go into baked goods, desserts, syrups, and preserves almost everywhere. In Europe, cloves are used as a pickling or mulling spice. The French press a single clove into an onion to flavor a stew, stock, or sauce; the Dutch use them more liberally in cheese and the English often too liberally in apple pie. In Germany, they are found in spiced breads, in the US in ham glazed with brown sugar. The candied walnuts of Turin have a clove stuck into one end. In the Middle East and North Africa, cloves go into spice blends used to flavor meat dishes or rice, often in combination with cinnamon and cardamom. In much of Asia, they appear in curry powders. In India, they are essential to garam masala, in China to five-spice powder, in France to quatre épices (with black pepper, nutmeg, and dried ginger). In Indonesia, cloves are mixed with tobacco for the very popular kretek cigarettes, which crackle as they burn and have a unique aroma.

Essential to quatre épices, five-spice powder, garam masala.

Good with apples, beets, red cabbage, carrots, chocolate, ham, onions, oranges, pork, pumpkin and other squashes, sweet potatoes.

Combines well with allspice, bay, cardamom, cinnamon, chili, coriander, curry leaves, fennel, ginger, mace, nutmeg, tamarind.

Five-spice powder

This Chinese blend of cloves, star anise, cassia, fennel seed, and Sichuan pepper goes well with chicken, duck, and pork (*recipe, p.284*).

CLOVES *grow in plantations of tall, dense trees that would produce remarkably delicate flowers if the buds were not*

picked before opening. The buds are still dried and sorted in the traditional way, without recourse to modern equipment.

ASAFETIDA

Ferula species

Asafetida is a dried, resinous gum obtained from three species of *Ferula*, giant fennel, a tall, fetid-smelling, perennial umbellifer native to the dry regions of Iran and Afghanistan, where it is also cultivated. Imported from Persia and Armenia, it was much appreciated in Roman cooking when silphium from Cyrenaica was no longer obtainable. It came to India via the Moghul empire and has remained a popular spice there, although it is only cultivated in the north, in Kashmir.

TASTING NOTES

Powdered asafetida has a strong, unpleasant smell, reminiscent of pickled garlic and as pervasive as that of truffles. The taste is bitter, musky, and acrid – nasty when sampled alone but becoming pleasantly onion-like when the spice is briefly fried in hot oil.

PARTS USED

Dried resin from the stems and rhizomes or taproots.

BUYING AND STORING

In India, asafetida is sold in a wide range of qualities; the lighter, water-soluble hing is preferred to dark, oil-soluble hingra. In the West, buy it in solid or powdered form. In an airtight tin (which also contains the smell), solid asafetida keeps for several years, while the powdered form lasts for about a year.

HARVESTING

Just before the flowering, the stems of plants at least 4 years old are cut and earth scraped away to expose the large taproots, which are also cut. A milky latex exudes; this hardens and darkens to a reddish-brown on exposure to the air. Care is taken to shield this process from sunlight, which would spoil the juice. The gum is collected and more cuts are made until the root dries up, usually after about 3 months.

Whole tears and lumps
Asafetida is available either as "tears," small individual pieces, or "lumps" consisting of tears processed into a uniform mass. Solid asafetida has little smell, but crushing releases the sulfur compounds in the volatile oil responsible for the odor.

Culinary uses

Asafetida is essentially an Indian spice. In western and southern India, it flavors soups, vegetable and legume dishes, pickles, relishes, and sauces. Its flavor is particularly appreciated in the cooking of the Brahmin and Jain sects, whose diet forbids the use of garlic or onions. It is very good in many fish dishes. In its native Iran, it is not used at all, and in Afghanistan it is only used, with salt, to cure meat that is dried in the sun for winter use.

Asafetida should always be used sparingly. It can be used in any cooked dish where garlic would be appropriate; even a tiny amount enhances the flavor of a dish or spice mix, such as sambhar powder. A piece could be rubbed on a grill or griddle before cooking.

Essential to chat masala, some curry powders, sambhar powder.

Good with fresh or salted fish, grains, grilled or roasted meat, legumes, most vegetables.

CRUSHED TEARS
Solid asafetida is prepared for use by grinding it in a mortar with an absorbent powder such as rice flour. Only a small piece is needed for an individual dish.

GROUND TEARS
Asafetida is most widely available as a powder, mixed with a starch or gum arabic to keep it from lumping. Brown powder is coarse and strong; yellow powder (which owes its color mostly to added turmeric) is more mellow.

MUSTARD

Brassica species

Black mustard, *B. nigra*, and white or yellow, *B. alba*, are native to southern Europe and western Asia, brown, *B. juncea*, to India. White mustard has long been naturalized in Europe and North America. The Romans, who made prepared mustard, introduced the plant to England. In medieval Europe, mustard was the one spice ordinary people could afford. The French started to add other ingredients in the 18th century, while the English refined the powder by removing the husks before grinding the kernels.

TASTING NOTES

Whole mustard seed has virtually no aroma. When ground it smells pungent, and cooking releases an acrid, earthy aroma. When chewed, black seeds have a forceful flavor; brown ones are slightly bitter, then hot and aromatic; the larger white seeds have an initial sickly sweetness.

PARTS USED

Dried seeds.

BUYING AND STORING

White and brown mustard seed is widely available. Black is hard to find; brown can be used instead but is less potent. Ground white mustard is relatively coarse as it contains the husk. Mustard powder is the finely sifted flour of seed kernels; its bright color is due to added turmeric. All forms keep well, provided they are kept scrupulously dry.

HARVESTING

Mustard is harvested by cutting the stems when the seeds are fully developed but not quite ripe, to avoid the pods bursting open and spilling their contents. Black mustard is particularly prone to this, which is why it has largely been replaced by brown in commercial production. The stems are dried, then threshed.

Whole seeds
Mustard's pungent taste is determined by an enzyme, myrosinase, which is activated by water.

WHITE SEEDS
Sandy-yellow mustard seeds are much larger than the brown or Asian variety.

BLACK SEEDS
Black seeds are larger than brown and are oblong rather than round. Their heat affects the nose and eyes as well as the mouth.

Culinary uses

In Western cooking, whole white mustard seeds are used primarily as a pickling and preserving spice, and in marinades.

Brown seeds (known as rai) have increasingly taken the place of black in much Indian cooking. They figure prominently in the cooking of southern India, where whole seeds are usually first dry-roasted or heated in hot oil or ghee to bring out an attractive nutty flavor for a tadka or baghar. The dishes are not pungent because the hot oil does not activate myrosinase. In Bengal, ground raw seed is used in pastes for curries, especially fish in mustard sauce. Mustard oil – viscous, deep golden, and quite pungent – is made from brown mustard seed and several lesser varieties. It is widely used as a cooking oil, most of all in Bengal, where it is heated to smoke point to reduce the smell, then cooled before use. Its piquant flavor contributes to the distinctive taste of many Indian dishes.

Powdered mustard flavors barbecue sauces and meat dishes and works well with most root vegetables. Add it toward the end of cooking because heat dissipates its strength fairly quickly.

The seeds are not the only part of the mustard plant to be used. Fresh sprouted shoots are often used in salads. In Japan, and now in Europe, the beautiful, feathery mizuna is grown as a salad herb; it makes its appearance alongside Chinese red mustard and other varieties in gourmet mixtures. Shredded leaves make a pleasant garnish for root vegetables, and potato and tomato salads. In Vietnam, leaves are used to wrap stuffings of pork, shrimp, and herbs.

MUSTARD OIL
Mustard oil is easier to digest after brief exposure to a very high temperature.

BROWN SEEDS
Brown seeds have a long-lasting pungency, almost as intense as that of black seeds.

Prepared mustards

To prepare blended mustards, the seeds are soaked in water to activate the enzyme myrosinase; once the required heat has been achieved the enzyme's activity is stopped. The resulting flavor is determined largely by the acidic liquid used – vinegar gives a mild tang, wine or verjuice a more spicy pungency, beer a real heat. Water gives the sharpest, hottest taste, but will not stop the enzyme's activity and therefore does not make a stable mustard. Prepared mustards are best stored at room temperature even when opened; they will keep for 2–3 months, but they may dry out a little and will steadily lose their flavor.

French mustards, milder than the English, are made in three forms. Bordeaux is brown, although made from white seed, and contains sugar and herbs, usually tarragon. Dijon, made from brown (but husked) mustard seed and white wine or verjuice, is paler and stronger, with fewer additives. Meaux is quite hot, made from crushed and ground grains, a step toward the many wholegrain mustards, some of them made more fiery by the addition of green peppercorns or chili peppers.

In Germany, Bavarian mustard is of the Bordeaux type, but Düsseldorf mustard is a pungent version of Dijon. Zwolle, in Holland, makes a mustard flavored with dill that would be great with gravad lax. Mild and runny American mustard is made from white mustard, with rather too much turmeric. The aromatic, mild Savora mustard was developed in England around 1900 and is popular throughout South America. English mustard powder is made up with cold water, then left

MEAUX MUSTARD
The town of Meaux has produced mustard since the 17th century. Usually sold in stoneware jars, this grainy mustard has a bite followed by a mouth-filling roundness. An excellent table mustard.

BORDEAUX MUSTARD
In Bordeaux mustard some of the hulls are left in the mixture, giving a darker appearance. It is mildly spicy with a hint of sweetness, and is good with sausages and in cheese dishes.

DIJON MUSTARD
Dijon mustard has an appellation contrôlée; the name refers to a style of mustard that is pale, smooth, and clean-tasting. The classic mustard for sauces and salad dressings, it is highly prized throughout the world.

for about 10 minutes to develop its clean and pungent taste. Once made up it will not keep.

Prepared mustards are mainly used as a condiment with oxtail or other meat casseroles, or a "tracklement" with roast beef, ham, and other cold meats. The various kinds are equally good in many cold sauces, from vinaigrette to mayonnaise, as dressings for green or other salads, vegetable dishes, and plain cooked or smoked fish. Added toward the end of the cooking process, they will spice up a wide variety of casseroles, such as rabbit with mustard sauce. They also go well with many cheese dishes. Sweet mustards, made with honey or brown sugar, make good glazes for chicken, ham, or pork, and can be a piquant addition to some fruit salads.

Essential to panch phoron, sambhar powder.

Good with roast and grilled beef, cabbage, strong cheeses, chicken, curries, dals, fish and seafood, cold meats, rabbit, sausages.

Combines well with bay, chili, coriander, cumin, dill, fennel, fenugreek, garlic, honey, nigella, parsley, pepper, tarragon, turmeric.

Other mustards

B. juncea has a yellow variety, used in Japan in cooking (stuffed into lotus roots fried in tempura batter) and as a condiment, made English-style and very hot, to go with oden, a fishy stew, and in dressings and pickles.

Field mustard, *B. campestris*, and **rapeseed**, *B. napus*, are both used to produce oil.

AMERICAN MUSTARD
Mild, sweet American mustard has devoted followers among hot-dog fanciers, but the turmeric that colors it bright yellow can also make the taste dusty.

MOUTARDE AU CASSIS
This wholegrain mustard from Dijon contains crème de cassis liqueur, which gives it a rich, fruity flavor and its red color.

ENGLISH MUSTARD
English mustard powder is a mixture of finely ground brown and white seeds, rice or wheat flour, and spices. Fiery and slightly acidic, it is good with roast beef and oxtail stew.

TARRAGON MUSTARD
Tarragon mustard is made by adding tarragon and sometimes green food coloring to a pale mustard. It is good in sauces for fish and chicken dishes.

CHILI PEPPERS

Capsicum species

Native to Central and South America and the Caribbean islands, chili peppers (or chile or hot peppers) have been cultivated there for thousands of years. Columbus took plants back to Spain, and the Spaniards named them *pimiento* (pepper) because of their pungency. Capsicum fruits are still called peppers even though they are not related to the pepper vine. Today chili peppers are the biggest spice crop; hundreds of different varieties are grown in all tropical regions and eaten daily by about a quarter of the world's population.

Whole fresh chili peppers
Chilies come in many colors, shapes, and sizes; they can be as tiny as a young pea or as long as 12in (30cm). Many of them stimulate the appetite not only with pungency but with fruity, floral, smoky, nutty, tobacco, or licorice flavors.

TASTING NOTES

Chili peppers range in taste from mild and tingling to explosively hot. The fruits of *C. frutescens* are generally hotter than those of *C. annuum*, and those of *C. chinense* are hottest of all. Large, fleshy varieties tend to be milder than small, thin-skinned peppers.

PARTS USED

Fresh and dried fruits. Immature chilies are green; they ripen to yellow, orange, red, brown, or purple, and may be used fresh or dried.

BUYING AND STORING

All fresh chilies should be shiny, smooth-skinned, and firm to the touch. They keep in the refrigerator vegetable crisper for a week or more. They can be blanched and frozen, but if frozen raw most lose their flavor and piquancy. Dried chilies vary in appearance according to the variety. A specialist merchant will tell you the country of origin, the type, flavor characteristics, and heat level. Dried chilies keep almost indefinitely in an airtight container.

HARVESTING

Most chilies are grown as annuals. Green chilies are picked 3 months after planting; varieties normally used ripe are left longer on the plant. Chilies may be dried in the sun or artificially.

Culinary uses

Chili peppers are an excellent source of vitamins A and C, and provide that added benefit to the millions of people who eat them as a cheap means of pepping up a bland and unvarying diet. Chilies are used extensively in their native region, throughout Asia, in Africa, and in the American southwest. India is the largest producer and consumer of chilies, fresh green or dried red (which are usually ground), and each region uses its local varieties. Mexican cooking makes the most sophisticated use of chili peppers, both fresh and dried.

The pungent bite of chilies is due to the presence of capsaicin in their seeds, white fleshy parts, and skin. The capsaicin content depends on the variety of chili pepper and its degree of ripeness; removing seeds and veins will reduce the heat of the chili. Capsaicin stimulates the digestive process and the circulation, which induces perspiration and has a cooling effect on the body.

Essential to berbere, chili powder (which is actually a combination of spices), curry powders and pastes, harissa, jerk seasoning, kimchi, moles, nam prik, pipián, romesco sauce, sambals.
Combines well with most spices, bay, coriander, rau ram, coconut milk, lemon and lime juice.

The heat of chili peppers is rated on a scale of 1–10, from 1 for mild peppers to 10 for extremely hot scotch bonnets.

GROUND HOT CHILI
Ground chili is made from dried hot red chilies. Heat rather than flavor is often the characteristic of these products, **5–9/10** on the heat scale, depending on the variety.

DRIED CHILI OR PEPPER FLAKES
Produced from mild to moderately hot chili peppers, **2–5/10**, these are often used as a table condiment in Hungary, Turkey, and the Middle East. Hotter chili flakes are used as a condiment in Korea and Japan.

CHILI THREADS
Red chili peppers are an essential Korean ingredient. Very fine chili threads are used as a garnish.

WHOLE DRIED CHILI PEPPERS
Drying changes the flavors of chilies. Similarly, the taste of green, immature chilies alters as they ripen and redden.

Chili products

Ground chili, chili pastes, sauces, and oils are produced worldwide. Good-quality ground chili smells fruity, earthy, and pungent and contains traces of natural oils that will stain the fingers slightly. A light orange color indicates the inclusion of a high proportion of seeds, which makes for a sharper taste. Thin, pungent sauces are labeled salsa picante or hot pepper sauce; some combine chilies with astringent ingredients such as limes or tamarind. Thick sauces, based on tomatoes, onions, garlic, and herbs, may be mild or hot and are often sweetened. Indonesian sambals and Thai chili jam are among the hottest. The Chinese use soy sauce, black beans, ginger, and garlic to create medium to hot sauces. Korean gochu-jang is a sticky condiment made with chilies, soybean paste, and rice flour.

CHILI POWDER
This blend of ground chili, cumin, dried oregano, paprika, and garlic powder is used to flavor chile con carne and other southwestern dishes. **1–3/10**

CHILI OIL
Seasoning oil made with dried red chilies is available commercially, but it is easy to make your own: fill one-third of a bottle with dried chili peppers, top up with sunflower oil, close tightly, and leave for 1 month. In Sichuan, crushed dried chilies are added to very hot oil, left to cool for several hours, then strained to produce a bright red oil, used in many cold sauces and on its own as a dip.

YELLOW GROUND CHILI
The color of ground chilies ranges from yellow to red and mahogany. Yellow ground chili is used in South America; it can be mild or hot.

CAYENNE OR RED PEPPER
The most common ground chili, cayenne is made from small, ripe chili peppers grown worldwide. The flavour is tart, slightly smoky, and intensely pungent. **8/10**

THIN SAUCES
Thin sauces are made from crushed chilies blended with spices and vinegar to produce fiery liquids. Tabasco sauce is the best-known example.

CHILI SAUCES
Chili sauces are made in most regions where chili peppers are grown. The simplest types are made from whole chilies preserved in brine or vinegar. Thick sauces, which may be cooked or made from raw ingredients, are used as dips and condiments.

CHILI JAM AND SAMBAL
Chili pastes and thick sauces enliven stir-fries and slow-cooked dishes. At the end of this book are recipes for chili jam (*p.299*) and sambals (*pp.300–301*).

Mexico

In Mexico, fresh and dried versions of a chili pepper often have different names. Specific chilies are required for specific dishes; using the wrong one can alter the balance of flavors. Large, fleshy poblanos are used as a vegetable, often stuffed; jalapeños and serranos appear in salsas, stuffings, and pickles; dried anchos and pasillas are often ground to thicken a sauce. When used fresh, green chili peppers tend to be preferred, and they are often charred and peeled before being used.

Serrano *C. annuum*

Mid-green, cylindrical, crisp-textured, with a concentrated, fresh, grassy flavor and very pungent seeds and veins. It ripens to bright red. Commonly used in sauces. **6–7/10**

Jalapeño *C. annuum*

Bright green, some with dark patches, torpedo-shaped, quite fat with crisp, thick flesh. Sometimes roasted and peeled. Jalapeños have a light flavor and are medium-hot. Red and fully ripe they are sweeter and less hot. Also sold canned en escabeche (pickled) and widely used as a table condiment. **5–6/10**

Habanero *C. chinense*

Lantern-shaped, mid-green ripening to yellow, orange, and deep red, thin-fleshed, and fruity. Mostly used in Yucatán, raw or roasted, to flavor beans and sauces. For a hot sauce, blend roasted habaneros with salt and lime juice. **10/10**

Chilaca *C. annuum*

Thin, deep red and shiny, with vertical ridges. The deep flavor has a hint of licorice. Roasted and peeled, they are used in vegetable dishes, with cheese, and in sauces. Sometimes available pickled. **6–7/10**

OTHER CHILI PEPPERS
Mulato (*C. annuum*) is similar to ancho, but chocolate brown; the taste is full-bodied, sweeter than ancho, with notes of dried cherries, and mild to medium-hot. Mostly toasted and ground for sauces. **3–5/10**
De arból (*C. annuum*) is seldom found fresh; it remains bright red when dried. Slender, curved, and pointed, with thin flesh and a smooth skin, it is searingly hot and has a somewhat tannic flavor. Soaked and then puréed, de arbóls are used in stews and as a table sauce. **8/10**
Poblano (*C. annuum*) is dark green and shiny, with a ridge around the base of the stem. The shape is triangular and tapering, and the flesh is thick. Roasted and peeled, poblanos are stuffed or fried. They pair well with corn and tomatoes, and have a rich flavor. **3–4/10**
Pasilla (*C. annuum*) is the dried chilaca, slender, wrinkled, and almost black. It has an astringent yet rich flavor with herby notes that is complex and long-lasting. Toasted and ground it is used in table sauces or in cooked sauces for fish. **6–7/10**
Güero (*C. annuum*) is pale yellow, smooth, long, and pointed, with thin flesh. The taste is lightly floral, mild to medium-hot. Güeros are used fresh in salsas and moles. **4–5/10**

Cascabel *C. annuum*

This is round and brown-red, with a smooth, translucent skin; the seeds rattle when you shake it. It has a lightly acidic, smoky flavor and is agreeably nutty after toasting. Moderately hot, it is toasted and blended with tomatoes or tomatillos to make a salsa, and crumbled in stews. **4–5/10**

Chipotle *C. annuum*

The smoke-dried jalapeño. Tan to coffee-colored, wrinkled, leathery, it has a smoky, sweet, chocolate smell and taste. Often used whole to flavor soups and stews. Soaked and puréed, it goes into sauces. Available canned in a light pickle for use as a condiment. **5–6/10**

Ancho *C. annuum*

This is a dried poblano. Deep red-brown, wrinkled, fruity, and sweet with rich flavors of tobacco, prune, and raisin, and slightly hot. Anchos are toasted and ground for sauces, or can be stuffed. Also available as powder and blocks of paste. The most popular dried chili pepper. **3–4/10**

Guajillo *C. annuum*

This is long and slender, with a blunt point; maroon with brown tones and a smooth, tough skin, it has high acidity, giving a tangy, pleasantly sharp taste. It is soaked and blended for enchilada sauces or crumbled into stews. It colors foods well. **4/10**

Southwest US and Caribbean

West Indians tend to prefer hot chili peppers for marinades, relishes, and stews. Early hot sauces mixed chilies and cassava juice; now garlic, onion, and other spices give depth to Caribbean chili sauces. In the American southwest, Mexican varieties are used in Mexican-inspired dishes, but the local New Mexican chili, used green, red, and dried, is mild. These chilies are hung out to dry in colorful ristras; once dried they are often ground and sold as Chimayo chili powder or chile colorado.

Jamaican hot *C. chinense*

Bright red and squat with thin flesh, this tastes sweet and very hot. Use in salsas, pickles, and curries. **9/10**

New Mexico *C. annuum*

Bright green or a deep, intense red, this has a sweet, earthy flavor. It is roasted and peeled, and keeps well if frozen after roasting. Green is good in guacamole, tacos, and tamales; red goes into sauces, soups, and chutneys. Dried, this has rich, dried-fruit flavors. It is used for red chili sauce and other relishes. **2–3/10**

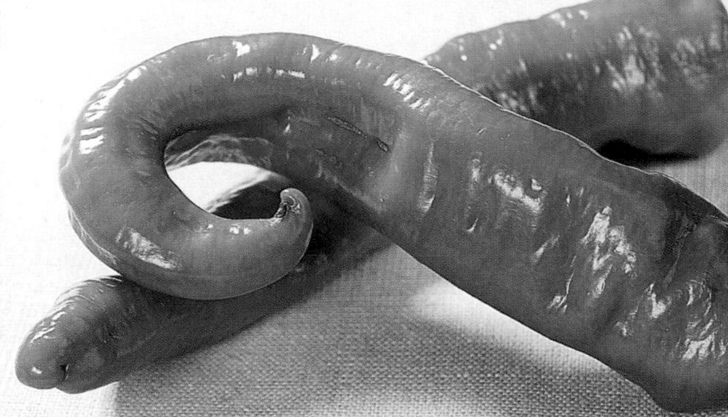

Scotch bonnet *C. chinense*

Yellow-green to orange-red, similar in appearance to the closely related habanero but with a wrinkled top and flattened base. Very hot and with a deep, fruity, smoky flavor. Used in many Caribbean hot sauces and in jerk seasoning. **10/10**

Tabasco *C. frutescens*

Thin-fleshed and yellow, turning orange or red when ripe, this has a sharp, biting taste with a hint of celery. It is mostly used for Tabasco sauce. **8/10**

Latin America

Called ají, chili peppers are much used in the Andean countries as a flavoring and as a condiment; a bowl of uchu llajawa – a fiery salsa of hot chilies and quillquiña (a local "cilantro") – is always on the table. Many varieties have only local names; some are mild, some bitter, particularly the yellow ones, and some dried chilies have rich flavors of raisin and prune. Chilies are also important in the cooking of Bahia in Brazil; elsewhere bottled chili sauce is more common.

Rocoto *C. pubescens*

Native to the Andes; plump and rounded, yellow to orange-red, rocotos are always used fresh in sauces and condiments, or as a vegetable, often stuffed with meat and cheese. **8–9/10**

Ají amarillo *C. baccatum*

Common in Peru, both fresh and dried, when it is called cusqueño. Pointed and hot with raisiny aromas, it is used with potatoes and other root vegetables, guinea pig (the local specialty), ceviche, and other seafood dishes. **7/10**

Mirasol *C. annuum*

This is popular in Peru and also found in Mexico, where the dried form is known as guajillo. Used green, yellow, or at its ripe, red-brown stage. Fruity and lively, it colors dishes well. Good with meats, beans, and vegetables. **5/10**

OTHER CHILI PEPPERS

Ají dulce (*C. annuum*) is sweet, mild, musky, and herbal-like. It is used extensively in Central America, Colombia, and Venezuela, especially with beans. **1/10**

Rocotillo (*C. chinense*) is a mild Andean chili pepper, bright red and squashed-looking, that is eaten as a condiment with corn, beans, root vegetables, and roast meats. **3–4/10**

Malagueta (*C. frutescens*) is pale or mid green, thin-fleshed, tapered, and tiny. It is native to Bahia in Brazil and widely used in Afro-Brazilian cooking and as a table condiment. Malagueta is also the name given in Portugal to small hot chilies pickled in vinegar. **8/10**

Asia

Asian chili peppers are even harder to pinpoint by name than Latin American ones. They are usually distinguished by types: large red and green ones, which are roasted and used in dips and sauces in Southeast Asia; medium-sized, shiny-skinned chilies, moderately hot, used in Indonesian and Malay cooking; and more pungent varieties for Thai and Indian curries. Japanese santakas and hontakas resemble cayennes.

Thai *C. annuum*

Used fresh and dried, these are slender, and dark green or bright red, with meaty flesh and lingering heat. Add whole to curries and stir-fries or chop for pastes and dips. **8/10**

Korean *C. annuum*

The bright green, curved, Korean chili pepper is related to the Thai. Fresh ones are cooked in fish, meat, and vegetable stews, in stir-fries, or stuffed and fried. **6–7/10**

Bird *C. frutescens*

The tiny green, orange, and red chilies are all used, often whole, to give a "finishing" flavor to a dish. They are fiercely hot. **9/10**

Kashmir *C. annuum*

Grown not only in Kashmir but in other parts of India, this is deep red and has sweet notes yet a distinct bite. In India, it is called lal mirch. **7/10**

Europe

A few chili peppers are specific to Europe, although many more are used in imported dishes. Hungary, Spain, and Portugal are the countries where local chilies are most used, and they are usually only mildly hot.

Peperoncino *C. annuum*

These are slender, wrinkled, and often curved, with thin flesh. Used fresh, green or red, in pickles and tomato-based dishes, the flavor is sweetish. **1–4/10**

Guindilla *C. annuum*

Brick-red and smooth, this long, tapering Spanish chili is used dried. Large pieces are soaked and added to a dish for extra piquancy; remove before serving. **5/10**

Banana *C. annuum*

Yellow-green ripening to red, curved, with a waxy skin, this mild chili is related to the hotter Hungarian wax. Use fresh in salads, stews, roasted whole, with legumes or potatoes, pickled, and as a garnish. **1/10**

Ñora *C. annuum*

This is mild and pleasantly earthy. It is soaked and used to flavor rice dishes and stews. Ñoras are essential to romesco sauce and for sweet paprika. The larger, bell-shaped choricero is similar and, as its name suggests, is used to flavor chorizo and other meat products. **1–2/10**

OTHER CHILI PEPPERS

Cherry (*C. annuum*) is orange to deep red when fresh, mahogany when dried, with a thick flesh and lots of seeds. It has a fruity flavor and ranges from mild to medium-hot. It is often sold pickled. **1–5/10**

Peri peri (*C. annuum*) is the Portuguese name for small chili peppers. It crops up in those parts of the world colonized by the Portuguese. In Africa, it is used for the jindungo chili, which is similar to the bird chili. **9/10**

Piment d'Espelette (*C. annuum*) from the Basque country has an appellation contrôlée. Bright red, wide-shouldered, and tapering, it is sweetly fruity and mildly piquant. Available dried, whole or as a powder, and also as a purée or coulis. **3/10**

preparing spices

BRUISING, GRATING, SLICING, AND SHREDDING SPICES

Many spices need some preparation before being added to a dish or used in a spice blend or paste. Bruising, cutting, and grinding serve to release the volatile oils and perfume of a spice. Large, bruised pieces of a spice are intended only for flavouring and should be removed before a dish is served. Mild spices are sometimes cut into bite-sized pieces and eaten as part of the dish; otherwise, spices should be grated, finely sliced, or shredded.

Bruising spices

Soft-textured fresh spices such as lemon grass, ginger, galangal, aromatic ginger, and zedoary (white turmeric) are often bruised before cooking to release their flavours, then added whole for later removal.

1. ▲ Remove the upper stalk of lemon grass (or peel a knob of the other spices).

2. ▶ Crush the lower part of the lemon grass stem (or the peeled knob) using the back of a heavy knife or a wooden kitchen mallet.

Slicing and shredding spices

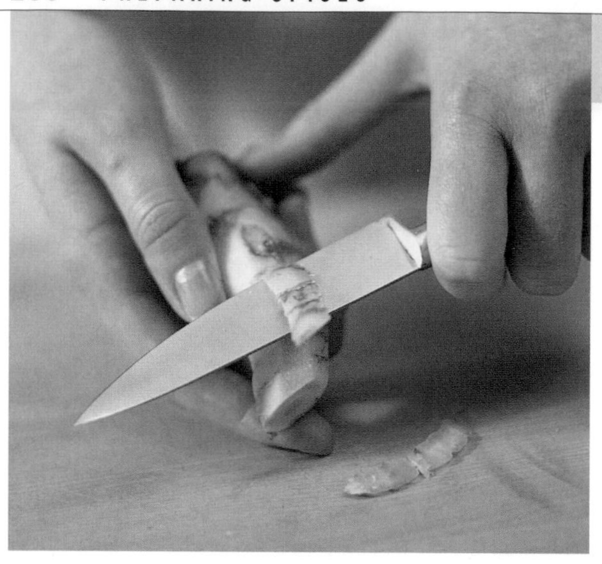

Some dishes require disks of fresh spices, while others call for spices to be shredded or chopped. The procedure for spices such as ginger, galangal, or zedoary (white turmeric) is given below. Lemon grass is cut into fine rings from the base, stopping when the texture becomes fibrous. Kaffir lime leaves should be shredded as fine as a needle if they are to be eaten.

1 Peel as much fresh rhizome or root as you need, cutting off any woody or dry bits.

2 Using a sharp knife, slice the root thinly across the grain into a series of fine disks.

3 Stack the disks, press down firmly, and shred them into fine slivers.

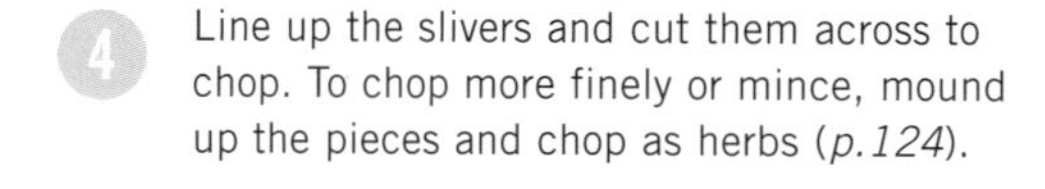

4 Line up the slivers and cut them across to chop. To chop more finely or mince, mound up the pieces and chop as herbs (*p. 124*).

Grating fresh spices

Fresh roots and rhizomes, such as wasabi and horseradish, and ginger and its relatives, are best grated. A Japanese oroshigane, designed specifically for grating wasabi and ginger (*p.115*), grates more finely than any Western grater.

Grating galangal ▶
A very sharp Western grater will produce a pulp that is suitable for some purposes, such as extracting the juice.

Extracting juice from ginger

Many Asian dishes call for the pure flavor of ginger juice, which can be quickly extracted from a fresh root.

1. Grate the ginger or chop finely in a food processor.
2. ◀ Wrap the shavings in a piece of cheesecloth or a dish towel and squeeze the juice into a bowl.

Grating dry spices

Although most spices are ground, some of the larger ones are more easily grated. For nutmeg use a nutmeg grater or the finest holes of a normal grater.

Grating dried ginger ▶
Dried ginger, turmeric, and zedoary (white turmeric) are very hard and therefore best grated on a fine citrus grater or rasp.

DRY-ROASTING AND FRYING SPICES

Roasting whole spices in a dry frying pan is especially common in Indian cooking. The process intensifies the flavors and makes the spices easier to grind. Other dishes call for spices to be fried before other ingredients are added. Frying brings out the flavor, which is imparted to the oil. The aroma of fried spices permeates a dish more fully than that of raw spices, but once a liquid is added the amount of fragrance they release is reduced.

Dry-roasting spices

Some seed spices, notably mustard seeds, tend to jump about as they roast, so have a lid available to cover the pan. A tablespoon of spices will be ready in 2–3 minutes, whereas a large quantity can take up to 8–10 minutes to brown evenly. With large quantities, roast each spice separately.

1. ▲ Heat a heavy pan until it feels hot when you hold your hand over it.

2. ▶ With the pan over a medium heat, toss in the spices. Stir them or shake the pan constantly. Let the spices darken and smoke a little, and they will soon give off a heady aroma. If they are changing color too quickly, lower the heat and make sure they do not burn.

3. Pour the spices into a bowl and let cool before grinding them.

Dry-roasting in an oven or microwave

Dry-roasting in an oven ▶
Dry-roasting a large quantity of spices may be easier in an oven preheated to 500°F (250°C). Spread the spices on a baking sheet and roast in the oven until they darken and are aromatic, shaking and stirring from time to time. Let cool before grinding.

Dry-roasting in a microwave
Spread the spices in one layer on a plate or dish and cook uncovered on high. Roasting 2–4 tbsp will take 4–5 minutes. Stir the spices once during cooking. Let cool before grinding.

Frying spices

Prepare all the ingredients of a dish before frying its spices. Some spices are fried for only a few seconds, others for up to a minute. All will darken, and some, such as cardamom pods, will puff up. Remove the pan from the heat to add more ingredients, and stir quickly to prevent them from burning in the oil.

1. ▲ Pour a thin film of sunflower oil into a heavy frying pan and heat until you can see a faint haze rising over the pan.

2. ▶ Fry whole spices before ground ones, adding them in the order they appear in the recipe. Spices should sizzle when they hit the hot oil and brown almost instantly. Watch them closely to prevent burning.

GRINDING, CRUSHING, AND MAKING SPICE PASTES

Freshly ground or crushed spices are always more aromatic than spices bought ready-ground. You will soon appreciate the difference if you take the trouble to grind, say, a teaspoon of coriander seeds and put them to one side for an hour or two. Then grind another spoonful. Smell the older batch and then the freshly ground seeds – you will find that some of the aroma of the first batch has already dissipated.

Grinding spices

Some whole spices – allspice, cinnamon, and cloves, for example – are aromatic, but most need to be crushed or ground to release their aroma. A blender can be used for a large quantity, but most spices are too hard to grind evenly in a food processor.

Using a mortar and pestle ▶
Choose a mortar that is deep, sturdy, and roughly textured, because many spices are very hard and considerable force is needed to grind them by hand.

Using an electric mill
Most spices can be ground in a spice mill, or coffee grinder kept specially for the purpose, although a few, such as anardana (*see p.169*), are too sticky.

Crushing spices

Some spices need only to be crushed, rather than pulverized to a powder. A mortar and pestle works well because you can easily see and control how much the spice is broken up – and you can enjoy its fragrance at the same time.

Using a rolling pin ▶
Put the spice in a plastic bag, spread out the seeds on a hard surface, then crush firmly with a rolling pin.

Making spice pastes

Spice pastes are made by crushing fresh spices (such as garlic, ginger, galangal, or zedoary) together with dry spices or herbs and sometimes a little liquid. The technique is widely used in India and Southeast Asia, and in Mexico. Use a mortar and pestle or the small bowl of a food processor.

1. ▶ If using any dry spices, grind them first, either in the mortar or in an electric mill.

2. ▼ Crush the garlic or ginger, then work in the ground spices, and finally the liquid if needed.

FRESH CHILI PEPPERS

Chili peppers come in many shapes, colors, and sizes, and the flavor changes from the young, green state to the mature, red or red-brown state. When chilies are dried, their flavor changes again. Often fresh chili peppers are used whole or sliced in a recipe, but sometimes they benefit from seeding or roasting, especially if they have tough skins.

Roasting fresh chili peppers

Most chilies can be used without peeling, but some are roasted and peeled because the skin is tough or because peeling will improve the texture and give a pleasant charred flavor. Small chilies can be roasted on a preheated dry griddle or heavy frying pan. Turn them until they darken and soften.

1. Hold large chilies directly over a gas flame, turning from time to time so that they are charred evenly and the flesh doesn't burn. Or, lay them on a grill that rests above an electric burner. Alternatively, hold them close to the the preheated element of the broiler and turn them as they blister and blacken.

2. ▲ Once they are evenly charred, put the chilies into a plastic bag or a bowl covered with plastic wrap and let sweat for 10–15 minutes.

3. ▶ Carefully peel off the skin and rinse. Dry the chilies on paper towel.

Freezing chili peppers

Fresh chilies can be frozen after roasting. There is no need to peel them because the skin will come off when the chilies have thawed.

Freezing unroasted chili peppers ▶
Blanch unroasted chilies with stems intact for 3 minutes, then drain in a colander. Let cool completely, place in a plastic bag, and freeze.

Removing seeds and veins from fresh chili peppers

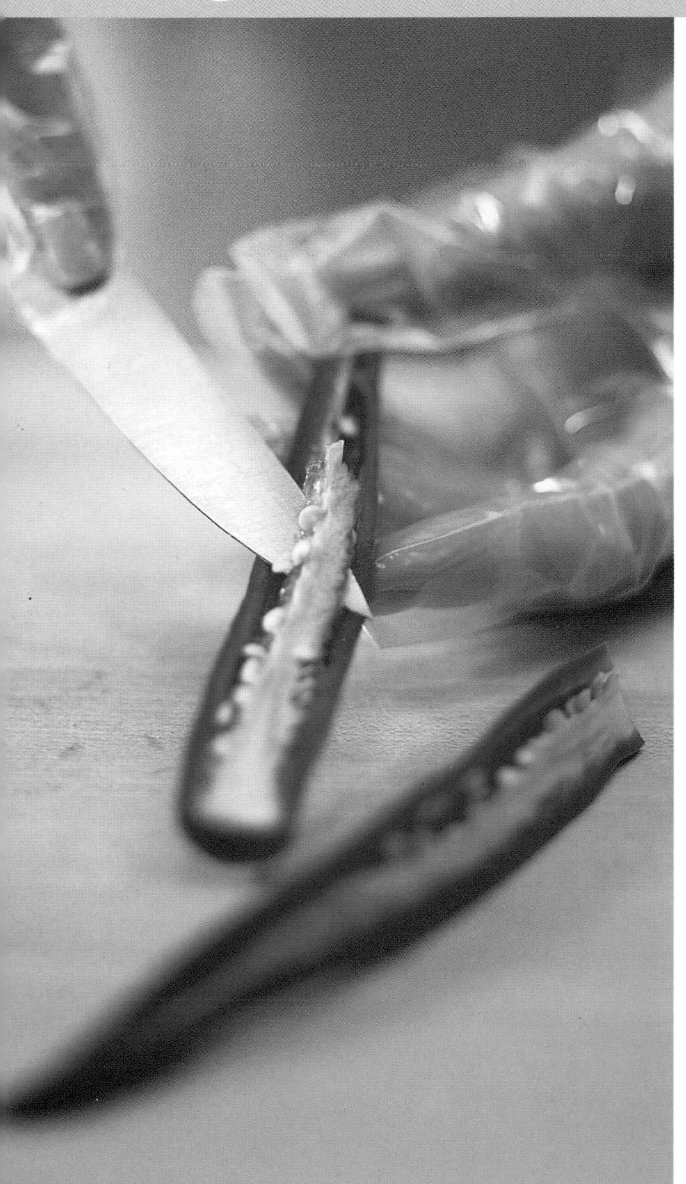

Capsaicin, the pungent principle that gives chilies their heat, is present in varying degrees in the seeds, white veins, and skin. Capsaicin can sting the skin and eyes (*see below*). Removing seeds and veins before cooking reduces the heat of a dish.

1. Cut off and remove the stems, and slice each of the chilies in half.
2. ◀ Cut out the veins and scrape out all the seeds, then rinse.

CAUTION

- If you are not used to handling chilies or have any cuts or a sensitive skin, wear thin rubber or plastic gloves to protect against the capsaicin.
- Remember that the seeds and veins are the hottest part of chilies. Avoid rubbing your eyes – if you do, rinse them at once with cold water.
- When you have finished handling chilies, use soapy water to wash your hands thoroughly, as well as the work surface and any utensils.
- If your hands do suffer chili burn, put them in a bowl of cold water or light vegetable oil.
- If you burn your mouth when eating a chili, a drink of water will make it worse. Instead, chew a piece of bread or try yogurt or milk.

DRIED CHILI PEPPERS

Large dried chili peppers, widely used in the cooking of Mexico and the southwestern US, are usually toasted, then soaked and puréed before use in a sauce. Toasting enhances their flavor; for a milder dish, the chilies are just soaked. In Mexico, smaller varieties of dried chilies are frequently ground or puréed straight into a sauce. Asian cooks are more likely to toast small dried chilies before grinding them.

Removing seeds and veins from dried chili peppers

As with fresh chilies, removing the seeds and veins from dried chilies before use reduces the heat of the dish. Seeds and veins are best removed before toasting, so that the chilies are ready for soaking or grinding immediately after they have been toasted.

Shaking out seeds ▶
Wipe the chilies clean, then either tear them apart or break off the stems and shake out the seeds.

Toasting dried chili peppers

Toasted dried chilies darken in color, blister, and crackle as they release their aroma. Don't let them scorch or they will taste acrid and bitter. Once toasted they are ready for soaking or grinding.

◀ Using a griddle
Place cleaned dried chilies on a preheated griddle or heavy frying pan for 1–2 minutes, turning them so that they don't burn. Alternatively, toast them for 2–3 minutes in an oven preheated to 500°F (250°C).

Soaking dried chili peppers

If you need small, soaked dried chilies for an Asian spice paste, tear them into pieces and add to water. They should be ready for use in 15 minutes.

1. ▲ Place toasted or cleaned, dried chilies in a bowl and cover with almost-boiling water. Keep the chilies submerged by setting a saucer or plate on top of them and let soak for 15 minutes or until soft – large, thick ones may need longer.

2. ▶ Rub the soft chilies through a wire strainer to remove the tough skins, then make a sauce by blending them with other ingredients and some of the soaking liquid.

Grinding dried chili peppers

Wipe the chilies clean, remove the stems, and tear the skins into pieces. Retain the seeds and veins if you need additional heat in the dish; otherwise remove them before grinding.

Using an electric mill ▶
Dried chilies can be ground to a fine consistency in an electric spice mill or coffee grinder. Better results are obtained if the dried chilies are first toasted.

recipes

HERB MIXTURES

Dried or fresh herbs can be used in many combinations. The composition of even the classic mixtures is usually determined by the kind of dish they are to go with – a guiding principle, whether in European bouquets garnis, Iranian blends, or Latin American blends in which spices are often included with the herbs.

Bouquets garnis

A bouquet garni is a little bundle of herbs used in classic French cooking to flavor slow-cooked dishes. Tied with string, or wrapped in cheesecloth, the bouquet garni is removed before serving. A basic bouquet garni consists of a bay leaf, 2–3 fresh parsley stems, and 2–3 sprigs of thyme, but flavorings can be varied according to the dish to be cooked. Here are a few suggestions:

FOR BEEF

Bay, parsley, thyme, and an outer piece of leek

Oregano, bay, garlic, and a strip of orange peel

Thyme, savory, marjoram, and a little hyssop

FOR PORK

Sage, celery, parsley, and thyme

Lovage, rosemary, and savory

Orange thyme, tarragon, and bay

FOR LAMB

Rosemary, garlic, oregano or marjoram, and thyme

Lavender, savory, and myrtle

Lemon thyme, mint, and parsley

FOR POULTRY

Parsley, bay, tarragon, and bruised lemon grass

Marjoram, rosemary, and savory

Lemon thyme, lovage, parsley, and an outer piece of leek

FOR GAME

Parsley, juniper berries, thyme, and bay

Lemon balm, marjoram, mint, and celery

Rosemary, myrtle, and a strip of orange peel

FOR FISH

Parsley, tarragon, thyme, and a strip of lemon peel

Fennel, bay, and lemon thyme

Dill, parsley, welsh onion, and lemon balm

FOR VEGETABLES

Oregano, thyme, parsley, and sage

Celery, savory, tarragon, and parsley

Bay, lovage, rosemary, and marjoram

Fines herbes

Another classic mixture from French cooking, fines herbes is a blend of delicately flavored summer herbs: chervil, chives, parsley, and tarragon, with equal proportions of the first three and half the amount of tarragon. The chopped herbs make an excellent seasoning for omelettes and other egg dishes, for cream sauces, and for salads of soft leaves.

Persillade

Chop together finely 1 garlic clove and a small handful of flat-leaf parsley sprigs. Stir the mixture into a dish a few minutes before serving or scatter, raw, over the dish before it goes to the table. Persillade makes a fresh-tasting topping for poultry, fish, and vegetables. Mixed with bread crumbs, it can also be pressed over a rack of lamb toward the end of cooking.

Gremolata

Prepare a persillade (*above*) but include the grated rind of half an unwaxed lemon. The classic garnish for Milanese osso buco, gremolata is also good with grilled or baked fish, lentil and bean soups, and salads. It is also sprinkled over or stirred into meat and poultry stews.

Herbes de Provence

This is traditionally a variable blend of dried herbs, but there is no reason not to use fresh when available. One version is described below, but fennel seed, sage, basil, bay, and hyssop are also used. Use for braised meat and game dishes, especially those cooked in a red-wine sauce, and with tomato dishes and root vegetables.

3 tbsp dried thyme

2 tbsp dried marjoram

1 tsp dried rosemary

1 tbsp dried savory

1 tsp dried lavender flowers

Crumble or grind the herbs and store in an airtight jar for 2–3 months.

Winter herbs

This is a simple blend Richard Olney used regularly, as I found when staying with him one summer and helping him prepare his winter supplies. Coarsely crumble or grind roughly equal amounts of dried thyme, oregano, and winter savory, and store. I have also used marjoram instead of oregano on occasion.

Farcellets

Farcellet is the Catalan word for a little bundle, and these little bundles, tightly bound in bay leaves, contain sprigs of dried savory, oregano, and thyme. Use to flavor long-cooked dishes of meat, poultry, or vegetables. Remove before serving.

Herbed pepper

1 tbsp dried rosemary

1 tbsp dried winter savory

1 tbsp dried thyme

1 tbsp dried marjoram

1 tbsp ground black pepper

1 tbsp ground mace

Crush or grind all the herbs finely. Sift and combine with the pepper and mace. Store in an airtight jar for 2–3 months. The blend is good with root vegetables, as a stuffing for chicken, and in winter soups. A clove of crushed garlic and a little grated lemon rind can be used with the herbed pepper to good effect.

Garlic and herb paste

4 garlic cloves

salt

2 tsp coarsely ground black peppercorns

4 tbsp finely chopped mixed fresh herbs (choose from basil, marjoram, parsley, rosemary, sage, tarragon, thyme)

1–2 tbsp olive oil

Crush the garlic to a paste with a little salt in a mortar. Add all the other ingredients and mix well. Use to coat ham, or pork or lamb chops to be grilled.

Cuban adobo

In the Spanish-speaking Caribbean islands, many dishes start with a sofrito, a mixture of herbs, spices, and vegetables cooked together to give the basic flavoring to a dish. The other means of flavoring is to make an adobo, which may be either dry, to use as a rub, or liquid, to use as a marinade. To use this recipe as a rub, omit the orange juice. Adobos occur throughout Central- and South-American cooking.

1 tbsp fresh thyme leaves

1 tbsp fresh oregano leaves

2 handfuls of cilantro – leaves and sprigs

3 garlic cloves, crushed

1 tsp ground cumin

2 tsp ground black pepper

7 tbsp (100ml) bitter orange juice or lime juice

Blend everything in a food processor and keep in a non-reactive jar in the refrigerator for 4–5 days. Use as seasoning (*p.283*).

Chilean aliño

Aliño means seasoning or dressing and is used throughout South America for herb and spice mixtures, either to rub onto meat, poultry, or fish, or to flavor soups and casseroles. In every market you can buy bundles or little packets of aliño. This version comes from *Three Generations of Chilean Cuisine* by Mirtha Umaña-Murray.

1 tbsp dried thyme

1 tbsp dried rosemary

1 tbsp dried oregano

1 tbsp dried sage

1 tbsp dried mint

1 tbsp dried lemon balm

1 tbsp dried marjoram

1 tbsp dried tarragon

Mix and crush the herbs, and store in an airtight container.

Khmeli-suneli

This mixture is from the Republic of Georgia. Many varieties of mixed herbs and spices are sold under the name khmeli-suneli in markets in Tbilisi. Every region and every family has its own version of khmeli-suneli. Here is one:

1 tbsp ground coriander

1 tsp dried fenugreek leaves

1 tsp ground marigold petals

1 tsp dried mint

1 tsp dried dill

1 tsp dried summer savory

½ tsp fennel seeds

½ tsp ground cinnamon

large pinch of ground cloves

Pound or grind all the ingredients to a powder. Store in an airtight container for 2–3 months. Use the mixture in a marinade for or rubbed on meats to be grilled, and in vegetable dishes, soups, and stews.

Green masala

This Indian masala is excellent with fish or chicken.

2oz (60g) fresh ginger

2 garlic cloves

4–6 hot green chili peppers

large handful of cilantro – leaves and young stems

½ tsp salt

Peel and chop the ginger and garlic; remove seeds from the chilies and slice the flesh. Put all the ingredients into a food processor and blend to a paste with a little water.

The mixture will keep for up to 2 weeks in a tightly closed container in the refrigerator, or it can be frozen for up to 3 months. A simpler masala can be made without the cilantro, if you prefer.

SEASONING

Seasoning is a paste used for flavoring meat, poultry, and fish in the English-speaking Caribbean islands. Ingredients and recipes vary from island to island and cook to cook, but they commonly include fresh herbs: parsley, mint, thyme, celery, oregano, cilantro, culantro, chives, welsh onions, and garlic. Spices used include ginger, cloves, cinnamon, allspice, curry powder, paprika, pepper, and chili peppers, along with other flavorings such as Worcestershire sauce, bitter orange juice, lime juice, vinegar, and oil.

Seasoning is most often used as a marinade, but it can also be used in sauces or stirred into a stew. To use as a marinade, rub the seasoning onto food and leave for 1–2 hours for small fish and seafood; up to 3–4 hours for large, whole fish, pieces of chicken, or meat; and up to 12 hours for large pieces of meat or a whole chicken.

Bajan seasoning

As its name indicates, this version of seasoning comes from Barbados.

6–8 scallions, coarsely chopped
4 garlic cloves, crushed
handful of fresh parsley – leaves and small stems
1 tbsp fresh thyme leaves
small bunch of fresh chives
1 scotch bonnet chili pepper, seeded and coarsely chopped
4 tbsp lime juice

Combine all the ingredients in a food processor and blend to a paste. Taste and add more lime juice if necessary, plus salt if you wish. Refrigerate in a non-reactive jar for 4–5 days.

Trinidad seasoning

6–8 scallions, coarsely chopped
1 small onion, coarsely chopped
3 garlic cloves, crushed
bunch of culantro or cilantro leaves, coarsely chopped
small handful of fresh mint leaves
small piece of fresh ginger, coarsely chopped
1 hot green chili pepper
good grinding of black pepper
4 tbsp lime juice

Blend all the ingredients to a paste in a food processor. Taste and add more lime juice as necessary. Salt may also be wanted. Store as Bajan seasoning (*above*).

Jamaican jerk seasoning

This seasoning is spice- rather than herb-based. It is used primarily as a rub for pork and chicken.

3–6 scotch bonnet chili peppers, seeded and coarsely chopped
4–6 scallions, coarsely chopped
3 shallots, quartered
3 garlic cloves, crushed
small piece of fresh ginger, coarsely chopped
3 tbsp fresh thyme leaves
1 tbsp ground allspice
2 tsp ground black pepper
1 tsp ground cinnamon
½ tsp grated nutmeg
½ tsp ground cloves
3–4 tbsp sunflower oil

Combine all the ingredients in a food processor and blend. If necessary, add a little water or more oil. Store, refrigerated, for up to 6 weeks.

MIXED HERB PLATTERS

A bowl of herbs accompanies almost every Iranian meal. The freshest possible herbs – mint, chives, scallions, parsley, dill, tarragon – are put on the table as an appetizer or to eat with other dishes.

In Lebanon, a platter of fresh vegetables and herbs is always part of a mezze table: cucumbers, radishes, tomatoes, romaine lettuce, parsley, purslane, watercress, mint, and scallions are those most often encountered.

The Vietnamese share this passion for fresh herbs. No meal is complete without a bowl of fresh herbs: basil, cilantro, rau ram, red and green perilla, mint, cucumber, and lettuce leaves.

IRANIAN HERB MIXTURES

The Iranian passion for herbs carries over to their cooked dishes. Large quantities of fresh herbs are used in summer; in winter dried herbs are used. Herbs dry well in Iran's hot climate, retaining their flavor and color; they are available from Iranian markets.

Rice mixture (sabzi polo) has equal quantities of parsley, cilantro, chives, and sometimes dill.

Stew mixture (sabzi ghormeh) includes parsley, chives, and cilantro with a little fenugreek; powdered dried lime is invariably included, and sometimes dill and mint.

Soup mixture (sabzi âshe) has parsley, chives, and cilantro as staples, and sometimes mint and fenugreek.

SPICE MIXTURES

The art of blending spices has been practiced for centuries in many parts of the world. In much of China, Japan, the Indian subcontinent, the Middle East, Africa (especially East and North Africa), the Caribbean islands, and Latin America, these mixtures are an important element in distinguishing regional cuisines.

Japan

In Japanese cooking emphasis is placed on bringing out the pure flavors of the food itself. A number of aromatic ingredients – soy products, seaweeds, dashi, dried bonito – are used, but few spices. Wasabi, sansho, chili, mustard, ginger, and sesame are used in moderation.

Seven-spice powder

Shichimi togarashi, often just called shichimi, translates as "seven-flavors chili." Plain ground chili is ichimi togarashi; shichimi is chili with six additions. There are variations to the formula depending on the region; perilla, mustard seeds, toasted and dried chili may all be used. Even if there are more than seven ingredients, the name doesn't change. Hemp seeds are usual in Japan, but hard to find elsewhere, so I have used poppy seeds.

The aroma is primarily of tangerine peel with iodine notes from the nori (laver); chili is the dominant but not overwhelming flavor, and the texture is gritty. The mixture can be bought mild or hot, so adjust the amount of chili to your taste when making your own. Yuzu peel may be added to seven-spice powder to give it a tart note. Use as a condiment for spicing udon (wheat noodles), soups, nabemono (one-pot dishes), and yakitori (chicken pieces broiled on a skewer).

2 tsp white sesame seeds

1 tsp crushed dried tangerine peel

2 tsp nori flakes (aonori)

2 tsp dried hot chili flakes

1 tbsp sansho

1 tsp black sesame seeds

1 tsp poppy seeds

Grind the white sesame seeds and tangerine peel coarsely. Add the nori and chili flakes and grind again. Stir in the remaining ingredients and store in an airtight container.

Goma shio

Goma means sesame and this simple mixture is used as a condiment for rice, vegetables and salads.

4 tsp black or white sesame seeds

2 tsp coarse sea salt

Dry-roast the sesame seeds lightly for a minute or two, stirring and shaking the pan. Cool, then grind briefly with the salt to keep a coarse texture. Store in an airtight jar. Sesame is a popular flavoring in Korea, and a similar Korean blend would use up to 2oz (60g) toasted sesame seeds to 2 tsp salt.

China

Chinese cooks use single spices, five-spice powder for a more complex flavor, and a rich blend of mixed spices with soy sauce and sugar to flavor the broth for slow-cooking pork or beef.

Five-spice powder

In Chinese culture the balance of the five flavors (salty, sour, bitter, pungent, and sweet) ensured medicinal and culinary potency. Five-spice powder is sometimes extended to seven with the addition of dried ginger, cardamom, or licorice. Use sparingly to flavor slow-cooked dishes, in marinades, and to season meat or poultry to be roasted or grilled.

6 star anise

1 tbsp Sichuan pepper

1 tbsp fennel seeds

2 tsp whole cloves

2 tsp ground cassia or cinnamon

Grind all the spices together to a powder. Sift, and store in an airtight container.

Thailand

The success of Thai cooking depends on the complex combination of flavors in a curry paste, sauce, soup, or dip. The skillful blending of herbs, spices, and other flavorings, such as fish sauce, dried shrimp, and shrimp paste, gives zest to vegetables, fish, meat, and poultry. Curry pastes differ from region to region and from house to house; they are usually prepared when needed and not stored, but these pastes will keep for about 2 weeks in a closed jar in the refrigerator, or can be frozen in small pots if you prefer to make larger amounts.

Red curry paste

10 dried hot red chili peppers

1 tsp shrimp paste (kapi)

1 tbsp coriander seeds

2 tsp cumin seeds

5 garlic cloves, chopped

6 shallots, chopped

2 lemon grass stalks, lower third only, sliced

6 slices of galangal

1 tsp grated kaffir lime peel

2 tbsp chopped cilantro roots

1 tsp ground black pepper

Cut the chilies and soak them in a little warm water for 10–15 minutes. Wrap the shrimp paste tightly in foil and dry-roast for 1–2 minutes on each side. Dry-roast the coriander and cumin seeds, cool and grind.

Put the chilies and their water into a food processor with all the other ingredients and blend to a smooth paste, or pound in a mortar. Red curry paste goes well with beef, game, duck, and pork.

Green curry paste

Green curry paste is the hottest type you can make, but you can reduce the number of chilies or leave out the seeds. Green curry paste is good with fish and seafood, chicken and vegetables.

2 tsp coriander seeds

1 tsp cumin seeds

1 tsp shrimp paste (kapi)

2 tsp chopped galangal, or 1 tsp dried

2 tsp chopped fingerroot (krachai), or 1 tsp dried

2 lemon grass stalks, lower third only, chopped

1 tsp grated kaffir lime peel

4 shallots, chopped

3 garlic cloves, chopped

1 tsp ground black pepper

½ tsp grated nutmeg

small bunch of cilantro – leaves, young stems, and roots, chopped

4 tbsp chopped fresh Thai basil leaves

15 small hot green chili peppers, chopped

Dry-roast the coriander and cumin seeds until they darken; cool, then grind. Dry-roast the shrimp paste, wrapped tightly in foil, for 1–2 minutes on each side. Let cool.

Combine all the ingredients and blend in a food processor or with a pestle and mortar until you have a smooth paste.

Massaman curry paste

This paste derives its name from the Muslim traders who brought spices to Thailand. Some of its spices are more commonly used in India and it has a rich, warm flavor.

2 tbsp coriander seeds

2 tsp cumin seeds

6 green cardamom pods

½ cinnamon stick

6 whole cloves

10 dried hot red chili peppers

½ tsp grated nutmeg

½ tsp ground mace

1 tsp shrimp paste (kapi)

2 tbsp sunflower oil

5 shallots, chopped

4 garlic cloves, chopped

1 tbsp chopped galangal

1 tbsp chopped cilantro root

2 lemon grass stalks, lower third only, sliced

Dry-roast all the whole spices and chilies; let cool, then remove the pods from the cardamoms and grind all to a powder. Combine with the nutmeg and mace. Wrap the shrimp paste in foil and dry-roast until its aroma rises.

Heat the oil and lightly fry the shallots and garlic until they start to color, then add the galangal, cilantro root, and lemon grass. Fry for a minute or two longer, then transfer to a food processor or mortar.

Add all the other ingredients and blend or pound to a smooth paste. Use with meat and poultry.

India

The first requirement of an Indian cook is to become a good masalchi, or spice-blender. A masala is a blend of spices; it may contain two or three, or a dozen or more. It may be added to the dish, whole or ground, at different stages of cooking. For rice and some meat dishes, whole spices are traditional; the most common ground mixtures are the garam masalas (hot spices) used in northern cooking. A garam masala is usually added toward the end of the cooking time to draw out the flavors of the other ingredients and preserve the aromas. Indians have taken their masalas to other parts of the world where they have settled: Malaysia, South Africa, and the Caribbean islands. Curry powder originated in Chennai (Madras), where local cooks working for British households in the 18th century introduced Indian dishes to the newcomers.

Standard garam masala

This masala and its variations are best for meat and poultry dishes, especially those cooked in tomato or onion gravy. It also makes a good flavoring for spiced bean or lentil soups.

2 tbsp black cardamom pods

1½ cinnamon sticks

4 tbsp coriander seeds

3 tbsp cumin seeds

2 tbsp black peppercorns

1 tbsp whole cloves

2 tejpat leaves, crumbled

Extract the seeds from the cardamom pods and discard the pods. Break the cinnamon. Dry-roast all the spices over a medium heat – this will probably take 8–10 minutes.

Let the spices cool, then grind them to a powder and sift. The masala will keep in an airtight jar for 2–3 months.

VARIATIONS

Gujarati masala

Add 1 tbsp sesame seeds, 2 tsp fennel seeds, 1 tsp ajowan seeds, and 3–4 dried hot chili peppers.

Kashmiri masala

Use black cumin seeds and green cardamom instead of black, and add 2 blades of mace and ¼ nutmeg, grated.

Punjabi masala

Reduce the coriander to 2 tbsp and black cardamom to 1 tbsp. Add 1 tbsp green cardamom pods, 2 tsp fennel seeds, 2 blades of mace, 1 tbsp black cumin seeds, 2 tsp ground ginger, and 1 tbsp dried rose petals.

Aromatic garam masala

This masala blend is mild, with a subtle emphasis on cardamom. It is used for kebabs and classic moghul dishes made with butter and cream or yogurt.

2 tbsp green or 3 tbsp black cardamom pods

½ cinnamon stick

2 mace blades

2 tsp black peppercorns

1 tsp whole cloves

Remove the seeds from the cardamom pods and discard the pods. Break the cinnamon into pieces. Combine all the spices in an electric mill and grind to a powder, then sift. Store in an airtight container for 2–3 months.

Bombay masala

This masala has richness and texture from the use of coconut and sesame and poppy seeds. It is particularly good with lentils and vegetables. If it is added to the dish at the beginning, it will give a subtle flavor; for a more pronounced taste, add it when the cooking is almost completed.

8 green cardamom pods

small piece of cinnamon stick

2 tejpat leaves or 1 sprig of curry leaves

1 tsp black peppercorns

2 tsp coriander seeds

1 tsp cumin seeds

6 whole cloves

2 tbsp unsweetened shredded dried coconut

2 tsp sesame seeds

1 tbsp poppy seeds

Take the seeds from the cardamoms and discard the pods. Break up the cinnamon; crumble dried tejpat leaves or strip curry leaves from the stem. Dry-roast the cardamom seeds, cinnamon, leaves, peppercorns, coriander, cumin, and cloves until lightly colored. Let cool.

Dry-roast the coconut and sesame and poppy seeds over gentle heat until they color; the coconut should be dark brown. Let cool, then grind with the spices. Store in an airtight container for 2–3 months.

Dhana jeera powder

This simple mixture of 4 parts coriander seeds to 1 part cumin is a common seasoning in Gujarat and Maharashtra, and is often used ground as the basis for masalas.

Tandoori masala

Tandoori chicken is one of the dishes most Westerners think of when Indian food is mentioned. The smoky flavor of tandoori meat or fish comes from the clay oven in which it is cooked, the slightly sour flavor from the spicing and the yogurt marinade. You can use the masala for food cooked in the oven or on a grill. To get the deep red color of restaurant tandoori food, you will need some red coloring from an Indian market.

Black salt is a rock salt, sold as a pink powder or in reddish lumps in Indian markets. It has a pronounced sulfurous smell that dissipates in cooking. If you can't find it, use a little extra sea salt.

½ cinnamon stick

1 tbsp coriander seeds

2 tsp cumin seeds

6 whole cloves

3 mace blades

2 tsp ground turmeric

2 tsp ground ginger

1 tsp ground hot chili

1 tsp amchoor

1 tsp black salt

1 tsp sea salt

Crush the cinnamon lightly and dry-roast the whole spices until they darken and start to smoke. Let cool, then grind them. Combine all the spices with the salts.

To use, stir scant 1 cup (200ml) plain yogurt and combine with 2–3 tsp of the masala.

Chat masala

This masala is used in small quantities with fruit and vegetable salads. It has a fresh, sourish taste.

1 tsp cumin seeds

1 tsp black peppercorns

½ tsp ajowan seeds

1 tsp anardana

1 tsp black salt (*see above*)

1 tsp coarse sea salt

1 tbsp amchoor

¼ tsp asafetida

½ tsp crushed dried mint leaves

½ tsp ground hot chili

Grind all the whole spices and salts to a powder, then stir in the remaining ingredients. Store in an airtight container for 2 months.

Masala for fish

1 tbsp cumin seeds

2 tbsp coriander seeds

½ tsp ajowan seeds

1 tbsp ginger juice (*p.239*)

Grind the spices and combine with the ginger juice. Add a little water if the mixture is too dry. Rub into the fish and leave to marinate for up to 1 hour before cooking.

Madras curry powder

2 dried hot chili peppers

4 tbsp coriander seeds

2 tbsp cumin seeds

1 tsp mustard seeds

1½ tbsp black peppercorns

6 curry leaves

½ tsp ground ginger

1 tsp ground turmeric

Roast the whole spices in a dry frying pan and let cool. Dry the curry leaves in the pan briefly, then add to the whole spices. Grind to a powder, sift, and stir in the ginger and turmeric. Keep in an airtight container for 2 months.

Sambhar powder

This powder is much used in south Indian cooking, which is mostly vegetarian, to flavor legumes, vegetable dishes, sauces, and soups. The dal in the blend serve as a thickening agent and provide a nutty taste.

4 tbsp coriander seeds

2 tbsp cumin seeds

1 tbsp black peppercorns

1 tsp mustard seeds

2 tsp fenugreek seeds

10 dried hot chili peppers

¼ tsp asafetida

1 tbsp ground turmeric

1 tbsp channa dal (yellow split peas)

1 tbsp urad dal (split black lentils)

1 tbsp sunflower oil

Dry-roast the whole spices for 5–8 minutes. When the spices have darkened and give off their aroma, add the asafetida and turmeric, and stir for 1 minute. Transfer to a bowl.

Fry the dal in the oil until they darken. Keep stirring to prevent burning. Add them to the spices, mix well and let cool, then grind. Store in an airtight container and use within 2 weeks.

Tamil curry powder

This southern Indian blend is used to flavor rice or is stirred into a vegetable curry just before serving.

10 sprigs of curry leaves
1 tbsp sunflower oil
1 tbsp coriander seeds
3 dried hot chili peppers
pinch of asafetida
1 tsp toor dal (yellow lentils)
1 tsp urad dal (split black lentils)

Strip the leaves from the stems and fry in the oil until lightly colored. Remove from the pan and fry the other items until they change color, stirring and shaking the pan. Let cool.

Grind the curry leaves; add the other ingredients and grind to a powder. Store in an airtight container for up to 2 weeks.

Bengali panch phoron

This mixture of whole spices is used to flavor legumes and vegetarian dishes.

1 tbsp cumin seeds
1 tbsp fennel seeds
1 tbsp mustard seeds
1 tbsp nigella seeds
1 tbsp fenugreek seeds

Combine all the spices and store in an airtight container. Use to flavor hot oil before other ingredients are added, or to spice ghee (clarified butter) that is poured over dal before serving.

Massalé

Massalé is the spice blend of the French islands of the Indian Ocean – Mauritius and Réunion. The proportions of ingredients vary. It is used, with turmeric, to flavor dishes variously called caris, curries, or massalés.

2 tbsp coriander seeds
2 tsp cumin seeds
2 tsp black peppercorns
1 tsp cardamom pods
1 tsp whole cloves
small piece of cinnamon stick
1 tsp ground hot chili
1 tsp grated nutmeg

Dry-roast the whole spices until lightly colored and let cool. Grind finely, then stir in the chili and nutmeg. Store for 2–3 months in an airtight jar.

Sri Lankan curry powder

1 tbsp uncooked rice
2 tbsp coriander seeds
½ cinnamon stick
3 green cardamom pods
3 whole cloves
1 tsp black peppercorns
1 tbsp cumin seeds
2 sprigs of curry leaves

Dry-roast the rice. Add the spices and curry leaves, stripped from the stems. Stir over low heat to prevent burning, until all the spices turn dark brown.

Let cool, then grind finely and sift. Stir a teaspoon or two into a curry just before serving. Fenugreek and chili can be added to the blend.

Malay curry powder

Malay curry spices show the influence of the large Indian population. The curries are usually cooked in coconut milk; lemon grass and garlic are sometimes added.

½ cinnamon stick
5 dried hot chili peppers
1 tsp green cardamom seeds
6 whole cloves
1 tsp cumin seeds
1 tbsp coriander seeds
2 tsp ground turmeric
1 tsp ground galangal

Grind the whole spices to a powder and stir in the turmeric and galangal. Store for 2–3 months in an airtight container.

Malay curry paste

2 lemon grass stalks, lower third only
thumb-sized piece of galangal, chopped
6 garlic cloves, chopped
2 shallots, chopped
6 hot chili peppers, seeded and chopped
1 tsp ground mace
1 tsp black peppercorns
1 tbsp sunflower oil
½ tsp salt
1 tbsp ground turmeric

Blend all the ingredients in a food processor, adding a little more oil or water if necessary to make a smooth paste. Store in a closed jar in the refrigerator for a week.

Middle East and North Africa

Iranian spicing tends to be mild, using sesame, saffron, cinnamon, rose petals, coriander, and small amounts of cardamom, caraway, and cumin. Souring spices such as sumac, dried limes, barberries, or pomegranate also play an important part. Spice mixtures (advieh) vary greatly from the Gulf to the central plateau, and are prepared for specific dishes.

The peoples of the Gulf have a taste for highly spiced food. Each country has its spice blends, called baharat (meaning spice). Enthusiasm for spicing spreads throughout the Arab countries to Israel and Turkey, where spices and herbs are often combined in milder blends; the widely used dried chili flakes may be fiery or subtle. The spicing of the eastern Mediterranean continues in North Africa, where sophisticated blends are used, particularly in Tunisia and Morocco.

Pickling spice blend

1 tsp coriander seeds

1 tsp ground ginger

1 tsp golpar

2 tsp powdered dried lime

1 tsp anise seed

1 tsp ground cinnamon

1 tsp cumin seeds

1 tsp nigella seeds

This blend is used for mixed pickled vegetables and fruit: green beans, carrots, cauliflower, cucumber, unripe tomatoes, pears, quinces, apricots, and medlars are most commonly used. The vegetables and fruits are cooked or salted, then combined with the spices and boiled vinegar.

Advieh for rice

2 tbsp ground cinnamon

2 tbsp ground dried rose petals

1 tbsp ground cumin or green cardamom seeds

Combine the spices and use to flavor steamed rice or rice cooked with herbs in the Iranian way (*p.321*). Store in an airtight jar for 1 month.

Advieh for stews

2 cinnamon sticks

2 tbsp coriander seeds

1½ tbsp green cardamom pods

1 tbsp black peppercorns

1 tbsp cumin seeds

2 tsp grated nutmeg

2 tsp powdered dried lime

Break the cinnamon into pieces. Grind all the whole spices, sift, and combine with the nutmeg and lime powder. Keep in an airtight container for 1 month.

Saudi baharat

2 tbsp black peppercorns

1 tbsp coriander seeds

small piece of cassia or cinnamon stick

2 tsp cumin seeds

2 tsp whole cloves

seeds from 6 green cardamom pods

2 tsp ground ginger

½ nutmeg, grated

2 tbsp paprika

1 tsp ground hot chili

Grind all the whole spices and mix with the ginger, nutmeg, paprika, and ground chili. Sift and store in an airtight container for 2 months. Fennel seed and turmeric are sometimes added to baharat.

The mixture is used in kibbeh, in meat stuffings for pastries, in tomato and other sauces, and in stews and soups.

Bizar a'shuwa

This blend comes from Oman, thanks to Philip Iddison, and is based on a recipe from *Al Azaf, the Omani Cookbook* by Lamees Abdullah Al Taie.

1 tbsp cumin seeds

1 tbsp coriander seeds

1 tbsp cardamom seeds

2 tsp ground hot chili

½ tsp ground turmeric

2–3 tbsp vinegar

2 garlic cloves, crushed

Grind the whole spices and mix with the chili and turmeric. Combine with enough vinegar and the garlic to make a stiff paste. Add to slow-cooked dishes or use as a rub for meat or chicken.

Yemeni hawaij

This blend is recommended for soups, grilled meat, and vegetable dishes.

1 tbsp black peppercorns

1 tbsp caraway seeds

1 tsp green cardamom seeds

1 tsp saffron threads

2 tsp ground turmeric

Combine all the ingredients in an electric mill and grind to a powder. Store for up to 2 months.

Yemeni zhug

This paste is a combination of garlic and peppers plus whatever spices the cook chooses. It is popular in Israel, where it has spread beyond the cooking of Yemeni Jews. There are red versions, as this one, and green ones with more cilantro and also parsley instead of sweet peppers.

2 small red sweet peppers

2 hot red chili peppers

8 garlic cloves

2 tsp coriander seeds

1 tsp cumin seeds

seeds from 6 green cardamom pods

handful of cilantro – leaves and young stems

Remove the seeds from the sweet and chili peppers, then cut them into pieces. Chop the garlic roughly. Blend all the ingredients to a paste in a food processor. Store in a closed jar in the refrigerator for 1–2 weeks, covered by a layer of oil.

Zhug is used as a condiment and a sauce for grilled fish or meat, and is added to soups and stews just before serving. A spoonful or two of zhug can be added to hilbeh (*below*).

Yemeni hilbeh

2 tbsp ground fenugreek seeds

large bunch of cilantro – leaves and small stems

4 garlic cloves, crushed

sea salt and freshly ground black pepper

seeds from 3–4 cardamom pods, crushed

¼ tsp caraway seeds

2–4 hot green chili peppers, seeded and chopped

juice of 1–2 lemons

Soak the ground fenugreek in plenty of hot water and leave overnight, or for at least 8 hours. It will separate into clear liquid at the top and a gelatinous mixture in the bottom of the bowl. Pour off the liquid, then set aside. Blend the cilantro, garlic, and all the other ingredients with the juice of 1 lemon. Add the fenugreek and blend again. Taste and add more lemon juice or salt if necessary. A little water can be beaten in to thin the mixture; it should be like a soft paste. The texture should be slightly frothy from the fenugreek, and the taste pungent and slightly bitter.

Hilbeh is stirred into stews at the end of cooking, or served at room temperature as a condiment to accompany dishes, or simply eaten with Middle-Eastern flatbread. Chopped tomatoes are sometimes added; in the Jewish community in Calcutta, where it is popular, a little fresh ginger is used. Store covered in the refrigerator for up to a week.

Taklia

This mixture of garlic and coriander is used to flavor soups and stews just before they are served. Popular throughout the Arab world, it is widely used in Egypt with melokhia, a dish that is virtually the national soup.

3 garlic cloves

salt

2 tbsp sunflower oil

1 tbsp ground coriander

½ tsp cayenne

Crush the garlic with a little salt and fry in the oil until golden. Stir in the coriander and cayenne, mix to a paste and fry, stirring, for 2 minutes. Use at once.

Za'atar

Za'atar is a generic name for a number of herbs with a thyme-savory-oregano aroma (*p.102*). This mixture is popular in the Middle East, sprinkled on meatballs, kebabs, and vegetables, or used as a dip. Mixed to a paste with olive oil, it can be spread over bread before baking.

2oz (60g) sesame seeds

1oz (30g) ground sumac

1oz (30g) dried za'atar or thyme, powdered

Dry-roast the sesame seeds for a few minutes, stirring frequently. Let them cool, then mix with the sumac and za'atar or thyme. Store in an airtight jar for 2–3 months.

Tunisian bharat

The simplest Tunisian mixture uses equal amounts of ground cinnamon and ground dried rosebuds, sometimes with the addition of a little black pepper. It is used for fish, roast and grilled meat, couscous, and tagines.

Aleppo blend

This mixture is used for grilled and roast chicken and lamb, and for preparing köfte and kibbeh.

1 tbsp black peppercorns

1 tbsp allspice berries

seeds from 5 green cardamom pods

½ nutmeg

1 tsp coriander seeds

1 tsp cumin seeds

1 tbsp ground cinnamon

1 tbsp Turkish or Aleppo red chili flakes (or paprika)

1 tsp sumac

Grind all the whole spices and blend with the cinnamon, chili flakes, and sumac. Store in an airtight jar for 2–3 months.

Tabil

Tabil means coriander, and it is also the name of a spice blend found only in Tunisia, as far as I can discover.

3 tbsp coriander seeds

1 tbsp caraway seeds

2 garlic cloves, crushed

2 tsp ground hot chili

Pound or grind all the ingredients together coarsely, then dry in the sun if you live in a hot place, or dry in a low oven, 250°F (130°C), for 30–45 minutes. When quite dry and cooled, grind to a fine powder.

Tabil is used for stews, sautéed and stuffed vegetables, and beef dishes. Store in an airtight container for 1–2 months.

Dukka

This Egyptian nut and spice blend varies from family to family. It is served at breakfast or as a snack later in the day. It has also become fashionable as a nibble with drinks and an appetizer in Australia.

4oz (120g) sesame seeds

⅔ cup (90g) hazelnuts

2oz (60g) coriander seeds

1oz (30g) cumin seeds

salt to taste

olive oil, to serve

Dry-roast all the ingredients separately until the sesame is golden, the hazelnuts are losing their skins, and the coriander and cumin darken and give off their aroma. For large quantities use a hot oven, 500°F (250°C). Let cool.

Remove loose skins from the hazelnuts. Put the ingredients into a food processor and grind to a coarse powder. Don't overwork or the oil from the nuts and sesame will be released and turn it into a paste. Store in an airtight container. Serve at room temperature with Middle-Eastern bread and olive oil. Dip the bread into the oil and then into the dukka.

Qâlat daqqa

This blend of five spices is from Tunisia, where it is used primarily with lamb and vegetable dishes. It is particularly good with pumpkin and other winter squashes, eggplant, spinach, and chickpeas and other legumes.

2 tsp black peppercorns

2 tsp whole cloves

1 tsp grains of paradise

1 tsp ground cinnamon

1 tbsp grated nutmeg

Grind the whole spices to a powder and combine with the cinnamon and nutmeg. Store in an airtight jar for 2–3 months.

La kama

This Moroccan mixture is used for harira, the soup eaten to break the Ramadan fast, for stews, and as a seasoning for chicken.

1 tbsp ground black pepper

1 tbsp ground ginger

1 tbsp ground turmeric

1 tsp grated nutmeg

2 tsp ground cumin

Combine all the spices and store in an airtight container for 1–2 months.

Ras el hanout

Ras el hanout is a Moroccan mixture of 20 or more spices. Many versions contain aphrodisiacs as well as herbs and spices. A typical blend could include allspice, ash berries, black and green cardamom, cassia, chufa nuts, cinnamon, cloves, cubebs, galangal, ginger, grains of paradise, lavender, mace, monk's pepper, nigella, nutmeg, orris root, black pepper, long pepper, rosebuds, ground turmeric, and the potentially hazardous belladonna and cantharides (Spanish fly). Exported ready-ground blends tend to be less exotic. In Tunisia, ras el hanout is a simpler blend of rosebuds, black pepper, cubebs, cloves, and cinnamon.

Ras el hanout is usually sold whole, and ground as required. It is used with game, lamb, couscous, and rice.

Africa

On the Horn of Africa and down the east coast, people have always looked eastward for their flavorings. In West Africa, chilies tend to dominate, together with local herbs and spices; in South Africa, Indian and Malay communities have influenced the cooking, with curries, sambals, and blatjangs.

West-African pepper blend

Pepper blends are used as a seasoning for fish, meat, and vegetables. They may be used as a dry mixture or made into a paste with the addition of onion, garlic, tomatoes, sweet red peppers, dried shrimp, and palm oil.

2 tbsp black peppercorns

2 tbsp white peppercorns

1 tbsp cubebs

1 tbsp allspice berries

2 tsp grains of paradise

2 tsp ground ginger

1 tbsp dried hot chili flakes

Grind the whole spices and combine with the ginger and chili flakes. Store in an airtight container for 2–3 months.

South-African curry powder

This mixture comes from the Cape. It is used with a paste of ginger and garlic pounded with salt; 2 tsp ground turmeric could be added.

2 tsp fennel seeds

2 tsp coriander seeds

2 tsp cumin seeds

small piece of cinnamon stick

seeds from 5 cardamom pods

Grind all the ingredients and store for 2–3 months in an airtight container.

Berbere

Berbere is a fiery mixture used in Ethiopia and Eritrea. Rather like garam masala (*p.286*), it is a complex blend of spices made to suit the dish and the taste of the cook. It is used primarily to flavor stews (called wats) of meat, vegetables, or lentils, but also to coat foods to be fried or grilled, or served as an accompaniment. The key spices are chili peppers, ginger, and cloves; others vary, and some are not found outside the region.

15–20 dried hot red chili peppers

1 tsp coriander seeds

seeds from 6 green cardamom pods

12 allspice berries

1 tsp cumin seeds

1 tsp fenugreek seeds

8 whole cloves

½ cinnamon stick, broken

½ tsp ajowan

1 tsp black peppercorns

1 tsp ground ginger

Heat a large, heavy frying pan and dry-roast the chilies for 2–3 minutes, turning and stirring. Add the other whole spices and roast for a further 5–6 minutes, stirring constantly, until all the spices have darkened.

Let cool, then grind, including the ginger, to a powder. Store in an airtight container for 2–3 months.

Wat spices

This is a simple blend and quick to prepare.

3 long peppers

1 tbsp black peppercorns

1 tbsp whole cloves

½ nutmeg

2 tbsp ground hot chili

2 tsp ground ginger

1 tsp ground cinnamon

Dry-roast the peppers, peppercorns, cloves, and nutmeg, and grind them when cool. Stir in the chili, ginger, and cinnamon. Add to a wat (stew) toward the end of cooking. The spice mixture will keep in an airtight jar for 2–3 months.

Europe

Early European food for the rich was spiced predominantly with pepper, cinnamon, cloves, and ginger, sweetened with honey, or later with sugar, and moistened with vinegar. By the 16th century the sweet element had diminished, and when, in the 17th and 18th centuries, spices became more widely available they were used less ostentatiously. Cookbooks of the 19th century began to record curry powders (from recipes sent home by colonial administrators) and mixtures that were often called kitchen pepper. Today few European spice blends are still in use, although Europeans consume quantities of spiced foods from other parts of the world.

Quatre épices

The classic French blend is used primarily for charcuterie and other meat products. It is useful to flavor a glaze for baked ham and to season fresh pork before cooking.

2 tbsp black or white peppercorns

1 tsp whole cloves

2 tsp grated nutmeg

1 tsp ground ginger

Grind the peppercorns and cloves finely, then combine with the nutmeg and ginger. Store in an airtight container for 1–2 months.

Cinnamon sometimes replaces ginger, and I have also come across mixtures that use allspice instead of cloves, and mace instead of nutmeg.

Italian spice mixture

This blend is good sprinkled on chicken or pork chops to be grilled or baked, to flavor a loin of pork to be stuffed and roasted, and rubbed onto a shoulder of lamb to be slow-roasted, wrapped in foil with apricot leather or other dried fruits.

1 tbsp white or black peppercorns

½ nutmeg

1 tsp juniper berries

¼ tsp whole cloves

Grind all the spices in an electric mill (it may be easier if you crush the nutmeg first with a rolling pin). Store the powder in an airtight container for 3–4 months.

Kitchen pepper

Kitchen pepper used to be made in bulk; here is an up-to-date version in a manageable quantity. Use it for stews and winter soups, bean dishes and spiced red cabbage, or to sprinkle over root vegetables before roasting them.

1 tbsp black peppercorns

2 tsp whole cloves

2 nutmegs, crushed with a rolling pin

2–3 pieces of dried ginger

1 tbsp anise seed

1 tbsp coriander seeds

Grind all the spices in an electric mill and store in an airtight container for 3–4 months.

Sweet baking spice

This English mixture, sold as mixed spice, is used for cookies, fruit cakes, mincemeat, and baked or steamed puddings. The selection and proportions of spices vary according to individual taste; some cooks add ginger to the blend, but I prefer this version.

½ cinnamon stick

1 tbsp allspice berries

1 tbsp coriander seeds

2 tsp whole cloves

4 mace blades

2 tsp grated nutmeg

Grind the whole spices to a fine powder and mix with the nutmeg. Store in an airtight container for 2–3 months.

Pickling spices

This is an English mixture of whole spices used when pickling fruits and vegetables in vinegar.

2 tbsp pieces of dried ginger

1½ tbsp yellow mustard seeds

2 tbsp mace blades

3 tbsp allspice berries

2 tbsp black peppercorns

2½ tbsp whole cloves

2 tbsp coriander seeds

Combine all the spices and use to flavor the vinegar that is to be used in making the pickles. The spices can be added directly or put into a cheesecloth bag for later removal.

The Americas

Many culinary influences can be traced in the Americas. In the US and Canada, English and French spice blends once predominated in the north, but now Mexican, Caribbean, and African ideas are widely popular. The Caribbean islands show a variety of colonial traditions (Spanish, French, and English) as well as immigrant influences – notably African, Indian, Sri Lankan, and Chinese – in the development of their cuisines. Mexico has maintained strong pre-Columbian food styles. Much of South America shows some vestiges of Spanish or Portuguese culinary traditions, combined with Indian food patterns in the Andes and with African traditions in Brazil.

Ají paste

This potent paste of chilies and garlic comes from Bolivia, where it is used as the base flavoring for stews and thick soups. Fresh herbs – cilantro or quillquiña, basil, and oregano – are usually added just before the dish is served.

2oz (60g) dried hot chili peppers, seeds removed

4 garlic cloves

½ tsp salt

5–6 tbsp water

3 tbsp sunflower or olive oil

Soak the chilies in hot water for 30 minutes, then drain and tear into pieces. Crush the garlic with the salt.

Blend all the ingredients to a smooth paste. Store for up to 1 month in the refrigerator under a layer of oil.

Barbecue spice

This is a medium-hot spice blend to rub onto meat before grilling.

1 tsp black peppercorns

½ tsp cumin seeds

½ tsp dried thyme

½ tsp dried marjoram

½ tsp cayenne

2 tsp paprika

1 tsp mustard powder

½ tsp salt

1 tbsp light brown sugar

Grind the peppercorns and cumin; crumble or grind the herbs if necessary; and combine all the ingredients. Spread the mixture over the meat and leave for 2–3 hours before cooking.

Cajun seasoning

The gumbos and jambalayas, blackened fish and grilled meats of the Cajun and Creole cooks of Louisiana are flavored with aromatic herbs, hot chilies, and other spices. Commercial blends use dried garlic and onion, which I find have a synthetic taste, so I mix the dry ingredients and add fresh garlic and onion.

1 tsp paprika

½ tsp ground black pepper

1 tsp ground fennel seed

½ tsp ground cumin

½ tsp mustard powder

1 tsp cayenne

1 tsp dried thyme

1 tsp dried oregano

½ tsp dried sage

½ tsp salt

1–2 garlic cloves

½ small onion

Combine all the dry ingredients. Crush the garlic and onion in a mortar and add to the dry ingredients.

Rub the mixture onto meat or fish and let marinate for up to 1 hour, then grill or fry to form a crisp crust. Alternatively, stir some of the mixture into rice dishes or gumbos.

Virgin-Islands spiced salt

The Virgin Islands were once an important stop for the British Royal Navy, and salt-based curing and seasoning is still practiced there, while salt is harvested at Salt Island in the British Islands.

3 tbsp sea salt

2 tsp black peppercorns

¼ tsp whole cloves

½ tsp grated nutmeg

¼ tsp dried thyme

2 garlic cloves, crushed

½ small onion, chopped

2 sprigs of fresh parsley

Grind all the ingredients in a mortar or food processor and store in the refrigerator. Use to rub onto fish or steak before grilling, or over a chicken before roasting.

For a dry mix omit the garlic, onion, and parsley and add a crumbled, dried bay leaf and ¼ tsp dried rosemary to the blend. This will keep for 2–3 months in an airtight container.

Poudre de Colombo

Colombo is the name of a curry made on the French Caribbean islands, originally by indentured workers from Sri Lanka. The curry powder does not have the heat of those from some of the other islands, and is very similar to Sri-Lankan curry powder (*p.288*).

1 tbsp uncooked rice
1 tbsp cumin seeds
1 tbsp coriander seeds
1 tsp black peppercorns
1 tsp fenugreek seeds
1 tsp black mustard seeds
4 whole cloves
1½ tbsp ground turmeric

Dry-roast the rice until lightly browned, stirring frequently. Put it aside to cool and add the whole spices to the pan. Roast until they give off their aroma and darken in color. Let them cool.

Grind the rice and spices to a powder in an electric mill, then stir in the turmeric. Store in an airtight container for 2–3 months.

West-Indian masala

Just as laborers from Sri Lanka took Colombo powder to the French islands, Hindus from the subcontinent took their masalas with them to Trinidad and Tobago. This recipe comes from Trinidad.

3 tbsp coriander seeds
1 tsp anise seed
1 tsp whole cloves
1 tsp cumin seeds
1 tsp fenugreek seeds
1 tsp black peppercorns
1 tsp black mustard seeds
1 tsp ground turmeric
ground hot chili to taste
3 garlic cloves, crushed
1 medium onion, chopped

Dry-roast the whole spices and let cool. Grind them finely, then combine with the turmeric and, if you wish, some ground chili.

Pound together with the garlic and onion, or blend in a processor to a smooth paste. If necessary, add a little water, tamarind water, or lemon juice. Store in the refrigerator for 3–4 days.

Steak recado

Spice pastes called recados are essential to the cooking of the Yucatán peninsula in southern Mexico, which is itself firmly rooted in Mayan traditions. On market stalls bowls are piled high with red, black, and khaki pastes; similar pastes are found in Cuba. This is a khaki version.

8 garlic cloves, crushed
1 tsp allspice berries
1 tsp black peppercorns
¼ tsp cumin seeds
½ cinnamon stick
1 tsp coriander seeds
4 whole cloves
2 tsp dried oregano
½ tsp salt
1 tbsp cider or wine vinegar

Combine all the ingredients in a food processor and blend to a paste. Store in the refrigerator; the flavors will develop if kept for a day before using, and the mixture will keep for several weeks.

The recado is used to rub on steaks for grilling or frying, but even more commonly in chicken and other dishes preserved in escabeche (a lightly spiced pickle).

Recado rojo: red achiote paste

1½ tbsp achiote seeds
½ tbsp coriander seeds
½ tbsp black peppercorns
½ tsp cumin seeds
3 whole cloves
2 tsp dried oregano
5 garlic cloves
1 tsp salt
1–2 tbsp wine vinegar or Seville orange juice

Grind the first 6 ingredients to a powder in an electric spice mill. Achiote seeds are very hard, so it will take a little time. Crush the garlic with the salt in a mortar, then gradually work in the ground spices. A hot red chili pepper could be added; crush it with the garlic. Moisten with the vinegar or bitter orange juice so that you have a smooth paste.

Form the paste into small disks or balls and let them dry, or put the paste into an airtight jar. Whether dried or as a paste, the recado will keep for several months if refrigerated.

To use, mix with more Seville orange juice. The recado is essential to the local specialty, pollo pibil (chicken wrapped in banana leaves and steamed or baked). Fish and pork can be cooked in the same way, and the mixture gives depth to soups and stews.

SAUCES AND CONDIMENTS

Most regions of the world have developed their favorite sauces – as a dip, to accompany dishes, or as an integral part of the cooking process. East India Company traders introduced relishes and ketchups to Britain, and condiments and sauces based on herbs and spices were among the first foods to be manufactured commercially.

Salsa verde

2 handfuls of fresh parsley sprigs, chopped

a few sprigs of fresh mint or basil, chopped

1 garlic clove, crushed

1 tbsp capers, chopped

4 anchovy fillets, chopped

approx ⅔ cup (150ml) extra virgin olive oil

salt and freshly ground pepper

Blend the herbs, garlic, capers, and anchovy fillets to a coarse paste in a food processor. Scrape down the sides and trickle in enough oil through the feed tube to make a smooth sauce. Season to taste. Serve with poached or baked fish, grilled meats, or with artichokes, cauliflower, or broccoli.

Pesto

This Genoese sauce for pasta also goes well with vegetables and as a dip or a spread for bruschetta; a thin version makes a good sauce for fish.

4 handfuls of fresh basil leaves

1 large garlic clove, crushed

¼ cup (30g) pine nuts

¼ cup (30g) grated Parmesan or pecorino cheese

5–6 tbsp extra virgin olive oil

Put all the ingredients except the olive oil into a food processor and blend. Scrape down the sides and add the oil slowly through the feed tube until you have a thick, green sauce. For a thinner sauce, add more olive oil. If you don't have a processor, put the basil and garlic in a large mortar and pound with a pestle. Add the pine nuts, a few at a time, then the cheese and oil alternately until you have a thick paste. Add more oil to obtain the consistency you want.

VARIATIONS

Cilantro pesto

Use cilantro instead of fresh basil and walnuts in place of pine nuts.

Parsley pesto

Replace the basil with parsley and use either pine nuts or blanched almonds.

Arugula pesto

Replace the basil with arugula and use walnuts or pine nuts.

Parsley and lemon sauce

1 tbsp Dijon mustard

juice of 1 lemon

⅔ cup (150ml) extra virgin olive oil

salt and freshly ground pepper

1½ cups (90g) finely chopped fresh parsley

2 shallots, finely chopped

Whisk the mustard into the lemon juice, add the oil, season, and stir in the parsley and shallots. Serve with grilled fish, seafood, or chicken.

Basil, mint, and red pepper sauce

3–4 sprigs of fresh mint

large handful of fresh basil leaves

1 red sweet pepper

1 small garlic clove, minced

salt and freshly ground pepper

2 tbsp red wine vinegar

3 tbsp olive oil

Strip the leaves from the mint sprigs and chop them finely with the basil. Scorch the red pepper over a gas flame or under the broiler until blackened all over. Put it into a plastic bag and let cool, then rub off the skin. Remove seeds and membrane, rinse, pat dry, and chop the flesh finely.

Mix the garlic and seasoning into the vinegar, then add the oil. Stir in the herbs and red pepper. This sauce goes well with cold fish, such as poached turbot or salmon.

Horseradish and apple sauce

This Austrian sauce (Apfelkren) makes a change from the standard horseradish cream. It goes well with beef, with smoked meats and sausages, and with smoked eel and trout. For a milder sauce, use more cream or add a few fresh bread crumbs to the mixture.

2 tbsp lemon juice

½ cup (60g) grated fresh horseradish

1 large tart apple

salt and sugar to taste

scant ½ cup (100ml) whipping cream

Stir 1 tbsp lemon juice into the horseradish so that it doesn't discolor. Peel, core, and grate the apple, and stir it into the horseradish with the remaining lemon juice. Season with a little salt and sugar, and let stand for 15 minutes. Whip the cream lightly and fold it into the horseradish mixture.

Yogurt and herb dressing

This can be used as a salad dressing, for baked potatoes, or as a dip. Use one or two of these herbs, which all combine well with yogurt: chives, cilantro, dill, lemon balm, lovage, marjoram, mint, parsley, or tarragon.

⅓ cup chopped fresh herbs

1 garlic clove, crushed

1–2 tbsp lemon juice

1 cup (250ml) thick, plain yogurt

salt and freshly ground pepper

paprika

Stir the herbs, garlic, and lemon juice into the yogurt and season with salt, pepper, and paprika.

Tartar sauce

To 1¼ cups (300ml) mayonnaise add 1 tsp each of chopped parsley, shallot, capers, gherkins, and green olives. The sauce is good with all fish and seafood, whether served hot or cold.

Remoulade sauce

Into 1¼ cups (300ml) mayonnaise work 1 tsp Dijon mustard and 1 pounded anchovy, then stir in 2 tsp each of chopped parsley, chervil, tarragon, capers, and gherkins. The sauce goes well with lobster and other seafood.

Ravigote sauce

To ⅔ cup (150ml) vinaigrette add 1 tbsp chopped capers, 1 tbsp chopped shallot, 2–3 tbsp chopped fresh herbs (parsley, chives, chervil, tarragon). This sauce is good with potato salad and grilled fish.

Béarnaise sauce

This sauce is the classic French accompaniment for grilled steak.

⅔ cup (150ml) dry white wine

3 tbsp white wine or tarragon vinegar

3 shallots, finely chopped

5 sprigs of fresh tarragon

freshly ground white pepper

1½ sticks/¾ cup (180g) unsalted butter

3 egg yolks

salt

1 tbsp finely chopped fresh tarragon leaves or a mixture of tarragon and chervil

Put the wine, vinegar, shallots, tarragon sprigs, and a good grinding of pepper into a small, heavy pan over low heat. Simmer, uncovered, until the liquid has reduced to 2–3 tbsp. Strain through a fine sieve, pressing the shallots and tarragon well to extract maximum flavor. Return the liquid to the pan.

Melt the butter gently in another pan and set aside. When it has cooled to lukewarm, pour off the clear liquid to use later; discard the white residue.

Set the pan with the wine and vinegar infusion over very low heat and whisk in the egg yolks and a little salt. Add the melted butter, a tablespoon or so at a time, whisking continuously. Wait until each spoonful is absorbed before adding more butter. Remove the pan from the heat before adding the final spoonful; it will be hot enough to go on cooking the sauce. Stir in the chopped tarragon and check that the seasoning is to taste.

The sauce can be kept warm for a short time in a bowl placed over a pan of hot, but not boiling, water.

VARIATION

Sauce paloise

Replace the tarragon with mint and serve the sauce with poached fish, grilled chicken, or lamb.

Sorrel sauce

Sorrel sauce can be made quickly to accompany fish and eggs. A thick version is also good with lamb chops.

7oz/about 2 cups (200g) sorrel leaves

1 tbsp (15g) butter

scant ½ cup (100ml) crème fraîche or whipping cream

salt and freshly ground pepper

Remove any thick stems from the sorrel and cook the leaves gently in the butter. They will wilt quickly. Stir in the cream a little at a time; sorrel is acidic, so it is important to balance the sorrel and the cream. Taste and find the balance that suits you. Season with a little salt and pepper.

Romesco sauce

This famous Catalan sauce is particularly popular in Tarragona. Serve it with fish and chicken, and with grilled vegetables.

2 ñora chili peppers

1 small, dried hot chili pepper

2 tbsp blanched almonds

2 tbsp hazelnuts

6 tbsp olive oil

3 garlic cloves

1 slice of white bread, without crusts

2 piquillo peppers or 1 red sweet pepper, roasted, peeled, and diced

2 tsp tomato paste

1 medium ripe tomato, peeled, seeded, and chopped

2 tbsp white wine vinegar

salt and freshly ground pepper

Break open the chilies, remove the seeds, and soak the flesh in hot water for 30 minutes.

Dry-roast the almonds and then the hazelnuts. Rub the skins from the hazelnuts in a cloth.

Heat 2 tbsp oil and fry 2 of the peeled garlic cloves until lightly colored. Remove the garlic, and fry the slice of bread in the same oil. Remove when lightly browned.

Put the drained chilies, all the garlic, the bread, nuts, roasted pepper, and tomato paste into a food processor or blender. When you have a smooth sauce transfer it to a bowl and stir in the tomato, the remaining oil, and the vinegar. Taste and season. If the sauce is too thick, add a little more olive oil or vinegar, or a little water. The sauce will keep for 2–3 days, covered, in the refrigerator.

Green mojo

Green mojo is a dipping sauce from the Canary Islands, usually served with papas arrugadas (wrinkled potatoes): Put unpeeled new potatoes in a pan and almost cover with cold water. Add ⅓ cup (100g) salt for each pound (500g) of potatoes. Bring to a boil, then lower the heat and cook until the potatoes are done, about 15 minutes. Drain but leave the potatoes in the pan over low heat, shaking them from time to time. They will be wrinkled and salty on the outside, but soft and tender inside.

Served with this mojo, they are decidedly more-ish. The mojo is also good with fish, meat, and salads.

1 green sweet pepper

3 hot green chili peppers

10 garlic cloves

1 tsp coarse salt

leaves from a bunch of fresh parsley

1 tsp ground cumin

4 tbsp wine vinegar

6 tbsp olive oil

Remove the seeds and veins from the sweet and chili peppers, then chop coarsely. Crush the garlic with the salt. Blend all the ingredients in a blender or processor, or pound in a mortar, until you have a smooth paste. Thin with water if you wish. Covered with a layer of oil in a closed jar, the sauce keeps for 2 weeks in the refrigerator.

Tomato sauce

This spicy sauce uses the Saudi baharat mixture (*p.289*). It goes well with roast or baked meat and with rice.

2 tbsp olive oil

6 garlic cloves, crushed

2lb (1kg) ripe tomatoes, peeled and chopped

1–2 tsp salt

2 tsp Saudi baharat

Heat the oil in a heavy pan and lightly fry the garlic for 1 minute. Do not let it color too much. Add the tomatoes and salt to taste, and simmer, covered, for 20–30 minutes. Stir in the Saudi baharat. Leave the pan uncovered and cook for 3–4 minutes longer.

Harissa

This fiery chili sauce is found throughout North Africa, but it is especially popular in Tunisia. It is usually made with dried chilies; the local chili pepper resembles the slender guajillo of Mexico. If you prefer to use fresh chilies for a table sauce, substitute the same quantity as dried and omit the soaking. Harissa is used in cooking and as a condiment with eggs, couscous, and tagines.

3½oz (100g) dried hot chili peppers

2 garlic cloves, peeled

½ tsp salt

½ tsp ground cumin

1 tsp ground caraway

olive oil

Break the chilies into pieces and discard the seeds. Soak the flesh in almost-boiling water for about 30 minutes, until soft. Meanwhile crush the garlic with the salt.

Drain the chilies and pound or process with the garlic and spices. Add 1–2 tbsp olive oil, or more, to lubricate the mixture. Store in a jar under a layer of olive oil for 3–4 weeks.

Harissa is usually thinned with oil and lemon juice, water, or a few spoonfuls of hot stock from the dish with which it is to be served.

Preserved lemons

Preserved lemons are a specialty of Morocco, although they are used elsewhere in North Africa. Traditionally used as a flavoring for meat, fish, and vegetables, they have a distinctive, slightly salty taste that is also good in salads, salsas, and dressings.

10 unwaxed lemons

coarse sea salt

Cut 5 of the lemons lengthwise into quarters, but stop short of separating the quarters completely by leaving the lemons uncut at the stem end. Gently pull the lemons open and sprinkle salt, about 1 tbsp per lemon, onto the exposed flesh; close up the lemons again and put them into a canning jar. Press down well and put a weight (a clean, heavy stone will do) on top, then close the jar.

After 2–3 days the lemons will have released some of their juices. Pour in enough juice from the remaining 5 lemons to cover them completely and leave for 1 month. If a piece of lemon is exposed to the air it may develop a harmless white mold that can be washed off.

The lemons will keep for up to a year; the flavor mellows with keeping. Only the chopped skin is used; discard the flesh and seeds when you take the pieces from the jar.

Thai chili jam

This relish, called nam prik pad in Thai, is similar to Indonesian sambals. It is served as a condiment or stirred into soups, stir-fries, and rice dishes.

1 tsp shrimp paste (kapi)

8 large, hot red chili peppers, fresh or dried

8 garlic cloves, cut in half

8 shallots, cut in half

¼ cup dried shrimp

3 tbsp sunflower oil

1 tbsp fish sauce

2 tbsp palm sugar

2 tbsp tamarind water (***p.163***)

Wrap the shrimp paste in foil and dry-roast in a pan, or in a preheated oven at 400°F (200°C), for a few minutes.

Remove stems and, if you wish, seeds from the chilies. Dry-roast the chilies, garlic, and shallots separately in a heavy pan, or in the preheated oven. Do not let them burn. When the chilies, garlic, and shallots are soft, put them into a food processor with the shrimp paste and blend, scraping down the sides if necessary. Pound the dried shrimp and add them to the mixture.

Heat the oil and fry the paste until it smells fragrant, then add the fish sauce, sugar, and tamarind water, and cook until all is well mixed and slightly reduced. Let cool, then store in a jar in the refrigerator for 2–3 weeks.

Nam prik

This sauce, which translates literally as "chili water," is popular throughout Thailand. Served with rice, fish, and raw or lightly cooked vegetables, it includes dried shrimp, shrimp paste, chilies, and garlic pounded with palm sugar, fish sauce, and lime juice. Shallots, peanuts, small eggplants, and unripe fruits are also used. Nam prik is made in minutes, to individual taste.

4 hot red chili peppers, seeded and chopped

4 garlic cloves, chopped

2 tbsp dried shrimp

1 tbsp palm or granulated sugar

1 tbsp water

2 tbsp fish sauce

lime juice

Pound the chilies, garlic, dried shrimp, and sugar in a mortar or blend in a food processor with the water. Gradually add the fish sauce and enough lime juice, probably 3–4 tbsp, to give a well-blended consistency. Taste. In a closed jar the sauce will keep for 1–2 weeks in the refrigerator.

Roasted nam prik

1 tsp tamarind concentrate

2 tbsp peanuts

5 garlic cloves, unpeeled

5 shallots, unpeeled

5 hot red chili peppers

thin slice of shrimp paste (kapi)

1 tbsp palm or granulated sugar

Dissolve the tamarind in 2 tbsp hot water. Heat a heavy frying pan and quickly dry-roast the peanuts. Set them aside. Dry-roast the garlic and shallots until the skins are dark brown and the insides soft. Wrap the chilies in foil and dry-roast until they soften. At the same time, wrap the shrimp paste in a tightly closed foil parcel and dry-roast for 1–2 minutes on each side, or until it darkens.

Peel the garlic and shallots; remove the seeds from the chilies, if you wish, and chop the flesh. Pound or process everything (including the sugar) to a paste. Store for a week or two in a closed jar in the refrigerator.

Nuoc cham

Nuoc cham is the dipping sauce served with every Vietnamese meal. There are different styles according to the region: in the north the sauce is often a simple one of fish sauce (nuoc mam) and water with chopped chilies, whereas in the south garlic, sugar, and lime juice are added. Bird chili peppers are best, but if you can't find them you can substitute other fresh hot chilies.

2 tbsp lime juice

3 tbsp fish sauce

3 tbsp water

2 tbsp sugar

1 bird chili pepper, seeded and finely chopped

1 garlic clove, minced

Combine the liquids and sugar, stirring until the sugar has dissolved. Add the chili and garlic.

VARIATIONS

Peel and finely chop a small piece of fresh ginger and add to the sauce.

Replace the fish sauce with soy sauce and reduce the sugar to 1 tbsp.

Sweet chili sauce

This easy sauce is good with fried or grilled fish and seafood or spring rolls.

½ cup (120ml) water

6 tbsp sugar

4 medium, hot red chili peppers, seeded and finely sliced

2 garlic cloves, minced

small piece of fresh ginger, cut into fine strips

5 tbsp rice or cider vinegar

1 tbsp fish sauce

3–4 tbsp chopped cilantro

Heat the water and sugar together to make a syrup. Let it thicken a little, then stir in all the ingredients except the cilantro. Bring to a boil and simmer for 3 minutes.

Pour the sauce into a bowl and let cool, then stir in the cilantro. Taste for seasoning and add a little salt if necessary; I find that the fish sauce makes it salty enough.

SAMBALS

Unlike curry pastes or masalas, Indonesian bumbus (spice mixtures) are an integral part of each dish. They usually have a base of onion and garlic with coriander, cumin, soy sauce, and tamarind or lime juice. The other spices and herbs vary according to the dish. Indonesians also make aromatic, chili-based table sauces called sambals, some of which are very hot.

Sambal ulek

The chilies used in this simple sambal are lomboks, but other fresh red chilies can be substituted. A large quantity can be made; it will keep in the refrigerator for 2–3 weeks in a closed jar, or can be frozen in small pots.

1lb (500g) hot red chili peppers

2 tsp salt

1 tbsp lemon juice

Discard the stems and dry-roast the chilies briefly until they soften. Do not let them burn. Let cool, then remove seeds if you wish. Transfer the chilies to a food processor with the salt and lemon juice, and process to a paste.

VARIATIONS

Sambal kemiri

Make half the quantity of sambal ulek. Dry-roast and grind 10 candlenuts, and add when processing.

Sambal manis

Add 2 tsp palm sugar to half the quantity of sambal ulek.

Sambal bajak

This sambal is made with large chilies and is fairly mild and quite sweet because of the addition of shallots, garlic, and coconut milk. It goes well with rice dishes such as nasi goreng.

10 large, medium-hot red chili peppers
8 shallots, chopped
5 garlic cloves, chopped
1 tsp shrimp paste (terasi)
5 candlenuts
1 tsp tamarind concentrate
½ tsp powdered galangal
2 kaffir lime leaves, shredded
2 tbsp sunflower oil
1 tsp salt
2 tsp palm sugar
1 cup (250ml) coconut milk

Discard the stems and, if you wish, the seeds of the chilies before chopping them coarsely. Process the chilies, shallots, garlic, shrimp paste, candlenuts, tamarind, galangal, and lime leaves to a paste.

Heat the oil and fry the paste for 10 minutes. Add the remaining ingredients and cook gently for 20–25 minutes, until the mixture thickens and has a visible layer of oil. Stir the oil into the sambal, let cool, and then store in jars in the refrigerator for 2–3 weeks.

Korean dipping sauce

Koreans have a number of dipping sauces based on combinations of sesame, chili, vinegar, and soy sauce. They are served with dumplings and pancakes, with raw fish, vegetables, and grilled meats.

1 tsp sugar
¼ cup soy sauce
2 tsp rice or cider vinegar
1 tsp toasted sesame oil
2 tsp toasted sesame seeds
1 scallion, very finely sliced
½ tsp ground hot chili

Stir the sugar into the soy sauce and vinegar. When it has dissolved, add all the other ingredients. The sauce will keep in the refrigerator for several days.

Pili pili sauce

This table condiment is popular in West Africa.

8oz (250g) hot red chili peppers
1 small onion
1 garlic clove
juice of 1 lemon

Remove stems, and seeds if you wish, from the chilies, then blend all the ingredients together until smooth.

Lime and chili sauce

There are different versions of this sauce throughout the Caribbean. This one is from Guadeloupe.

2 hot red chili peppers
1 tbsp sea salt
1 cup (250ml) lime juice

Remove the seeds from the chilies and slice finely. Dissolve the salt in the lime juice. Pack the chilies into a jar and pour in the lime juice. This is best after 2–3 days, but will keep for up to 1 month. Serve with fish or grilled vegetables.

Mole verde

Moles are Mexican cooked sauces, flavored with chilies and herbs. Green mole is good with poached chicken breast and sautéed duck breast.

⅔ cup (100g) pumpkin seeds
6 tomatillos, fresh or canned
2 garlic cloves, crushed
1 small onion, chopped
10 romaine lettuce leaves, torn
3 tbsp chopped cilantro
leaves from 3 sprigs of fresh epazote, or 1 tbsp dried
4 serrano chili peppers, seeded and chopped
¼ tsp ground cumin
2 tbsp sunflower oil
1 cup (250ml) chicken stock

Dry-roast the pumpkin seeds, stirring to prevent burning. Let cool, then grind. If the tomatillos are fresh, remove the husks and chop the flesh. Blend the tomatillos with the vegetables, herbs, and spices. Heat the oil in a pan and cook the sauce, stirring constantly, over high heat so that it thickens, about 5 minutes. Set aside.

Stir the pumpkin seeds into the stock and add to the sauce. Very gently heat it, avoiding boiling or it will lose its color. Let it barely simmer for 15 minutes, stirring regularly.

Chimichurri

This Argentinian herb sauce is served with grilled meats. It goes well with pies and vegetables, and in soups.

4 garlic cloves, minced

1 tsp ground black pepper

½ tsp dried hot chili flakes

1 tsp paprika

2 tsp finely chopped fresh oregano leaves

large handful of fresh parsley leaves and sprigs, finely chopped

7 tbsp (100ml) olive oil

5 tbsp red wine vinegar

salt to taste

Mix all the ingredients together in a jar and shake well. Leave for 3–4 hours before using.

Cuban mojo

A mojo is a table sauce, akin to a Mexican salsa. Seville (sour) orange juice is most often used; lime juice on its own or with a little sweet orange juice can be substituted.

¼ cup olive oil

2 garlic cloves, minced

1 shallot, finely chopped

½ tsp salt

1 tsp dried oregano

1 tsp ground cumin

7 tbsp (100ml) Seville orange juice, or 4½ tbsp sweet orange juice and 2½ tbsp lime juice

3 tbsp chopped cilantro

Heat the oil and gently fry the garlic and shallot until lightly browned. Remove from the heat and add the salt, oregano, cumin, and orange juice. Stir well and let cool.

Transfer to a bowl and stir in the cilantro. The mojo will keep in a bottle or jar in the refrigerator for 2–3 weeks, but it tastes best when fresh. Good with steak, chicken, vegetables.

Mango and papaya mojo

1 ripe mango

1 ripe papaya

2 scallions, finely sliced

small piece of fresh ginger, finely chopped

2 tbsp chopped fresh mint leaves

7 tbsp (100ml) lime juice

Cut the flesh of the mango and the papaya into small cubes and combine with the other ingredients. Serve with grilled fish, seafood, or chicken.

Ajilimójili

This Puerto Rican garlic and pepper sauce is made with mild ají dulce chilies. It is served with tostones (fried green plantains), but also goes well with fried or grilled fish or meat. This version is from *The Complete Book of Caribbean Cooking* by Elisabeth Lambert Ortiz.

3 hot red chili peppers

3 red sweet peppers

4 black peppercorns

4 garlic cloves, crushed

2 tsp salt

⅔ cup (150ml) lime juice

⅔ cup (150ml) olive oil

Remove the seeds and veins from the chili and sweet peppers, and chop them roughly. Reduce them to a coarse purée in a processor with the peppercorns, garlic, and salt.

Add the lime juice and olive oil and process until smooth. Store in the refrigerator in a closed jar for 3–4 weeks.

Peruvian parsley salsa

This salsa is served with corn, potatoes, and meat dishes.

1 small onion, finely chopped

1 tsp fresh oregano leaves

salt and freshly ground black pepper

wine vinegar

3 handfuls of fresh parsley leaves

1 tomato

Put the onion and oregano into a bowl, season, and add vinegar to cover. Let marinate for at least 30 minutes, then drain off the vinegar. Chop the parsley leaves to a paste in a food processor and add it to the onion and oregano.

Dip the tomato in boiling water and remove the skin. Grate the flesh into the salsa, or chop very finely and then add it. Stir well to combine all the ingredients.

Salsa fresca

This is the standard salsa found throughout Mexico.

4 tomatoes, peeled, seeded, and chopped

1 red onion, finely chopped

4 jalapeño chili peppers, seeded and sliced in thin rings

5 tbsp chopped cilantro

5 tbsp lime juice or sherry vinegar

salt

Combine all the ingredients and let stand for at least 30 minutes before using.

Green mango relish

1 large green mango, about 1lb (500g)

1 garlic clove, minced

1 small hot green chili pepper, finely chopped

½ tsp salt

1 tbsp olive oil

handful of fresh parsley or mint leaves, chopped

Chop the mango finely and mix with the other ingredients. This will keep for 2–3 days if you put it in a closed jar with a layer of oil over the top and store in the refrigerator.

Nepali mint chutney

large handful of fresh mint leaves, finely chopped

2 garlic cloves, minced

¼ tsp ground hot chili

½ tsp salt

juice of 1 lemon

2 tbsp mustard or sunflower oil

½ tsp fenugreek seeds

½ tsp ground turmeric

Combine the mint, garlic, ground chili, salt, and lemon juice; set aside. Heat the oil and fry the fenugreek seeds until they are very dark; add the turmeric and stir for a moment. Let cool, then stir into the mint mixture. Serve with rice or bread, or pakoras.

Cucumber sambal

Sambals with hot, sweet, and sour flavors are popular condiments in Indonesia and Malaysia. This one goes well with chicken satay, grilled fish, and vegetables.

1 hothouse cucumber

1 tbsp finely chopped onion

1 small, hot red chili pepper, seeded and cut in shreds

1 tbsp chopped fresh parsley or cilantro

½ tsp ground fennel seed

1 tsp sugar

salt and freshly ground pepper

2–3 tbsp lemon juice

2 tbsp sunflower oil

Remove the seeds from the cucumber and cut the flesh into short, thin strips. Mix with the onion, chili, and parsley or cilantro. Stir the fennel, sugar and seasoning into the lemon juice, then add the oil and toss with the cucumber mixture.

Tomato sambal

4 shallots, sliced

3 hot chili peppers, seeded and sliced

3 large tomatoes, chopped

3 tbsp chopped fresh mint or basil

juice of 1 lime or lemon

salt to taste

Combine all the ingredients and serve at room temperature. Good with chicken or pork satay.

Cilantro chutney

This chutney goes well with kebabs, samosas, pakoras, and fried or grilled vegetables. Vary the number of chilies to suit your taste.

6½ tbsp (60g) sesame seeds

1 tsp cumin seeds

8oz/about 4 cups (250g) cilantro – leaves and young stems

2–6 hot green chili peppers, seeded and chopped

1 tbsp chopped fresh ginger

salt

juice of 1 lemon

Dry-roast the sesame seeds and cumin seeds separately. Put all the ingredients except the salt and lemon juice into a food processor and blend to a paste.

Scrape down the sides of the bowl if necessary. Add salt to taste and enough lemon juice to loosen the paste a little; it should remain quite thick. In a closed jar the chutney will keep for a week in the refrigerator.

Garlic purée

Put 6 heads of young garlic in a pan and cover with boiling water. Simmer for 15–20 minutes until soft. Drain and let cool, then peel and blend in a food processor with a little salt. Mix in 4–6 tbsp fruity olive oil and transfer to a jar. Cover with a layer of olive oil, then the lid, and refrigerate. Add a fresh layer of oil each time you use the purée. It will keep for up to 2 weeks.

MARINADES

Marinades tenderize and enhance flavor, and they also preserve food. They are useful in preparing fish, meat, and poultry to be grilled, roasted, or fried. Mix the ingredients in a container that will not react with acid (glass or ceramic, for example). Immerse the food in the marinade, turning it periodically. Keep in the refrigerator, but bring to room temperature before cooking. Marinate fish for 1–2 hours, shellfish for up to 1 hour; allow 3–4 hours for pieces of meat or chicken; large pieces of meat or a whole chicken can be left overnight. A marinade can be used to baste food while it is cooking, but never keep it for re-use. Some of the other mixtures can also be used as marinades – see Cuban adobo and Chilean aliño (*p.282*), Seasoning (*p.283*), Masala for fish (*p.287*), and the Barbecue and Cajun mixtures (*p.294*).

Ginger and lime marinade

Use for salmon and firm, meaty fish such as swordfish.

small piece of fresh ginger, finely chopped
2 garlic cloves, crushed
grated rind of 1 unwaxed lime
¼ cup lime juice
2 tbsp soy sauce
1 tbsp toasted sesame oil
1 tbsp dry sherry

Yogurt marinade

Use for lamb or chicken.

scant 1 cup (200ml) plain yogurt
1 garlic clove, crushed
2 tbsp chopped fresh mint
2–3 tsp tandoori masala (*p.287*) or massalé (*p.288*).

Pernod marinade

Use for fish and seafood.

3 tbsp lemon juice
1 tbsp fennel seeds or a handful of fresh fennel leaves
4 tsp olive oil
small glass of dry white wine
3 tbsp Pernod or other anise-based drink

Red wine marinade

Use for large cuts of beef and venison and for hare.

½ bottle of red wine
2 tbsp olive or sunflower oil
1 onion, sliced
1 celery stalk, sliced
2 bay leaves
sprig of fresh rosemary
2 sprigs of fresh thyme
8 crushed black peppercorns
4 crushed allspice berries

Mediterranean marinade

Use for lamb, chicken, or pork. You could substitute 1 tbsp herbes de Provence (*p.281*) for the sprigs of herbs, and 1 tsp Italian spice mixture (*p.293*) could be used instead of the black pepper.

1 garlic clove, crushed
2–3 sprigs of fresh thyme or lemon thyme
3–4 sprigs of fresh lavender or rosemary
1 tsp crushed black peppercorns
juice of 2 oranges
juice of 1 lemon

Barbecue marinade 1

Use for steaks, pork chops, and spareribs.

2 shallots, chopped
¼ tsp ground cloves
¼ tsp ground allspice
3 tbsp sunflower oil
1 tbsp honey
2 tbsp soy sauce
3 tbsp dry sherry

Barbecue marinade 2

2 shallots, chopped
1 tbsp chopped cilantro
2 tsp crushed black peppercorns
2 tbsp Dijon mustard
3 tbsp sunflower oil

Asian marinade

Use for spareribs, poultry, or fish.

2 shallots, chopped
small piece of fresh ginger, chopped
1 hot chili pepper, sliced
2 tsp sugar
¼ cup chopped cilantro – root, leaf, and stem
¼ cup lime juice
2 tbsp fish sauce
5 tbsp rice vinegar

Adobo for pork

This marinade for a loin of pork is from Chile. The meat can be left as a rack or boned, stuffed and rolled before cooking. The adobo is rubbed over all the surfaces and the pork is marinated overnight.

3–4 tbsp wine vinegar
3–4 tbsp olive or sunflower oil
2 tsp crushed fresh oregano leaves
1 tsp ground cumin
1 tbsp (or to taste) ají paste (*p.295*)
4 tsp Spanish paprika
½ tsp salt

Dry adobo

Dry rubs of this kind are common in the Spanish-speaking Caribbean islands.

2 tbsp cumin seeds
¼ cup coarse sea salt
1 tbsp fennel seeds
½ tbsp black peppercorns
2 tbsp dried hot chili flakes
1 tbsp dried oregano

Dry-roast the cumin until lightly colored. Let cool, then grind with the salt, fennel, and peppercorns, and combine with the chili and oregano.

Lightly coat meat or poultry to be grilled with the mixture. The adobo will keep in an airtight jar for 3–4 months.

Mexican marinade

Use this marinade for meat that is to be grilled or broiled.

3 pasilla chili peppers
½ tsp ground cumin
1 tbsp dried oregano
1 tbsp dried thyme
juice of 1 lime and ½ orange
½ small onion, sliced
2 garlic cloves
¼ cup olive oil

Discard stems and seeds from the chili peppers. Toast the chilies in a preheated, heavy frying pan for 1–2 minutes. Transfer them to a bowl and just cover with boiling water; let soak for 30 minutes.

Blend the other ingredients in a food processor, then add the chilies and blend with enough of their soaking liquid to make a marinade of pouring consistency.

Juniper and wine marinade

Use for duck and game birds.

10 juniper berries, lightly crushed
10 black peppercorns, crushed
sprig of fresh rosemary
1 cup (250ml) red or white wine
3 tbsp brandy
3 tbsp olive oil

SOUPS AND LIGHT DISHES

Leek and herb soup

A well-flavored soup with an attractive pale green color. It can be enriched by adding cream for the last few minutes of cooking.

FOR 6

¼ cup olive oil

2lb (1kg) leeks, thickly sliced

juice of ½ lemon

salt and freshly ground pepper

2 cups (125g) shredded spinach

2 cups (125g) shredded lettuce

a handful of arugula or salad burnet, chopped

¾ cup (125g) shelled or frozen peas

1½ quarts (1.5 liters) water

1 tbsp chopped cutting celery

1 tbsp chopped fresh parsley

1 tbsp chopped fresh mint

Heat the olive oil in a heavy saucepan and add the leeks and lemon juice. Season, cover, and cook gently until the leeks are soft, about 20 minutes.

Stir in the spinach, lettuce, arugula or burnet, and peas, and cook for a minute or two. Add the water, bring to a boil, and simmer for 15 minutes until all the vegetables are tender.

Blend and sieve, then reheat gently, adding a little more water if the soup is too thick. If you want to use cream, add a few tablespoons now. Stir in the celery, parsley, and mint, and serve.

Tarragon soup

FOR 4

5 cups (1.25 liters) chicken or beef stock

2 tbsp chopped fresh tarragon

2 tbsp grated Parmesan cheese

Heat the stock gently with the tarragon, and stir in the cheese just before serving. This simple, well-flavored soup is from Elizabeth David's *Summer Cooking*.

Watercress, tomato, and sole soup

This light soup is made in the Cantonese manner. Any fine-textured fish in the flounder/sole family can be used.

FOR 4

7oz (200g) sole fillet, skinned

5 cups (1.25 liters) fish or chicken stock

1 tbsp rice wine or dry sherry

5 thin slices of fresh ginger

1½ cups (125g) small watercress sprigs

2 tomatoes, peeled, seeded, and diced

salt and white pepper

2 tsp soy sauce

½ tsp toasted sesame oil

1 welsh onion or scallion, very finely sliced

Cut the fish into thin strips across the grain. Bring the stock slowly to a boil. Add the rice wine or sherry and the ginger, and simmer for 5 minutes. Add the watercress and tomatoes, season, and bring back to a boil. Simmer for 2–3 minutes.

Add the pieces of fish to the soup. Remove the pan from the heat, cover, and leave for about 4 minutes, until the fish turns white and is lightly cooked. Season with the soy sauce and sesame oil, stir in the onion, and serve.

HERB SALADS

Salads vary according to what is in season, and most green salads are enhanced by the addition of herb leaves and flowers. Alternatively, you can compose a salad entirely of herbs, offsetting mild leaves with bitter or peppery ones. Choose from anise hyssop, arugula, basil, borage, calamint, chervil, chicory, chives, the cresses, dill, fennel, lemon balm, lovage, marjoram, mint, mint-scented marigold, miner's lettuce, mitsuba, orach, parsley, perilla, purslane, salad burnet, sorrel, sweet cicely, and tarragon. Garnish with herb flowers such as bee balm, borage, lavender, marigold, nasturtium, rosemary, sage, and thyme. Use small sprigs or single leaves, especially of the potent herbs, and taste as you prepare the salad to balance the flavors.

Other ingredients might include anchovies, chopped walnuts, toasted slivered almonds or pine nuts, shrimp, feta cheese, thinly sliced mushrooms, black olives, and tomatoes. Dress the salad with a vinaigrette made with one part wine vinegar to three parts extra virgin olive oil, or with a simple cream dressing.

Fattoush

The essential ingredients in this Lebanese salad are sumac, fresh herbs, and bread. You can use watercress or more mint and parsley if you have no purslane.

FOR 6

1 pitta bread

1 hothouse cucumber

3 tomatoes, cut in chunks

handful of radishes, cut in half

6 scallions, sliced

a few lettuce leaves, torn if large

large handful of fresh flat-leaf parsley, coarsely chopped

large handful of fresh mint, coarsely chopped

sprigs and leaves from a small bunch of purslane

1 tbsp sumac

salt and freshly ground pepper

6 tbsp lemon juice

6 tbsp olive oil

Split open the pitta bread and toast with the open side to the broiler until lightly golden and crisp. Break it into small pieces.

Cut the cucumber into four lengthwise, and then into pieces. Put all the vegetables and herbs into a bowl and scatter the bread over the top.

Whisk the sumac, salt, and pepper into the lemon juice, then whisk in the oil. Pour the dressing over the salad, toss, and serve at once before the bread gets soggy.

Pomegranate, olive, and walnut salad

This salad comes from Gaziantep in southeastern Turkey, where all the ingredients grow on the hills around the town.

FOR 4

2 pomegranates

1 cup (125g) pitted and coarsely chopped green olives

bunch of cilantro, chopped

2–3 shallots, chopped

1 cup (125g) coarsely chopped walnuts

4 tsp lemon juice

3 tbsp olive oil

½ tsp dried hot chili flakes

salt

Cut the top from each pomegranate, insert your thumbs and pull it apart. Take out the seeds, discarding all the beige pith. Put the seeds into a bowl with the olives, cilantro, shallots, and walnuts.

Make a piquant dressing with the remaining ingredients and add any juice from the pomegranates. Pour this over the salad, toss, and serve with bread. If you have any left over, it will keep for a day or two in the refrigerator.

Salad of crab, beans, and pickled ginger

FOR 4

12oz (350g) thin green beans

2 tbsp sherry vinegar

2 tbsp sunflower oil

salt and a grinding of Sichuan pepper

8oz (250g) white crab meat

2 tbsp slivered pickled ginger ***(p.240)***

Cook the beans in boiling water until they are firm but have no trace of rawness. Drain and refresh them in cold water. Drain again.

In a shallow bowl, whisk together the vinegar and oil, and season well. Arrange the beans in the dish, place the crab in the center, and put the slivers of ginger over the top. Toss before serving.

Tuna tartare

FOR 4

½ hothouse cucumber

salt and freshly ground pepper

10oz (300g) very fresh tuna fillet

juice of 1–2 lemons

1–2 tsp wasabi paste

1 tbsp rice vinegar

2 tbsp extra virgin olive oil

1 tbsp chopped fresh chives

1 tbsp chopped mitsuba or parsley

Peel alternate strips from the cucumber, cut it in half lengthwise, and remove the seeds. Slice very thinly and spread in a colander. Sprinkle the layers of cucumber with salt and let drain for 1 hour.

Remove the skin from the tuna and dice the flesh with a very sharp knife. Put the fish into a bowl. Combine the lemon juice and wasabi with a little salt and pour over the fish. Lift the fish with your fingers to mix it well with the dressing. Cover, refrigerate, and let marinate for 1 hour.

Rinse the cucumber and dry on a cloth. Make a vinaigrette with the vinegar, olive oil, and pepper, and stir in the cucumber and chives. Spoon a flattish circle of cucumber onto a serving plate. Drain the tuna and mound it on top. Garnish with the mitsuba or parsley.

Larp

This warm chicken dish comes from northern Thailand and Laos, where a version is also made with steak tartare.

FOR 4–6

2 tbsp uncooked rice

14oz (400g) chicken breast, skinned and boned

3 tbsp lime juice

⅔ cup (150ml) chicken stock

3 tbsp fish sauce

1–2 tsp ground hot chili

1 medium red onion, chopped

2 lemon grass stalks, bottom third only, finely sliced

2 tsp grated kaffir lime peel (optional)

4 lime leaves, shredded

fresh mint and cilantro or culantro

Put the rice in a dry frying pan and toast over medium heat until the grains turn pale brown. Shake the pan from time to time. Let cool, then grind in a spice mill.

Dice the chicken or chop it roughly in a food processor. Bring the lime juice, stock, and fish sauce to a boil in a wok or large pan. Put in the chicken and toss until the meat turns white.

Transfer to a bowl and add the rice, chili, onion, lemon grass, and lime peel and leaves. Stir thoroughly to mix all the ingredients well. Garnish with mint and cilantro or culantro, and serve.

Vietnamese spring rolls

At first attempt these rolls are a bit tricky to make, but they have a lovely fresh, crisp taste. Wrappers can be bought in Asian markets. For a vegetarian version, use strips of red sweet pepper to replace the shrimp. If you have a supply of Vietamese balm or rau ram, add some to the filling.

FOR ABOUT 20 ROLLS

1 small hothouse cucumber, seeded and cut in julienne strips

1–2 carrots, cut in julienne strips

1 heaped cup (125g) bean sprouts, tails trimmed

grated rind and juice of 1 unwaxed lime

6 garlic chives, cut in short lengths

small handful of fresh Thai basil leaves, coarsely chopped

small handful of cilantro, coarsely chopped

1 tsp sambal ulek or chili jam (*p.300*)

12oz (350g) cooked shrimp

20–25 rice paper wrappers

sprigs of fresh herbs for garnish

Combine the vegetables with the lime rind and juice, herbs, and sambal, and leave for 30 minutes so that the flavors blend. Peel and devein the shrimp, and cut each one in half, or in smaller pieces if they are large.

Pour some warm water into a large bowl and soak a rice paper wrapper until it is pliable, then put it on a board. Put a few pieces of shrimp on one side of the wrapper, and top with a spoonful of the vegetable mixture. Press the filling to flatten it a little, then fold in the sides of the wrapper and roll up. Put it seam-side down on a platter, sprinkle with a little water, and cover with a damp cloth or plastic wrap.

Make the other rolls in the same way. Garnish with the herbs and serve with sweet chili sauce or nuoc cham (*p.300*).

Note: rice wrappers become brittle if they are not kept moist, so continue to sprinkle water on them as you make them, or if they are kept for some time before serving.

Middle-Eastern herb omelette

This substantial omelette, something like a Spanish tortilla, is called a kookoo in Iran, an eggah in the Arab countries. A tablespoon of barberries can be added to the filling. The omelette can be baked or cooked on top of the stove.

FOR 4–6

5oz (150g) fresh flat-leaf parsley

5oz (150g) fresh dill

2oz (60g) cilantro

small bunch of fresh chives

3–4 lettuce leaves

3–4 spinach leaves

2 small zucchini, chopped (optional)

4 scallions, chopped

¼ cup chopped walnuts

pinch of saffron threads

6 eggs

salt and freshly ground pepper

2 tbsp (30g) butter

If you intend to bake the omelette, heat the oven to 350°F (180°C).

Discard the coarse stems from the parsley, dill, and cilantro, and chop these herbs with the chives, lettuce, and spinach. Combine with the zucchini, scallions, and walnuts. Crush the saffron in a small mortar and stir in 2 tsp warm water. Beat the eggs well, add the saffron liquid, season, and stir in the herb mixture.

To bake the omelette, butter a shallow, baking dish, pour in the mixture, and bake for 45–50 minutes, until the omelette has a golden-brown crust.

Alternatively, heat the butter in a frying pan, coating it well on the bottom and sides, pour in the mixture, and cook over low heat for about 25 minutes. Turn the omelette by reversing it onto a plate held over the pan, and cook the other side for 10–15 minutes.

Serve hot or at room temperature, cut in wedges, with a bowl of thick yogurt.

FISH

Gravad lax

FOR 8–10

1½ cups (200g) coarse sea salt

1 tbsp white peppercorns, crushed

large bunch of fresh dill, chopped

2 tbsp vodka or brandy

7 tbsp (85g) sugar

4lb (2kg) middle cut of salmon, scaled, boned, and filleted

3 tbsp Dijon mustard

1 egg yolk

⅔ cup (150ml) sunflower oil

1 tbsp lemon juice

3 tbsp chopped fresh dill

Combine the salt, peppercorns, dill, vodka, and all but 2 tsp sugar. Put a quarter of this cure into a shallow dish just large enough to hold the fish. Put in one fillet, skin-side down, and cover with most of the remaining cure. Place the other fillet on top, skin-side up. Spread with the rest of the cure.

Cover with plastic wrap and a weighted plate. Refrigerate for at least 18 and up to 48 hours, turning the fish once or twice.

Wipe the salmon and slice it thinly on the diagonal with a sharp, thin knife. Discard the skin. It will keep 5–6 days if refrigerated.

To make the sauce, whisk the mustard and 2 tsp sugar into the egg yolk. Beat in the oil as if making mayonnaise. Stir in the lemon juice and dill.

Shrimp and coconut curry

FOR 3–4

1lb (500g) large raw shrimp, peeled

salt

½ tsp mustard seeds

½ tsp ground turmeric or zedoary

2 tsp ground coriander

1 tsp ground anise

3 tbsp sunflower oil

2 tbsp green masala (*p.282*)

2 onions, thinly sliced

1¾ cups (400ml) coconut milk

Devein the shrimp, rub with salt, and set aside. Dry-roast the mustard seeds quickly, then add the other spices. Stir and shake the pan; when the aroma rises, remove the spices from the pan and let cool.

Heat the oil in a heavy pan and fry the green masala paste for 2–3 minutes. Add the onions and stir for a few minutes more. Add the spices and the coconut milk, and simmer, uncovered, for 8–10 minutes, stirring frequently. Put in the shrimp and simmer for 4–6 minutes, until they are cooked through. Do not overcook or they will be tough. Serve with rice.

Seychelles fish curry

FOR 4

2lb (1kg) snapper or monkfish fillet

salt and freshly ground pepper

3 tbsp sunflower oil

2 onions, chopped

2 tbsp massalé (*p.288*)

½ tsp ground turmeric

2 garlic cloves, chopped

small piece of fresh ginger, chopped

3 tbsp tamarind water (*p.163*)

leaves from 2 sprigs of fresh thyme

½ tsp anise seed

scant 2 cups (450ml) fish stock or water

Cut the fish into bite-sized pieces, season with salt and pepper, and set aside.

Heat the oil in a heavy pan and fry the onions until golden. Stir in the massalé and turmeric, and fry lightly. Put in the pieces of fish and all the other ingredients. Bring to a simmer and cook for about 10 minutes until the fish is done. Serve with rice.

Baked sea bass with star anise

FOR 4

1 sea bass, weighing 3lb (1.5kg)

1 tbsp chopped fresh ginger

2 tbsp rice wine or dry sherry

1 tsp five-spice powder (*p.284*)

4 welsh onions or scallions, finely chopped

1 tbsp soy sauce

1 tsp toasted sesame oil

salt

3 star anise

oil

Make two diagonal slits in each side of the bass. Combine the ginger, rice wine, and five-spice powder, and rub the fish with the mixture. Let marinate for 1 hour. Heat the oven to 425°F (220°C). Combine the onions, soy sauce, and sesame oil with a little salt, and use this mixture and the star anise to stuff the fish.

Spread a piece of foil big enough to wrap the fish on a baking sheet and oil it lightly. Lift the sides and wrap the fish, folding the edges at least double; pinch them closed.

Bake the sea bass for about 35 minutes. Open the parcel. If the flesh flakes when a knife is inserted near the bone, it is ready. Serve with the juices.

Snapper with chermoula

FOR 4

3 garlic cloves

1 tsp salt

1 small onion, finely chopped

small bunch of cilantro, chopped

small bunch of fresh parsley, chopped

1 tsp paprika

½ tsp chili powder

½ tsp ground cumin

6 tbsp olive oil

juice of 1 lemon

2 small snappers, each weighing about 1½lb (800g)

1½lb (800g) ripe tomatoes

1 cup (150g) cracked green olives

Chermoula is a Moroccan seasoning for fish. Crush the garlic with the salt and combine with the onion, herbs, and spices. Add the olive oil and lemon juice to make a paste.

Slash the sides of the fish in two or three places and rub the fish well with the chermoula, putting some into the slashes and the cavity. Put the fish into a dish, cover, and refrigerate for at least 2 hours, or even overnight, to allow the flavors to develop.

Take out the fish 30 minutes before it is to be cooked and place it in a baking dish. Heat the oven to 375°F (190°C). Slice the tomatoes and put them over the fish. Salt lightly, scatter the olives over, and spoon on any remaining chermoula.

Cover with foil and bake the fish for 35–45 minutes, depending on its thickness. The fish is cooked if the flesh flakes when a knife is inserted near the backbone. Serve directly from the dish.

Mussels with lemon grass and ginger

FOR 4

4lb (2kg) mussels

6 tbsp water

2 lemon grass stalks, lower third only, finely sliced

2 garlic cloves, chopped

4 kaffir lime leaves

small piece of fresh ginger, chopped

freshly ground pepper

scant 1 cup (200ml) coconut milk

3 tbsp chopped cilantro

Scrub the mussels, pull out the beards, and discard any that are broken or remain open when tapped firmly. Put them into a large pot (you may need to cook them in batches) with the water, lemon grass, garlic, lime leaves, ginger, and pepper. Cover and cook over high heat, shaking the pan now and then until the mussels open, about 2–3 minutes.

Lift out the mussels and put them into a warmed serving bowl. Boil the cooking liquid to reduce by half. Pour in the coconut milk, bring to a boil to thicken it slightly, and pour over the mussels. Remove the lime leaves, stir in the cilantro, and serve.

MEATS

Slow-cooked leg of lamb with Oman spices

This dish is based on shuwa, a celebratory dish of a whole baked lamb served in Oman. For a leg of lamb, halve the quantity of bizar a'shuwa blend given on p.289.

FOR 6–8

1 leg of lamb

bizar a'shuwa spice mixture (*p.289*)

Heat the oven to 275°F (140°C). Remove as much fat as possible from the meat and rub the bizar a'shuwa spice mixture into all the surfaces. Wrap the meat in a lightly oiled sheet of foil, then enclose the parcel in a second layer of foil.

Put the lamb into a large, heavy casserole or a roasting pan with a lid and cook for about 5 hours. Check to see that it is not drying out; the meat should remain moist and come loose from the bone. Cook longer if necessary. To keep warm, turn off the oven and open the door, but leave the meat in its wrapper and pan. Serve with rice and, if you wish, tomato sauce (*p.298*).

VARIATION

Spiced leg or shoulder of lamb with apricots

*Use 1½–2 tbsp of Aleppo blend, qâlat daqqa, or la kama (*all p.291*) instead of the bizar a'shuwa. Wrap the meat in 2–3 sheets of apricot fruit leather, or finely chop some moist dried apricots and put them around the meat before you wrap it. A half leg or half shoulder will take about 3½ hours to cook.*

Lamb korma

In this Moghul dish the lamb is cooked in a spiced yogurt sauce thickened with poppy seeds and almonds.

FOR 6–8

scant 2 cups (450ml) thick plain yogurt

small piece of fresh ginger, chopped

4 hot green chili peppers, seeded and chopped

4 garlic cloves, chopped

3 tbsp water

2 tbsp blanched almonds

2 tbsp poppy seeds

small piece of cinnamon stick

3 mace blades

½ tsp cumin or black cumin seeds

4 whole cloves

seeds from 4 brown cardamom pods

10 black peppercorns

3 tbsp sunflower oil or ghee

1 large onion, sliced

2lb (1kg) lean boneless lamb, cubed

¼ tsp powdered saffron soaked in 1 tbsp water

salt

3 tbsp chopped cilantro

Set a fine strainer over a bowl and strain the yogurt in it for 1 hour. Discard the whey in the bowl. Blend the ginger, chilies, garlic, and water to a paste. Grind together the almonds and all the spices.

Heat the oil or ghee in a large, heavy pan and fry the onion until golden. Stir in the ginger paste and the ground almonds and spices, and fry for 2–3 minutes more. Add the meat and stir well to coat it with the spices. Add the yogurt and saffron, season with salt, and cover the pan tightly.

Simmer over very low heat for 1½–2 hours, until the lamb is tender. Stir frequently to make sure it is not sticking; if necessary, add a little water. Garnish with the cilantro.

Pumpkin bredie

A bredie is a South African stew, usually made with lamb and a single vegetable, with a variety of herbs and spices as flavorings.

FOR 6

2 tbsp sunflower oil

2 large onions, chopped

2lb (1kg) lean boneless lamb, cubed

3 garlic cloves, chopped

2 hot green chili peppers, seeded and sliced

small piece of fresh ginger, chopped

4 whole cloves

½ cinnamon stick

salt

1½lb (750g) pumpkin or butternut squash

Heat the oil in a heavy pan and fry the onions gently until golden brown. Add the lamb and fry for 10–15 minutes, turning to brown the pieces on all sides. Add the garlic, all the spices, salt, and enough water to prevent the meat from sticking. Cover the pan and simmer on low heat for 1 hour. Stir occasionally and add more water if necessary.

Peel the pumpkin and cut into cubes. Add to the pan. Bring to a boil, lower the heat, and cover. Simmer for a further hour until the pumpkin is cooked and the lamb is tender.

Braised beef with licorice

FOR 4

2lb (1kg) boneless beef rump roast

red wine marinade (*p.304*)

7oz (200g) shallots

7oz (200g) carrots

salt and freshly ground black pepper

flour

3 tbsp olive oil

3 tomatoes, peeled and chopped

grated rind of 1 unwaxed orange

2 pieces of licorice, about ¾in (2cm) long

3 whole cloves

½ tsp ground coriander

Put the meat into a glass or china bowl just large enough to hold it, and pour the marinade over. Cover and let marinate in the refrigerator for 24 hours. Turn from time to time. Bring the beef to room temperature at least 1 hour before cooking.

Heat the oven to 300°F (150°C). Remove the meat and dry it with paper towel. Strain the marinade and set aside; discard the vegetables. Halve the shallots and cut the carrots to the same size.

Season the beef with salt and pepper and coat lightly with flour. Heat 2 tbsp oil in a heavy casserole and brown the meat on all sides. Remove the meat, lower the heat, and sauté the shallots and carrots. Pour in the reserved marinade and bring it to a boil. Stir in the tomatoes, orange rind, and spices, and put back the meat. About one-third of the meat should be submerged in the liquid. Cover the casserole tightly, with a piece of foil under the lid if necessary, and cook in the oven for 2½ hours. Turn the meat once or twice during this time.

Remove the meat from the casserole and let rest, closely covered, in a warm place for 10 minutes. Remove the vegetables from the casserole and keep them warm. Scoop out the whole spices and discard. Bring the cooking liquid to a boil and skim off any fat. Boil rapidly to reduce to a sauce.

Slice the meat, put the vegetables around it, and serve with the sauce. Mashed potato or a celery root and potato mash goes well with this dish.

Osso buco

FOR 4

1½ tsp Italian spice mixture (*p.293*)

salt

4 meaty slices of veal shank

2 garlic cloves

1 unwaxed lemon

flour

3 tbsp olive oil

2 tbsp chopped fresh parsley

large glass of dry white wine

Rub the spice mixture and salt into both sides of each slice of veal. Let stand while you chop the garlic and slice half the lemon thinly, removing any seeds.

Sprinkle the meat with flour on both sides. In a heavy, shallow pan that will hold the pieces side by side, heat the olive oil and brown the meat lightly. Scatter the garlic and most of the parsley over, then lay the lemon slices over the meat. Pour in the wine and enough water to come almost to the top of the meat. Bring to a simmer, cover, and cook over very low heat for about 1½ hours.

Check after 1 hour to see how well the meat is cooked and how much liquid is in the pan. If necessary leave the pan open to reduce the liquid a little. There should be enough to serve 2–3 tbsp with each piece of meat. The sauce will be quite sticky from the juices released from the veal.

Grate the rind of the remaining half lemon, combine it with the remaining parsley, and scatter over the meat 5 minutes before serving. A saffron risotto (*p.323*) is the classic Italian accompaniment for this dish.

Malaysian rendang

FOR 6

8 shallots, chopped

4 garlic cloves, crushed

5 hot red chili peppers, seeded and sliced

small piece of fresh galangal, chopped

4 cups (1 liter) coconut milk

2lb (1kg) chuck steak, cubed

2 tbsp ground coriander

1 tsp ground cumin

1 tsp ground turmeric, or 1 tbsp chopped fresh

1 lemon grass stalk, bottom third only, crushed

2 tsp sugar

1 tsp tamarind concentrate, soaked in a little warm water

First prepare the spice paste: blend the shallots, garlic, chilies, and galangal to a smooth paste with 2–3 tbsp coconut milk. Tip it into a wok, add the beef, and stir well to coat it with the mixture.

Add the remaining spices and pour in the rest of the coconut milk. Stir well and bring to a boil, then simmer uncovered over gentle heat for about 1½ hours, until most of the liquid has evaporated and the meat is tender.

When the oil from the coconut starts to separate out, stir constantly until it is absorbed by the meat. Stir in the sugar and tamarind, and remove from the heat.

Rendang has little liquid and is served with rice. Like most stews, it improves if made a day in advance and reheated.

Thai beef curry

FOR 4

2 tbsp sunflower oil

2 tbsp red curry paste (*p.285*)

1½lb (750g) boneless sirloin or rump steak, cut in strips

3 cups (750ml) coconut milk

2 tbsp fish sauce

4 kaffir lime leaves

2 hot red chili peppers, seeded and sliced

1 tbsp palm or brown sugar

¼ cup roasted peanuts, crushed

2 tbsp chopped cilantro

Heat a wok, add the oil, and stir in the curry paste. Fry until it is fragrant. Add the beef and toss until it browns. Pour in the coconut milk and add the fish sauce, lime leaves, and chilies. Bring to a boil and simmer for about 20 minutes, until the beef is tender.

Stir in the sugar and peanuts. Transfer to a serving dish, and scatter the cilantro over. Serve with jasmine rice.

Massaman curry paste (*p.285*), with its flavors of Indian spices, could be used instead of red curry paste.

Pork chops with juniper and rosemary

FOR 4

4 pork chops

salt and freshly ground pepper

2 tsp juniper berries, crushed

1 sprig of fresh rosemary, finely chopped

1 tbsp olive oil

2 shallots, finely chopped

1 glass of port

about ½ cup (100ml) stock or water

Heat the oven to 350°F (180°C). Trim excess fat from the chops, and season with salt and pepper. Combine the juniper and rosemary. Rub the mixture into the meat on both sides. Lightly oil a baking dish and put in the shallots and the chops. Pour the port over and add enough stock or water to cover the meat. Cover and bake for 30 minutes.

Remove the lid and bake for a further 20–25 minutes, until the chops are well cooked and the sauce reduced. The chops are ready when they offer no resistance to a skewer; the cooking time depends as much on thickness as on weight. They go well with lightly fried apple slices.

Pork tenderloin with tarragon and mustard

FOR 4

2 pork tenderloins, each about 1lb (500g)

salt and freshly ground pepper

2 tbsp Dijon mustard

leaves from 10 sprigs of fresh tarragon

2 tbsp (30g) butter

large glass of dry white wine

1¼ cups (300ml) whipping cream

2 shallots, finely chopped

Trim the tenderloins and season with salt and pepper. Rub one side of each with ½ tbsp mustard and spread two-thirds of the tarragon leaves over the mustard. Put the mustard and tarragon sides of the two tenderloins together and tie with string.

Heat the butter in a heavy pan into which the pork just fits, and brown the meat on all sides. Pour the wine over, cover the pan tightly, and cook over very low heat for 40–45 minutes. Turn the meat once or twice and baste it. While the pork is cooking, chop the rest of the tarragon finely. Pierce the thick part of the meat with a skewer toward the end of the cooking time; when juices run clear, the pork is ready. Lift it out of the pan and let stand, covered, in a warm place for at least 5 minutes, then slice and keep warm.

While the pork is resting, make the sauce. Boil the cream in a nonstick pan until it bubbles fiercely with small bubbles and is thick but still pourable. Heat the shallots and the strained cooking liquid in another pan. Simmer for 4–5 minutes until the shallots are soft. Stir in the remaining mustard, the chopped tarragon, and cream. Taste and adjust the seasoning and simmer for a few minutes, then serve with the pork.

Pot-roasted chicken with Indian spices

FOR 4

4 tsp aromatic garam masala (*p.286*)

thick slice of fresh ginger, finely chopped

1 garlic clove, crushed

½ tsp salt

2 tbsp (30g) butter

3lb (1.5kg) chicken

3 tbsp sunflower oil or clarified butter

Prepare the chicken 2–3 hours before you want to cook it. Mix the garam masala, ginger, garlic, and salt, then work the mixture into the butter to make a paste.

Work your fingers under the skin of the chicken over the breast and then the legs, loosening but not breaking the skin. Push the spice paste under the skin, rubbing it into the flesh. Leave for 2–3 hours for the flavors to penetrate the meat. Heat the oven to 375°F (190°C).

Heat the oil in a heavy casserole that will just hold the chicken. Put in the chicken on its side, cover tightly, and bake for 30–35 minutes. Turn the chicken over on its other side and bake for 30 minutes or so. Finally, turn it breast uppermost, baste with the pan juices, and bake uncovered for 10–15 minutes so it browns. Pierce the thickest part of the thigh with a skewer; if the juices flow clear, the chicken is ready.

Spoon the juices from the casserole over the chicken when it is carved. Serve with lemon wedges, a chutney or yogurt and herb dressing, and a bowl of rice.

Chicken wat

Ethiopian wats are well-spiced stews, usually served with flatbread, but rice or couscous make a good alternative.

FOR 6

3–4lb (1.5–1.8 kg) chicken pieces, skinned

4 tbsp (60g) butter

4 large onions, chopped

3 garlic cloves, minced

1 heaped tbsp berbere or wat spices (*p.292*)

14oz (400g) ripe tomatoes, chopped, or 1 can

salt

Lightly score each piece of chicken with a sharp knife so the flavors of the sauce will penetrate. Heat the butter in a large, heavy pan and fry the onions until golden. Add the garlic and fry for a minute or two longer. Add the spice mix and stir it into the onions, then add the tomatoes.

Cover and simmer for 15 minutes until you have a thick sauce. Put in the chicken pieces and bring back to a simmer; add a little water if necessary. Cover and cook for 40–45 minutes, until the chicken is tender. Taste and add salt if you wish.

Caribbean chicken Colombo

This curry from the French Caribbean islands is made with kid, lamb, beef, or pork as well as chicken.

FOR 6–8

3lb (1.5kg) chicken pieces, skinned

3 tbsp sunflower oil

2 onions, chopped

4 garlic cloves, chopped

small piece of fresh ginger, chopped

2 tbsp poudre de Colombo (*p.295*)

2 tbsp tamarind water (*p.163*)

10oz (300g) peeled pumpkin, cut in chunks

10oz (300g) sweet potatoes, peeled and cut in chunks

1 chayote or eggplant, peeled and cut in chunks

2½ cups (600ml) chicken stock

salt

1 tbsp lime juice

bunch of fresh chives or 3 scallions, chopped

Sauté the chicken pieces in the oil in a large, heavy pan until they are lightly colored on both sides. Remove them to a plate. In the oil remaining in the pan, sauté the onions until golden. Add the garlic, ginger, and poudre de Colombo, and stir for 3–4 minutes until the aromas rise from the spices. Return the chicken to the pan. Add the tamarind, vegetables, and stock, and season with salt.

Cover and bring just to a boil, then simmer gently until the chicken and vegetables are tender, about 45 minutes. Just before you serve, stir in the lime juice and scatter the chives or scallions over. Serve with rice.

The Colombo can be made in advance and reheated, but wait to add the lime juice and garnish.

Chicken tikka

FOR 4

1¼lb (600g) boneless chicken

scant 1 cup (200ml) plain yogurt

1 tbsp tandoori masala (*p.287*)

2 tbsp sunflower oil

2 lemons

small handful of cilantro or fresh mint

Cut the chicken into 2in (5cm) cubes. Whisk the yogurt and stir in the masala and the oil. Marinate the chicken in the yogurt for at least 2 hours. When you are ready to cook, heat the oven to 450°F (220°C), or heat the broiler or a charcoal grill. Thread the chicken pieces onto skewers.

Bake the chicken for about 12 minutes, or broil or grill for about 10 minutes, turning the skewers once. Serve with lemon wedges and chopped cilantro or mint.

VEGETABLES

Eggplant with preserved lemon

FOR 4

2 long eggplants

1 preserved lemon (*p.299*)

1 tbsp sunflower oil

¼ tsp paprika or ground hot chili

3 tbsp pine nuts

Heat the oven to 350°F (180°C). Cut the eggplants in half lengthwise, and make some deep slits in the flesh of each piece. Take the peel from the preserved lemon and cut it into slivers. Discard the pulp. Push the lemon peel into the slits, then brush the cut surface of each aubergine half lightly with oil and season with paprika or chili (the lemon will provide salt). Distribute the pine nuts over each piece.

Wrap each half in foil and bake for 20–25 minutes, until they are soft. Let cool. Serve at room temperature.

Paprika potatoes

FOR 6

2 tbsp (30g) butter

5 shallots, chopped

2 tsp Hungarian paprika

4 tomatoes, peeled and chopped

salt

⅔ cup (150ml) sour cream

2lb (1kg) potatoes, sliced medium-thick

1¼ cups (300ml) vegetable or chicken stock

Heat the oven to 400°F (200°C). Melt the butter in a heavy pan and cook the shallots gently until soft. Stir in the paprika and cook for 2–3 minutes. Add the tomatoes, season with salt, and cook until the mixture thickens. Stir in the sour cream.

Spread a layer of potatoes in a gratin dish and cover with some of the tomato mixture; repeat the layers. Pour the stock over. Cover the dish and bake for 1 hour. Uncover, return the dish to the oven, and continue to bake until the potatoes are tender and the liquid is almost all absorbed.

Spiced lentils

FOR 4

1¼ cups (250g) French lentilles de Puy

2 bay leaves

1 tsp ground coriander

¾ tsp ground cumin

crushed seeds from 2 cardamom pods

1 medium onion

3⅔ cups (900ml) water

salt

¼ cup whipping cream or extra virgin olive oil

1 garlic clove, crushed with a little salt

1 tbsp chopped fresh mint

1 tbsp chopped fresh basil, preferably Thai or anise basil

Put the lentils into a large pan with the bay leaves, spices, and whole onion. Add the water and bring to a boil, then simmer, partly covered, until the lentils are tender, about 20 minutes. Add salt to taste in the last 5 minutes of cooking.

Drain thoroughly and discard the bay leaves and onion. Heat the cream or olive oil, stir in the garlic, and pour over the lentils, turning to coat them well. Stir in the herbs, and serve.

Slow-cooked red cabbage

FOR 6

1 medium red cabbage

4 tbsp (60g) butter

1 red or white onion, finely sliced

2 tsp kitchen pepper (*p.293*) or 1 tsp ground coriander and 3 cloves

salt

¼ cup red wine vinegar

2 tbsp water

½ cup (90g) chopped prunes

1–2 tbsp sweet chutney (optional)

Cut the cabbage in four, remove the core, and shred the leaves. Heat the butter in a heavy pan and cook the onion and cabbage for 2–3 minutes, stirring to coat them well. Season with kitchen pepper, or coriander and cloves, and salt. Pour in the vinegar and water, cover the pan, and simmer for 45–50 minutes, until the cabbage is tender.

Stir in the prunes, and chutney if you are using it, and cook for a further 15 minutes or so, to allow the flavors to blend. If there is too much liquid, cook uncovered at this stage to evaporate it.

Braised fennel with star anise

FOR 4

4 fennel bulbs

2 garlic cloves, sliced

2 star anise

¼ cup olive oil

1¼ cups (300ml) vegetable stock or water

salt and freshly ground pepper

1 tbsp chopped fresh chives

Trim the fennel tops and bases, and peel off the outer leaves. Put the bulbs into a heavy pan, side by side, with the garlic and star anise. Pour in the olive oil and stock. Season with salt and pepper.

Cover and bring to a boil, then lower the heat and braise gently for 30–40 minutes, turning the fennel once. It is ready when it can be pierced with a knife, but don't overcook it – fennel tastes better with a slight bite. Remove the bulbs from the pan and cut in half. Spoon a little cooking liquid over and sprinkle with the chives.

Mushrooms with bacon

FOR 4

14oz (400g) button mushrooms

¼ cup olive oil

½ tsp ground mace

salt and freshly ground pepper

4 Canadian bacon slices, cut into squares

3 garlic cloves, slivered

glass of red wine

3 tbsp chopped fresh parsley

Wipe the mushrooms and cut off the stems. Heat the oil in a heavy pan and sauté the mushrooms until they are lightly browned and start to give up their liquid. Season with mace, pepper, and only a little salt, since the bacon may be salty.

Add the bacon and garlic to the pan and sauté for 2–3 minutes more, then add the wine. Bring to a boil quickly, then reduce the heat and simmer for 4–5 minutes, until the wine is reduced to a tablespoon or two of sauce. Stir in the parsley and serve hot or at room temperature.

Glazed carrots with marjoram

FOR 4

1lb (500g) carrots, thinly sliced

salt and freshly ground pepper

4 tbsp (60g) butter

2 tsp chopped fresh marjoram

juice and grated rind of ½ unwaxed orange

Cook the carrots in boiling, salted water until just tender, about 4–5 minutes, then drain. Melt the butter and add the carrots, pepper, marjoram, and orange rind and juice. Toss over the heat for 1–2 minutes, then serve.

PASTA, NOODLES, AND GRAINS

Ravioli filled with saffron ricotta

FOR 4–6

½ tsp saffron threads

1 tbsp milk

1½ cups (375g) ricotta

grated rind of 1 unwaxed orange

2 eggs

salt and freshly ground pepper

nutmeg

1lb (500g) sheets of fresh pasta

1 stick/½ cup (125g) butter

fresh sage leaves

2 slices prosciutto, cut in thin strips (optional)

Crush the saffron and soak it in the milk for 20 minutes. Mix it into the ricotta with the orange rind and 1 egg. Season with salt, pepper, and a little freshly grated nutmeg. Whisk the other egg lightly with 1 tbsp water. Spread out a sheet of pasta and cut into rounds with a 2in (5cm) pastry cutter.

Brush the outer edge of each circle of pasta lightly with the beaten egg. Put a teaspoonful of the filling in the middle of each circle and carefully fold over one side of the pasta to form a half-moon shape. Press the edges together firmly to seal. Repeat with the rest of the pasta and the filling. Put the ravioli in a cool place until you are ready to cook.

Bring a large pan of salted water to a boil. Carefully put in the ravioli (in batches), bring back to a boil, and simmer for 4–5 minutes, until they puff up slightly and rise to the top of the pan.

While they are cooking, melt the butter and flavor it with a few whole sage leaves and, if you wish, the strips of prosciutto. Toss the drained ravioli in the sage butter and serve.

Tagliatelle with horseradish, dill, and smoked trout

FOR 2

8oz (250g) fresh tagliatelle, or 5oz (150g) dried

1 tbsp (15g) butter

1 onion, thinly sliced

2 garlic cloves, chopped

2 tsp grated horseradish

1 tbsp capers, rinsed

scant ½ cup (100ml) whipping cream

salt and freshly ground pepper

2 tbsp lemon juice

3oz (80g) smoked trout, flaked

2 tbsp chopped fresh dill

If you are using dried pasta, put it to cook now. To make the sauce, melt the butter and gently soften the onion until it is translucent. Add the garlic and cook for 1–2 minutes more. Stir in the horseradish, capers, and cream. Season and let the sauce simmer very gently.

If you have fresh pasta, cook it now. While it is in the pan, stir the lemon juice into the sauce and keep stirring so that it thickens slightly. Add the smoked trout and let it heat through. At the last moment, stir in the dill. When the pasta is cooked al dente, drain well and tip it into a warmed dish. Toss with the sauce and serve.

Linguine with herbs

This dish is only worth making if you have good, fresh herbs and extra virgin olive oil. Chop the herbs by hand rather than in a processor to achieve a better texture.

FOR 4

4 sprigs of fresh basil

6 sprigs of fresh flat-leaf parsley

3 sprigs of fresh marjoram

1 sprig of fresh rosemary

1 small sprig of fresh hyssop

7 tbsp (100ml) extra virgin olive oil

salt and freshly ground pepper

1 shallot, finely chopped

3–4 tbsp fresh bread crumbs

1¼lb (600g) fresh linguine or 14oz (400g) dried

Discard the large stems from the herbs, and chop the leaves and fine stems. Make sure that the sharp leaves of the rosemary and hyssop are chopped small. Mix the herbs with 5 tbsp of the oil in a large serving bowl. Season, giving a good grinding of pepper, then let infuse.

Heat the remaining oil and sauté the shallot and bread crumbs until the bread crumbs are crisp. Cook the linguine al dente and drain well. Toss the pasta in the oil and herb mixture, scatter the shallot and bread crumbs over, and serve.

Laksa

Laksa is a fresh-tasting Malay dish of noodles in a spiced coconut-milk broth. Candlenuts are hard, oily nuts with a slightly bitter taste, used as a thickening agent; sweeter macadamia nuts can be substituted. Candlenuts and dried shrimp are available from Asian markets.

FOR 6

14oz (400g) fresh rice noodles

2 garlic cloves

3 lemon grass stalks, lower third only

2in (5cm) piece of fresh ginger or galangal

3 hot red chili peppers, seeded

8 shallots

2 tsp fresh turmeric or ½ tsp ground

5 candlenuts

2 tbsp dried shrimp, soaked in a little water

3 tbsp sunflower oil

2 cups (200g) bean sprouts, tails trimmed

2½ cups (600ml) fish or chicken stock

2½ cups (600ml) coconut milk

14oz (400g) white fish fillet, cut into 1½in (4cm) pieces

10oz (300g) peeled, cooked small shrimp

salt

juice of 1 lime

2 scallions, finely sliced

2 tbsp chopped rau ram or cilantro

Blanch the noodles in a large pan of unsalted, boiling water. Drain and rinse thoroughly in cold water.

To prepare the spice paste, roughly chop the garlic, lemon grass, ginger, chilies, shallots, fresh turmeric, and candlenuts. Blend them in a food processor with the dried shrimp (and ground turmeric if that is what you are using). Add a little oil if necessary to make a smooth paste. Blanch the bean sprouts for 1 minute, drain, and rinse – this helps to keep them crisp.

Heat the remaining oil in a large pan or wok. Add the spice paste and fry, stirring constantly, until the paste is fragrant and the oil separates from the solids, about 5 minutes. Add the stock, bring to a boil, and stir to blend it with the paste. Lower the heat, add the coconut milk and simmer for 2–3 minutes. Then add the fish and stir until it is almost cooked. Add the shrimp and season with salt and lime juice.

Serve laksa in deep bowls. Divide the noodles and bean sprouts among them and ladle in the broth and seafood. Garnish with scallions and rau ram or cilantro.

Noodles with beef and broccoli

FOR 2

10oz (300g) boneless sirloin steak

3 tbsp soy sauce

2 tbsp rice vinegar

1 tsp chopped garlic

1 tsp chopped fresh ginger

1 tsp sugar

4 tbsp sunflower oil

8oz (250g) egg noodles

7oz (200g) small broccoli florets

4 scallions, finely sliced

3 tbsp chopped cilantro

1 tbsp toasted sesame seeds

Slice the steak across the grain into thin strips. Combine the soy sauce, vinegar, garlic, ginger, sugar, and 2 tbsp oil, and marinate the beef for 30 minutes.

Cook the noodles in plenty of unsalted boiling water until just tender. Drain and rinse them under cold water.

Heat a wok, put in the remaining oil, and swirl to coat the bottom and sides. Stir-fry the broccoli for 2 minutes, then add the noodles and toss them for 2 minutes. Add the beef and its marinade, and stir-fry for another 2 minutes, stirring in the scallions and cilantro. Transfer to a warmed serving bowl, sprinkle the top with the sesame seeds, and serve.

Rice with herbs

This is a beautiful dish – the green herbs cling to the rice and the crisp, golden crust on the bottom of the pan is a delightful surprise. Fresh herbs are best for this Iranian dish, but you can use dried: 4–6 tbsp (15–20g) will flavor 3 cups (500g) rice. Fresh herbs must be completely dry when they are added to the rice, so put them through a salad spinner or dry them carefully in a dish towel before chopping.

FOR 4–6

3 cups (500g) basmati rice

salt

7 tbsp (100g) butter or 6 tbsp sunflower oil

3 tbsp water

1¼ cups (80g) finely chopped fresh dill

1⅓ cups (80g) finely chopped fresh parsley

1⅓ cups (80g) finely chopped cilantro

¾ cup (80g) finely chopped fresh chives

Put the rice into a large pan, pour in cold water, swirl around, then drain and rinse until the water runs clear. Return the rice to the pan and soak in salted water for at least 2 hours; the longer it soaks, the better.

Drain the rice. Put 2½ quarts (2.5 liters) of water and 1 tbsp salt in the pan and bring to a boil. Add the rice, stirring to ensure it does not stick. Simmer, uncovered, for 2–3 minutes, then test to see if it is done: it should be tender but with a firm core. Drain and rinse in lukewarm water.

Put half the butter or oil and 3 tbsp water into a nonstick pan if you have one large enough for the rice; otherwise, rinse the pan the rice was cooked in and use that. When the butter has melted or the oil is hot, put in a layer of rice and then a third of the mixed herbs. Repeat this layering, making each layer a bit narrower than the one before, so that you make a cone-shaped mound in the pan. Finish with a layer of rice. With the handle of a wooden spoon, poke two or three holes through the cone down to the bottom of the pan, so that steam can escape. Pour the rest of the melted butter or oil over the rice.

Cover the pan with a folded dish towel and the lid (flip the ends of the towel up over the lid to keep them away from the heat). Cook on high heat for 3–4 minutes, until the rice is steaming, then turn the heat very low and steam for 30 minutes. The cloth will absorb excess steam and keep the rice grains separate. Once done, the rice will keep hot for 20–30 minutes, provided the cloth and lid are left in place. To serve, turn the rice into a warmed dish with a wooden fork. Lift out the crust with a spatula and put it around the rice.

Jambalaya

Louisiana is known for its highly seasoned gumbos and rice dishes; for jambalaya a mixture of seafood and meat is common.

FOR 4

2 tbsp sunflower oil

1¼ cups (180g) chopped smoked ham

1 large chicken breast half, skinned and cubed

1 onion, chopped

2 celery stalks, sliced

1 green sweet pepper, seeded and diced

2 tsp Cajun seasoning (*p.294*)

3 large tomatoes, peeled and chopped

¼ cup chopped fresh parsley

2½ cups (600ml) chicken stock

¼ tsp cayenne

salt

1¼ cups (200g) long-grain rice

20 large cooked shrimp, peeled

Heat the oil in a large, heavy pan and gently fry the ham and chicken for 5–6 minutes. Remove the meats and add the onion, celery, and green pepper. Let them start to brown, then add the Cajun seasoning and stir until the aroma is released.

Return the meats to the pan, and add the tomatoes, half the parsley, and the stock; season with the cayenne and a little salt. When the liquid comes to a boil, stir in the rice. Let it come back to a boil, then cover and lower the heat. Simmer for about 20 minutes, until the rice is tender, but still has a bite.

Stir the shrimp into the mixture with a wooden fork and simmer, uncovered, for 5 minutes, until they are heated through. Check the seasoning, stir in the remaining parsley, and serve.

Malabar pilaf

This pilaf comes from the southwestern hills of India, where spices grow in profusion. It makes an excellent accompaniment for braised chicken or lamb, or a vegetable stew. The pilaf is served with its spices, but only the cumin seeds are eaten.

FOR 4–6

3 cups (500g) basmati rice

2 tbsp sunflower oil or clarified butter

1 large onion, chopped

8 green cardamom pods

1 cinnamon stick

8 whole cloves

1 tsp cumin seeds

12 black peppercorns

1 tsp salt

1–2 tbsp sunflower oil or melted butter (optional)

Wash the rice in cold water and drain, then rinse until the water runs clear. Let soak in cold water for 30 minutes or so.

Heat the oil in a heavy pan and fry the onion until golden. Bruise the cardamoms lightly, and break the cinnamon in three. Add all the spices to the onion and fry gently for about 30 seconds, until the spices are slightly puffed and have darkened a little.

Drain the rice and add it to the pan. Fry for 2–3 minutes, stirring, until the rice becomes translucent. Add 3¾ cups boiling water, season with salt and bring back to a boil. Reduce the heat to very low, cover the pan, and simmer for 15 minutes. The water will be absorbed and the surface of the rice will be covered with tiny steam holes. If you wish, add the oil or butter to the rice now.

Fold a dish towel, put it over the pan and put on the lid (fold up the corners of the towel over the top). Leave the rice to steam for 5 minutes longer, then remove from the heat and let steam undisturbed for a further 5–10 minutes. Turn the rice out onto a warmed serving dish with a wooden fork, fluffing the rice as you do so.

Saffron risotto

This risotto will serve 4 as a first course, or 6 if it is to accompany a meat dish such as osso buco. Measure the rice and use twice the volume of liquid.

FOR 4–6

about 3½ cups (800ml) chicken or vegetable stock

½ tsp saffron threads, ground to a powder

7 tbsp (100g) butter

2 shallots, finely chopped

1¾ cups (400g) carnaroli or arborio rice

glass of white wine (optional)

salt and freshly ground pepper

2 tbsp freshly grated Parmesan cheese

Heat the stock and keep it simmering. Steep the saffron in 3 tbsp hot stock for about 5 minutes. Heat half the butter in a heavy pan and gently fry the shallots until golden. Add the rice and stir for 2–3 minutes until the grains are glistening with butter.

Pour in the wine if you are using it (or a ladleful of stock). Stir gently with a wooden fork, and wait until the liquid is absorbed. Add a ladleful of stock, the saffron liquid, and salt and pepper, stirring as you do so. When this is absorbed, add another ladleful of stock and stir it in. Continue to do this until the rice is tender and creamy but still retains a slight bite in the center; it will take about 18–20 minutes to cook. Take the pan from the heat and stir in the remaining butter and the Parmesan cheese.

Couscous with seven vegetables

In this traditional dish the vegetables could be varied: pumpkin, peas, potatoes, artichokes, or other vegetables in season can be used instead of those given below.

FOR 6

3 tbsp olive oil

1 tsp freshly ground black pepper

1 tbsp paprika

1 tbsp tabil (*p.291*) or ground cumin and coriander

2 onions, coarsely chopped

3 tomatoes, peeled and chopped

⅓ cup (60g) dried chickpeas, soaked overnight, or ½ can chickpeas, rinsed

3⅔ cups (900ml) water

2 carrots, thickly sliced

2 zucchini, thickly sliced

3 small white turnips, quartered

1¼ cups (200g) shelled or frozen fava beans

7oz (200g) cabbage heart, cut in pieces

2 red sweet peppers, cut in squares

handful of cilantro, chopped

salt

1⅓ cups (300g) quick-cooking couscous

harissa (*p.299*)

Heat the oil in a large pan, put in the spices and onions, and fry over medium heat for 3–4 minutes; then add the tomatoes and fry for a few minutes more.

If you are using soaked chickpeas, drain them and add to the pan with the unsalted water. Bring to a boil, cover, and leave to boil for 40 minutes. Then add the other vegetables, the cilantro, and salt, and cook for a further 20–30 minutes, until all the vegetables are done.

If you are using canned chickpeas, add them along with the other vegetables, the cilantro, salt to taste, and the water. Bring to a boil and simmer for 20–30 minutes until all the vegetables are cooked.

When the stew is almost ready, prepare the couscous according to the directions on the package. To serve, mound the couscous in a warmed serving dish, put the vegetables around it, and spoon some of the broth over. Use a ladleful of broth to thin the harissa, and pour the rest into a separate bowl. Serve the couscous with the extra broth and the harissa.

DESSERTS AND DRINKS

Pears baked with bay leaves

FOR 4

4 hard pears

handful of fresh bay leaves

2 tbsp water

1 tsp sugar

12 crushed black peppercorns

This recipe comes from Lynda Brown. Heat the oven to 180°F (90°C). Peel the pears thinly and remove the stems. Crush the bay leaves lightly to release their aroma.

Put the water, sugar, and half the bay leaves in a heavy casserole that will hold the pears snugly. Put in the pears. Drop the peppercorns in between them, and put the rest of the bay between and over the pears.

Cover tightly and bake for about 3 hours, until the pears are very soft and almost transparent. Serve hot or cold.

Baked figs with port and cinnamon

If you have figs that aren't quite ripe, this is a good way of using them. The flavorings can be varied: use seeds from 4–5 cardamom pods or 1 tsp lavender flowers instead of the cinnamon, a muscat or other sweet wine instead of the port, and orange juice and a little sugar instead of syrup. Firm peaches and nectarines also bake well.

FOR 6

7 tbsp (100ml) water

5 tbsp (60g) sugar

6 tbsp port

½ cinnamon stick

12 figs

Heat the oven to 400°F (200°C). Heat the water and sugar in a small saucepan until the sugar has dissolved, then simmer the syrup for 3–4 minutes. Pour the syrup into a baking dish just big enough to hold the figs in one layer. Pour in the port. Break the cinnamon in two. Put the figs into the dish and tuck the cinnamon between them.

Bake for 20–30 minutes, depending on the ripeness of the figs. Lift out the figs to a serving dish. Transfer the liquid to a pan, boil to reduce a little, and then strain this sauce over the figs. Serve at once or leave until cold.

Cinnamon cookies

FOR ABOUT 30 COOKIES

2 cups (300g) all-purpose flour

2 tsp ground cinnamon

1 tsp baking powder

¾ cup (150g) packed light brown sugar

6 tbsp (80g) butter

1 egg

3 tbsp (60g) golden or light corn syrup

blanched almonds or walnut pieces

Sift the flour, cinnamon, and baking powder into a large bowl and stir in the sugar. Cut the butter into small cubes and rub these into the flour with your fingertips until it looks like bread crumbs. Beat the egg, add the syrup, and beat until smooth.

Make a well in the center of the flour mixture and pour in the egg and syrup. Mix to a smooth dough; if it seems too stiff, add 1 tsp milk. Shape the dough into a ball, wrap in plastic, and chill for 30 minutes.

Heat the oven to 350°F (180°C). Roll out the dough on a lightly floured surface to ¼in (5mm) thick and cut out 2in (5cm) rounds with a cookie cutter. Put a blanched almond or a piece of walnut in the center of each cookie. Put them onto a baking sheet and bake for about 12 minutes. They will still feel soft but will harden on cooling. Let cool on a wire rack.

Vanilla ice cream

FOR 6

scant 2 cups (450ml) milk or light cream

1 vanilla bean, split lengthwise

4 egg yolks

¾ cup (150g) sugar

⅔ cup (150ml) whipping cream

Put the milk or light cream and the vanilla bean into a heavy pan and bring slowly to a boil. Remove from the heat, cover, and let infuse for 20 minutes. Take out the vanilla bean and scrape the seeds into the liquid.

Beat the egg yolks and sugar until thick and pale. Gently reheat the milk or cream and beat a little of it into the egg yolks. Pour the egg mixture into the cream and return the pan to a low heat. Stir until the custard is thick enough to coat the back of a spoon; it will take several minutes. Do not let it boil.

Remove the pan from the heat and continue to stir until it has almost cooled. Whip the whipping cream lightly and fold it into the custard. Freeze in an ice cream maker following the manufacturer's instructions.

VARIATIONS

Cardamom ice cream

Replace the vanilla bean with 8 lightly crushed cardamom pods. Infuse for 30 minutes, then strain .

Cinnamon ice cream

Replace the vanilla bean with 1 tbsp finely ground cinnamon. There is no need to infuse.

Lavender ice cream

Replace the vanilla bean with 3 tbsp fresh lavender flowers. Infuse for 1 hour, then strain. Add 1 tsp finely chopped lavender flowers just before the whipped cream.

Pineapple and ginger cooler

FOR 3–4

2oz (60g) fresh ginger

1 large pineapple

juice of 2 lemons and 2 oranges

sugar

This Ethiopian recipe comes from Mariam Kruss. Peel the ginger and slice thinly. Peel the pineapple, remove the eyes and the core, and slice thinly. Blend the ginger and pineapple with the citrus juice. Add sugar to taste, about ⅔ cup (125g) per quart (liter) of liquid, and blend to mix. Strain, chill, and serve diluted with water if too thick.

Sol kadhi

Along the tropical Malabar coast of India, this refreshing drink is often served at the end of a meal. It can also be served to accompany rice and fried fish.

FOR 4–6

15 pieces of kokam

5–6 tbsp warm water

2 hot green chili peppers, chopped

2 garlic cloves, crushed

2½ cups (600ml) coconut milk

salt

2 tbsp chopped cilantro

Soak the kokam in the warm water for 10–15 minutes; the water should be colored pink and taste slightly sour. If necessary, leave the kokam to soak longer.

While the kokam is soaking, pound or blend the chilies into the garlic. Strain the kokam liquid into the coconut milk, and stir in the garlic and chili paste, salt to taste and the cilantro. Chill. Stir well before serving.

Mojito

A refreshing long drink, popular in Cuba.

light rum

lime juice

superfine sugar

sprigs of fresh spearmint

For each serving mix equal measures of rum and lime juice with sugar to taste. Stir well and add 2 sprigs of spearmint with crushed stems and ice cubes; top up with water.

BIBLIOGRAPHY

Andrews, Jean
Red Hot Peppers
New York, Macmillan, 1993
Peppers: the Domesticated Capsicums
Austin, Univ. of Texas Press, 1984

Arndt, Alice
Seasoning Savvy
New York, Haworth Press, 1999

Bayless, Rick
Authentic Mexican Cooking
London, Headline, 1989

Bharadwaj, Monisha
The Indian Pantry
London, Kyle Cathie, 1996

Boulestin, Marcel & Jason Hill
Herbs, Salads and Seasonings
London, Heinemann, 1930

Bown, Deni
Encyclopedia of Herbs
London, Dorling Kindersley, 1995

Boxer, Arabella
The Herb Book
San Diego, Thunder Bay Press, 1996

Braudel, Fernand
The Mediterranean and the Mediterranean World in the Age of Philip II (two volumes)
London, Collins, 1972–73

Bremness, Lesley
The Complete Book of Herbs
London, Dorling Kindersley, 1988

Brennan, Jennifer
Thai Cooking
London, Jill Norman & Hobhouse, 1981

Brierley, Joanna Hall
Spices: The Story of Indonesia's Spice Trade
Kuala Lumpur, Oxford Univ. Press, 1994

Capus, G. & D. Bois
Les Produits Coloniaux
Paris, Armand Colin, 1912

Choi, Trieu Thi & Marcel Isaak
The Food of Vietnam
Hong Kong, Periplus, 1997

Clair, Colin
Of Herbs & Spices
London, Abelard-Schuman, 1961

Clébert, Jean-Paul
Le Livre de l'Ail
Paris, Barthélemy, 1987

Corn, Charles
The Scents of Eden
New York, Kodansha, 1999

Cost, Bruce
Asian Ingredients
London, Ebury Press, 1990
Ginger East to West: a Cook's Tour
Los Angeles, Aris, 1984

Dalby, Andrew
Dangerous Tastes: The Story of Spices
London, British Museum Press, 2000

David, Elizabeth
Dried Herbs, Aromatics and Condiments
London, the author, 1967
Spices, Salt and Aromatics in the English Kitchen
London, Penguin Books, 1970

De Jordan, Nelly
Nuestras Comidas
Cochabamba, the author, 1990

Delaveau, Pierre
Les Epices: Histoire, Description et Usage
Paris, Albin Michel, 1987

DeWitt, Dave & Nancy Gerlach
The Whole Chile Pepper Book
Boston, Little Brown, 1990

Dunlop, Fuchsia
Sichuan Cookery
London, Michael Joseph, 2001

E(velyn), J(ohn). Acetaria
A Discourse of Sallets
London, B. Tooke, 1699; (facsimile with index and glossary), Totnes, Prospect Books, 1994

Farrell, Kenneth T.
Spices, Condiments, and Seasonings
Gaithersburg MD, Aspen, 1999

Gilbertie, Sal
Kitchen Herbs
New York, Bantam, 1988

Goldstein, Darra
The Georgian Feast
New York, Harper Collins, 1993

Grieve, M.
A Modern Herbal
London, Cape, 1974
(on-line at www.botany.com)
Culinary Herbs and Condiments
New York, Dover, 1971

Grigson, Sophie
Herbs
London, BBC Worldwide, 1999

Guinaudeau, Z.
Fes Vue par sa Cuisine
Oudaia, J. E. Laurent, 1966

Halıcı, Nevin
Turkish Cookbook
London, Dorling Kindersley, 1989

Harris, Jessica B.
The Africa Cookbook
New York, Simon & Schuster, 1998

Heal, Carolyn & Michael Allsop
Cooking with Spices
Newton Abbot, David & Charles, 1983

Hemphill, Ian
Spice Notes: A Cook's Compendium of Herbs and Spices
Sydney, Macmillan, 2000

Hemphill, Rosemary
Herbs and Spices
Harmondsworth, Penguin Books, 1966
Herbs for all Seasons
London, Angus & Robertson, 1972

Holt, Geraldene
A Taste of Herbs
London, Conran Octopus, 1991

Hom, Ken
Asian Ingredients: A Guide with Recipes
Berkeley CA, Ten Speed Press, 1996

Hosking, Richard
A Dictionary of Japanese Food, Ingredients & Culture
Rutland VT, Tuttle, 1996

Humphries, John
The Essential Saffron Companion
London, Grub Street, 1996

Hutson, Lucinda
The Herb Garden Cookbook
Houston TX, Gulf, 1992

Hutton, Wendy
Tropical Herbs & Spices
Hong Kong, Periplus, 1998

Jacquat, Christiane
Plants From the Markets of Thailand
Bangkok, Duang Kamol, 1990

Jump, Meg
Cooking with Chillies
London, The Bodley Head, 1989

Kennedy, Diana
The Art of Mexican Cooking
New York, Bantam, 1989

Khawam, René R.
La Cuisine Arabe
Paris, Albin Michel, 1970

Kouki, Mohamed
La Cuisine Tunisienne
Tunis, the author, 1967

Kowalchik, Claire & Wm H. Hylton (ed.s)
Rodale's Illustrated Encyclopedia of Herbs
Emmaus PA, Rodale, 1987

Lancellotti, Angelo.
Le Erbe Aromatiche in Cucina
Lodi, Bibl. Culinaria, 2001

Landry, Robert
Les Soleils de la Cuisine
Paris, Robert Laffont, 1967

Larkcom, Joy
Oriental Vegetables
London, John Murray, 1991

Loewenfeld, Claire & Philippa Back
The Complete Book of Herbs and Spices
Newton Abbot, David & Charles, 1978

Manfield, Christine
Spice
Ringwood Vict., Viking, 1999

Miller, J. Innes
The Spice Trade of the Roman Empire
Oxford, Univ. Press, 1969

Miller, Mark
The Great Chile Book
Berkeley CA, Ten Speed Press, 1991

Milton, Giles
Nathaniel's Nutmeg
London, Hodder Headline, 1999

Misia-Peta
Nueva Cocina Peruana
Lima, Mercurio, 1997

Norman, Jill
Aromatic Herbs
London, Dorling Kindersley 1989
Salad Herbs
London, Dorling Kindersley, 1989
Spices: Roots & Fruits
London, Dorling Kindersley, 1989
Spices: Seeds & Barks
London, Dorling Kindersley, 1990
The Complete Book of Spices
London, Dorling Kindersley, 1990
The Classic Herb Cookbook
London, Dorling Kindersley, 1997
Cooking with Spices
London, Dorling Kindersley, 1998

Ortiz, Elisabeth Lambert
The Complete Book of Caribbean Cooking
New York, M. Evans, 1973

Owen, Sri
Indonesian Food and Cookery
London, Prospect Books, 1986

Page, Mary & Wm T. Stearn
Culinary Herbs (3rd ed.)
London, RHS, 1992

Panjabi, Camellia
50 Great Curries of India
London, Kyle Cathie, 1994

Parry, J. W.
The Spice Handbook: Spices, Aromatic Seeds and Herbs
Brooklyn NY, Chemical Publ. Co., 1945

Pham, Mai
Pleasures of the Vietnamese Table
New York, Harper Collins, 2001

Phillips, Roger & Martyn Rix
Herbs for Cooking
London, Pan, 1998

Pruthi, J. S.
Spices and Condiments
New Delhi, National Book Trust, 1979

Pursglove, J. W. (and others)
Spices (two volumes)
Harlow, Longman Scientific, 1981

Raichlen, Steven
The Caribbean Pantry Cookbook
New York, Artisan, 1995

Rocha, Rui
A Viagem dos Sabores: A Voyage around Tastes
Lisbon, Inapa, 1998

Roden, Claudia
A New Book of Middle Eastern Food
London, Viking, 1985
The Book of Jewish Food
London, Viking, 1997

Rohde, Eleanour Sinclair
Culinary and Salad Herbs
London, Country Life, 1940
Herbs and Herb Gardening
London, Medici Society, 1936

Rosengarten, Frederic
The Book of Spices
New York, Livingston, 1969

Sahni, Julie
Classic Indian Cooking
London, Dorling Kindersley, 1986

Schlesinger, Chris & John Willoughby
Salsa, Sambals, Chutneys & Chowchows
New York, Wm Morrow, 1993

Schönfeld, Sybil & Ute Lundberg
Paprika: Gewürz und Gemüse
Füssen, Teubner, 1993

Scotto, Elisabeth
La Cuisine des Parfums
Paris, Ed. du Chêne, 1996

Shaida, Margaret
The Legendary Cuisine of Persia
Henley-on-Thames, Lieuse, 1992

Siewek, Fred
Exotische Gewürze
Basel, Birkhäuser, 1990

Singh, V. S. & Kirti
Spices
New Delhi, New Age, 1996

Small, Ernest
Culinary Herbs
Ottawa, NRC Research Press, 1997

Solomon, Charmaine
Encyclopedia of Asian Food
Port Melbourne, Wm Heinemann, 1996

Sotti, M. L. & M. T. Della Beffa
Le Piante Aromatiche
Milano, Mondadori, 1989

Stella, Alain
The Book of Spices
Paris, Flammarion, 1999

Stobart, Tom
Herbs, Spices and Flavourings
London, David & Charles, 1970

Teubner, Schönfeldt, Gerhardt, Rühlemann
Kräuter und Knoblauch
Füssen, Teubner, 1993

Tidbury, G. E.
The Clove Tree
London, Crosby Lockwood, 1949

Traunfeld, Jerry
The Herbfarm Cookbook
New York, Scribner, 2000

Tropp, Barbara
The Modern Art of Chinese Cooking
New York, Wm Morrow, 1982

Tsuji, Shizuo
Japanese Cooking - a Simple Art
Tokyo, Kodansha, 1980

Tucker, Arthur O. & Thomas Debaggio
The Big Book of Herbs
Loveland CO, Interweave Press, 2000

Uhl, Susheela R.
Spices, Seasonings, & Flavorings
Lancaster PA, Technomic, 2000

Vilmorin-Andrieu & Cie
Les Plantes Potagères: Description et Culture des Principaux Légumes des Climats Tempérés
Paris, Vilmorin-Andrieux, 1925

Walter, Eugene
Hints & Pinches
Atlanta GA, Longstreet, 1991

Waters, Alice
Chez Panisse Vegetables
New York, Harper Collins, 1996

Wolfert, Paula
The Cooking of the Eastern Mediterranean
New York, Harper Collins, 1994
Moroccan Cuisine
London, Grub Street, 1998

SOURCES OF HERBS AND SPICES

Adriana's Caravan
409 Vanderbilt Street
Brooklyn, NY 11218, USA
Fax: 718 436 8565
www.adrianascaravan.com
"1,500 spices, condiments, and other ingredients from around the world."

Arne Herbs
Limeburn Nurseries
Chew Magna
BS18 8QW, UK
Tel/Fax: 01275 333 399
www.arneherbs.co.uk
"Suppliers of authentic plants for the recreation of historic gardens."

Bristol Sweet Mart
80 St Marks Road
Bristol BS5 6JH, UK
Tel: 0117 951 2257
Fax: 0117 952 5456
www.sweetmart.co.uk
"The biggest seller of ethnic foodstuffs in southwest England."

City Herbs
New Spitalfields Market
Sherrin Road
London E10 5SQ, UK
Tel: 020 8558 9708
Fax: 020 8558 6909
Good suppliers of all sorts of herbs and imported vegetables.

A Cook's Wares
211 37th Street
Beaver Falls, PA 15010, USA
www.cookswares.com
Online company has a comprehensive range of herbs, spices, and cookware.

Cool Chile Co.
PO Box 5702
London W11 2GS, UK
Tel: 07973 311 714
Fax: 020 7229 9360
www.coolchile.co.uk
Has most of the dried Mexican and Spanish chili peppers.

Essbare Landschaften
Gutshaus Boltenhagen,
18516 Süderholz,
Germany
Tel: 038326 46335
Fax: 038326 46337
www.essbare-landschaften.de

Halcyonseeds
10 Hampden Close
Chalgrove OX44 7SB, UK
Tel/Fax: 01865 890 180
www.halcyonseeds.co.uk
Good suppliers of salad and other herb seeds.

Herbie's Spices
745 Darling Street, Rozelle,
NSW 2039, Australia
www.herbies.com.au
Australia's leading supplier of dried herbs and spices, run by Ian Hemphill
(*see* Bibliography, *p.326*).

Highdown Nursery
New Hall Lane
Small Dole, Henfield
West Sussex BN5 9YH, UK
Tel: 01273 492 976
Supplies "*well-grown herbs*" in 3½-in and 1-quart pots.

Iden Croft Herbs
Frittenden Road
Staplehurst
TN12 0DH, UK
Tel: 01580 891 432
Fax: 01580 892 416
www.herbs-uk.com
Has an excellent range of plants, herbs, and seeds.

Jekka's Herb Farm
Rose Cottage
Shellards Lane
Alveston, Bristol
BS35 3SY, UK
Tel: 01454 418 878
Fax: 01454 411 988
www.jekkasherbfarm.com
Suppliers of organic herb plants and seeds.

Kalustyans
123 Lexington Avenue
New York, NY 10016-8120, USA
Tel: 212 685 3451
Fax: 212 683 8458
www.kalustyans.com
"*The best Asian grocer in Manhattan*"; offers a very good range of Indian and other spices.

Laurel Farm Herbs
Main Road, Kelsale,
Saxmundham,
Suffolk IP17 2RG, UK
Tel: 01728 668 223
Fax: 01728 668 468
www.theherbfarm.co.uk
Has a wide range of top-quality herb plants immaculately packed for shipping.

LER's World-Herb Shop
16245 SW 304 Street
Homestead, FL 33033, USA
www.ethnobotany.com
Tel: 305 242 0877
LER (Legendary Ethnobotanical Resources) sells many dried herbs that are hard to find elsewhere.

Libanus
www.libanus.com
French-language website selling all varieties of Middle-Eastern herbs and spices.

Maggie's Herb Farm
11400 County Road 13 North
St Augustine, FL 32092 USA
Tel: 904 829 0722
Sells 4-in and larger potted plants and fresh cut herbs.

MSK
PO Box 1592
Dronfield, South Yorkshire
S18 8BR, UK
Tel: 01246 416 486
Fax: 01246 419 371
Has excellent saffron, vanilla, paprika, and other spices at reasonable prices.

Pacific Gourmet
PO Box 2071
San Rafael, CA 94912, USA
Tel: 415 641 8400

Peppers By Post
Sea Spring Farm
West Bexington
Dorchester, Dorset
DT2 9DD, UK
Tel: 01308 897 892
Fax: 01308 897 735
Has fresh (in season) and dried peppers.

Renaissance
262 Hakone Road, Warnervale,
NSW 2259, Australia
Tel: 02 4392 4600
Fax: 02 4393 1221
"*Growers of Renaissance herbs and romantic cottage plants.*"

Richters Herb Specialists
Goodwood, Ontario,
Canada L0C 1A0
Tel: 905 640 6677
Fax: 905 640 6641
www.richters.com
The leading herb growers in Canada, from whom all of Small's (*see* Bibliography, *p.327*) specimens were obtained.

Seasoned Pioneers
101 Summers Road
Liverpool L3 4BJ, UK
Tel: 0800 068 2348
www.seasonedpioneers.co.uk
Good spice merchant, stocking a wide range of less familiar spices and blends.

Francesco Sirene
PO Box 1051, Peachland,
BC, Canada V0H 1XO
www.silk.net/sirene
"A *purveyor of goods for historical cookery and living.*"

The Spice House
1512 N. Wells Street
Chicago, IL 60610, USA
Tel: 312 274 0378
Fax: 312 274 0143
www.thespicehouse.com
Started by William Penzey Sr in the 1950s and now run by the next generation. The biggest and best spice and dried herb mail-order business in the US.

Suffolk Herbs
Monks Farm, Coggeshall Road
Kelvedon, CO5 9PG, UK
Tel: 01376 572 456
Fax: 01376 571189
Particularly good for seeds.

Suma Wholefoods
Dean Clough
Halifax, HX3 5AN, UK
Tel: 0845 458 2290
Fax: 01422 349 429
A big wholesaler of foods with a good list of dried herbs and spices.

Vanilla Venture
Ruysdaelkade 161
1072 AS Amsterdam
Holland
Tel: 020 676 9146
email postbus@vanilla-venture.demon.nl
Good-quality vanilla.

Well-Sweep Herb Farm
205 Mt Bethel Road
Port Murray, NJ 07865, USA
Tel: 908 852 5390
www.wellsweep.com
Has a wide variety of herbs "*and related herbalware.*"

West Dean Gardens
West Dean
Chichester, Sussex
PO18 0QZ, UK
Tel: 01243 818210
Fax: 01243 811342
www.westdean.org.uk
Has the best collection of chili peppers in the UK and also sells herbs.

INDEX

The index is divided into three parts Common and botanical names (*p.330*); Recipes (*p.333*); and Techniques and miscellaneous (*p.335*).

Common and botanical names

(a reference to a recipe indicates that the ingredient is essential to that recipe)

Acacia spp. 143
achiote 214–15; recipe 295
Aframomum spp. 196–97
agastache 68–69
Agastache spp. 68–69
ají 263; recipe 294
ajowan 218–19
ajwain 218
akudjura 158
alexanders 87
alligator pepper 234
Allium ampeloprasum 80
Allium canadense 80
Allium fistulosum 81
Allium sativum 76–80
Allium schoenoprasum 82
Allium tuberosum 83
allspice 244–45; recipe 292
Aloysia citriodora 54
Alpinia spp. 178–79
amb halao 210
amchoor 172–73; recipe 287
Ammi majus 219
Amomum melegueta 197, 234–35
Amomum spp. 196–97
amsul 170
anardana 168–69
ancho 260–61
Anethum graveolens 64–65
angelica 39
Angelica arcangelica 39
anise (seed) 186–87
anise hyssop 68–69
annatto 214–15
Anthriscus cerefolium 60–61
Apium graveolens 84–85
Armoracia rusticana 116–17
aromatic ginger 180
Artemisia dracunculoides 63
Artemisia dracunculus 62–63
Artemisia vulgaris 121
arugula 112–13; recipe 296
asafetida 250–51; recipe 287
asem 163
Ashanti pepper 229
Atriplex hortensis 27
avocado leaf 231

Backhousia citriodora 181
bai gaprow 34
bai horopa 34
bai manglak 35
balm 50, 52, 53, 74
banana chili pepper 265
Barbarea verna praecox 119
barberry 166–67
basil 30–35; recipes 296
bay 36–37; recipe 324
bee balm 50
beefsteak plant 25
Benin pepper 229
beni-shoga 240
Berberis vulgaris 166–67
bergamot 50–51
betel pepper 230
bird chili pepper 264
bishop's weed 219
bitter orange 182–83; recipes 282, 302
Bixa orellana 214–15
black cardamom 196–97; recipes 286
black mangosteen 170
black mint 29
black onion seed 140
Boesenbergia pandurata 180
Bohnenkraut 105
borage 22
Borago officinalis 22
Brassica spp. 252–55
bunching onion 81
Bunias orientalis 113
Bunium persicum 199
burnet 23
bush tomato 158

calamint 74
Calamintha spp. 74
Calendula officinalis 28–29
caper berries 217
capers 216–17; recipe 319
Capparis spp. 216–17
Capsicum annuum spp. 160–61, 256–65
Capsicum baccatum 263
Capsicum chinense 256, 260, 262–63
Capsicum frutescens 256, 263–64
Capsicum pubescens 263
caraway 200–201
cardamom 194–97; recipes 286, 325
carom 218
cascabel 261
Carthamus tinctorius 223
Carum carvi 200–201
cassia 146–47
catmint 75
catnip 75
cekur 180
céleri bâtard 86
celery 84–85
chaa phluu 230
chadron benee 110
Chenopodium ambrosioides 120
cherry chili pepper 265
chervil 60–61
chicory 89
chilaca 260
chili peppers 256–65
  dried, recipes 285, 292, 294, 298, 299
  fresh, recipes 283, 285, 299, 300–301, 302
Chinese celery 84–85
Chinese chives 83
Chinese keys 180
Chinese parsley 108–109
chipotle 261
chives 82; recipe 319
choricero 265
Cichorium intybus 89
cilantro 108–109
  recipes 290, 296, 303, 307
Cinnamomum spp. 144–47
cinnamon 144–45; recipes 289, 324, 325
citron 182
citrus 182–83
Citrus hystrix 176–77
Citrus spp. 182–83
claytonia 21
Claytonia perfoliata 21
cloves 246–49
coriander (seed) 148–49;
  recipes 286, 291
Coriandrum sativum (herb) 108–109
Coriandrum sativum (spice) 148–49
Costa Rican mint 106
cress 118–19
Crocus sativus 190–91
Cryptotaenia japonica 26
cubeb 229
culantro 110
cumin 198–99; recipe 286
Cuminum cyminum 198–99
Curcuma longa 208–209
Curcuma spp. 210–11
curry leaf 212–13; recipes 287, 288
cusqueño 263
Cymbopogon citratus 174–75

daun kesom 111
de arból 261
desert raisins 158
dhana-jeera 148, 198; recipe 286
dill 64–65; recipes 310, 319

Diplotaxis muralis 113
Dorrigo pepper 233
elephant garlic 80
Elettaria cardamomum 194–95
Elsholtzia ciliata 53
emperor's mint 107
epazote 120; recipe 301
Eruca vesicaria subsp. *sativa* 112–13
Eryngium foetidum 110
Ethiopian cumin 219
Eugenia polyantha 231
Eutrema wasabi 114–15

fagara 236
false Queen Anne's lace 219
fennel 66–67; recipe 304
fenugreek 220–21; recipe 290
Ferula spp. 250–51
fingerroot 180; recipe 285
fish mint/plant 58
flower pepper 236
Foeniculum vulgare 66–67

galangal 178–80
Galium odoratum 48
Gänsekraut 121
Garcinia spp. 170–71
gari 240
garlic 76–80; recipes 281, 290, 294, 296, 298, 299, 303
garlic chives 83
geranium 40–42
giant hyssop 68
ginger 137, 269
  dried ginger 242–43
  fresh ginger 238–41; recipes 304, 311, 325
  pickled ginger 240; recipe 308
  preserved ginger 241
Glycyrrhiza spp. 188–89
golpar 93
grains of paradise 197, 234–35; recipe 291
guajillo 261, 263
güero 261
guindilla 265
Guinea pepper 234

habanero 260
hajikami-shoga 240
Heracleum persicum 93
hierba buena 106
hoja santa 230–31
hontaka 264
horsemint 51
horseradish 116–17; recipes 297, 319
houttuynia 58
Houttuynia cordata 58
huacatay 28, 29
Hungarian wax chili pepper 265
hyssop 88
Hyssopus officinalis 88
Illicium verum 184–85
Imeretian saffron 29
Indian arrowroot 211
Indian bay 147
Indian mint 106

jalapeño 260, 261
Jamaican hot chili pepper 262
Jamaican mint 106
Jamaica pepper 244
Japanese chervil 26
Japanese horseradish 114
Japanese leek 81
Japanese parsley 26
Japanese pepper 236
Java pepper 229
jeera 199
jindungo 265
juniper 150–51; recipes 293, 305, 315
Juniperus communis 150–51

kadhi patta 212
kaffir lime 176–77; recipes 285, 308, 311
kala jeera 199
Kampferia spp. 180
kangaroo apple 158
kari patta 212
kemangie 35
kencur 180, 210
kha 178
khamin khao 211
kinome 236, 237
kokam 170–71; recipe 325
Korean chili pepper 264
Korean mint 68, 69
krachai 180; recipe 285
kun choi 85

laksa leaf 111
lá lót 230, 231
laos 178
Laurus nobilis 36–37
Lavandula spp. 44–45
lavender 44–47; recipe 325
lemon balm 52
lemon grass 174–75, 267; recipes 285, 311
lemon myrtle 181
lemon verbena 54
lengkuas 178
Lepidium sativum 119
Levisticum officinale 86–87
licorice 188–89; recipe 313
Ligusticum scoticum 87
lime 182–83; recipe 301
  dried, recipe 289
Limnophilia aromatica 59
Lippia graveolens 93
long cilantro 110
lovage 86–87
love-in-a-mist 140

mace 202–207; recipe 293
mahlab 142
Mahonia spp. 166–67
Majorana spp. 90
makrut lime 176–77; recipes 285, 308, 311
malagueta 263
Mangifera indica 172–73
mango powder 172–73
marigold 28–29; recipe 282
marjoram 90–93; recipe 318
mastic 222
meetha neem 212
melegueta pepper 234
Melissa officinalis 52
Mentha spp. 70–73
methi 221
Mexican tarragon 29, 63
micromeria 107
Micromeria spp. 107
miner's lettuce 21
mint 70–73; recipes 296, 297, 303, 325
mioga ginger 241
mirasol 263
mitsuba 26
mizuna 253
Monarda fistulosa var. *menthifolia* 93
Monarda spp. 50–51
mountain balm 74
mountain pepper 232–33
mountain spinach 27
mugwort 121
mulato chili pepper 261
Murraya koenigii 212–13
mustard 252–55
  prepared mustard 254–55; recipes 310, 315
Myristica fragrans 202–207
Myrrhis odorata 43
Myrtus communis 38
myrtle 38

nasturtium 118, 119
Nasturtium officinale 118, 119
Nepeta cataria 75
nepitella 74
New Mexico chili pepper 262
Nicolaia elatior 241
nigella 140, 199
Nigella sativa 140, 199
ñora 265; recipe 298
nutmeg 202–205; recipe 293
Ocimum spp. 30–35

Oenanthe javanica 84
Oman lime 183
onion, bunching 81
  green 81
  Welsh 81
orach 27
orange peel 182
Oregon grape 167
oregano 90–93
oriental bunching onion 81
Origanum spp. 90–93
Oswego tea 51

pandan 49
Pandanus spp. 49
Papaver somniferum 141
paprika 160–61; recipe 317
parsley 18–19; recipes 201, 296, 298, 302
pasilla 260, 261
pebre d'aï 105
Pelargonium spp. 40–42
pennyroyal 73
peperoncino 265
pepper 224–28; recipes 281, 292, 293
peppermint 70, 72, 73
perilla 24–25
Perilla frutescens 24–25
peri peri 265
Persea americana 231
Petroselinum crispum 18–19
piment d'Espellette 265
Pimenta dioica 244–45
pimento 244
pimentón 160
pimienta 244
pimiento 256
Pimpinella anisum 186–87
pink pepper 159
Piper spp. 224–30
Plectranthus amboinicus 93
poblano 260, 261
poivre d'âne 105
Poliomintha longiflora 93
Polygonum odoratum 111
pomegranate 168–69; recipe 307
poppy 141
Portulaca spp. 20
pro hom 180
Prunus mahaleb 142, 222
Punica granata 168–69
purslane 20; recipe 307
Pycnanthemum pilosa 73

quillquiña 263

rai 253
ramps 80
ramsons 80
rapeseed 255
rau diep ca 58
rau kinh gio'i 53
rau ngo 59
rau om 59
rau ram 111; recipe 320
recao 110
resurrection lily 180
Rhus coriaria 164–65
rice paddy herb 59
rígani 90
rocambole 80
rocotillo 263
rocoto 263
rokka 113
roquette 112–13
Rosa spp. 152–53
rose 152–53; recipe 289
rosemary 94–95; recipe 315
Rosmarinus officinalis 94–95
Rumex spp. 56–57

safflower 223
saffron 190–93; recipes 319, 323
sage 96–99
salad burnet 23
salam 231
Salvia spp. 96–99
sandleek 80
Sanguisorba minor 23
sansho 236–37
santaka 264
sassafras 55
Sassafras albidum 55
Satureja spp. 104–106, 107
savory 104–106
sawleaf herb 110
scallions 81
scented geranium 40–42
Schinus terebinthifolius 159
Scotch bonnet 262
screwpine 49
serrano 260
sesame 138–39; recipes 284, 290, 301
Sesamum orientale 138–39
shado beni 110
shiso 24–25
Sichuan pepper 236–37; recipe 284
silphium 250
smallage 84
Smyrnium olusatrum 87
Solanum spp. 158
sorrel 56–57; recipe 298
spearmint 70–72, 106
spiny cilantro 110
star anise 184–85; recipes 284, 311, 318
sumac 164–65; recipes 290, 307
sweet cicely 43
Syrian oregano 93, 102
Syzygium aromaticum 246–47

tabasco 262
Tagetes spp. 28–29
tailed pepper 229
tamarind 162–63
Tamarindus indica 162–63
tangerine peel 182–83; recipe 284
tarragon 62–63; recipes 297, 306, 315
Tasmannia spp. 232–33
tejpat 147; recipe 286
temu kunci 180
Thai chili pepper 264
Thai parsley 110
thryba 102, 106
Thymbra spicata 102
thyme 100–103
Thymus spp. 100–103
tikor 211
Trachyspermum ammi 218–19
trefoil 26
Trigonella foenum-graecum 220–21
Tropaeolum majus 119
Turkish saffron 223
turmeric 208–209

vanilla 154–57; recipe 325
Vanilla planifolia 154–57
vap ca 58
Vietnamese balm 53
Vietnamese celery 84
Vietnamese cilantro 111
Vietnamese fish mint 58
Vietnamese mint 111

Waldmeister 48
wasabi 114–15; recipe 308
water celery 84
watercress 118; recipe 306
wattle 143
Welsh onion 81
"white turmeric" 210–11
winter purslane 21
winter tarragon 29
woodruff 48

yerba buena 106
yomogi 121
yuzu 182–83

za'atar 93, 102; recipe 290
za'atar farsi 103
Zanthoxylum spp. 236–37
zedoary 210–11
Zingiber spp. 238–43

Recipes

Page numbers in **bold** refer to illustrations

adobo
  Cuban 282
  dry 305
  for pork 305
achiote paste 295
advieh
  for rice **153**, 289
  for stews 289
agastache honey 69
ajilimójili 302
ají paste 294
  in adobo 305
Aleppo blend 291
  in slow-cooked leg of lamb 312
aliño, Chilean 282
Apfelkren 297; and see 117
aromatic garam masala **207**, 286
  in pot-roasted chicken 315
arugula pesto 296
Asian marinade 305
Australian dry rub for lamb 233

baharat
  Saudi 289
  Tunisian 290
Bajan seasoning 283
baking spice **245**, 293
barberry rub 167
basil, mint, and red pepper sauce 296
barbecue marinades 305
barbecue spice 294
béarnaise sauce 297
bee balm salsa 51
beef braised with licorice 313
beef curry, Thai 314
beef and broccoli,
  noodles with 321
berbere 292
  in chicken wat 316
bharat 290
bizar a'shuwa 289
  in slow-cooked leg of lamb 312
Bombay masala 287
bouquet garni 280
  for beef **37**
  for fish **63**
  for pork **97**

Cajun seasoning 294
  in jambalaya 322
cardamom ice cream 325
carrots, glazed, with marjoram 318
chat masala **219**, 287
chermoula 311
chicken Colombo 316
chicken
  pot-roasted with Indian spices 315
chicken tikka 316
chicken wat 316
chili jam, Thai 299; and see 259
chili oil 258
chili sauce
  sweet 300
  with lime 301
chimichurri 302
chutney
  cilantro 303
  Nepali mint 303
cilantro chutney 303
cilantro pesto 296
cinnamon cookies 324
cinnamon ice cream 325
couscous with seven vegetables 323
Cuban adobo 282
Cuban mojo 302
cucumber sambal 303
curry
  Seychelles fish 310
  shrimp and coconut 310
  Thai beef 314
curry paste
  green 285
  Malay 288
  massaman 285
  red 285
curry powder
  Madras 287
  Malay 288
  poudre de Colombo 295
  South African 292
  Sri Lankan 288
  Tamil 288

dhana jeera 286
dipping sauce, Korean 301
dry adobo 305
dry rub for lamb 233
dukka 291

eggah 309
eggplant with preserved lemon 317

farcellets 281
fattoush 307
fennel braised with star anise 318
figs baked with port and cinnamon 324
fines herbes **61,** 281
fish curry 310
five-spice powder **247**, 284
  in baked sea bass 311

garam masala
  aromatic **207**, 286
    in pot-roasted chicken 315
  standard **197**, 286
garlic and herb paste 281
garlic purée 303
geranium leaf syrup 41
ginger and lime marinade 304
goma shio 284
gravad lax 310; and see 65
green curry paste 285
green mango relish 303
green masala 282
  in shrimp and coconut curry 310
green mojo 298
green mole 301
gremolata 281
Gujarati masala 286

harissa 299
  with couscous 323
hawaij 290
herbed pepper 281
herbes de Provence **95**, 281
herb omelette, Middle Eastern 309
herb mixtures 280–83
herb salads 307
hilbeh 290; and see 221
horseradish and apple sauce 297

ice cream 325
Iranian herb mixtures 283
Italian spice mixture 293
  in osso buco 314

jambalaya 322
jerk seasoning, Jamaican 283
juniper and wine marinade 305
juniper rub 151
Kashmiri masala 286
khmeli-sumeli 282
kitchen pepper 293
  in slow-cooked red cabbage 318
kookoo 309
Korean dipping sauce 301

la kama 291
  in slow-cooked leg of lamb 312
laksa 320
lamb
  Australian dry rub for 233
  korma 312
  with Oman spices 312
larp 308
lavender ice cream 325
leek and herb soup 306
lemon, preserved **182**, 299
lentils, spiced 317
lime and chili sauce 301
linguine with herbs 320

Madras curry powder 287;
  and see 286
Malabar pilaf 322
Malay curry paste 288
Malay curry powder 288
mango and papaya mojo 302
marinade
  adobo 305

marinade *contd.*
- Asian 305
- barbecue 305
- ginger and lime 304
- juniper and wine 305
- Mediterranean 304
- Mexican 305
- Pernod 304
- red wine 304
- yogurt 304

masala
- Bombay 286
- chat masala 287
- for fish 287
- garam masala 286
- green 282
- Gujarati 286
- Kashmiri 286
- Punjabi 286
- tandoori 287
- West Indian 295

massalé 288
- in Seychelles fish curry 310
- in yogurt marinade 304

massaman curry paste 285
- in Thai beef curry 314

Mediterranean marinade 304
Mexican marinade 305
mint chutney, Nepali 303
mixed herb platters 283
mojito 325
mojo 183
- Cuban 302
- green 298
- mango and papaya 302

mole verde 301
mushrooms with bacon 318
mussels with lemon grass and ginger 311

nam prik 299
- roasted 300

nam prik pad 299
noodles with beef and broccoli 321
nuoc cham 300

osso buco 314

panch phoron, Bengali 288
papas arrugadas 298
paprika potatoes 317
parsley and lemon sauce 296
parsley pesto 296
parsley salsa, Peruvian 302
pears baked with bay leaves 324
pepper
- herbed 281
- kitchen 293
- West Indian blend 292

Pernod marinade 304
persillade 281
pesto 296
pickling spices
- English 293
- Middle Eastern **187**, 289

pili pili sauce 301
pineapple and ginger cooler 325
pomegranate, olive, and walnut salad 307
pork chops with juniper and rosemary 315
pork tenderloin with tarragon and mustard 315
poudre de Colombo 295
- in Caribbean chicken Colombo 316

preserved lemons **182**, 299
- in eggplant recipe 317

pumpkin bredie 313
Punjabi masala 286

qâlat daqqa **135**, **235**, 291
- in slow-cooked leg of lamb 312

quatre épices **243**, 293

ras el hanout 291
ravigote sauce 297
ravioli filled with saffron ricotta 319
recado
- for steak 295
- rojo **215**, 295

red cabbage, slow-cooked 318
red curry paste 285
- in Thai beef curry 314

red wine marinade 304
- in braised beef with licorice 313

remoulade sauce 297
rendang, Malaysian 314
rice with herbs 321
risotto, saffron 323
romesco sauce 298

sabzi âshe 283
sabzi ghormeh 283
sabzi polo 283
saffron risotto 323
salad of crab, beans, and pickled ginger 308
salad of pomegranate, olive, and walnut 307
salsa fresca 302
salsa, Peruvian parsley 302
salsa verde 296
- with sorrel 57

sambal
- bajak 301
- cucumber 303
- kemiri 300
- manis 300
- tomato 303
- ulek 300
  - in spring rolls 309

sambhar powder 287
sauce paloise 297
Saudi baharat 289
- in tomato sauce 298

sea bass baked with star anise 311
seasoning
- Bajan 283
- Cajun 294
- Jamaican jerk 283
- Trinidad 283

seven-spice powder **237**, 284
shichimi togarashi **237**, 284
shrimp and coconut curry 310
snapper with chermoula 311
sol kadhi 325
sorrel sauce 57, 298
South African curry powder 292
spice mixtures 284–95
spiced salt, Virgin Islands 294
spring rolls, Vietnamese 309
Sri Lankan curry powder **213**, 288
sweet baking spice **245**, 293
sweet chili sauce 300

tabil **201**, 291
- in couscous with seven vegetables 323

tagliatelle with horseradish, dill, and smoked trout 319
taklia 290
Tamil curry powder 288
tandoori masala 287
- in chicken tikka 316
- in yogurt marinade 304

tarragon soup 306
tartar sauce 297
Thai beef curry 314
Thai chili jam 299; and see 259
tomato sambal 303
tomato sauce 298
Trinidad seasoning 283
tuna tartare 308
Tunisian bharat 290

vanilla ice cream 325
vanilla sugar 155

watercress, tomato, and sole soup 306
wat spices 292
- in chicken wat 316

West African pepper blend 292
West Indian masala 295
winter herbs 281
wrinkled potatoes 298

Yemeni hawaij 290
Yemeni hilbeh 290
Yemeni zhug 290
yogurt and herb dressing 297
yogurt marinade 304

za'atar 290; **165**
zhug 290; **109**

Techniques and miscellaneous

aliño criollo 215
allicin 76
Al Taie, Lamees Abdullah 289
aonori 284
Asian (sesame) oil 139
attar of roses 152

bagaar 213
Belgian endive 89
black salt 287
bredie 313
Brown, Lynda 324
bstilla 145
bumbu 175

cacik 71
candlenuts 320
Capitulaire de Villes 94
capsaicin 257
cayenne pepper 256, 258
Charlemagne 94
chiffonade (making) 125
chile colorado 262
chili powder 257, 258, 262
chili peppers (preparing dried)
  deseeding 276
  grinding 277
  soaking 277
  toasting 276
chili peppers (preparing fresh)
  deseeding 275
  freezing 275
  roasting 274
chili flakes 257
  in seven-spice powder 284
chili oil 258
chili powder 258, 262
chili threads 257
Chimayo chili powder 262
chorek 142
coumarin 48

dashi 115
David, Elizabeth 151, 306
drop 189

eugenol 34, 144, 244
Evelyn, John 16

fennel pollen 66, 67
fesenjan 169
filé powder 55
flaoune 71, 222

Gerard, John 108
gheimeh 209
ghormeh sabzi 221
ginger juice 239, 269
gingili oil 139
givre 155
glycyrrhizic acid 188
gochu-jang 258
gumbo filé 55

herba 8
herb butter 129
herb oil 128
herbs (preserved)
  dried 17
  freeze-dried 11
  in oil 11
herbs (processing)
  chopping 17, 124
  drying 17, 126–27
  freezing 126
  pounding 17, 125
  stripping 123
herb vinegar 128
hydroxicitrate 171

ichimi togarashi 284
Iddison, Philip 289

kapi 285, 299, 300
keftedes 71
kewra essence/water 49
kheer 195
khoresh 145
kimchi 239
kokam saar 171
korma 195
Kruss, Mariam 325
kulfi 195

lassi 153
linalool 34

ma'amool 142
matsutake no dobinmushi 26
menthol 70
methyl chavicol 34
Miller, Philip 16
mishmisheya 145
mochi 121
Monardes, Nicolas 50
muhammarah 169
mustard oil 253
myrosinase 254

nabemono 26, 183
nuoc mam 300

oden 255
Olney, Richard 281
oroshigane 115, 269
Ortiz, Elisabeth Lambert 302

paan 195
pastirma 221
pho 185
pipián 215
pollo pibil 215, 295
pomegranate molasses 169
Pontefract cakes 189
pulegone 107

rose water 152, 153

safrole 55
salt substitute 87
sesame oil 138, 139
shukta 141, 221
shuwa 312
sofrito 110, 161
species 8
spice butter 129
spice paste (making) 273
spices (using)
  bruising 267
  crushing 272
  dry-roasting 270–71
  frying 137, 272
  grating 137, 269
  grinding 137, 272
  shredding 268
  slicing 268

tadka 213
tahini 138, 139
terasi 301
thymol 218
til laddoo 139
til oil 139
tom kha kai 179
tostones 302
tsoureki 142, 222

uchu llawaja 263
Umaña-Murray, Mirtha 282
umeboshi 25

vanilla extract 154, 155

wasabi-joyu 115
witloof 89

yubeshi 183

ACKNOWLEDGMENTS

Author's acknowledgments

Thanks first to my husband, Paul Breman, who helped with research, and encouraged me constantly throughout the writing of the book. He also compiled the index.

Many friends generously provided information or samples from their own part of the world or their own area of expertise; thanks go to Lynda Brown, Vic Cherikoff, Nevin Halıcı, Ian Hemphill, Richard Hosking, Philip Iddison, Aglaia Kremezi, Myung Sook Lee, Maricel Presilla, Diny Schouten, Maria José Sevilla, Margaret Shaida, David Thompson, Yong Suk Willendrup, Paula Wolfert, and Sami Zubaida.

William Penzey of The Spice House in Milwaukee generously provided a wealth of spices and information; Dr P.S.S. Thampi of the Spices Board of India provided useful contacts in Kerala; Summa Navaratnam and N.M. Wickramasinghe helped on cinnamon production; Patricia Raymond of Aust & Hachmann gave help on vanilla; the Hungarian Trade Office and Foods from Spain on paprika and pimentón; Sarah Wain of West Dean Gardens took me through their impressive collection of chilies; Kevin Bateman of MSK provided samples of Kashmiri saffron and bourbon vanilla; Chris Seagon of Laurel Herb Farm provided herbs; Jason Stemm sent me statistics from the American Spice Trade Association, and A.C. Whitely of the Royal Horticultural Society and Dr Mark Nesbitt of the Royal Botanic Gardens at Kew helped me to identify golpar.

At Dorling Kindersley publisher Mary-Clare Jerram, art director Carole Ash, and their team conceived an exciting and ambitious book; Gillian Roberts has been an exemplary managing editor; Frank Ritter and Hugh Thompson have been painstaking and constructive in their editing; Toni Kay and Sara Robin have produced a handsome and imaginative design; and Dave King has produced lively and informative photographs of all the herbs and spices. My thanks go to all of them.

Publisher's acknowledgments

Dorling Kindersley would like to thank Marghie Gianni and Jo Gray for design assistance; Sarah Duncan for picture research; Jo Harris for research and styling; Nancy Campbell for research and sourcing items for photography; Jim Arbury for his splendid Hamburg parsley; Patty Penzey of The Spice House; Debbie Yakeley at Richters in Ontario; and all those who helped us in Florida, making it possible to photograph many fresh herbs and chilies when they were unobtainable in the UK – Linda Cunningham in Jacksonville and Maggie at Maggie's Herb Farm, Della and Tim Baldwin at Palm Valley Peppers, and Paul Figura.

Picture acknowledgments

The publisher would like to thank the following for their kind permission to reproduce the photographs:

a=above; b=below; c=centre; l=left; r=right; t=top;

Anthony Blake Photo Library: Sue Atkinson 79br; Martin Brigdale 205r; Graham Kirk 226; Andrew Pini 79 bl.

Jacques Boulay: 157br, 192–193.

Corbis: Jonathan Blair 46bl; Chris Bland 47tl; Michael Busselle 79tr; Dean Conger 204b, 205bl; Ric Ergenbright 192bl; Owen Franken 78b, 157tr, 248tl, 249tl, 249tr; Michael Freeman 156–157b; Lindsay Hebberd 248–249; Chris Hellier 47tr, 156bl; Dave G Houser 226cl; Earl & Nazima Kowall 193tl; Gail Mooney 227tl; Caroline Penn 193tr; Kevin Schafer 156t.

Flowerphotos: Barbara Gray 204tl.

Garden Picture Library: David Cavagnaro 78–79; Brigitte Thomas 157tl; Michel Viard 227tr, 227br, 248tr.

Oxford Scientific Films: Deni Bown 205tl; Alain Christof 46–47; Bob Gibbons 227bl; TC Nature 249br.

The Dorling Kindersley picture library contains over 2.5 million images, including travel photography, food, and drink. For more information, visit www.dkimages.com